16⁵⁰

Jan. 1964

Donald Clark
Bounty,
Sask

1596

THE WILDERNESS
OF DENALI

THE WILDERNESS

OF

DENALI

❧ *Explorations of a Hunter-Naturalist*
in Northern Alaska

by CHARLES SHELDON

With an Introduction by C. HART MERRIAM, M. D.
RESEARCH ASSOCIATE SMITHSONIAN INSTITUTION

New York ❧ CHARLES SCRIBNER'S SONS

Contents

APPENDICES

by CHARLES SHELDON

by THE EDITORS

Introduction

Among the hunter-naturalists of America, Charles Sheldon occupied a unique position. For "notwithstanding his attitude of self-effacement"—as well expressed by George Bird Grinnell—"he was our most famous big-game hunter." Choosing his hunting grounds in some of the most remote and inaccessible parts of the continent; possessed of physical strength and endurance almost beyond belief, of unbounded enthusiasm, of powers of observation second to none, and endowed with a conscience intolerant of exaggeration, the accounts of his hunts abound in vivid descriptions of localities not previously explored, while his circumstantial studies of the habits of animals rank among the most valuable of the contributions thus far made to the life histories of many species— particularly the mountain sheep, caribou, moose, grizzly bear, and wolverine.

Of independent means and unhampered by government restrictions, he was able to choose his own hunting grounds and outfit his own expeditions. Moreover, by his enthusiasm and influence, others, chiefly young sportsmen, were led to make their hunting trips contribute specimens of permanent value to our great museums.

While his personal interest centered chiefly in the larger game animals, Sheldon nevertheless appreciated the importance of collecting the smaller mammals and took the trouble to trap, prepare, and label large numbers of mice, lemmings, shrews, and other small species, all of which he presented to the Biological Survey, for permanent deposit in our National Museum. These specimens have been of inestimable help to naturalists engaged in defining and mapping the ranges of the smaller mammals and besides have brought to light a number of species previously unknown. And it should be borne in

ix

mind that while the major part of his field work was done in
Alaska and Yukon Territory, he also made important col-
lections and field notes in British Columbia, Arizona, and
northern Mexico.

In most localities in which he hunted he was a pioneer—
there being no one to tell him where or how to go, or what to
expect when he got there. He modestly mentions the fact that
nearly all the mountains on which he hunted "were untrodden
by foot of white man or Indian. The wilderness was primeval.
. . . It was not possible to find guides, for there were none.
It was necessary not only to search out a route to the mountains but also to find the ranges occupied by sheep." And it
may be added that in several instances his explorations led
not only to discoveries in the field of natural history but also
to extensions of geographic knowledge.

The mountain sheep of all the big animals of America appealed most forcibly to his imagination. This is clearly stated
in the first chapter of his *Wilderness of the Upper Yukon,*
where he writes:

The mountain sheep of America are among the noblest of our wild
animals. Their pursuit leads the hunter into the most remote and inaccessible parts of the wilderness and calls into play his greatest skill and
highest qualities of endurance.

My first experience with sheep was in northern Mexico, where they
dwell among the isolated groups of rugged mountains that rise abruptly
from the great waterless deserts—deserts beautiful in their wealth of
color, weird in the depth of their solitude, impressive in their grim desolation. It was there that I became fascinated by the exhilaration of the
sport of hunting the wild sheep, and dominated by the desire of following them in other lands.

I was familiar with what had been written about the white sheep,
Ovis dalli, of Alaska, and the darkest of the American sheep, *Ovis
stonei,* of the Stikine water-shed in northern British Columbia; and
when in 1901 still another form of sheep, *Ovis fannini,* was described
from the ranges of the Canadian Rockies in Yukon Territory—an animal with a pure white head and gray back—I decided to explore for
it if the chance ever offered. Indeed, so little was known about the
variation, habits, and distribution of the wild sheep of the far northern wilderness, that my imagination was impressed by the possibilities
of the results of studying them in their native land. There was, besides,
the chance of penetrating new regions, of adding the exhilaration of

exploration to that of hunting, and of bringing back information of value to zoologists and geographers, and of interest to sportsmen and lovers of natural history.*

After studying the white sheep for three or more seasons in the mountains of Yukon Territory and in the Alaska Range he realized that important facts in their life history—particularly concerning the seasonal ranges and breeding habits— were still unknown. In order to obtain this information he undertook still another long journey, again visiting the Upper Toklat and Mount Denali—the Indian name for Mount McKinley—where he remained through the summer, fall, winter, and following spring. This he did at great personal sacrifice of time, money, and labor. His reward was the satisfaction of success, for by unceasing exertion he succeeded in filling the previous gaps in the knowledge of the lives of these remarkable animals. In obtaining these facts he did an almost unbelievable amount of severe and often perilous climbing, visiting bands of sheep on the steep declivities of tremendous mountains—not alone in summer and fall, but also during nearly every day of the severe cold and storms of the Arctic winter—accomplishing tasks that few of the most hardy hunters would deem possible.

Of high value to students of American game animals are his graphic illustrations showing the colors and markings of sheep. Nine patterns or intensities of coloration are exhibited by these animals in the different mountain regions of Alaska and Yukon Territory, and the areas occupied by each were graphically shown on maps. Sheldon alone possessed the knowledge necessary to do this.

When studying sheep and grizzly bear he risked his life a hundred times—day after day, week after week, and month after month—in penetrating unknown canyons, fording swirling torrents, and scaling perilous cliffs, that he might fill gaps in our knowledge of the habits and movements of these animals. Some of his escapes were little less than miraculous, but

* "The Wilderness of the Upper Yukon," pp. 3-4, and map and plate facing p. 298. Scribners, 1911.

he secured what he went for and lived to return—evidence of his determination, his powers of endurance, and his skill as a mountaineer.

When hunting, he hunted alone, well aware of the annoyances and failures attending the presence of a companion. But when in camp he enjoyed the comradeship of those interested in like pursuits. On one of his Alaska expeditions he took with him Wilfred H. Osgood, then of the U. S. Biological Survey (later head of the Mammal Department of the Field Museum in Chicago), Carl Rungius, the celebrated mammal artist of New York; and for a part of the season was joined by the late F. C. Selous, the eminent and much beloved British hunter-naturalist whose writings on big-game animals of Africa and Canada are well known.

Sheldon was a splendid type of vigorous manhood, self-reliant, courageous, of pleasing personality, possessed of sober earnest dignity, unassuming, simple in tastes, kindly, generous, and when estimating others always fair, giving due weight to their environment and opportunities. He was a staunch friend, undemonstrative but true.

In his natural history investigations, he had no patience with guesswork or inference. He wanted exact facts, verified by repeated observation and recorded with painstaking fidelity. When out with gun and glass, it was his practice to focus attention on certain habits of the animal studied and to record what he saw with scrupulous detail. Unwilling to rely on memory, he sometimes wrote while actually watching the animal, and at all times penned his account immediately after reaching camp, no matter at what hour of the night or how fatigued he might be. His journals show that after many an arduous hunt, often encumbered by a heavy load, he returned in the darkness of night—descending precipitous slopes, feeling his way through slippery canyons, wading treacherous torrents—and after reaching camp and eating a late supper, immediately proceeded to record the day's experiences. Many pages, as stated by his camp man, Henry Karstens, were written between midnight and morning.

His observations on the amazing power of scent of bears

and caribou contrasted with the power of sight of the sheep;
on the breeding habits and periods of sheep and caribou, on
the prodigious physical strength of the wolverine, on the bru-
tality of the Canada lynx in tearing out the eyes of sheep, on
the familiar winter habits of the Alaska Canada jays about
his cabin; on the breeding antics of the ptarmigan and of the
short-eared owls—these and many others are among the notable contributions of the present volume.

Although familiar with a large proportion of the mammals
and birds of the United States and Alaska, he always dis-
claimed technical knowledge. Still, a few years ago he undertook a technical study of the mountain sheep. This, unfortunately, he did not live to complete.

His appreciation of scenic grandeur and his delight in remote solitudes are evident throughout his writings. He not
only loved wild places but in his contemplation of them—as
in hunting—he preferred to be alone. He was deeply sensitive
to color, whether of foliage, mountain, or sky, many pages
attesting his appreciation of the varying tints of cliffs, peaks,
and mountain pastures, of the evanescent hues of Arctic auroras, and more particularly, of the extraordinary colors en-
shrouding the great "Denali" when the winter sun shone low
and cold in the west.

During his several years in Mexico (from 1898 to 1902)
Sheldon acquired the Spanish language, became interested in
the people, the country, and the game animals. He hunted in
the Sierre Madre and other parts of northern Chihuahua, at
that time "the best field for big-game hunting in all Mexico."
The Sierre Madre, many readers may be surprised to learn,
is clad in forests of stately pines and cleft by canyons, some
more than a hundred miles in length and, according to Sheldon, almost if not quite equaling the Grand Canyon of the
Colorado; while on the east is a vast desert covered by yuccas,
cactus and mesquite trees.

In the timbered mountains he hunted the mountain sheep,
the small Mexican grizzly, the black bear, and the small white-
tail or Coues deer (which also inhabited the lower country),

and noted the abundance of cougars; while in the brushy and open deserts to the east he found the desert mule deer and the antelope.*

It was his early experiences with sheep in the Sierre Madre, as already pointed out, that led to the study of these fascinating animals in a number of mountain ranges in Yukon Territory and Alaska, in the course of which his interest in the group became so intense that he determined to secure specimens from as many disconnected mountains as possible in the United States, Canada, and Mexico. With this in view, he persuaded the Biological Survey to send hunters to a number of localities in the Far West while he personally undertook the task of obtaining specimens from the extreme southwestern limit of sheep in the Desert Ranges of Mexico. He had already hunted in the Grand and Havasu Canyons of northern Arizona where, accompanied by the aged chief of the Havasupai Indians, he had killed several fine specimens for the Biological Survey.

Learning later that Carl Lumholtz had seen sheep tracks along the base of Sierra del Rosario† and believing that the complete isolation of this range would prevent sheep from crossing the broad desert leading to it, Sheldon felt that the species would be likely to differ from that of the mountains farther north. Anxious to determine this, in March, 1916, he made a special trip to El Rosario, whose rugged crests attain an elevation of 1,500 to 1,700 feet. Yet, as he ascertained, "there is not a drop of water in the whole range," so he was obliged to carry a small quantity from Tinajas Altas in the Gila Range, twenty miles away. He rode a horse there from Wellton in three days and "remained alone for eight days, climbing the crags and hunting for sheep." He finally succeeded in killing an adult ram and in finding the bleached skull of a mature ewe. The species proving distinct, was named *Ovis sheldoni* in his honor.‡ As might be expected

---

* "The Big Game of Chihuahua," Mexico, in volume entitled "Hunting and Conservation," the Book of the Boone and Crockett Club, pp. 138-181, 1925.

† Lumholtz, "New Trails in Mexico," Scribner's, 1912.

‡ "Proceedings Biological Society of Washington," vol. 29, pp. 129-132, September 6, 1916.

from its inhospitable environment, it is the smallest of the American sheep.

In 1921 Sheldon visited the little-known Sére Indians at their home on the remote and desolate Tiburon Island in the Gulf of California. He had been warned against going because of their reputation for killing white visitors, but he was unafraid. Finding them in a half-starved condition, he went with the chief into the far interior and killed for them one of the rare and little-known Tiburon mule deer. The chief, by means of signal smokes, summoned several of his men from their home on the coast many miles away to bring water—for they had become very thirsty—and to carry back the meat. While on the island no white man was with him—his only companions, the Indians. He visited their headquarters, became interested in their rude habitations and mode of life, and brought back examples of their tiny effigies and crude basketry.*

Sheldon's earlier books tell of most of his hunts north of the United States except in the area now embraced in Mount McKinley National Park—the subject of the present volume. They tell of his work along the great Yukon, the MacMillan, the Pelly and Ross rivers, and in the adjacent mountains of Yukon Territory; of his big bear hunts on Montague and Admiralty Islands, his mountain goat hunt on the Katzehin River, a tributary to Lynn Canal in southeastern Alaska; his search for the rare Dawson caribou on Queen Charlotte Islands, and his hunt for the coast elk in the dense rain forest of Vancouver Island. Thus *The Wilderness of Denali* completes the account of his hunting expeditions in the Far North. A book published by the Boone and Crockett Club tells of his work in Chihuahua, Mexico. But nowhere except in his precious journals may be found accounts of his sheep hunts in the Grand and Havasu Canyons of Arizona and those on the desert mountains of Sonora, nor of his visit and deer hunt with the Sére Indians of Tiburon Island in the Gulf of California.

---

* On February 7, 1923, he lectured before the Anthropological Society of Washington on his visit to the Sére Indians, and exhibited a number of lantern-slides of the people and their homes on Tiburon Island.

In view of his natural tastes and extensive field experience it is not surprising that Sheldon should have become an enthusiastic supporter of the National Parks, National Forests, and National Game Refuges. He stood also for *rational* game conservation and became one of the leaders of the movement. But he was not an extremist, for, as stated by E. W. Nelson, "He was a thorough believer in the *reasonable* utilization of surplus game by the people where it occurs, and by the sportsmen; yet he was a strong advocate of adequate protection of wild life to insure its perpetuation in *reasonable* numbers." [Italics by the editor.]

After much thought he formulated a plan for the conservation and increase of game animals in the United States. He proposed that the states having national forests within their borders voluntarily relinquish the control of game therein, turning its administration over to the Forest Service; and that outside the national forests the control be placed in the hands of the State Game Commissions with full powers. This policy, he believed, "would result in greatly increased financial advantage to the states."*

Recognizing the need of a central national organization for the consideration of the general subject of field, forest and game, Sheldon consulted with other leaders and succeeded in bringing about the National Conference on Outdoor Recreation; and he was one of the founders of the Wild Fowlers League.

His appreciation of stupendous mountain scenery, coupled with his desire to perpetuate under natural conditions the white sheep, caribou, moose, grizzly bear, and other wild animals of the North, led him to urge upon the Government the desirability of setting aside the area now known as Mount McKinley National Park in northern Alaska. This Park was established by Congress in 1917, seven years after the similarly public-spirited labors of his friend, George Bird Grinnell, had resulted in the creation of Glacier National Park in western Montana.

The esteem in which Sheldon was held by co-workers is

* *Outdoor Life,* p. 99, Feb., 1925.

echoed by the important offices to which he was elected: Vice-president of the Boone and Crockett Club and Advisory Member of its Game Conservation Committee; Trustee and Member of the Executive Committee of the National Parks Association; Member of the Board of Directors of the American Forestry Association; Member of the Co-ordination Committee on National Parks and Forests; Chairman of the Commission on the Conservation of the Jackson Hole Elk; Chairman of the Permanent Wild Life Committee of the National Recreation Conference, and others of like interest and aims.

Sheldon's interest in big game led him to gather books on hunting and exploration in America and other lands. The collection grew until at the time of his death it numbered between six and seven thousand volumes. Since his death this incomparable library has been acquired by Yale University.

His interests were so broad that little escaped his inquiring mind. He tells of a variety of things, animate and inanimate, that caught his attention—songs of birds, actions of squirrels and mice, features of the landscape, doings of Indians. His hunting trips brought him in contact with Indians of many tribes, leading him to record facts of value to the anthropologist.

His contributions to the knowledge of the habits and ranges of American mammals, his continued efforts to secure adequate series of specimens for our great museums, and his struggle for the reasonable conservation of wild life are among the lasting monuments to his industry and understanding.

C. HART MERRIAM

THE WILDERNESS
OF DENALI

DENALI

PART I · *1906*

First Trip to Denali and the Upper Toklat.

Wishing to study the white or Dall sheep of Alaska, I determined to visit the northern slopes of the Alaska Range, in the vicinity of Denali—commonly called Mount McKinley. I reached Dawson June 28, 1906, and made preparations for the trip. It was my purpose to outfit in Fairbanks, Alaska, and engage a small steamer to take me a hundred and fifty or more miles up the Kantishna River to some point from which to reach the base of the mountain with pack horses. Five horses, together with packing equipment, were purchased in Dawson, and Jack Haydon, who had been in Yukon Territory for some years, was engaged as packer and assistant.

July 3. We embarked on the steamer *Seattle No. 3,* and arrived in Tanana the evening of July 6. Aside from the fascination of steaming down the wonderful Yukon, making long stops at the various 'cities,' and observing different tribes of Indians along the river, no unusual incident marked the trip. At that time of the year evidences of bird life, even on the Yukon Flats, were almost absent. Some distance below Eagle a lynx was seen swimming across the river—swimming with so much ease that I was surprised to see how well it was adapted to the water. It seemed to glide along the surface, its whole back remaining three or four inches above until, on reaching the bank, it stepped out and calmly sat down and watched the steamer.

The morning following our arrival at Tanana we started up the Tanana River. This stream is much less interesting than the Yukon, the current not so swift, the water extremely muddy, and the country bordering it flat. By noon, July 8, we had reached the mouth of the Kantishna River, where Haydon disembarked with the horses to await my return from

3

Fairbanks, which I reached on July 11 after a monotonous trip.

Fairbanks, then in the flush of mining activity, was 'wide open' and interesting. After some vexatious experiences I engaged the small steamer *Dusty Diamond* to take me up the Kantishna; and purchased provisions for the whole trip.

As I look back upon my experiences in Alaska and the Yukon Territory, I recall no better fortune that that which befell me when Harry Karstens was engaged as an assistant packer. Before he was twenty years of age he had left his home in Illinois bound for Alaska, and had reached Dawson during the early days of the Klondike gold rush. Later, after attempting mining on Seventy Mile Creek in Alaska, he had become a member of the small party of men who laid out the town site of Eagle. After the discovery of gold near Fairbanks he became a mail carrier, driving dogs between Fairbanks and Valdez and other points; and the winter before my arrival he carried mail by dog team between Fairbanks and the Kantishna mining district. He is a tall, stalwart man, well poised, frank, and strictly honorable. One of the best dog drivers in the north, and peculiarly fitted by youth and experience for explorations in little-known regions, he proved a most efficient and congenial companion.

Late in the evening of July 14 the *Dusty Diamond* left Fairbanks, and the next afternoon reached the mouth of the Kantishna, where Karstens joined Haydon. I remained on the boat, which went forty miles below to leave some freight at Bakers Hot Springs, where I passed the night. Here, hot springs flow from the hillside, and the ground is so favorable for farming that large vegetable gardens are cultivated, all the hardy vegetables fully maturing and growing to very large size. In the morning the boat returned and by noon reached the Kantishna, where my men and horses embarked, and we were soon steaming up that river—on the same day of the month as that on which I had entered the Pelly River the previous year. But the contrast was significant.

The Kantishna, then unmapped, is a silt-laden river with very muddy water two or three hundred yards or more in width, meandering with rather sluggish current through broad, flat, swampy territory. Except well up toward its source, only a few rolling hills diversify the scenery, until the Chitsea Range, of rather low relief, comes into view to the southeast above the mouth of the Toklat, fifteen or twenty miles from the Kantishna.

The journey was monotonous, the weather very hot, and mosquitoes were swarming, and the horses, cramped in a narrow space near the boiler, were continually tortured by both mosquitoes and big horse flies. No mammals were seen and birds were very scarce, the only species observed being hawks, ravens, gulls, mallard ducks, kingfishers, spotted sandpipers, and waxwings.* We steamed along at a fairly steady rate, stopping at intervals to cut wood, and now and then having some difficulty in crossing a bar, so that we did not reach the mouth of Bearpaw River until ten the next evening.

July 17. A passenger was aboard, destined for Bearpaw City, three miles up that river, where he intended to take a small gasoline launch that had been left there early in the summer and go up to Diamond City. The Kantishna mining district had been discovered the previous year when Jim Dalton found gold on Eureka Creek—a small tributary of Moose Creek, the main branch of the Bearpaw—about fifty miles in a straight line from the mouth of the Bearpaw. That discovery immediately started a rush, and during the fall and winter four or five hundred hardy men went into the district.

Two rival town sites were quickly established, each intended to be a distributing point for traffic on the Kantishna River to the 'diggings.' One was Bearpaw City, whose founders hoped to utilize the river of the same name for the navigation of small boats; the other was Roosevelt City, thirty miles farther up the Kantishna, nearer the mining locality, and much more favorably located for winter travel. At the head of navigation on the Bearpaw, Diamond City sprang up, and twelve miles beyond, on Glacier Creek and its tributaries, Glacier City was located. A small quantity of gold was taken from Glacier

* [Undoubtedly the Bohemian waxwing (*Bombycilla garrula*), the locality being far north of the range of the cedar waxwing (*B. cedrorum*).]

Creek, and the discovery claim on Eureka Creek was very successful; but, as the district in general failed to produce, within the year it was depopulated almost as quickly as it had been filled. Yet a few men were still scattered through it, some washing out small amounts of gold from their claims, others working in the hope of further discoveries.

July 18. We went three miles up the Bearpaw to Bearpaw City, then entirely deserted and consisting of nothing but several abandoned cabins. The next night we reached Roosevelt —a row of about thirty cabins, including two stores, a saloon, and a sawmill—on the southeast bank of the Kantishna thirty miles above the mouth of the Bearpaw. Only eight people, including two women, remained there, and these were about to return down river, leaving the place completely abandoned. We unloaded the horses and outfit, intending to go thirty miles by the winter trail to Eureka. From this point we hoped to fined a route to Denali, which in a direct course to the south is not more than thirty-five miles distant. We passed the night in a cabin and devoted the following day to making up the packs and resting the horses. A half-breed had fortunately just arrived at Roosevelt, having come over the trail from Eureka, with three horses. This gave me an opportunity to exchange one of my large horses, which was unsound, for a small mare that I thought had been accustomed to packing.

Our equipment consisted of a shelter tent and the usual provisions—flour, bacon, sugar, tea, butter in cans, salt, evaporated onions, dried fruit, and a few other things. We depended on killing game enough to provide food during the trip. Some of our animals were old stage horses that had been used between Whitehorse and Dawson until unfit for service, though still able to carry packs. These, with two bays, *Tuffy* and *Jimmy*, and two grays, *Coghlan* and *Alphonse*, together with the small mare, *Babe*, comprised the packtrain. *Babe* proved to be a splendid pack horse, but the others were unsuited to the work, and hence made traveling difficult.

July 20-22. On the morning of July 20 we started over the trail through a level country across a vast muskeg, very soft in places, full of 'nigger heads' in others, for thirty miles to Eureka, which we reached on the evening of the third day. These three days were most trying: the horses constantly bogged and lost their packs, mosquitoes swarmed continually, and the weather was very hot. Finally *Alphonse,* while climbing a bluff near Moose Creek, fell and rolled down a hundred feet with his pack, cutting such a gash on his leg that he was disabled for the rest of the summer.

Old moose signs were quite abundant on the flat, while in the woods there were red squirrels, a few sparrows, and the Alaska form of the Canada jay.

Eureka, consisting of about twenty tents and a few cabins, was situated on Moose Creek at the mouth of Eureka Creek, where Dalton had found gold the previous summer. His claim proved rich ground for a few hundred feet, the gold occurring at a depth of only three or four feet. At the time of our visit he employed about fifteen men, who were shoveling the gravel into a trough where the water carried it off, leaving the gold deposited over the riffles at the foot. These men were receiving fifteen dollars a day, besides their board, which, under the conditions, was an item of operation almost equally expensive. Dalton, although he controlled some ground higher up on the same creek (from which a small amount of gold was taken out for two or three subsequent years), exhausted the richest part of his claim that same summer. All the creeks in the vicinity had been staked, and a few men were working other claims, none of which, however, were successful.

In a region so remote and so difficult to reach, and in such a small camp, it was not strange that the saloon and the gambling establishment were missing. But to those familiar with the mining regions of the far North, it would indeed have been surprising not to have found in this camp that more persisting complement of the saloon and gambling place; and sure enough, it flourished in a large tent occupied by a single individual who, early in the summer, had left Fairbanks and penetrated this wilderness, to remain alone and absorb a large share of the miners' wages—the greater part of which in every mining camp in the northern country has fallen into the grasping hands of her kind.

Eureka is enclosed by fairly high mountains mostly devoid
of timber except along the creeks. The grating sound of the
shovels as they were forced into the gravel bar, the voices of
the miners, and the general bustle of a busy camp seemed
strangely out of harmony with the surrounding country, which
otherwise imparted a feeling of solitude and a sense of the
remote lonely wilderness.

July 23. As the horses had cast six of their shoes, a day
was given to shoeing them and to idling about camp. Since no
information could be obtained as to a good route toward the
great mountain, we decided to follow up Moose Creek for
three miles and then strike south across the mountain range.

July 24. Very early in the morning we started with four
horses along an old moose trail leading up Moose Creek. *Alphonse* was so badly disabled that we were obliged to leave
him at Eureka. Pushing through brush and swamp for nearly
three miles, we turned south up a mountainside free from timber and zigzagged upward without much difficulty. We could
soon look below on a fine lake [Wonder Lake], two or three
miles long, which lies in a low divide between Moose Creek
and the McKinley Fork of the Kantishna River. The outlet
of this lake discharges into Moose Creek. Before reaching the
top of the mountain we lunched and refreshed ourselves with
the luscious blueberries that were everywhere abundant. Soon
after starting again we caught glimpses of snowy peaks toward the south, and when we reached the top, Denali and the
Alaska Range suddenly burst into view ahead, apparently very
near.

I can never forget my sensations at the sight. No descrip-
tion could convey any suggestion of it. I have seen the mountain panoramas of the Alaska coast and the Yukon Territory.
In the opinion of many able judges the St. Elias range is one
of the most glorious masses of mountain scenery in the world.
I had viewed St. Elias and the adjacent mountains the previous year, but compared with the view now before my eyes
they seemed almost insignificant.

Three miles below lay the glacial bar of the Muldrow
Branch of McKinley Fork, fringed on both sides by narrow

lines of timber, its swift torrents rushing through many channels. Beyond, along the north side of the main Alaska Range,
is a belt of bare rolling hills ten or twelve miles wide, forming
a vast piedmont plateau* dotted with exquisite little lakes.
The foothill mountains, 6,000 or 7,000 feet in altitude and
now free from snow, extend in a series of five or six ranges
parallel to the main snow-covered range on the south. Carved
by glaciers, eroded by the elements, furrowed by canyons and
ravines, hollowed by cirques, and rich in contrasting colors,
they form an appropriate foreground to the main range.

Denali—a majestic dome which from some points of view
seems to present an unbroken skyline—rises to an altitude of
20,300 feet, with a mantle of snow and ice reaching down for
14,000 feet. Towering above all others, in its stupendous immensity it dominates the picture. Nearby on the west stands
Mount Foraker, more than 17,000 feet in altitude, flanked on
both sides by peaks of 10,000 to 13,000 feet that extend in
a ragged snowy line as far as the eye can see.

We traveled three or four miles down a gentle descent, and
in order to keep in view this tremendous panorama, camped
at 10 P. M. far above timber. Mosquitoes swarmed but we sat
inside a netting under the shelter. Thus far only a few old
moose tracks had been seen.

July 25. In less than an hour from camp we reached the
Muldrow Branch, and after much trouble in fording the
channels, struck across the plateau directly for the mountain.
The traveling, though at times through boggy ground, was
fairly good, though some difficulty was found in crossing a
canyon where numerous lakes had to be skirted. In the evening we descended directly from the ridges to the end of a
strip of timber which borders Muddy Fork or Peters Branch
of McKinley River, as far as the foot of the moraine of
Peters Glacier [called Hanna Glacier on recent Government
maps].

We decided to make a camp where we were, six miles from
Denali, at the base of the outside mountains. When the men

---

* *Piedmont plateau,* a term applied by geographers to the foothills or low
country at the base of a mountain range.

began to unpack the horses, I took my rifle and went to the river, which was rushing by in full volume, impossible to ford. On the skyline of the ridges beyond was a cow caribou. Returning to camp I saw another caribou, five hundred yards above, and quickly started to stalk it; but when I climbed the ridge it was nowhere to be seen.

That day, when we had crossed the Muldrow Branch and climbed the ridges of the plateau, caribou tracks were abundant, and the chatter of ground squirrels was heard on all sides. Ravens, golden eagles, willow ptarmigan, Hudsonian curlews, and black-bellied plovers were often seen.

Denali.

July 26. Rain fell nearly all last night and continued until three in the afternoon. Early in the morning I saw twelve or thirteen caribou on the ridge behind camp, and soon after, a large bull came down and entered the timber. As it was necessary to have meat as soon as possible, I climbed the ridge and circled around, but the caribou had moved and some time elapsed before I found them. They were traveling slowly and stopping at intervals to feed. In order to gain on them I cut across some foothills, and when I reached a point within three hundred yards of them, one evidently saw me; therefore I sat down and remained motionless for a while. As the wind was in my favor, I tried the experiment of waving a handkerchief, but with no other result than that of causing them all to watch the bandana. I was surprised to see them break into a run when I arose. Although two shots were fired before they disappeared, none were hit. Following in the direction they had taken, I saw them all trotting toward the mountains nearly a mile ahead. It was raining so heavily that I returned to camp. But after lunch, when the rain had slackened, I again climbed the hills and crossed a valley to the mountains, which were carefully examined for signs of sheep.

It was discouraging to find no evidences of them—not a track, nor even the appearance of a trail. Two miles ahead, between the ranges, eleven caribou cows and calves were feeding, while a single calf was slowly wandering over a ridge half a mile to their right. As I approached, a cow suddenly broke away from the band and ran in the direction of the calf, which apparently was lost, for the cow soon ran around in circles, stopping every few moments to look, until she was out of my sight. When she disappeared I hurried in that di-

11

rection, and after reaching the place where the calf had last been seen, seated myself to wait for the band that had then begun to move toward me. Suddenly the sound of hoofs striking the ground close behind me caused me to turn my head; it was the cow, still running swiftly though somewhat aimlessly—undoubtedly trying to find her calf. As she stopped a moment a hundred yards away, I fired and killed her. Her horns, being in the velvet, were very soft, and her pelage was thin and ragged. After dressing her, I took the udder (full of milk) and the heart, liver, and some of the meat to camp.

Bear diggings were abundant everywhere, and all the willows, wherever they grew, had been cropped by moose. Waxwings, chickadees, robins, and Alaska Canada jays* were common about the woods, while western tree sparrows, pipits [titlarks], and intermediate sparrows were on the ridges.

The Peters Branch of McKinley Fork emerges from Peters Glacier three miles above my camp, and flows eleven miles through a broad glacial bar to its junction with the Muldrow Branch [McKinley Fork]. Greatly swollen in the afternoon, owing to the more rapid melting of the glacier, it at that time discharges a heavy volume of water that rushes swiftly down a heavy gradient. The land on both sides of the bar is perfectly flat as far back as the ridges, which rise from two to five hundred feet parallel with the valley. This valley, incised in the piedmont plateau, varies from half a mile to a mile or more in width, and is covered with spruces and willows; its floor for the most part is hard. Spruce timber ends at the terminal of a newly formed moraine that stretches across the valley and reaches the base of Denali six miles away.

Our shelter was nicely situated near this moraine. Dry spruces for firewood were plentiful; a fine spring of water was at hand; and mosquitoes were at their worst. The mountain, though buried in clouds nearly all day, was visible when it cleared, directly south of the camp.

July 27. Early in the morning, when this wonderful mountain, free from clouds, towered above us, I started, in-

* The Alaska form of the Canada jay (*Perisoreus canadensis fumifrons*), the only jay of the region. Wherever the term *jay* occurs, this bird is meant.

tending to reach its slopes. Haydon accompanied me as far as
the caribou killed last evening in order to bring back the meat.

At the edge of timber on the banks of Peters Branch, we
found an old camp that had been occupied by Judge Wickersham. I kept on over the ridges east of Peters Glacier, determined to climb the lower slopes of the great mountain.
When I started, the huge white dome, lifting up into the
heavens, stood out boldly against a clear blue sky; but layers
of infant clouds began to creep across the slopes and rapidly
maturing, soon completely obscured the upper half of the
mountain.

Four or five outlying ranges, 6,000 or 7,000 feet in altitude, separated by V-shaped gorges or irregularly linked together by intersecting elevations, stand between the piedmont
plateau and the main mountain. They were bisected by the
newly formed dead moraine of Peters Glacier, which on the
west side of the glacier reaches to the base of the mountain.
The width of this moraine is two or more miles, while that
of the present ice of the glacier is only a few hundred feet.
At the extreme east of the moraine is a hard-beaten caribou
trail, over which a horse could be ridden, leading four miles
directly along the foot of the mountains, to the base of Denali
—and even for several hundred feet up the slope.

When I reached the mountains, a heavy rain began to fall;
but after an hour it ceased and the clouds about the main
peak began to thin away so that now and then the summit
was visible through the mist.

Conies, marmots, and ground squirrels were more abundant among the rocks of the moraine and on the adjacent
mountains than I have ever seen them elsewhere. After passing the first range and while crossing the wide gravel bar of
a swift torrent rushing down between two mountains, I saw
a big bull caribou with a magnificent pair of antlers, then in
the velvet, standing with head hanging down, close to the
river. The wind, blowing at my back, evidently reached his
nostrils two hundred yards away, for he threw up his head,
and with tail erect, trotted back and forth, quite confused as
to which direction to take. Finally he leaped into the creek,

crossed it, and trotted off up the draw, holding his head in such a way that the antlers almost rested on his back. While trotting, he constantly shook his head as if to keep it in a certain position of balance.

Going on, I penetrated short distances among the mountains and here and there climbed the slopes, scanning the surface everywhere, but could not find a sign of sheep. These mountains, covered with abundant feed, seemed ideal sheep ranges, but neither a sheep track nor any dung pellets could be found, nor was anything resembling a trail visible on the slopes. It was perfectly clear that for some reason this region directly south of Denali is inhospitable for sheep.

But I was in some degree compensated for my disappointment when I approached the base of the great mountain, for feeding on its basal slope were two cow caribou. Winding me at once, they galloped or trotted in an easterly direction until lost to sight among the canyons. So, my first start up Denali was made while caribou were fleeing before me.

I climbed a spur that flanks the east edge of the moraine of Peters Glacier and continues to the outside range. At the point where I climbed up, I found a tin cylinder half full of alcohol, a tower, a leather-covered valise box, two or three empty cans, a tent pole or two, and some wood that had been brought up there on horses. These proved to be part of the equipment left by Frederick A. Cook's party, which three years previously had attempted the ascent of Denali by following up Peters Glacier.

The slope became steeper as I zigzagged upward for nearly three hours until, having climbed a thousand feet in soft snow, I was obliged to stop where it rose almost perpendicularly. My aneroid barometer recorded 8,900 feet. As the clouds lifted, leaving the vast snow-mantled mountain clear, I seated myself and gazed for more than an hour on the sublime panorama. There was not a breath of wind, and no sound except the faint murmur of the creek far below, and the cannonading and crashing roar of avalanches thundering down the mountain walls.

Great masses of ice kept constantly breaking away from

far up near the summit. Starting slowly at first, they increased in momentum and size, accumulating large bodies of snow and ice, some of which during the rapidity of the descent were ground into swirling clouds resembling the spray of cataracts. When the sliding material pitched off the glacier cap and struck the bare walls below, enormous fragments of rock were dislodged and carried along with the mass, which finally fell on the dumping ground of the moraine. Then, before the clouds of snow had disappeared from the path of the avalanche, the rumbling of the echoes died away and silence was again supreme. During the four hours that I was there, nineteen avalanches fell—some of them of enormous proportions. Eleven were near by and visible throughout their descent.

Behind me reared the tremendous glacier cap in all its immensity. To my left Peters Glacier filled the deep valley between the north face of the mountain and a high adjoining range; to my right was the northeast ridge of Denali; and, as far as I could see, on both sides of me were the spired crestlines of the outside ranges.

Directly below was the newly formed moraine of Peters Glacier, the glacier itself appearing like a huge white reptile winding along the west side. Not yet smoothed by the elements, this moraine was one confused mass of drumlins, kettle holes, eskers and kames. Many miniature lakes glistened in the depressions; patches of green grass and dwarf willows along the water courses, with flowers and lichens, added a wealth of color to its desolate surface. Along the base of the mountain was the dumping ground of the avalanches—a wild disorder of débris.

Through bisected ranges of mountains I could see the rolling piedmont plateau, filled with hundreds of bright lakes, and still beyond could look over the vast wilderness of low relief all clothed in timber, until the vision was lost in the wavy outlines of rolling country merging into the horizon. Far to the northwest Lake Minchumina, reflecting the sun, fairly shone out of the dark timber-clad area surrounding it.

Alone in an unknown wilderness hundreds of miles from

civilization and high on one of the world's most imposing mountains, I was deeply moved by the stupendous mass of the great upheaval, the vast extent of the wild areas below, the chaos of the unfinished surfaces still in process of moulding, and by the crash and roar of the mighty avalanches.

The sun was low; a dark shadowy mantle was cast over the wild desolate areas below; the skyline of the great mountain burned with a golden glow; distant snowy peaks glistened white above sombre-colored slopes not touched by the light of the sun, which still bathed the wide forested region of the north. A huge avalanche ploughed the mountainside not a hundred and fifty yards to my left, while clouds of snow swept about me.

Awakening to a realization that I had been and was still in a path of danger, I slowly made the descent.

While wandering about the foot of the slope I observed a few very old tracks of rams, indicating that sheep, though they do not live within it, occasionally cross this area. Golden eagles had been in sight all day; bear diggings were numerous even on the lower slopes, where ground squirrels, conies, and marmots were plentiful; as were also fresh tracks of caribou. While returning I shot a fine marmot, and when outside the ranges I saw a band of cow caribou feeding on the ridges and two or three single bulls descending into the timber.

Reaching camp long after midnight, I was saddened by the thought that in order to find sheep I must move to new country. Nothing could have been more satisfactory than to have found them inhabiting these mountains. Hunting and stalking rams under the great dome would have been romantic indeed.

July 28. Rain fell all night and poured so hard in the morning that I did not leave camp until two in the afternoon, when I started with Haydon, who brought a .22 rifle for the purpose of collecting conies and marmots. When we reached the remains of the cow caribou I was surprised to see, standing near it, the calf, which at once caught sight of us, but stood still as I walked near enough to photograph it. It was a small calf, born that spring. Shortly after I pressed the kodak bulb, it began to circle round us until, when reaching a point where the wind blew from us toward it, it immediately threw up its tail and trotted off. Although the nostrils of this calf had never before known the scent of man, its actions from the time of seeing us to that of trotting off were similar to those of the adult.

As Denali was covered all day with dense clouds, we could not see even the base. Several conies, ground squirrels, and a marmot were shot with the .22 rifle. Again other parts of the mountains were examined without finding any signs of sheep; so I decided to move camp as early as the weather would permit. Once while approaching a small lake in a depression of the moraine, we saw two wandering tattlers flying about in alarm. One was killed by Haydon; the other alighted on a willow close to the lake. It kept constantly whistling and flying at us as we approached, and continued to fly from willow to willow in great distress while we searched for its young, which, judging by its actions, must have been near by.

July 29. Again rain fell heavily in the night and all the next day until six in the evening, preventing us from making a start. Numerous traps for mice had been put out, both in the timber and on the ridges, but not so much as a fresh sign of a mouse could we find.

For years I have looked back at the events of that evening with a feeling of shame and regret. It causes me no little humiliation to record them in my narrative, yet in submitting this case of bad judgment I can only plead a clear conscience as to my intentions. When I had taken my rifle and had gone about five hundred yards down the flat to a point where the timber was so scattered that I could see fairly well through it along the timbered slopes of the ridge, my eye caught a moving object which was immediately recognized as a large bull moose, standing among spruces and willows on a hillside two hundred yards away. He was rubbing his horns against a tree. Looking through the glasses, I was surprised to observe that all the points of his horns, for ten inches back, were apparently pure white—giving the impression that they were clear of the velvet. Knowing that it was altogether too early for velvet to be shed, I quietly seated myself to watch him and make sure of it. He kept constantly rubbing his horns on the willows, and also against a spruce. The antlers were huge, but as they could not be seen clearly through the brush, I watched them for five minutes through the glasses. So far as could be judged, even after making allowance for the season, the velvet appeared to be off and the horns white. The fact that the bull so persistently rubbed them confirmed this conclusion; hence believing this case an exception, I killed him.

I cannot express my chagrin at finding the antlers still in full velvet with all the points soft except two, from which the velvet had been rubbed off and which were fairly hard. But since the velvet on all the points, extending as far as the blades, was so light in color that it appeared white, and the remaining parts of the horns, which were seen in the brush, had been inconspicuous, I had been deceived. The antlers were magnificent, having a spread of sixty-seven inches. They probably would have spread over seventy in September. I called the men, who took many pounds of his fat and the whole of his nose for the purpose of eating it. His stomach contained mainly willow buds, with some *grass and green plants.*

I then ascended a knoll a hundred yards below and saw another big bull with large antlers quietly standing in the forest not a hundred yards distant, his head pushed forward, ears cocked up, while he looked straight at me. He silently backed a few steps, slowly turned, and almost crept out of sight into the woods. Two hundred yards farther on in the direction he had taken, the timber was scattered and I soon saw him going through it at a trot.

Then looking across the river, I saw another bull with equally large horns feeding among the willows a quarter of a mile away. This bull soon walked up to a steep bank and for a short time grazed on *grass.* Once or twice he struck his horns to the ground in evident anger, apparently because of finding difficulty in reaching the grass below.

Walking in a circle through the woods I came upon an old camp which had been occupied by some of the members of the Geological Survey party led by Alfred H. Brooks, who had crossed this country in 1902. Rain again fell as I reached camp and continued to pour all night.

Traveling Along the Alaska Range.

July 30–31. To study the mountain sheep of this region and collect specimens was the object of my trip; hence early in the morning we packed the horses and started in a north-easterly direction, keeping close to the base of the ranges. This gave an opportunity to examine the slopes for signs of sheep. We traveled on the piedmont plateau until late in the afternoon over fairly good ground, much of which was boggy, especially along the foothills close to the mountains. Numerous clear streams fringed with low stunted willows were crossed. All the pools in these creeks were full of grayling. The horses bogged frequently, causing much delay to adjust the packs. Some of the fords were rather dangerous, and in order to cross we often had to leap on the backs of the horses. A large carbuncle, beginning to appear on my left ankle, caused painful walking.

The first night we camped on a willow bar close to the mountains, and next day continued along their base until opposite Muldrow Glacier, where we crossed a high ridge directly north and descended to the south branch of the glacial river that flowed through several channels down the flat. Crossing these with some difficulty, we found ourselves in a magnificent meadow several square miles in area, covered with long nutritious grass. Proceeding two or three miles we camped in balsam poplars at the base of the dead moraine of Muldrow Glacier—a moraine similar in all respects to that of Peters Glacier. All the water flowing from the outside ranges between Peters Glacier and Muldrow Glacier is clear—indicating that none of it comes from glaciers of any size.

During these two days of arduous tramping I examined the mountains along the route without finding a sign indicating that they were inhabited by sheep. No sheep trails were

20

visible on the outer slopes and therefore I did not attempt to penetrate them.

The feature of the trip was the caribou; they were constantly in sight, both on the mountainsides and all about us on the rolling plateau—even on the river bars. In scattered bands of four to twenty, about 200 in all were casually observed, mostly young bulls, cows, and calves, though many old bulls were seen, always by themselves.

When we approached caribou with the wind, and still a long distance away, they would throw up their tails and trot off. If the wind were favorable, the pack-train would only excite their curiosity, and usually they either came trotting up to it, or ran off a short distance and came to a stand. After watching it awhile, in all cases they would begin to circle until they came into the wind. The moment they received the scent, they would give a great jump, erect their white 'flag,' exactly as would a deer, and trot off out of sight. Sometimes after scenting us they would gallop a short distance. The calves erected their tails exactly like the adults. Once, while we were eating lunch, two young bulls trotted up to the horses, which were feeding some distance away from us, and stampeded them. Other bands of caribou often came to within a hundred and fifty yards of the camp-fire and would circle until they received our scent, then leave in alarm. Another time, a bull came trotting toward the pack-train and stampeded the horses with their packs on.

Traveling through this piedmont plateau, close to the mountains, was like passing through a well-stocked cattle ranch in the West, except that here cattle were replaced by caribou.

As several bands of caribou were feeding in the great meadow where we camped, we had to hobble the horses when they were turned out to feed. All that day I had limped along, and by the time camp was made my ankle was so badly swollen that I knew it would not be possible to proceed the next day.

August 1–3. We were obliged to remain in this camp for three days, because the carbuncle had swollen to such proportions that I could not endure the least weight on my foot. The camp was so delightful, however, that patience was not overtaxed. We watched the horses blissfully feeding in the fine grass of the meadow, and enjoyed the glorious sight of the Alaska Range stretching away in the distance, its snowy crest-lines backed by a golden sky as the sun went low behind them. At this hour Denali's great bulk piercing the sky was usually clear. Until evening, except for one day, it was covered with clouds.

The abundant ground squirrels amused us, marmots whistled on the moraine, Canada jays flew about, the tree sparrows and intermediate sparrows sang continually, and waxwings and northern shrikes were particularly plentiful. White-tailed ptarmigan with broods of chicks were near; the wing-beats of ravens passing overhead hissed through the air; Arctic terns flew gracefully over the meadows; and golden eagles soared above the ridges. Old bear diggings were everywhere, but no large animal was seen except a big bull caribou which Haydon saw on the moraine. Our numerous traps failed to capture any mice, nor did we see any sign of these small mammals, always so interesting to the faunal naturalist.

August 4. Fortunately these three days were perfect. With a pocket knife, Karstens had finally succeeded in reducing my carbuncle, and on August 4 I was able to move camp. It was a beautiful day, and I followed the horses, limping along with the aid of a staff. After crossing the North Fork of Muldrow Branch, we ascended the ridge and circled round near the head of Moose Creek, with the magnificent panorama of the Alaska Range before us all day. This north fork is formed by the junction of two short branches above its entrance to the canyon, through which it runs for six or seven miles along the moraine. Late in the evening we descended to a vast glacial bar on one of these branches and followed it up to some willows, where made camp.

All that day caribou were as numerous as before. While lunching we noticed a calf, half a mile away, wandering along a side hill, and a cow on another ridge, half a mile to the right. Suddenly the cow began running in a swift gallop, taking various directions and circling in her efforts to find the strayed calf. At times she would lower her nose to the ground and seek to smell the calf's tracks, until finally she winded it and galloped in the right direction, circling about until she found it. Many times I have observed similar cases. Caribou are the only wild ruminants I have ever seen that constantly lose their young.

We were exploring a route close along the mountains, and being uncertain as to how far the country would permit pack-horse travel, I limped up on a mounatin near camp, and found it possible to proceed with the horses. Several bands of caribou were in sight, but as yet no signs of sheep. The whole country was carpeted with a profusion of beautiful wild flowers of various colors. Although we were among the mountains, none of the nights had been frosty.

August 5. The day was clear, balmy, and mild. Early in the morning we packed the horses and ascended a low ridge, from the top of which we saw nine caribou cows feeding on a nearby mountain and four more directly ahead. Enclosed by mountains on all sides, we worked our way along the side of a ridge which proved so boggy that the horse *Coghlan* broke through and became mired,* causing a delay to take off his pack and pull him out. After descending this ridge we were in a wide rolling pasture from which the waters drained into the Toklat River—an Indian name signifying 'Head of the Water.' Ten or twelve caribou cows were feeding on a hill to our right, while on the very top of a rounded summit ahead a large bull was lazily moving.

We then ascended a boggy ridge connecting two impassable mountains, and from its summit obtained a magnificent view of Denali, free from clouds, towering above the adjacent snowy peaks. I could now view its double summit from the east and distinctly see the great Muldrow Glacier falling down its eastern side from the snowfield between its two domes. That night I wrote in my journal: "The view from Bog Hill was magnificent and more complete of Denali than any I have yet seen. The south peak near the western extremity of the south dome is the highest point. A glacier [head

---

* This ridge proved so miry that the horses bogged several times, for which reason I named it *Bog Hill*.

of Harper Glacier of the Geological Survey Map] descends
between the south and the north summit-domes. I believe that
if the top of this glacier can be reached along its south edge
the mountain can be ascended. From my position it looked possible. But difficulties may be found below on parts of the
mountain I could not see."

It has interested me to learn that it was by this route that
three years later the party of Tom Lloyd made its ascent.

On the east slopes we stopped for a short time for lunch,
and I gave Haydon my rifle to shoot a small bull caribou to
replenish our stock of meat. He made a beautiful shot at three
hundred yards, dropping the bull dead. After lunch we crossed
a creek which is the Upper East Branch of Toklat River.
The mountains ahead and on both sides loomed high, rugged,
and imposing. We were traveling through a depression between two ranges, close to the snow-covered main Alaska
Range and not more than two or three miles distant. This depression continued, as far as I could see, for many miles
ahead. We had seen no spruce timber since leaving the vicinity of Peters Glacier, and on this branch of the Toklat even
willows were scant.

On a mountain to the right I saw a sheep trail and was
encouraged to feel that at last we had come to the edge of the
sheep country.

It was necessary to continue until timber could be found in
sufficient quantity to supply a camp. So we went on between
fine mountains, the slopes of which fall gently to the narrow
valley through which we were taking the horses. The highest
point of this valley forms a divide with the next branch of the
Toklat.

Exactly at four we passed over the top and were about to
descend to the creek flowing west, when a golden eagle
swooped, returned upward with wings spread, and continued
swooping at something hidden from my sight in one of the
numerous depressions.

Suddenly a white object came in view and moved along the
slope. Sheep at last! I thought. But the field glasses revealed
a grizzly bear walking along smelling the ground for squir-

rels or pawing a moment for a mouse. Under the bright sun its body color appeared to be pure white, its legs brown. It seemed utterly indifferent to the eagle, which again and again darted at it. Continuing, it often broke into a short run, pausing at times and throwing up its head to sniff the air— always searching for food.

After the long day's tramp I had difficulty in limping along, but with such game in sight I could not go on with the pack horses. So, taking the rifle, I jammed my staff in the ground and circled up the slope, hoping to anticipate the bear in a favorable wind. A year later I found this same staff still standing upright in the ground. My lame ankle was forgotten (much to my regret later), while I climbed as rapidly as possible. The bear had descended slightly and passed out of sight, but its course was disclosed by the eagle, which still continued to follow and swoop at it. Reaching a higher point I saw the bear going in a direction away from me. I climbed rapidly, and finally the bear, when still half a mile away, turned and came toward me. As observed through the glasses, it looked like a large male and I could see no cub following it.

I continued climbing to a point opposite two rough spurs projecting from the mountainside between me and the course of the bear, which though it had descended to a point near the end of the spurs, was still coming in my direction. Then I began a careful approach against the wind, lying flat when the bear's head pointed toward me, advancing more rapidly while its head was turned the other way. It advanced in such an irregular course that I never felt certain it would come within shot, and realized that it might pass above or below me. Still climbing, I found myself on the edge of a ravine three hundred yards wide, in the bottom of which was a creek divided into several channels. As the bear was still approaching I lay down, and wriggling over the skyline, worked down to the bars. The bear had then disappeared behind the spurs, so I walked rapidly to within a hundred and fifty yards and, cocking my rifle, sat down. If the bear should come around the foot of these spurs, my chance to kill it was excellent; but should it go over them, it would receive my scent.

For a few moments my anxiety was intense. The bear suddenly came in sight, running down the slope of the second spur and on reaching the foot turned directly toward me. As it came on rapidly, covering the ground with powerful strides, it looked indeed formidable. Its head was held low as it faced toward me, and as I wanted to avoid breaking the skull, so valuable for scientific study, I waited until it threw up its head to sniff the air; then fired at its shoulder. It gave one spring, grabbed the shoulder, twisted around three times low on the ground, and fell dead. Almost simultaneously, a response of exulting shouts came from the men who though they had watched the bear until it fell, had not once seen me.

Quickly going to it, I found it to be a female. The whole of the upper coat was pale buff, the legs were brown, the edges of the ears were even lighter than the coat, the eyes dark brown. The claws were shorter than those of grizzlies I had killed in the Yukon Territory.* Her teeth indicated an adult. Her body length was 58 inches; hind foot, 14½ inches; width of ball of forefoot, 5⅛ inches (130 mm.); width of hind foot, 4¾ inches (120 mm.). Her teats were shrunken, showing that she had not suckled a cub that season.

Haydon came quickly up the ravine and we took off the skin. The stomach contained the morning meal of grass, with three ground squirrels and a shrew, all partly digested. She had evidently been resting and had just begun to search for food. Though blueberries were abundant everywhere, her stomach did not contain a trace of them. Salmon had been running up Moose Creek, forty or fifty miles distant, but evidently she had not gone there to feed on them.

Karstens had made camp at the foot of the ravine. The horses, well hobbled, were feeding near on rich grass; a fire of dry willow twigs was burning, water was boiling ready to steep the tea; and over the coals a frying-pan was full of sizzling caribou steak.

Sitting down to appease a hunter's appetite, I looked toward the top of a mountain directly ahead and on a grassy

* See "The Wildnerness of the Upper Yukon," by Charles Sheldon. Scribners, 1911.

space just below the summit saw twelve sheep, which the glasses showed to be ewes and lambs. This was my first sight of sheep in the Alaska Range; how elated I felt! They soon worked a little lower to some rough rocks, where all lay down to pass the night. Two years before, after a long exploration in the Ogilvie Rockies, I had found my first sheep at the time of killing a grizzly bear. Here likewise, after an arduous exploration in the Alaska Range, I was rewarded with a similar experience.

Engulfed among mountains, we could look to the east between two ranges and see broad glacial valleys surrounded by irregular ranks of high crestlines. We slept without shelter and awoke eager for the onward march in search of spruce timber in which a convenient hunting camp could be made.

Head of the Toklat.

August 6. When we broke camp the sheep seen the night before were still in sight near the top of the same mountain, resting after their early morning meal. The way led down along the stony bottom of the creek, flanked on both sides by rough mountains, the steep slopes almost hanging over us. After going three miles we entered the wide glacial flats of the main Toklat and found ourselves at the limit of spruce timber, narrow bands of which fringed both sides of the river. Just before entering the woods I noticed, about three hundred yards out on the bar, a dark bulky object, its outlines blurred by the heat waves undulating under the hot sun. The glasses revealed a small grizzly bear standing half up on its hind legs, looking at us. As I reached for the rifle, which was tied on one of the pack horses, the bear turned, ran with great speed across the bar, plunged through the torrent of the glacial river, and continued running until lost to sight on the flat two miles beyond.

Finding an excellent spring of water at the edge of the timber we all set to work to make a comfortable camp. The shelter tent was placed outside the spruces, thus affording an unobstructed outlook over the broad flats, and was surrounded on all sides by inspiring mountains. The flat valley of the main Toklat, half a mile or more in width and bordered by high jagged ranges, runs nearly due north as far as the eye can see, and the belt of spruces reaches a hundred yards or so to the base of the mountains. Directly in front of our camp the two upper forks of the Toklat unite to form the main river. Between them is the magnificent mountain which from its position I named Divide Mountain. Both streams come from the south, each forking above and each coming from two small glaciers of the main range. East of the main Forks is a low pass [Polychrome Pass], beyond which, far in the distance, may be seen ranks of peaks belonging to the Teklanika Mountains.

Below our camp at the Forks the channels of the main Toklat descend swiftly over rocky bars a quarter of a mile or more in width. On the east side is the remnant of an ancient bar, now worn flat and covered with dryas and grass, with occasional patches of willows and dwarf birches close to the base of Divide Mountain. Our camp at the Forks was well situated. Nearby were plenty of dry spruces for fuel, an abundance of fine grass for the horses, and a fine spring of pure cold water. In addition, the conformation of the land on both sides gave excellent protection from the winds that swept up and down the valley. On the whole, this was the most attractive and convenient hunting camp I have ever occupied in the North.

The shelter tent was well erected, with a canvas stretched on inclined poles at one side to protect the provisions, and plenty of fuel wood was cut and piled near the fire. The bear skin was fleshed, salted, and hung over poles, and a hearty meal was eaten. Then I reclined before the fire, anticipating delightful days to come when I should be exploring the country for rams. Sheep were already in sight. Twelve could be seen far to the south on Divide Mountain, and four on the slope of a mountain to the north, all too distant to determine the sex. Ground squirrels were chattering near, red squirrels in the trees; and small traps for mice were set both in the woods and on the slopes above. Tree sparrows and intermediate sparrows were singing all around, jays were hovering near camp, and in the woods pigeon hawks were calling. Mosquitoes, which up to that time had swarmed as abundantly as elsewhere in the North, were now absent.

August 7. Early in the morning I crossed the river channels on the horse *Coghlan,* sending him back by Haydon, and went on toward Divide Mountain to see if the sheep then in sight three miles to the south were rams. For the next week my foot was extremely sore, but although painful it did not prevent me from tramping over the mountains. My moose-hide moccasins were not only a continual comfort, but ideal for summer hunting.

Bears had scratched all over the grassy flat for roots of the wild pea vines. I have never seen ground squirrels more abundant than they are all along the Alaska Range, where their chatter, even high on the mountains, is almost continuous. Before going far I saw six fine bull caribou feeding on a flat on the other side of the river, three of them carrying large antlers with the velvet still on. I contented myself with observing them, as they quietly grazed without much watchfulness or suspicion, although occasionally one or another would throw up his head to look. Although I walked for half an hour in plain sight, a quarter of a mile from them, not one noticed me.

Three sheep resting near the crest of Divide Mountain proved to be small rams. Returning to the foot of the slope I kept on, and coming near enough to scrutinize the other sheep, then lying down, saw that they also were rams. Their horns so well matched the background of rocks that, even through the field glasses, I could not determine the size. The majority of the rams, facing upward, maintained a careful watch above, while the others looked below constantly turning their heads in all directions. At times, some would stretch their necks out on the ground, lying half on their sides, their heads supported by their horns. Six others were idling about and picking up food near those lying down. In all, eighteen were in sight.

Not seeing a way of approaching them from this side of the mountain, I carefully circled round a projecting spur and when out of their sight began the ascent. It was difficult climbing over loose broken rock among cliffs and walls where the rock was loose and disintegrating. Finally, after working over the crest of the spur all the rams were seen lying down, a hundred and fifty yards below. With the exception of two that were four-year-olds, all were aged three years or less—not a head worth having among them, so they were left undisturbed. At no time did one take a position as a 'sentinel,' and about four in the afternoon all rose and fed for an hour before beginning to go lower down.

While feeding high they were alert like ewes, keeping a constant watch in all directions, but the moment they started downward their caution began to increase until finally, when reaching the lower slopes, they became so nervous that they could scarcely feed. As if taking extraordinary chances, two made a sudden dash downward for some small willows, but after snatching a leaf or two, ran back upward to the others. In fact, these small rams were so nervous when below that one or another was constantly rushing about and watching as if immediate danger threatened from all directions.

Several times when a marmot whistled, all raised their heads and became uneasy. Finally, after feeding for twenty minutes on the lower slope they began to climb up by runs and jumps, in the usual way. But once, while all slowly ran upward for fifty yards or more, each kept his mouth open as if panting.

August 8. The morning was very hot. I climbed the mountain behind camp and circled round it to the north side, but although wonderful views were had of rock-shattered slopes, deep basins, canyons, and alpine scenery, no sheep were found. On a mountain farther to the north, on the other side of the river, sixty ewes and lambs were feeding on a grassy slope, while one was lying down a hundred feet above them. Not waiting to observe whether this 'sentinel' would later join them, I returned to camp for lunch, and then went to the bear's carcass. Nothing had touched it. The sheep that had been seen on a mountain near it were still there peacefully feeding. Golden eagles, ravens, and marsh hawks were common, and I noticed a wolverine track on the bars of the creek.

When I returned in the evening it was cold, the sun was low, shadows fell about the mountains, and the lights playing on their summits were particularly beautiful. At camp, the roar of the river was the only sound breaking the silence that brooded over this wonderful wilderness. Daylight still lingered between ten at night and three in the morning. The first frost of the season occurred that night.

August 9. The horses, gentle and always easy to catch, had adopted as their feeding ground a flat two hundred yards from camp, where grass was long and nutritious. This place was chosen principally for the reason that from it they could see in all directions. Their experiences with caribou had made them extremely nervous, and they were constantly alert and watchful. While passing them in going from or returning to camp, I always observed them, and found without fail that they possessed senses as keen as those of any wild animal. We had been obliged to put short hobbles on them, yet in the morning they had wandered far up the creek, having evidently been frightened by caribou whose tracks we saw near the pasture. Haydon consumed the whole morning finding and bringing them back.

From the camp sixty ewes were in sight to the north, and ten or fifteen small rams to the south; also several other ewes on a mountain near the Forks. I visited and reset the mouse traps. That year mice had almost disappeared. In the woods we caught only two Dawson red-backed mice, and on the mountain slopes seven meadow mice. These proved to be a new subspecies and were described by W. H. Osgood under the name *Microtus miurus oreas.*

After lunch I rode across the river and tramped up the Upper East Branch, which, coming from the south along the east of Divide Mountain, curves westerly for three miles to the Forks. Bordering this branch on the east is a rugged range of richly colored rock which I called East Branch Range. Both it and the Divide Range [Divide Mountain] are long spurs from the main Alaska Range. Seeing nine sheep at the north end of the East Branch Range I climbed far enough to recognize them as ewes; at the same time more than seventy-five ewes and lambs were visible on the same range, farther to the south. Descending to the flat, I went near enough to watch them. Some were lying down, others feeding. A few small rams stood by themselves apart from the ewes, while the lambs kept running about in play. Six or

seven lambs, on some cliffs a hundred yards below, were leaping about the rocks, chasing each other and playing, entirely
separate from the ewes. More than a third of the ewes were
without lambs. The lambs varied so much in size that some
must have been at least a month older than others. No ewe at
any time acted the part of a 'sentinel,' but all were extremely
alert and watchful. Twice a golden eagle alighted on a rock
fifty yards from the band, yet none of the ewes paid any attention to it, nor did the eagle seem interested in them. While
hunting sheep in the Yukon Territory during the two previous years, and also while in the Alaska Range that summer,
I observed the relations between golden eagles and sheep, not
once noticing any antagonism between them—but only complete indifference. [See 1908 observations, pp. 367 and 382.]
After enjoying the sight of these sheep for an hour and a
half, I waded the ice-cold channels of the river and climbed
Divide Mountain. The large band of ewes opposite camp began to feed upward at seven in the evening, and at nine all
were lying down among high rocks near the crest.

Near the top of Divide Mountain were three widely separated pairs of small rams. I stalked to within a hundred yards
of one pair, consisting of four-year-olds, and pointed my rifle
at them, but did not care to kill them. Like all small rams,
they were nervous and alert. I tried some experiments to test
their sight. Going below to a distance of a hundred and fifty
yards from the rams, while they were not looking, I crept in
sight and remained motionless. My clothes were of a neutral
color. The rams often looked directly at me, but though they
seemed to recognize an unusual object, apparently did not
realize any danger. Then, when the chance offered, I sat up
and remained motionless. Again and again they looked toward me, but still did not recognize danger. Withdrawing, I
went three hundred yards below them, crept out in sight, and
waited without moving, but they paid little attention to me
even when looking in my direction. When their heads were
down I sat up, and when they next looked up I moved slowly.
The effect was immediate: they looked at me for a few seconds and then ran over the top.

From the top of Divide Mountain I could see on other mountains more than a hundred ewes and lambs, including the sheep on the East Branch Range. Four bull caribou were feeding below on the bar. By the time I reached camp after ten, the horses had again become frightened and had wandered off.

Searching for Big Rams.

August 10. Early in the morning a large band of ewes and lambs was seen on the outside range, six or seven miles to the north. Having seen ewes on all the mountains in that direction I concluded that the large rams must be on the main Alaska Range to the south. It may be recorded here that the character of the rock on all these mountains composed a background so contrasting to the white sheep of the region that at times they could easily be seen with the naked eye from a distance of three or four miles—often farther. On the outside range I first observed them from my camp as white spots six or seven miles distant. This was different from my experience while observing sheep in Yukon Territory where, in most places, their color blended better with the rocks.

After an early breakfast I headed south toward a deep narrow canyon that bisected a part of the divide range four miles from camp. While Haydon and I were riding over to the flat near the foot of the mountains, we saw a three-year-old ram lying down near the crest; it soon detected us, jumped up and ran over the top. I kept on alone and entering the canyon found myself in a deep narrow gorge, its rock walls rising several hundred feet on both sides not a hundred feet apart, eroded into fantastic shapes—gouged, pillared, and furrowed. Through the bottom flowed a swift clear creek in which no grayling were observed. In fact, none of the grayling, so abundant in the main river far below, ascend the silt-laden waters above until September, when the glaciers do not melt so rapidly and the river becomes low and clear. Grayling then run up and remain until spring, when the glaciers again send forth the silt-laden torrents that rush in raging turmoil over the bars.

This narrow precipiced canyon, penetrating the range for a quarter of a mile, leads to a wonderful circular basin. Steep, rough-hewn, craggy mountain slopes surround it—their sides fluted by canyons and gorges, with large fields of snow embanked below the summit crestlines, and tiny creeks dashing down in all directions. Walls, mounds, and pyramids of volcanic material—fantastic displays of disintegrating rock—are strewn irregularly about. I felt enclosed as though within the standing walls of a great mountain castle the interior of which had been demolished.

Coming from the canyon into the basin, I saw a four-year-old ram on a grassy knoll, and farther to the right another of the same age feeding with a three-year-old.

Our caribou meat was almost exhausted and we were all anxious for mutton; here was a chance to kill sheep where horses could be taken to the carcasses. The rams passed out of sight but when I had advanced to within a hundred and fifty yards of the spot, the first one reappeared. I shot offhand; the bullet passed through the middle of his body, shattering fragments from the rocks behind. At first I thought the shot had missed, but when the ram began to stagger I did not fire again. Then the other four-year-old ram appeared a hundred and seventy-five yards distant. At my shot fragments of rock flew behind him also, and in a moment he fell dead and rolled downward. His smaller companion, which had been close to him when I fired, looked down at the dead body, then at the wounded ram, and after watching both for some time, lay down.

Looking over the other slopes, I saw four more small rams near the crest of a mountain and two others in a different direction. Like all the sheep of the region, the two rams killed were pure white, although a search would usually reveal a few black hairs in the tail, and now and then a few scattered above it or along the back. Both rams were very fat; they were perfectly prime and in the best condition for eating. Their stomachs contained nothing but green plants.

The gorge where they were killed I named Ram Canyon. Through the field glasses a doubtful route was located up the mountains to the north, and after a hazardous climb of two hours the crest was reached. From the top several other small rams could be seen on the slopes surrounding the basin, which from my viewpoint revealed itself in all its wild beauty and grandeur. Mounting a pinnacle, I seated myself to lunch and enjoy the glory of the stupendous landscape. Ewes and lambs were visible in several directions, and on the bar below three bull caribou were standing at rest near the river, their heads hanging close to the ground. Two golden eagles were soaring along the crests; conies were bleating, and now and then the whistle of a marmot sounded, while slightly below, ground squirrels were running about.

The rugged snowy crest of the Alaska Range almost over-hanging me extends in a continuous sea of rough peaks and cones, flanked by the bare outer ranges, for fifty or fifty-five miles southwesterly to Denali, which, towering up in a clear sky, appeared only a few miles away. This wonderful range reaches eastward as far as I could see. Below are the wide valleys of the Toklat, its several channels shining under the sun; to the north, the outside ranges, and still beyond them the vast forested areas of the lower country. I could clearly see the whole top of the great mountain and again concluded that the west peak of the south dome is the highest point.

Following the irregular crest toward the main range, which joins it three miles to the south, I enjoyed the most enchant-ing kind of sheep hunting—walking along a high mountain crest, with the most wonderful landscape I had ever beheld unfolding before me.

The walking was very different from that on the high crests of the mountains in Yukon Territory. Here the ranges subordinate to the main range are composed of conglomer-ates, slates, and volcanic intrusions, nearly all in a state of active disintegration. Here and there are masses of limestone, but for the most part none of the other rock is solid, espe-cially where it rises in walls or cliffs. The crests are broken by deep gorges and cirques, the slopes exceedingly steep, the whole range carved irregularly, with great masses of talus reaching down a thousand feet from the summit.

While walking along the smoother parts, I experienced periods of supreme exhilaration, followed by periods of intense anxiety in realizing the difficulties and dangers of my position. As I climbed up and down the crags almost every foothold or handhold was on a loose rock, which several times gave way, making my position dangerous in the extreme. Every step and hold had to be carefully tested, but even then I could never feel sure that an apparently unyielding rock would not be dislodged when my weight bore upon it. Once, when halfway up an almost perpendicular wall of two hundred feet, the rocks under my feet loosened and fell; I was holding on with hands and knees, fearful that the rocks above also would give way. I could not retreat, and though finally managing to reach the top, was filled with doubt as to the possibility of a safe descent.

After several such experiences while winding among the crests above the cirques, I finally reached the last peak, the one adjoining a glacier in the main range, which is the source of the extreme east division of the Upper West Branch of the Toklat. Finding a sheep trail leading round this peak, I followed it through a rough cirque to some grassy benches near the glacier. Far below I spied a single ewe and the trail led toward her. She soon saw me and at once ran up the rocky side of the canyon, followed, to my surprise, by a tiny lamb not more than two or three weeks old. This was a positive proof that exceptionally some of the ewes mate well along in December or even in January.

Reaching the bottom of the cirque I found that the creek formed by the gathering streams from the snow above emerged, not through the narrow walled outlet of the cirque, but through a hole in the solid rock, from which it dropped fifteen feet to a gorge down which it cascaded to the glacial river below. Since the mountain at that end was limestone, I had no difficulty in following the slope down to the benches —exquisite green areas, set in fields of snow and ice. While coming down the slope of the cirque, I had caught a glimpse of several sheep on the side of a mountain across the river, and carefully climbing a bench, peeked over.

Before me was a glacier filling a depression in the mountain, with high rugged walls rising on all sides, the melting ice forming a river that plunged down a rocky channel. Just across from it was a mountain of impressive architecture—almost a true pyramid, with a single lofty spire shooting up from its summit—a pyramid that would tower high above those built by man in Egypt, emphasizing the insignificance of man's works compared with those of Nature.

But this was not all my eyes beheld in that remote wonderful mountain recess. On the grassy reaches near the glacier was a band of more than seventy-five ewes and lambs. And a short distance away were twelve rams, three and two-year-olds, while on the other side of the river, thirteen or fourteen more small rams were grazing close to the glacier. Not far below the glacier, well up on the mountain side, were sixteen or seventeen other ewes and lambs actively feeding.

For the first time, I had come upon large bands of ewes which, owing to the remoteness of their temporary abode, had to some degree relaxed their caution. They were at an elevation of nearly six thousand feet. It was a scene of evening peace, in a green spot, brightening the austere surroundings. Half the ewes were lying down, some of them even on the bar of the creek; others quietly feeding on the tender young dryas, while the lambs were continually bleating, frisking, butting one another, and now and then dashing up a wall of rocks where they leaped about in pure sport. Although I tried photographs, the light was too dull to get good results. The whole band was not a hundred yards from me. There was no sentinel, and although the ewes kept a careful watch in all directions, the extreme nervousness and alertness usually so characteristic of them were lacking.

I withdrew before any of them suspected my presence, and started down the creek, hoping soon to reach the river bars below; but because it flowed through a canyon, I was obliged to toil along the broken slope for two miles before descending and gaining the flat below. As I rounded the curve of the fork and came out in the broad flat valley, six bull caribou were lying down three hundred yards ahead, one of them with a wonderful pair of antlers. In order not to disturb them, I circled well around, and looking up on the range west of the Upper West Branch (which I call the West Branch Range), discovered twenty-five sheep lying down high up near the crest. During the dim hours of the night I tramped back seven miles to camp, while the sky above the main range glowed pink and gold and deathlike stillness brooded over the mountains.

August 11. Though the nights were now frosty, as yet none of the vegetation had been affected. The country was green and the flowers still displayed a wealth of color, painting the surface with brilliant hues. Both men started early with the horses to bring the meat from yesterday's kill while I pushed rapidly up the Upper East Branch to examine the main range at the head of the valley. Along the slopes of the East Branch Range eighty or ninety ewes were still feeding —the same animals I had seen two days before—now divided into two bands grazing some distance apart. Both bands were fairly low on the green slopes, presenting a peaceful scene of wild animal life, with the lambs gamboling about bleating, the mothers responding in deeper tones.

Some of the sheep were resting, others feeding; one band appeared to have a 'sentinel,' but the other did not. Although the sheep were rather sluggish, all were alert and watchful. In this region feed is so abundant that the large bands of ewes, in order to satisfy their hunger, do not have to travel so far and so often as in some other regions. On the green slopes all were exceedingly conspicuous, almost as much so as when the background is dark rock. Along the east slope of Divide Range thirty young rams, probably the ones I had already seen, were feeding near the crest, not one of them over four years old.

This valley was inspiring in its beauty, even more so than that of the Upper West Branch—the East Branch Range being more rugged, with an exquisitely tinted, broad irregular band of pink volcanic intrusion extending through the whole length of its west slope. Here also, areas of greenstone mingled with a wide variety of richly colored rock. The main

ranges at the head were thrown up in rougher outlines, and
the snow-capped peaks appeared to rise higher above the
ragged crestline. A high limestone mountain, the peak of
which dominates the Divide Range, links it with contrasting
color to the main range. It was on the other side of this limestone mountain that I had seen so many sheep the day before.
The valley widens into a broad area of bars and gravel flats
near the head, and there the Upper East Branch forks in a
manner similar to that of the Upper West Branch.

On a wide rocky bar, near where this fork divides, two
large bull caribou were standing at rest, heads hanging down
as usual, apparently indifferent to whatever enemy might approach. I have watched caribou standing in this attitude for
more than forty minutes before one would lazily raise its
head to look. Before these noticed me I walked to within
seventy-five yards and photographed them, but their bodies,
blending so well with the rocky background, did not appear
on the negatives. The wind was blowing from them to me,
but while I was trying to walk nearer they saw me, threw up
their heads in an alert attitude, gazed at me for a moment,
and then trotted or galloped off, neither throwing up his tail
as other caribou had done after scenting me. These bulls trotted along the base of the mountain not a hundred yards below
the sheep, all of which paused in their feeding, raised their
heads and looked at the passing caribou. When the latter had
gone past them a short distance, the sheep quietly resumed
feeding, evidently not having been in the least alarmed.

I was close to the main range, and noticed on one of the
mountains about thirty sheep resting not far below the snow;
but when near enough to distinguish them through the field
glasses, found that all were ewes and lambs. This was a great
disappointment and I began to realize that my camp might
not be in the vicinity of the haunts of the big rams. I continued to wander in various directions, but could not find
other sheep.

Late in the evening as I started back two bull caribou came
into view well below on the bar. They saw me from a long distance and trotted across the river to a mountain slope where

they remained in sight, feeding directly below the ewes that were resting up near the crest. Soon another bull caribou came down from the Divide Range. Without suspicion he crossed my morning trail and slowly walked across the bar, meeting and passing two others which likewise crossed my trail without noticing it, and disappeared in a small pocket in the mountains.

They were a long distance off, and when finally I approached the spot, the wind blowing strongly from me toward them evidently carried my scent past them without wafting it into the indentation. As I rounded a projection I surprised them lying down not forty feet away. Seeing me they quickly jumped up and galloped off for two hundred feet with *tails down*. But a little later, evidently when they came into my scent, *their tails went up at once;* they almost reared on their hind legs in terror. They were completely confused and rushed away in an S-shaped course for three hundred yards more, when they paused, apparently to look back in an effort to ascertain the cause of alarm. They continued to run, with similar pauses, to the mountain, their alarm evidently increasing, for they galloped without stopping from the foot clear over the crest. In contrast to the effect of my scent on these caribou, the two others, which had twice been frightened by the sight of me, were still quietly feeding at the foot of the mountain slope half a mile up the valley.

August 12. Camp was reached long after midnight, and in the morning I climbed the West Branch Range, zigzagged up its highest peak (7,400 feet in altitude) and traveled for several hours among its crests, seeing ewes and lambs on its slopes, also other ewes in various directions on adjacent mountains. But although many new areas were examined, not a ram did I find. While tramping among the savage rocks, inspecting slopes and canyons for sheep, bull caribou were seen below on the bars.

Reaching camp late in the afternoon just before a heavy thunder shower, my disappointment was very keen, for the range I had climbed that day seemed to be my last resource. All the other ranges within reach of camp were frequented only by ewes, lambs, and young rams. Not then familiar with the habits and haunts of the old rams, I believed that all the mountains in the vicinity were ewe mountains, and that the big rams must have their feeding grounds in another locality.

In order to catch the last steamer running up the Yukon, I had been advised that it was necessary to reach that river at least by September 15. To do this might require a trip of three weeks or more, and it was already near the middle of August. After searching these mountains for a distance of sixty miles and finally finding ranges where sheep were more abundant than I had ever imagined, I began to feel doubtful of the complete success of my long trip to Denali and the Alaska Range, the main object of which was to collect some large rams and study the habits of the sheep.

Twenty miles to the east could be seen the rugged crestline, topped by spired peaks, of a mountainous region. I decided to take a pack horse and one of the men, go there if possible, and after establishing a camp, send the man back with the horse, and remain alone. Not only did I long for solitude in this wonderful wilderness, but when completely alone, undisturbed by the numerous little diversions of camp life, men, and horses, I had always been able to put more energy into the hunting. Time could be saved in cooking, both morning and evening, the fire and smoke reduced to a minimum, and also the noise, so that in the vicinity of the camp, animals would be frightened as little as possible.

August 13. I planned to start this morning, but for the first time since leaving Denali, a severe rainstorm interfered with traveling. Nevertheless, Haydon and I strapped blankets on two of the horses, faced the rain, and rode over the divide of East Branch Range, to ascertain if a favorable route for pack horses could be found. After passing the divide and riding far enough to see that horses could easily be taken to the mountains, we returned to camp, completely drenched. The field glasses had revealed several large bands of sheep on the mountains ahead and I thought it might be possible that big rams might be found there without going to the more distant ranges that had been selected for the new camp.

August 14–15. These two days brought still more worry and disappointment, for storm, rain, and fog filled the forty-eight hours of impatient waiting. Whenever the fog lifted for a short interval, ewes and lambs could be seen on the mountains. In fact, while this camp was occupied there was never a moment that I could not stand outside the shelter and see sheep on some of the mountains.

August 16. The morning was cloudy, with a light drizzling rain; but the warm atmosphere and lack of wind were encouraging. We put a pack on *Tuffy,* Haydon mounted *Jimmy,* I *Babe,* and we started, leading both *Tuffy* and *Coghlan.* It was necessary to keep all the horses together, or they would stray off, for the purpose of finding each other.

My recollection of that day's travel is still vivid. After crossing the divide of the East Branch Range [Polychrome Pass] most of the way was soft and boggy, all the little depressions filled with water through which we slopped along, climbing and descending hills and ridges, passing through valleys, crossing wide bars, and going up creeks. After lunching on the wide bars of the East Fork of the Toklat—a stream equally as heavy in volume as the main Toklat and forking and flowing through glacial valleys in a similar manner—we crossed two divides. One of these led to a branch of the Teklanika River, the next to the main Teklanika which flows through a wide glacial valley resembling those of the branches of the Toklat. Late in the evening we descended to the bars at the limit of spruce timber, and there tied together two pack-cloths, threw them over inclined poles, cut some boughs, and camp was ready.

Shortly after we left camp the rain ceased, but showers fell at intervals all day. Several bands of sheep were observed, and just after crossing the first divide, we saw a beautiful cross fox. I fired at him at a distance of three hundred yards and he ran into a patch of willows as if wounded. I rapidly followed only to see him jump out twenty feet away and make off—this time with a gait that showed no evidence that the bullet had touched him.

All the mountains along our route could be clearly seen, and all were well sprinkled with sheep. There were large bands of eighty or more, and small bands of a few individuals. Some were resting, others feeding at different elevations—sheep on every mountain we passed. I could not count them, but 800 is a conservative estimate of the sheep seen that day, though I really believe that nearly a thousand came within my field of vision. Alas! all, with the exception of one band of twenty-four small rams, on a mountain near the last divide leading to the main Teklanika, were ewes and lambs. Many of these sheep saw us from a distance and hurried up the mountain side; others stood and looked at us for awhile before they began to walk slowly upward.

After leaving the East Fork of the Toklat we saw four large bull caribou lying down—the wind blowing from them to us—and approached to within two hundred yards before they noticed us and ran, tails down. Farther on seven small bull caribou were feeding very close to sheep near the foot of a mountain white with sheep, while a large bull was standing some distance away. It was with the greatest difficulty that we were able to keep the horses from stampeding when they saw these caribou; and their nervousness made it extremely hard to lead them over this rough wet country.

Although old bear diggings had been abundant everywhere in the region, I had not seen a bear since our arrival at the main camp. A few miles down the river moose were very plentiful, but as we were hunting just above the limit of their feeding ground, only a stray track here and there showed that one occasionally wandered up the river about as far as the limit of timber.

Where were the big rams? Were all the mountains of this region occupied exclusively by ewes and young rams? Had I chanced upon the wrong localities? During the few days I could remain to hunt was I facing failure to accomplish the main purpose of my long trip? These questions agitated me before I doubled under the same robe with Haydon and fell asleep, while heavy rain continued to beat on the canvas all night.

Head of the Teklanika.

August 17. Still raining this morning! My disgust was extreme. Haydon left early, taking all the horses with him. My little camp was situated well within the hospitable spruces, in a spot affording glorious vistas of mountains on all sides. The morning was spent completing my shelter, filling in the sides with small spruces, gathering more spruce boughs for the bed, chopping an abundant supply of wood for fuel, arranging everything in such order that in the future every possible moment could be used in hunting. A large pot of mutton soup was cooked, thickened to a mass with rice and meat—enough to last for several meals, requiring no more time than that necessary to warm it.

By noon everything was ready, but the rain still fell. Directly behind camp was the base of a rough range that rose in a rugged mass on the east side of the valley. This range is higher, more imposing, cleft by more canyons, scooped out by more cirques, eroded and sculptured in more chaotic outlines than any of those bordering the several forks of the Toklat. It extends with a bewildering crestline six or seven miles south to the main range at the head of the valley, where the mountains are not so imposing as those parts of the main range I had seen to the westward. The basin of the glacier at the head is so low as to form a fairly easy divide across the main range. The valley of the Teklanika is in a general way similar to other glacier valleys of the region—wide rocky bars cut into numerous channels by the river, bordered, usually on both sides, by flats of variable width, which in places extend with a gentle incline to the bases of the bordering mountains.

46

Opposite on the west side of the river is a high massive mountain [Sable Mountain of the U. S. Geological Survey map], its broken face fronting the valley, and with rugged pyramidal peaks rising from the crest. Its whole side is indented by deep canyons between projecting spurs and high precipices, with enormous masses of black rock isolated on its rough slopes—masses hewn and worn into strange resemblance to huge cathedrals. The rocks of this mountain present striking contrasts of color—black, pink, red, gray, green, and white—all occurring irregularly and producing a crazy-quilt effect, yet so patched on the great mass as to harmonize and give an impression of surpassing beauty. This is the outside mountain, north of which is the forested country of low relief.

This mountain is the eastern end of the range swinging westward to the Toklat, its south slopes facing my route of the day before. The range is cleft by branches of the Teklanika on the east and the Toklat on the west. To the south is a high ridge, rising rapidly for three miles to form the range at the extreme head of the Teklanika. [This ridge is the divide between Bull River, the main eastern branch of the Chulitna on the south, and the series of glaciers at the heads of the Toklat and Teklanika, and may be regarded as the northern part of the main Alaska Range.]

On the east side of the Teklanika, north of my camp, the spruces extend for a mile to a vast meadow where they become scattered and mixed with willows. This meadow spreads for two miles over a fairly wide area as far as another large branch of the river.

As the rain continued my hopes sank, for time was passing and I had to content myself with watching a dozen ewes and lambs not ten minutes' walk from camp. At 3 P. M. however the rain ceased, the mist cleared, and I was soon tramping north down the river to inspect the great mountain [Sable Mountain] on the opposite side. To the southwest, seventy-five ewes were visible; to the east a few sheep, too far off to determine the sex. Having gone a mile, the glasses showed twelve sheep high up near the north end of the mountain of many colors—Cathedral Mountain I called it. Viewed from

half a mile nearer, all were seen to be rams. Still nearer, and
the glasses revealed that some of them had large horns. Big
rams! After an arduous exploration of the country for more
than eight miles, including many days of toilsome tramping
over rough mountains, at last I had found old rams! I could
scarcely believe it, but after going a little nearer, the glasses
confirmed it. Among thirteen rams, nine had strikingly big
horns. Two more rams, one with a good head, came over the
crest, but the others assumed a threatening attitude and
would not permit these to join the band.

Seating myself, I studied the mountain with the field glass
in the hope of finding a reasonable route for stalking the rams.
The slope was exceedingly steep, the canyons were deep, the
talus in places seemed almost perpendicular. Here and there
between areas of talus were strips of slippery grassy ground.
The rams were near the crest, well toward the north end of
the mountain, feeding on the edge of a deep canyon whose
sides of shattered rock rose up in precipices, furrowed here
and there with depressions that possibly might be ascended.
But these routes of approach were below the rams and could
not be undertaken with any hope of success. It was impossible
to circle the crest directly above the rams because it was split
by the head of the canyon, leaving a gap of high unscalable
cliffs. Only one possible route seemed available, and even this,
since part of the approach would be in plain sight of the sheep,
was extremely doubtful. Half a mile to the south of the rams
I could keep out of sight while ascending the slope, until well
up near the heads of the intervening canyons, and then stalk
across the open slope directly toward them. It was obvious
that along such a route the probability of success would be
doubtful, but on the other hand, the next day the rams might
be far away. I realized also that the success or failure of the
whole trip might depend on the result of this stalk, and that,
since my time was so limited, the risk was worth taking. Moreover, my several years' experience in hunting sheep in Alaska
and Yukon Territory had taught me that with proper caution
it is sometimes possible to approach sheep, even when in
plain sight. This encouraged me to make the attempt. De-

scending from the high bluff bordering the river, extreme
caution was necessary while crossing the three hundred yards
of bars and the four intervening channels, which at that time
of the day, owing to the rapid melting of the glaciers, were
rushing and roaring at maximum height. As any of the rams
could easily detect me when moving on the flat, I slowly
crawled to the first channel, and after a look at the rams
through the field glasses, plunged at a selected moment into
the river. Once wading, I could not stop until across, and to
cross these channels without being seen by the rams was
not only doubtful, but was by far the most dangerous part
of the whole stalk. The moosehide moccasins afforded a weak
foothold and several times, when nearly up to my hips in the
swirling icy water, its leaping combers dancing around me, I
was nearly swept off my feet. The chances were that such an
accident would mean death. A long time was consumed in
reaching the fringe of spruces at the base of the mountain,
but it was finally accomplished without being observed by the
rams. Once, while crossing the bar, I saw the two new rams,
chased by three of the others, suddenly turn and run back
over the crest. I knew that they were outsiders, prohibited
from joining the others by the spirit of the band.

Not worried by the unlucky 'thirteen,' then quietly feeding in the same place, I went up rapidly through the spruces
to a grassy slope and hidden from the rams climbed as quickly
as possible, while rain, driven by a strong wind blowing from
the sheep directly toward me, began to fall. Finally, when half
a mile away, I turned and started directly toward them, the
light rain beating on my face.

A magnificent new landscape was spread about me, the
mountain panorama made wilder by the wind and rain; while
banks of clouds, filling the lower depressions, caused the
spired crestlines to loom as if suspended along a broken horizon. My position seemed almost to overhang the river below, from which the noise of the rushing torrents sounded
with a dull continuous roar.

For an hour and a half my advance along that steep broken
slope required all the caution and strategy that experience had

taught me. Often in plain sight of the rams, necessitating the most careful watchfulness, I moved only when all the heads were down or turned away; at other times depressions shielded me from their eyes. The grassy slopes were steep and slippery, the broken rocks loose and likely to fall with disastrous noise. Two canyons were crossed, both with extreme difficulty and danger.

During all this time the rams were quietly feeding in the way characteristic of old ones. They appeared fat and heavy, with short thick necks that protruded when their heads were up. Their movements were sluggish and expressive of supreme confidence. Ewes are more active, their motions more jerky; they impress the stalker as more alert and watchful. But to one who knows sheep well, the apparently indifferent actions of the old rams are not deceptive. They quietly raise their heads to look, their gaze is calm, one or another is nearly always looking either up, down, or sidewise. The experienced stalker knows that their very unconcern implies that their senses of sight and hearing are employed in a way far more effective than are those of ewes, which depend more on the collective sense of the band than on that of the individual members. But, even when with his band, each ram watches for himself, independent of the others—watches more carefully than do ewes, and with vision as keen. A band of rams usually detects approaching danger much sooner than does a band of ewes.

My advance, slow and difficult, was one of increasing suspense. I had succeeded in approaching so near that the chance of success would be ruined by the slightest mistake. Had one of the rams seen me in motion at any time during that stalk, at once all would have moved off. Many times one or another —sometimes several—were apparently looking right at me as I lay motionless on the slope. But even if they did see my bulk, not one suspected me as an enemy. Unless the stalker is very near, if he stands still, or if sitting upright remains motionless, sheep do not often become suspicious. But if they detect the slightest movement, they are suddenly alarmed. At any distance, even when motionless, the stalker must always avoid suspicious attitudes. This means that as he advances, he must continually observe the surface about him, and also the immediate background, in order that he may properly adjust his postures.

Before crossing the second canyon, I was only three hundred yards away, crawling on a slope of broken rock where it was necessary to feel carefully and select each knee and elbow rest. Finally, after mounting the opposite side of the canyon, I advanced foot by foot in the intervals of their watching. At other times many minutes were required to so arrange the small broken rocks as to prevent their falling or my slipping. As I climbed out of this canyon two marmots whistled, but on peering over the edge my anxiety was relieved by noticing that the rams were not disturbed. A golden eagle uttering shrill screams was soaring above the band but the rams paid no attention to it; nor did they to the querulous bleat of the conies or the chatter of ground squirrels. When I finally reached the brink of the canyon beyond which the rams were feeding, the rain had decreased to a drizzle but the wind was fairly strong. As the canyon walls were too precipitous to descend, my time for action had come.

Finding a slight depression at the edge I crept into it and lay on my back. Then slowly revolving to a position with my feet forward, I waited a few moments to steady my nerves. My two-hundred-yard sight had been pushed up, and watching my opportunity, I slowly rose to a sitting position, elbows on knees. Not a ram had seen or suspected me. I carefully aimed at a ram standing broadside near the edge of the canyon, realizing that the success of my long arduous trip would be determined the next moment. I pulled the trigger and as the shot echoed from the rocky walls, the ram fell and tried to rise, but could not. His back was broken. The others sprang into alert attitudes and looked in all directions. I fired at another standing on the brink, apparently looking directly at me. At the shot, he fell and rolled into the canyon. Then a ram with big massive wrinkled horns dashed out from the band and, heading in my direction, ran down into the canyon. The others immediately followed, but one paused at the brink and, as I fired, dropped and rolled below. Another turned and was running upward as I fired and missed him.

For a moment, after I had put a fresh clip of cartridges in the rifle and pushed down the sight, all was silence. I remained motionless. Then came a slight sound of falling rocks and the big ram appeared, rushing directly toward me—coming so fast that he crossed the slope to the brink of the canyon before I could get a bead on him. He dashed down the steep opposite side and came running up only twenty feet away, when I fired. He kept on, but fell at the edge of the canyon behind me. Two other big rams were following, but when I fired at him, they separated. One ran up the canyon and as he paused a moment, I killed him in his tracks. The other had gone below but at the sound of the shot, started back. When he reached the top I fired and he rolled down near the bottom. A smaller one ran up the slope near by, but I paid no attention to him.

Then another appeared on the edge of the canyon, where the first two had been shot. He had returned from the bottom of the canyon and seemed confused as to which way to run. Since his horns were large, I pushed up the two-hundred-yard sight, and brought him down. Another then came running out of the canyon directly toward me, and turned up the slope. As his horns were not very large, I let him go. The remaining three rams must have ascended through the bottom of the canyon for they were not seen again.

Seven fine rams had been killed with eight shots—and by one who is an indifferent marksman! My trip had quickly turned from disappointment to success.

The U. S. Biological Survey had intrusted me with the mission of securing the skulls of at least four adult rams, with some of their skins, for the study collection in the National Museum, and I desired four reasonably good trophies (the legal limit) for myself. Most of these were now before me.

The rain had stopped. I sat there smoking my pipe, enjoying the exhilaration following the stalk, while the beauty of the landscape about me was intensified by my wrought-up senses.

Although two of the rams, badly wounded, had fallen above the canyon, I could not see them, and finding a route to the bottom, mounted its farther wall. Near the top I found the first ram lying on his side. While I approached, he simply sat up, looked at me with a wild expression in his eyes, and expanded his nostrils, but did not offer resistance, struggle, or utter a sound as I dispatched him. Then, going above to the next one, I found him also practically unable to move, and promptly put him out of misery. I was obliged to descend the mountain in the dark (about 10.30), and after fording the river reached camp about midnight.

A fire was soon burning, the soup quickly warmed, and tea made. After satisfying my hunger I sat close by the fire to dry my clothes, which had been completely soaked since first I waded the river in the morning. The wind had ceased, the sky had become cloudless, the air frosty and clear. The sparks of the fire shot straight up through the spruce trees, while ghostly shadows danced among them as if to emphasize the inky blackness beyond. By candle-light at 1.30 in the morning I finished recording in my journal the success of that memorable day.

August 18. At this date dawn began at four. By five I had breakfasted and was tramping down the bar. The night had been very cold, many degrees below freezing, and the mountains were completely white with frost, which sparkling in the early sun presented a brilliant sight. On the slopes to the south were more than a hundred ewes and lambs, while several others were feeding low, just behind my camp. The cold had sealed the glaciers, so reducing the water in the river channels that it was hard to realize that later in the day torrents would again come rushing down. By the time I had climbed the mountain all the frost had melted, the sky was clear, the day calm, the sun very hot.

When I reached the rams several ravens were flying near.

Excepting an hour for rest in the middle of the day I worked on the rams continuously until after dark. Two whole skins, four scalps, and three skulls with big horns were roughed out and carried down to the foot of the slope. This took till ten in the evening. Then, caching all the skulls high in a spruce tree, I packed the skins and scalps to camp on my back.

Five of the seven rams had been shot through the heart. All were very fat, and their stomachs contained the usual food—young tender dryas and a variety of other young plants, but no grass. All were pure white except for a few black hairs in their tails, only observed by searching for them. The sheep of that district are typical *Ovis dalli.** The horns of all were large and massive—typical of the adult bighorns of that region—those of the old ram especially heavy and wrinkled. None exceeded fourteen inches in circumference, nor with one exception, thirty-four inches in length. One pair measured thirty-six inches in length and had a spread of nearly twenty-eight inches—thus representing the divergent type. The spread of all the others was under twenty-five inches, some under twenty.

August 19. I had to work hard the whole day, which was clear and calm, to prepare the material and carefully wash and salt it. The white pelage of all these rams was so badly stained by the soil that none of the skins could be washed clean, even by scrubbing with soap and water. All day numerous ewes and lambs were visible on mountains, and several jays were about camp chattering with their usual excitement when in the presence of meat.

August 20. Most of the morning was required, during a pouring rain, to construct a framework between trees and suspend a canvas over it to protect the skins from the weather.

In the afternoon I went five miles up the river. Although the rain increased and fog settled over the mountains, I saw a hundred and fifty sheep, but could not determine the sex. When I returned in the evening, Karstens was there with the horses, *Tuffy* and *Jimmy,* and a good meal was ready. He reported that nothing of note had occurred at the main camp.

---

* The White or Dall sheep of Alaska and Yukon Territory, described and named *Ovis dalli* by E. W. Nelson in 1884 from specimens collected by Indians in the mountains south of Fort Yukon, between the Yukon and Tanana Rivers. (Proc. U. S. National Museum, vol. 7, p. 13, June 3, 1884.)

August 21. Early in the morning we took both horses to bring back the skulls and meat of the rams. It was foggy, and in the afternoon, when the mists had lifted from the mountains, it rained at intervals. When the skulls were packed on the horses, I left Karstens and went up the large tributary [Calico Creek of U. S. Geological Survey map] that comes from the east and joins the main river two miles below the camp. I had not gone far before thirty or more ewes and lambs were in sight on a mountain to the south, and another band of eighty ewes high on a mountain ahead.

Three miles up from the junction of this creek with the main river, it is joined by a large creek. Turning up this branch, I followed it to the head. It flows through a gorge similar to that of Ram Canyon, and has its source in two basins, each occupied by a small glacier. Here is a small circular valley like that at the head of Ram Canyon, consisting of a vast chaos of rocks, precipices, boulders, and deep ravines— a jumble of disorder. Numerous cascades fell from the rugged walls of the surrounding mountains, and near each of two glaciers was a band of sixty or seventy ewes. The wind was favorable (blowing against me) but both bands saw me when a mile away and ran over the crest above the glaciers. These ewes, when approached openly in plain sight, acted like those of most of the bands already described.

As rain again began to pour I turned back, and soon after reaching the main tributary, saw five sheep on the mountain where ewes had been seen in the morning. Supposing them to be ewes, I went along carelessly until within half a mile, when they saw me and immediately began to run. The field glasses showed them to be rams of fair size, but since none were so large as those I had already killed, I made no effort to follow them.

The increasing rain prevented my climbing the mountains with any idea of continued hunting.

Old bear diggings were everywhere, and marmots, conies, and ground squirrels were as abundant as elsewhere. The common birds were the raven, golden eagle, Alaska Canada jay, chickadee, robin, and western tree sparrow. Besides these, the white-tailed and rock ptarmigan were fairly common on the mountain, the willow ptarmigan everywhere near willows both low and high on the slopes; and a kingfisher and a spotted sandpiper were often observed on the bars.

In this region along the base of the Alaska Range, at and above timberline, the variety of bird life was not great. In addition to the birds already mentioned, a green-winged teal was occasionally seen in some of the small lakes; upland plovers and Hudsonian curlews were fairly common in the rolling country above timber; in suitable places Wilson snipe were flushed; juncos, fox sparrows, northern shrikes, yellow-rumped warblers, pileolated warblers, and golden-crowned kinglets were not rare; pipits and intermediate sparrows were common.

Thirty miles below the range, along the rivers, and in the forest, bird life was probably more varied. A few species that I did not observe may have been in the higher regions, but during the summer, after the breeding season, birds are more silent and some are not often seen.

Experiences with Grizzly Bears on the Teklanika.

August 22. It rained very hard all night and the next day was cloudy with occasional patches of clear sky. I wanted one more large ram, and started very early for the main range at the head of the valley. When out on the bar I saw seven ewes on the opposite mountain across the river, and thirty on the slopes directly behind camp. Since all the mountains, halfway down, were covered with snow, it had been necessary to exchange moccasins for hobnail shoes. Farther up the river, ten or twelve more ewes were on the south end of the mountain opposite, and four miles above, on the mountain west of the valley, more than a hundred ewes and lambs were feeding near the foot of the slope. I stalked to within three hundred yards of the large band, and tried to photograph the sheep before they ran. Here a large creek, carrying a heavy volume of water from the high mountains on the west, enters the Teklanika.

Passing its mouth, I was well toward the head of the valley, where the Teklanika forks exactly like the headwaters of the main Toklat, one branch coming from a glacier to the east, the other heading in two fairly large glaciers, slightly separated.

Here the main range is imposing, the glaciers being wider and of lower altitude than those at the head of the Toklat. The surrounding peaks of the main range, not clustered quite so closely together, give an impression of greater space, and offer a landscape equally sublime. The mountains encircling the head of the valley were covered with sheep, all ewes and lambs, but as was the case everywhere, a few small rams were feeding close to, though separate from, the large ewe bands. Some of the bands were high on the slopes, some low, some

57

composed of a few members, others of many. Seventy or eighty sheep were near the west glacier, more than fifty were between the glaciers, sixty-four were on the gravel moraine at the foot of the glacier, more than ninety were just above the east glacier, and a very large band of more than a hundred—too many to be exactly counted—was on the mountains near the east fork. Six scattered groups of six to fifteen each were feeding between the large bands. I had become accustomed to viewing great numbers of sheep, but here, amid snowy mountains, glaciers, moraines, flats, and rugged rocky masses, this great assemblage was too wonderful to be neglected, so from a favorable spot I watched them for three hours.

By this time, I had observed enough sheep to know that the so-called 'sentinel,' so often mentioned as guarding bands of sheep, is a delusion—an erroneous interpretation of the facts due to incomplete or faulty observation. Only one or twice have I observed the alleged 'sentinel' remaining at its post long enough to properly perform that duty. When a large band of sheep is seen feeding, and near them—usually lying or standing above them—is a single sheep, apparently maintaining a careful watch, the case seems clearly that of a posted sentinel. One is even more impressed with this theory if he is trying to stalk the band and cannot do so, for the sole reason that he would be detected by the sheep watching from above the others. This is a common enough experience to settle the question in the mind of the casual observer, who forgets the more numerous cases where he has seen no 'sentinel' at all. Most observers have accepted without question the belief that some gregarious animals, including the wild sheep, have sentinels posted in a manner analogous to that of a drilled army of men. A little reflection however might lead one to suspect that no animal of this class, whatever the nature of its intelligence, has developed the degree of reason necessary in order to post individuals as a guard against danger.

My conclusions concerning sheep are based exclusively on personally observed facts. One of the most positive of these conclusions—one based upon a vast number of accurate observations—is that in many if not all cases, the so-called 'sentinels' are merely individuals that, after having satisfied their appetites, seek undisturbed _rest_. Sheep according to their nature commonly prefer to rest where there is a good lookout. Hence, while sheep are feeding, often one or more are resting, usually in places above the others. Quite as often, when a band is feeding, none at all are resting. Sometimes the resting 'sentinel' is above, at other times below the others. With the rarest exception the 'sentinel' after resting will leave its 'post' and mingle with the others, and the whole band will keep on feeding without any such 'protection.'

There is another class of so-called 'sentinels.' Each band of sheep comprises individuals that at different times in their lives have experienced attacks from enemies. These naturally are more cautious than others. Hence the degree of wariness among the individuals of a band is always unequal, some being hardly cautious at all, others continually on the alert. A few become habitually nervous, never relaxing their efforts to detect the approach of possible enemies. These individuals, whether alone or with a band, always seek a commanding spot in which to rest. _They_ are the ones commonly supposed to be doing guard duty. My observations have shown that such habits are the result of individual experiences, and that such 'sentinels' live and act with no thought of protecting others. It is wholly erroneous, therefore, to conclude that they are performing selected duties, imposed on them by an assumed organization of the band.

Mention should be made of the collective spirit shown by the ewe bands. This has probably developed as a result of the necessity of protecting the lambs. Large rams seldom gather in bands of more than twenty—often fewer than fifteen. Ewes, on the other hand, commonly gather with their lambs in large bands, not infrequently of as many as a hundred and fifty, though usually fewer than a hundred. While watching them, one is continually impressed by their collective action, their complete dependence on each other, and the fact that their ordinary movements are usually mass movements made by the band as a whole, and always guided by one or more experienced leaders.

At the heads of the valleys near the main range showers fall nearly every day, keeping the rocks and much of the surface wet or damp. Several times today sheep were seen rubbing themselves against rocks, often for fifteen minutes at a time. This accounts in part for the badly stained coats of all the sheep seen near the main range, and probably also for some of the staining of all northern sheep, for in other localities also I have often seen sheep doing the same thing. It gave me keen joy to watch the habits of these sheep, which were unconscious of my presence.

In the middle of the day I brought some dry willows for a fire to a hidden spot at the foot of a slope on the west side of the valley, made a cup of tea, and ate lunch. I must say a word here about these lunches, which are recalled as among the pleasantest features of my wanderings in the northern wilderness. In my rucksack were always a filled tea-ball, a small tin box of sugar, and an aluminum pint cup with cover and bale. After making a very small fire, I could hold or suspend the cup over it long enough to bring the water to the boiling-point; then the tea-ball was dropped in and soon the brew was ready for the sugar. This with less than a quarter of a small loaf of bread provided my lunch. Sometimes enough tea was brought for a second cup, and in case I was a long distance from camp, some of the bread was reserved for later refreshment. In the middle of the day after hours of vigorous tramping it was seldom that I failed to make a cup of tea and rest for an hour or more. Often, when going above the willows, enough dry sticks were carried in the rucksack to make a fire.

Always alone, with birds and animals for my only companions, I found in these hours inspiration from the sublime in nature as well as a refreshing renewal of bodily strength. It was an interval for reflection, for the appreciation of the glories that nature was so richly revealing, and for sensing the hidden spirit of the northern wilderness.

In the middle of the afternoon the glasses showed five sheep, apparently rams, near the crest of the south end of the range east of the valley. I started toward them, crossing the foot of both glaciers, each discharging swollen waters, which uniting in a common stream, rushed down along the east side of the valley. The torrent could not be crossed so near the glacier, and seeking a possible ford I walked a quarter of a mile down the river. The descent was abrupt, and the muddy torrent raced over its irregular rocky bed in a continuous boiling rapid. While standing at the edge, considering the chances of a ford, I looked at the five sheep, now somewhat nearer. They were rams, four with horns of medium size, those of the other much larger, but it was necessary to go nearer before they could be seen clearly.

I had decided that the stream was too dangerous to ford at that point, but before proceeding farther, glanced along a high ridge on the opposite side. My eyes were suddenly arrested by the movement of a huge spider-like creature that proved to be a moving grizzly bear. It was traveling rapidly toward the glacier, just below the top of the ridge, and was about to pass out of sight in a depression.

Without further hesitation I stepped into the rapids and waded forward before realizing my danger, which came only too soon as I sank to my hips and was swept off my feet. Fortunately, before starting down-stream I had slung the rifle on my back. Only those who have fallen in dangerous rapids can know my state of mind for a few seconds as I struggled for a footing and was hurled along toward a rock over which boiled a foot of water, swirling in foam.

Toward it I extended my feet, which struck it; the hobnail shoes held securely, while the force of the water pushed me into a standing position. Though the current fairly roared past my legs, I felt my footing secure and held it. It required a few moments to recover my courage, and many more to consider the situation. Almost in the middle of the narrow river, the angry muddy rapids whirling by on both sides, I could scarcely realize that I was standing firmly in their midst. The water was too deep for me to wade back toward the west bank, which I had left, but seemed shallower toward the east bank. As the icy water was forced well up on my legs, the cold began to have its effect and I felt it would be impossible to remain there very long.

Thus forced into action, I stepped from the rock with a feeling of great uncertainty, bracing myself to keep my footing, and knowing full well that the danger was extreme. The water did not quite reach my hips and the rocky bottom was very rough, so the hobnail shoes prevented slipping. I had to go twenty feet more to reach the bank. After three or four steps the water became slightly shallower and I waded ahead with more confidence, yet fearful of stepping into a depression, knowing that if the current should rise above my hips it would be impossible to stand. But the depth, even close to the bank, continued the same and I scrambled out with a feeling of intense relief.

The bear was still in sight pottering along in an irregular course, looking for ground squirrels. Through the field glasses it seemed to be a huge male grizzly of typical color—if any color is typical—being a silver-tipped brown. The rain had stopped and the mists lifted, leaving the mountains clear under a cloudy sky. The wind was blowing down the valley, probably driving my scent past the bear, which then was nearly opposite me. It was evidently necessary to circle and reach a position where the wind was more favorable. As the bear walked about, now going to a small gully and smelling for a ground squirrel, now changing its direction and often throwing up its head to sniff, I carefully watched and adjusted my movements to the direction of its head. After progressing a hundred yards down the river, I circled another hundred yards to the foot of the ridge, and then, while the bear was going away from me, worked upward more rapidly. It soon vanished over the top and I climbed in a wide circle to keep below the crest and also to avoid getting in an unfavorable wind should the bear change its course.

Reaching the top quite out of breath, I waited a few moments. The inclines on the east side were smooth, leading down to a deep canyon, beyond which the snowfields of exceedingly high mountains were grouped round a deep basin, with a glacier at its head—the source of the east branch of this tributary of the Teklanika. A hundred and fifty ewes and lambs were feeding on the mountain sides surrounding this wild and broken basin. Not seeing the bear on the east side of the ridge, I knew that it must be ahead either in one of the hollows on the top or somewhere below on the west slope.

The stalking of no other animal on the American continent is so exciting as the close approach to a grizzly bear. Its activity is astonishing; it is constantly on the move, and may suddenly turn and go in any direction. And when very close, one's nerves are at high tension, for in any small depression the hunter eagerly watching may suddenly meet the bear face to face.

My stalk was begun amid a wonderful setting of lofty mountains, glaciers, and snow-clad peaks. The direction the bear was taking was indicated by a band of ninety sheep on the mountain ahead, for one or another of them kept looking toward the side of the ridge. From this however I could not determine the bear's exact position. Since the east slope was broken by gullies through which rushed little creeks, many slight descents were necessary in order to see every part of the slope. The approach to each depression was intensely exciting as with rifle ready I looked over into the hollow.

Since the bear had not appeared, each advance became more interesting, and finally only one depression remained between me and the mountain. I knew the bear must be either behind the next swell or on the slope below it. Moving cautiously forward I looked into the hollow, but saw no bear. Then, descending a short distance, I suddenly saw it, facing me and busily engaged in digging out a ground squirrel exactly a hundred and seventy paces below. Immediately I seated myself, rifle in position, with a contented feeling that the bear was mine. Not two hundred yards to my left were ninety sheep, now all bunched, looking at me. I watched the bear, which was sitting on its hind quarters actively at work, throwing out the dirt vigorously in all directions. It dug indifferently with either front paw, while its face assumed a ludicrous expression of supreme contentment as though confident of its ability to capture the squirrel. With mouth open and tongue hanging out, it panted like a good-natured dog. Once, looking directly at me, it half rose on its hind quarters in order to better inspect the strange object. But since the object was motionless, the bear's suspicions were soon allayed and it again sat down to work. After watching it for several minutes I concluded the time had come to kill it; but try as I did, I could not bring the rifle sight on its foreshoulder, its head was so constantly in motion and always in the way. It would be better to lose the bear than ruin its skull, so valuable for scientific study.

After five minutes, it rose, turned a little, and threw up its head to sniff the air. It may have moved a little as I pulled the trigger, or more likely my aim was not quite accurate, for the bullet only grazed its throat and broke a fore leg. It grabbed the wounded leg, turned around once, and on three legs ran rapidly down hill. It fell as I heard my second bullet strike, but was up again and running when two more shots ended its career.

After photographing it I was disappointed to find it an old female. It looked so big, even when near, that I had felt sure it was a male. Later observations have emphasized the difficulty of distinguishing the sex of adult bears when alive in the mountains. Either when alone seems big. In fact, the traditional bear, observed from a short distance, is always a "big" one. This one was so wedged in the narrow bottom that I could scarcely move her, and with difficulty succeeded in pulling her down a few feet to a position where she could be skinned. It grew cold, sleet began to fall, and the water of the creek soaked the hide while it was gradually being taken off. After two and a half hours the head was cut off and the skin pulled up on a dry bank. The stomach contained only partly digested ground squirrels and round worms, nothing else. It seemed strange that she had not gone five miles below where blueberries were exceedingly abundant, or still farther down the rivers where thousands of dog salmon were running. She had not nursed a cub this season.

While stalking the bear, I had carefully observed the sheep. Though a large band was less than two hundred yards distant from the bear, none of them had given her any attention beyond that of looking toward her with indifference. They were not in the least frightened.

The water-soaked skin and head weighed not less than sixty pounds. Putting them in my rucksack I set out for camp, glad to warm up, for I was wet to the skin. It was near the twilight hour and the clouds had lifted. Many bands of sheep were visible resting near the crests in spots safe from danger. An exquisite glow of chocolate brown settled over the mountains. There was not a breath of wind, the sunset sky above the main range was soon suffused with a brilliant yellow glow, gradually changing into deep crimson. While with aching shoulders I toiled down the valley, the small obtruding rocks on the slopes looked in the dusk suspiciously like animals, and as darkness settled I flushed an English snipe and several willow ptarmigan. Camp was reached about midnight, and after a hearty meal I recorded the experiences of the day in my journal.

August 23. The day was cold and windy and was spent in camp preparing the skin of the bear. It was really a beautiful one, rich silver-tipped brown in color, the pelage fairly long, the hair so well set that I concluded it was the new fall coat.

Since we were out of meat, in the afternoon Karstens took my rifle, went up the river and killed a two-year-old ewe, which he brought to camp.

Chickadees were now flocking about the woods; on all sides their inviting notes welcomed us. The two horses were evidently in a continual state of alarm and though both were hobbled, kept wandering off, repeatedly causing Karstens much trouble in going out to find them and bring them back. Karstens had proved himself a splendid fellow, thoroughly efficient in all that pertained to practical life in the northern wilderness—a skilful packer of horses, a good traveler and woodsman, inventive and resourceful in any kind of constructive work, from sewing to mechanics and carpentering, and an excellent camp cook. And what counted more than anything else, he was brimful of good nature, thoroughly companionable, and agreeably interested in all that I was doing.

I had planned to collect three or four specimens of adult

bull caribou for the Biological Survey and counted on getting them easily as the large bulls had remained all summer in the valleys close to my other camp. This should require not more than three days. Then I must hasten back to the Yukon.

August 24. It was very cold in the night, many degrees below freezing, and in the morning a raw bleak wind blew down the valley. I had intended to go up the lower tributary in the hope of killing another ram, but after passing through the meadows opposite the mountain where I had killed the rams, a white object was seen moving near one of the carcasses. The field glasses revealed a grizzly bear with two cubs running about her, and a third cub following. The bear looked white, like the first one I had killed, and the cubs observed in the distance varied from white to dark brown. She was feeding on the slope of a spur, apparently eating grass or blueberries, both of which grew abundantly there. The cubs did nothing but run about in play. At once I circled to gain a favorable wind, and reaching a bluff overhanging the river, saw the bear about five hundred yards above.

She kept throwing up her nose to sniff the air, and finally seemed to catch a scent, for she started walking rapidly across the rocky slope, her head held high, continually sniffing, guiding her course by scent directly toward the canyon where I had killed the fifth and sixth rams. Reaching the edge, she fairly rushed down the steep side and stood at the lower carcass. One cub followed close, the two others loitered far behind, playing. She began to paw out the rocks near the carcass, scooping out a deep hollow, tumbling big rocks down the canyon and moving others to one side, apparently with no effort at all. Then, seizing the carcass with her jaws she dragged it into the hollow and pawed rocks all around it, completely covering it, so that nothing but a mound of broken rock was visible.

While the mother was so engaged the three cubs looked on with interest, though two of them often broke away and kept keeling over in play. The third never left her side but kept up a continual bawling. I know of no other animal voice in the northern wilderness that produces so weird an impression as the wailing cry of a grizzly cub.

The bear then ascended the canyon to the carcass above and buried it in a similar manner, all three cubs now running round her, watching with curiosity. When she started up the side of the canyon followed by two of the cubs, the other one, having discovered that the carcass was palatable, pawed off some of the rocks and remained behind, eating. When the old bear reached the top and looking back saw the cub, she rushed down and gave it a cuff, causing it to bawl loudly and run to one side. Then she pawed back the rocks and, followed closely by the three cubs, went to the top and started back across the slope.

She had not gone far when she suddenly turned, ran back to the edge of the canyon and gazed below as if to reassure herself that the carcasses were in no danger of being disturbed. Again she started across the slope, but again rushed back for another look. This she repeated fourteen times during twenty minutes, the last time running back at least a hundred yards. Then, taking a long look until satisfied that nothing was there to disturb the carcasses, she went a hundred yards directly down the slope, crossed back over the spur, descended into the next canyon and, without noticing two other sheep carcasses that were well above her, climbed the opposite slope and proceeded for about four hundred yards. There, looking carefully in all directions, she tossed her head, sniffed the air until certain that no danger was near, and lay down among the willows. Although I remained watching for more than an hour, neither she nor the cubs were seen. When they had been crossing the spur, the cubs ran ahead and fed on the grass, always remaining on the slope while the mother ran back to look into the canyon.

She was resting in a line directly north of the carcass of the first sheep I had killed, on a slope completely covered with willows, alders, dwarf birch, and small scattered spruces. The cover was so dense that unless she had come into a small clear space I should not have seen her again. The slope was exceedingly steep, rising directly from the river. Above her resting spot it rose almost sheer to a broken precipiced face of a spur, projecting from the extreme north peak of the mountain. While she was constantly in motion there had been no chance of a stalk with any hope of success. Knowing that later she would rise and go to the carcasses to feed, I decided to return to camp, only two and a half miles above, and later in the afternoon come back with Karstens, who in case I should kill her, would assist in taking off the skin.

The possibility of catching one of the cubs led me to prepare a lariat with one of the sling ropes, which was put in the rucksack. We left camp at 3.30, a cold wind blowing strongly down the river. In an hour we reached the bluff opposite where the bear had lain down, and hidden by some spruces, scanned the mountain side through the field glasses, but without detecting the bear. About fifteen minutes later, however, I caught a glimpse of her in the willows a hundred yards south of her resting place. She was digging, the cubs watching her. It was hard to understand why, with so much meat near at hand, she should seek ground squirrels. In a short time she went up a little higher and lay down, but the cubs were not then in sight. I was still more puzzled by her actions. In about an hour she again arose, pottered about a few moments, tossed her head several times to sniff the air, and after digging for a moment, stood and looked about several times, then lay down again. The cubs, however, remained where she had been digging, moving about the spot with evident interest.

I then began to suspect that she had dragged one of the carcasses there, and my suspicions were confirmed when later she rose, walked back to the same spot, dug a moment and began eating. The surrounding brush was too dense to permit me to see what she was really feeding on, still I felt sufficiently sure to take a chance, and at 6.40 P. M. began a stalk. My rucksack, containing field glasses, kodak, and rope, was left with Karstens, who had been instructed to keep out of sight and watch me. If he should see me shoot the bear he was to climb toward the spot as quickly as possible, and approach cautiously until he received a signal.

I planned to circle round on the other side of the mountain and come up on the peak behind the bear, from which point I hoped not only to see her, but also to be near enough for a reasonable shot. Reaching the bar, it was necessary to go down the river very cautiously while in plain sight for three hundred yards until, coming to some bluffs that hid me, I was able to go more rapidly to find a fording place. Again nearly swept off my feet by the rapids, I was soaked to above my hips. Fighting my way upward through the tangled thicket of willow and alder, I finally circled round behind the peak. This I climbed and then carefully looked over, but a short spur prevented me from seeing the spot I had marked as the one where the bear had been feeding.

Having crept down the spur, I rose to a sitting position, carefully elevated my head and looked. I could see the bear indistinctly, lying down in the thick brush, two hundred yards below. None of the cubs were visible.

Holding the rifle in position I whistled. The bear elevated her head, and another whistle brought her to her feet, revealing the three cubs. Though she could not be seen distinctly in the brush, I fired and heard the bullet strike. She gave a great jump downward and cuffed one of the cubs, causing it to bawl so loudly that the sound echoed among the rocks of the canyon. She then rushed a few feet forward and as I fired again, stood in plain sight looking *downward*. She instantly dropped dead.

By holding on to the willows for support I descended to a less precipitous part of the slope, circled against the wind and cautiously advanced until within twenty feet of the body of the dead sheep, and peeked over. There I saw a great mound of earth piled over the carcass, with only the two hind legs sticking out. Within a circle fifteen feet in diameter the willows had been uprooted and the earth scooped out to cover the remains. The dead bear lay just below and the three cubs were playing right on top of it. One was on her hind quarters, sitting erect on its hind legs; another, on his back stretched across the mother's side, with one paw elevated to ward off an expected blow from the other; the third was standing with its front paws on the mother's head, watching the others. Oh for my kodak! Why had I left it with Karstens? Never before or since have I needed it so much.

The cubs began to play. They tumbled, they danced on their hind legs, they wrestled, they lost their tempers, they leapt on and off the mother—in short, they performed every conceivable antic. I could not resist watching them. But they were likely to see me at any moment and escape. So, watching my chance, with two quick shots I killed the two darker cubs. The other, the largest, the one that appeared almost white, was confused a moment. It walked about, ran to a dead cub and cuffed it as if to make it play, then jumped on the other one; but getting no response, looked at each for a short time and then slowly walked to the body of its mother, sat on its hind quarters, placed its paws on her back, its head between them, and went sound asleep, quite unconscious of the tragedy that had taken place.

By this time Karstens was near, toiling up through the willows. Not being clear as to my exact position he shouted, and I was fearful that he would alarm the cub. But it paid no attention and slept on. Slowly rising, I saw Karstens, and by signaling, gave him to understand that he must approach quietly against the wind, and also that there was a possibility of capturing a cub. He soon arrived and handed me the rope. I arranged the noose and carefully approached the cub from behind. It was still sleeping as I lowered the loop in front of its nose. At the touch of the rope the cub elevated its head, the noose fell back, I gave a jerk and he was fast. He sprang up and for five minutes fought the rope with a force and fury that surprised me, bawling loudly all the time.

During this rough and tumble, Karstens had taken the kodak and snapped it twice. The cub struggled against the rope without noticing me, until it was badly choked. Yet it still fought so hard that we had to almost strangle it in order to tie its feet and make a knot in the noose to prevent choking it. It was then tied to a willow. Up to that time it had paid no attention to us, but only sought escape from the rope. In a few moments it had fully recovered its strength and rushed at me with such a furious charge that in a quick effort to avoid its claws and teeth I stumbled over the body of its mother. Having chewed off the thongs from its feet it paid no more attention to the rope but turned all its strength and rage against us, rushing savagely at whoever attempted to approach.

As the twilight sky warned us that it was too late to skin the bears, Karstens took the rope to lead the cub down the mountain. But our lack of experience in handling cubs was soon painfully apparent. We should have cut a pole and attached it to the noose round the young bear's neck in order to keep it at a safe distance. It was a male, born the preceding winter, large and strong, with teeth and claws long and sharp enough to inflict severe punishment. As Karstens, at the end of the twenty-foot rope, pulled, the cub charged him. Karstens dropped the rope and I seized it while the cub followed him. This was the beginning of a lively struggle that lasted all the way down the mountain.

The cub continually charged, fought the rope, became entangled in the brush, bawled, rolled over, rushed sideways or lay down, and balked every inch of the way. Some of our situations were amusing. In a space somewhat free from willows, when Karstens was ahead pulling at the end of the rope, the cub suddenly rushed toward him, gained rapidly and sprang at him, just missing him as he ran and fell, rolling over—the cub still pursuing. I was on hand to pick up the rope and check the cub, which again lay down and fought the noose.

If ever an animal showed gameness it was this cub. He fought without relaxing as long as any strength was left in him. When I pushed a frying pan full of water toward him he grabbed it savagely and bit it, but tasting the water, at once began to drink.

August 25. It was still colder last night and the frost was heavy in the morning. The day was cold and clear as we went up on the mountain and skinned the bear and the two cubs. All were badly swollen. Their stomachs contained nothing but meat and a few pieces of grass—no signs of blueberries, which were abundant on all the slopes in that vicinity. It was a great disappointment to find that the second bullet had struck the skull of the old bear, badly shattering it behind. She was very old and, for a female, very large. The fur was pale buffy in color like the first bear I had killed, and was ragged. She was so stiff and contorted we could not measure her. The colors of the three cubs provide interesting phases of variation. The male we had captured was pale buff like the mother. A second male was silver-tipped brown; the third, a female (slightly smaller than the others), was exactly inter- mediate in color. The pelage of all three was new and long, and probably would not have changed in color before they denned up in October.

The old bear had dragged the carcass of the first sheep three or four hundred yards across the steep slope, through the thick willows, to the hidden spot where she had buried it, always carefully covering it with earth after each feeding [doubtless to keep off marauders]. There were no entrails left in the sheep carcass, and part of the hind quarters had been eaten.

As we worked, sheep were continually visible on all the mountains.

That night the cub began to bawl and ran about fighting the rope. It kept this up all night and I rose several times to make sure that he would not escape. Each time I approached with the wind, he would charge at me to the end of his rope. We slept but little.

August 26. Leaving Karstens to flesh the bear skins I went again to the tributary, still hoping to kill another ram. The mountains were covered with ewes and lambs, but not a good ram could be found. It was a windy day, but this did not affect the movements of the sheep. My ample observations had already shown that sheep feed and travel indifferently with or against the wind. It has often been asserted that they always feed against the wind, but the habits of these animals, from British Columbia north, absolutely contradict any such assertion. I must have seen 250 ewes along and at the head of this tributary, which is a large branch of the Teklanika River.

August 27. The cub again bawled all night and in the morning, to my great disappointment, I felt obliged to shoot him.

Looking for Caribou.

August 28. This morning we packed the horses and returned to the camp on the Toklat. Sheep, in numbers equal to those observed on my previous trip, were on the mountains along the route, but not a caribou was seen. Now, all the country was resplendent with fall colors. A rich brown spread over the mountains, the dwarf birches were carmine, the blueberry bushes deep scarlet, the willow leaves yellow, crimson, and various shades of green; the rocks of the mountains were black, white, green, purple, pink, and some were golden yellow. The blending of colors in the landscape was very beautiful.

Haydon reported no incident of note had occurred during our absence, nor had he seen any game, except sheep.

August 29. Last night there was no frost. In the morning I went up the Upper West Branch to try to kill at least two of the big bull caribou I had seen up there. It was a perfect day, and I went to the head of the valley, climbed the slopes to scan every area, but did not see a single caribou. The usual numbers of sheep, feeding as high as the snow, and on some of the slopes almost at the foot, were on all the mountains. Once a three-year-old ram descended from the West Branch Range, crossed the flat and the bars in a succession of runs, plunged without hesitation into the river, and finally ran up the slopes of Divide Mountain. Since one of this ram's horns was deformed, I recognized him as the solitary animal I had observed on Divide Mountain every day I had been near it. Plenty of young rams were banded farther along the range, and several times this ram tried to join them, but they would not permit it. He was probably a stray from the West Branch Range, and the neighboring rams would not yet admit him into their band.

A band of about a hundred and twenty-five ewes was feeding low down; later they ran across the bar and plunged through the rapids of the river, not seeming in the least to mind the swift water. Another and smaller band was stalked and photographed. It became dark before 9.30. The stars were shining brilliantly when I reached camp, to find great satisfaction in its comfort compared with that of the little shelter I had been occupying.

August 30. Thinking the caribou might have moved down the valley, I started down river early in the morning and carefully inspected all the country along the route. Many sheep were on the mountains—all ewes and lambs. Four miles below, I came to a fine flat of spruce trees—really a wooded island, for it was surrounded by earth-covered ancient bars. At the lower end of the spruces, near the edge, was an elevated old Indian cache, still in a good state of preservation. Many years before, a family of Indians from Tanana River had been in the habit of coming to this point in winter, probably for the purpose of trapping foxes. Some time ago the Indians abandoned all their trapping grounds on the upper parts of these rivers, and at present even the lower parts of this mountain country remain practically undisturbed. The Indians never hunted the upper reaches, having always found game abundant enough below to satisfy their needs. The thought then occurred to me that this patch of woods would be an ideal place in which to build a cabin and spend a winter.

Three miles farther down I came to the south face of the outside mountain [apparently Cabin Divide Mountain]—a vast high mountain, cut by deep canyons and carved into most irregular forms, though the crestline was more regular than those of the mountains nearer the main range. Along its north base, at the mouth of a lively creek from the east, were signs of an old camp of white men, with three or four fair-sized rams' skulls—all too mutilated for preservation. Later I learned that during the previous winter three prospectors from the Kantishna district had spent a short time there.

Following up this creek for a couple of miles I found myself on a divide [Cabin Divide] leading to the East Fork of the Toklat, between the outside mountain [Cabin Divide Mountain] and the one next south [Cabin Peak]. A large band of sheep was feeding on the slope of each of these mountains, also several smaller bands—ewes and lambs—in all about two hundred. In speaking of bands of ewes and lambs I always mean to include a few young rams, those under three years of age.

Neither caribou nor fresh signs were observed. In order that a wider area might be seen, I climbed to the top of the range to the south—a range almost as high as the outside mountain but, except at its east end, smoother in outline. From the summit a wide expanse of new country was brought into view, but no caribou were in sight.

A short distance below were six or seven ewes. I made an unsuccessful effort to photograph them, but at the snap of the kodak they saw me and dashed down a very steep incline. Their gait down-hill was the typical gait of frightened sheep —a series of short jumps, the forefeet lightly touching the ground, all the weight being taken on the hindfeet, which usually land ahead and outside of the forefeet.

Descending the south face of this mountain to another divide between the branches of the Toklat, I followed it and descended into a wonderful draw with rugged peaks clustering at its head, where eighty ewes and lambs were feeding. A good-sized creek flows to the Toklat a couple of miles beyond, but instead of following it, I cut diagonally across the mountain to better inspect the country, and reached camp just before dark. Not a fresh sign of caribou had been seen. Now all thoughts of getting another ram were banished, and my sole aim was to collect some adult bull caribou.

August 31. The frost was heavy last night and in the morning all the little creeks were more or less frozen and the mountains were white as I tramped to the west, following our route into this country [through Highway Pass of the map]. The bear carcass remained untouched. The slopes of the bordering range to the south [West Branch Range] were traversed for three miles, thus expanding the outlook for a better inspection of the country. About forty ewes were observed,

but not a sign of caribou. I reached the extreme West Fork of
the Toklat (also called Stony Creek), which comes from a
small glacier in the main range, and followed it to its head,
but saw nothing, and returned to camp after dark. To my
increasing doubts about finding caribou, anxiety was now
added, for only one more day could be spared to hunt from
this camp, and the East Branch valley afforded the only remaining chance. Caribou had always been there before when
I had visited it.

September 1. I left camp very early in the morning with
the feeling that some caribou would surely be loitering there.
It had snowed during the night, the ground about camp was
white, and the snow fairly sparkled as the sun dispelled the
early mist. The rest of the day was clear, cloudless and balmy.
A fair wind blew up the valley—a most unusual thing, as the
winds generally blew down all these rivers. While the snow
remained I carefully inspected it for tracks of mice, but could
see none. It was clear that in the upper country mice were
almost extinct this year. On the lower slopes the snow soon
melted, leaving an exquisite brown in contrast to the white
above. Not a caribou was seen all day, though the whole valley was carefully inspected.

About noon I entered a small indentation from which a
caribou had formerly been frightened, and then made a cup
of tea. I had gone most of the way along the slopes, always
taking advantage of the ground, to avoid my scent blowing up
the valley. Nearly every book on hunting gives advice, including a solemn warning to "hunt against the wind." Many
of us were taught that maxim before we could carry a gun,
and had it drilled into us long before we were old enough to
read printed instructions. Practical experience, however, has
proved that it is often necessary to hunt with the wind. My
narrative is not a book of advice, so I will only remark that
many times conditions will permit successful hunting directly
with the wind, without the carrying of one's scent to the keen
nostrils of the game.

I kept on up the valley and at three in the afternoon saw
sheep scattered about the flat near its head. On the East

Branch Range seventy or eighty ewes were placidly feeding high, with another band of sixty near the south end on the same slope. After carefully advancing for an hour, I saw about fifty small rams; they were scattered in a semicircle across the flat, and just east of them were six or seven ewes and lambs. These sheep were in several detached bands, each feeding independently of the others. They fed back and forth, gradually working ahead *with* the wind. Most of them were undoubtedly the young rams I had so often seen on Divide Mountain, now after the first snows, feeding low. Having assured myself that no caribou were ahead, I deliberately stalked to within five hundred yards of the rams in order to test the effect of my scent on them.

Seating myself on the flat, behind a low rock, with the wind blowing strongly from me toward them, I watched for an hour—meanwhile twice smoking a pipeful; but not once did any sheep show any indication of scenting me. I then moved two hundred yards nearer, but still they did not show alarm.

After watching them for fifteen minutes, I noticed a band of six a little ahead to my right, feeding on the flat at the foot of the slope. This band was led by a ram with fine large horns, affording a chance to kill the ram I wanted. The wind was blowing practically toward them, and I had to circle to the right to keep out of sight and get a little nearer. This brought me in a wind blowing directly toward them, but still they showed no signs of noticing danger. As I approached nearer, they slowly fed up the slope. Two small detached rams then came out of a hollow between me and the band, not seventy-five yards away, and walking slowly to the bar, crossed the river. My scent was blowing directly to them, but neither showed the least suspicion. The band I was stalking disappeared in a slight depression and I hurried forward feeling certain they would wind me and run. When within a hundred and fifty yards I could see the tips of their horns; then they seemed to catch my scent, for they suddenly walked upward, not much alarmed, but looking about as if suspicious. I was already seated, and at once fired at the one with the big horns.

He pitched forward a little, walked a few yards, and stood still while the others ran upward. Through the glasses I could see a red spot low on his belly, and quickly putting up the two-hundred-yard sight, fired again, and he fell shot through the heart.

It was a beautiful sight to see the other sheep running about in confusion, constantly changing direction in their uncertainty, the members of each band keeping together, still independent of the others. The whole flat was at once alive with sheep until they finally ran up the mountains on both sides of the valley. One small band of ewes, more distant than the others, after running about and looking, finally began to feed again, although all the rams had kept on running.

It must not be inferred that these observations are intended to prove that sheep are never frightened by the scent of man. Sometimes they are very badly frightened, but the subject is too intricate for discussion here.

Going to the dead ram, I found a fine pair of horns with seven age rings and a basal circumference of nearly thirteen and a half inches. After photographing him and skinning one side I paused to look over the country. At the very head of the wide gravel flat more than a mile distant a dark moving object caught my eye, and the glasses revealed a small brown grizzly bear walking rapidly in my direction. Hastily scrambling down the slope I made a wide circle out on the bar so that my scent would be blown, if possible, to the east of the bear's approach. This was an unfortunate necessity for the bear was coming diagonally toward the place where I had skinned the ram. I was afraid that after it should have reached a point almost opposite me—where I could approach it without danger of being winded—I might not be able to follow it fast enough to get within shot.

I watched it from the bar. On it came without once pausing. My interest was the more aroused when I saw it heading toward five sheep that were feeding at the foot of the big limestone mountain. Here was an excellent opportunity to observe the actions of sheep when a bear was approaching. I turned the glasses on them and my surprise was still greater to behold large rams, four of the five carrying massive horns. Where had they come from? Why, during all my hunting in that locality, had I not seen them before? The bear traveled rapidly with powerful strides, breaking into a gallop every few steps. A wild grizzly traveling among the mountains looks formidable indeed, his shaggy coat making him appear much larger than he really is, and his activity indicating the power that he actually possesses.

The rams soon saw him approaching and at first regarded him with complete indifference, continuing their quiet feeding. Now and then one or another looked at him—but they looked equally in other directions. When he had come to within two hundred yards of them, for the first time all five rams looked at him, but only for a moment; then their heads went down and their feeding was quietly resumed. He kept on directly toward them, and when a hundred yards nearer they still seemed indifferent, but more often threw up their heads to look at him. When he was fifty yards nearer, the rams, scarcely appearing to notice him, slowly walked upward and stood on a rock fifty feet up the slope where all stood looking at him. As he passed, the rams were less than seventy-five feet from him. When exactly opposite them he broke into a gallop for a few feet, and all the rams ran about twenty feet farther up, then turned, and remained looking until he had passed well beyond, when they quietly resumed feeding. During the bear's approach to and beyond the rams I carefully watched his actions through the field glasses. When within a hundred yards of them he first noticed them, and merely cocking up his ears, looked at them a moment as he advanced. He did not notice them again until they began to walk upward, when he gave them an indifferent glance and did not pay the least attention to them again.

The bear soon reached a point where it was safe for me to advance without my scent reaching him, but my approach was nearly at right angles and he was still traveling swiftly. When he passed me, three hundred yards away, I put up the rifle sight, seated myself, and fired. Evidently the bullet struck, for he grabbed his side, whirled frantically about several times, and ran directly toward the mountain, where he disappeared in a depression and was not seen again.

My attention had been so absorbed by the bear that I had not kept track of the rams, and now that I looked for them, they were not in sight.

Just below the point where the bear had disappeared was a deep canyon walled on both sides with lofty precipices. Here, near the entrance, the bear's trail was found. Following it between the towering walls, I reached a rugged basin and immediately saw the five rams, not a hundred yards ahead feeding low on the slope. One carried more beautiful horns than any I had killed and three others had massive well-curved horns, larger than those of the ram I had just skinned. Not suspecting my presence, they were completely at my mercy. After watching them awhile I imitated the whistle of a marmot and they at once bunched, stood rigid, heads up, necks swelled out, alarmed and ready to run, but paused to *see* the source of danger. They presented that wonderful picture of big rams standing alert against a background of sculptured crags and jagged peaks. I purposely moved. Quickly seeing me, they ran up over the crest. This was my last sight of big rams that season.

There was no blood in the trail of the bear, and toward the head of the basin its tracks were lost and I knew that it had escaped. After measuring the distance between the tracks of the bear and those of the rams, I returned to my skinning.

The wind soon died down and a deep twilight calm pervaded the valley. Numerous sheep were resting near the crests. Above the peaks the sky glowed in sunset colors, first light pink, gradually changing to yellow gold, then into crimson. A purple haze overspread the mountains, objects in the valley grew faint, and darkness finally obscured all except the white mountain tops looming against the starry sky. Long before this, I had finished skinning the ram and was walking down the valley toward camp, nine miles ahead.

Just at dusk when all objects, both on the bars and on the mountains, looked suspiciously like animals, my eye caught a

small black object on the bar only fifty feet ahead. Little attention was paid to it until suddenly it began to move. My
rifle was cocked as an exquisite black fox began to run.
Though unable to see the sights, I fired twice, but the fox
kept on running.

During the two-hour walk in darkness that night I reached
the conclusion that I knew very little about the habits of
sheep. The haunts of rams were still a mystery—else why had
I not before found this group, seen to-day for the first time?
I did not know. Undoubtedly these rams had been feeding
about the small basin all summer, scarcely moving to other
slopes. It was not until two more seasons had been spent
among the northern sheep that I really learned the habits of
the old rams and felt some confidence in my ability to find
them in a region still unexplored. Long field experience in
different localities is necessary—experience enough to often
have one's conclusions contradicted—in order to realize how
little one knows about the haunts of rams.

It was after midnight when I reached camp. After taking
food and tea, Karstens and I prepared and salted the sheep
skin, and at 2.30 in the morning I wrote my journal.

September 2. The day was spent in breaking camp and
making preparations for the return journey. A heavy rain
falling all the afternoon did not encourage the hope that the
bear and sheep skins, which were still soft, would be well preserved.

September 3. The morning was clear and cold. Sheep were
in sight on all the mountains, when shortly after daylight I
turned my back on that enchanting valley and left this wonderful country behind. My feelings of sadness and regret cannot be expressed. The men were to bring the horses to our
camp of August 4, and I was to travel ahead, getting at least
two hours' start of them. All the caribou had left the upper
waters of the Toklat, but I felt sure of finding them still plentiful in the country through which we had passed August 3
and 4. The cold of the last few days had checked the melting
of the glaciers, and all the rivers that before had been rushing in torrents through the bars, were now only small clear

creeks. I had crossed the Upper West Branch of the Toklat. Signs of approaching winter were everywhere.

If I had been asked where I had seen the most caribou I should have said between the camp of August 4 and the Upper West Branch of the Toklat—the region westward from the Toklat, where sheep are very scarce. But that day, reaching the camp of August 4 by two in the afternoon and having specially looked all along the route for caribou, here and there climbing to positions from which I could more thoroughly inspect the country, not a caribou or even the fresh sign of one was observed—all had departed.

After lunch, I went two miles across the flat and climbed high on the slopes of a mountain that curves round to Muldrow Glacier. This is the outside mountain, bordering the piedmont plateau on the north. I had not advanced far before a band of ten caribou was seen three miles out on the flat. Hastening down and going near enough to distinguish their horns, I was disappointed to find that the band consisted of seven cows, two calves, and a very young bull, about three years old—not mature enough to be worth preserving as a specimen. He was vigorously attempting to perform the duties of an older bull at the approach of the rut, for he had herded the cows and was holding the herd intact. The cows were feeding and the little bull strutted round among them keeping them together. If a cow wandered a little away from the band, he would extend his head forward, his small horns resting on his withers, his mouth wide open, and drive her back to her companions. Occasionally a cow, as if sporting with him, would break away on a run, but each time he pursued and drove her back, sometimes after a chase of several hundred yards. Not once did any of the calves attempt to separate from the band or to follow a cow.

After watching them for an hour, during a heavy rain, I again climbed the mountain alongside the Muldrow Glacier, and went far up to the point where the glacier turned west. No animals except ground squirrels and marmots were seen. All the higher mountains were blotted out by the clouds—only the miniature mountain landscape of the vast dead moraine being visible.

The men were in camp when I arrived long after dark. The willow growth was so scanty it did not provide a fire large enough to dry my clothes. On the way the others had seen no animals of any kind.

September 4. At daylight I again crossed the flats ahead of the others without seeing a caribou anywhere. Climbing to the top of the moraine I attempted to cross its four miles of cones and depressions, but after a hundred yards of continual climbing up and down, circling the little ponds, most of the time unable to view the country anywhere, it became evident that to continue would not only be profitless in the search for caribou, but would consume most of the day. Turning back, therefore, I followed the river six miles through the canyon and found even this rough enough. At two in the afternoon I reached our poplar camp near the foot of Muldrow Glacier, and after stopping for lunch, tramped up the West Fork of the Muldrow Branch, as far as the glacier ice. Not a caribou was seen all day. The men were not in camp on my return at dark, but came in half an hour later reporting that at the head of the canyon one of the horses had bogged so badly that it was only with the greatest difficulty and by two hours of hard work that they had been able to extricate him.

The bad condition of all the horses provided a good excuse to take the risk of losing the last steamer up the Yukon by remaining at this camp a couple of days to hunt caribou. Perhaps my failure thus far to find them, as well as my desire to obtain specimens, was the real reason for this decision.

For more than a week nearly all the grass had been frost killed, and dead grass in this northern country retains little nutriment. Fortunately, much of the long meadow grass near camp was still alive, and since we knew that there was little grass at Eureka and that the country as far as Glacier City was hilly and very boggy, it was really a wise precaution to give the horses a chance to feed and recuperate.

A large flock of little brown cranes flew over camp at daylight, heading southeast, directly over the Muldrow Glacier —a positive sign that winter was approaching. All men in the country say "when the cranes begin to fly, look out for ice running in the rivers." Like other weather aphorisms, however, this one does not always hold true.

The morning was perfect and I climbed the ridges south of the river, now entirely outside the mountain ranges, where I fully expected at last to find caribou. The whole glory of Denali, spotlessly white and clear in outline, with the high peaks clustered about it, and the crestline of the range stretching far away, were before me. No words can convey any impression of the sublimity of that wonderful sight, which that day compensated me for my failure to find a bull caribou.

Blueberries were abundant everywhere, still full of flavor. Willow ptarmigan, now turning white, were massing in large flocks; ravens, golden eagles, and occasional English snipe were the only other birds observed, except a pigeon hawk that chased and actually caught a tree sparrow.

Two caribou were seen three miles beyond Clearwater Creek, and later another. One was a very small bull accompanying a cow; the other, also a small bull, was continually kept at a distance by the former. On the ridge, about three miles farther west, were two other caribou, too far off to distinguish the sex.

Heavy showers fell all the afternoon as I climbed the ridge and proceeded along the crest. Finally, a cow caribou was seen in the distance, and then another, but no bull. As I returned along the top of the ridge a cow caribou appeared, trotting, tail up—an indication of fright. Every few moments she would stop and look back as if alarmed and continued to do so until lost in the distance. Not far from where I first saw her she had crossed my trail—either the morning trail, or the one made early in the afternoon, and must have been frightened by the scent. If anything had been pursuing her I should have seen it. All day I had been able to look over a wide sweep of treeless country, but had seen no animals other than those mentioned.

September 6. Since the big bulls must be somewhere in this country, outside the ranges, my disappointment may be imagined when the morning dawned in a heavy fog and pouring rain, obscuring the vision in all directions. Part of the day

I could not leave camp. After three in the afternoon, though rain still fell, the fog lifted and in the hope of seeing something before dark, I went down the meadow. About three miles below the Muldrow Glacier a wide strip of willows crosses the middle of the meadow. On reaching this I saw an animal's ears outlined above the bushes not a hundred feet ahead. They were held in such a position that I knew the animal had detected me. The ears disappeared and a young bull moose skulked across an open space, his small spikelike horns showing him to be about three years old. He was slightly crouching, his head pushed forward, horns laid back on his shoulders as he glided away, slowly and noiselessly, among the willows. Later, he was seen crossing the bar half a mile farther down, going on a full trot toward the ridges.

September 7. Leaving the men to take the horses to Eureka, I started at daylight for the ridges north of the river. Mounting the crest, I followed it for six or seven miles, all the way to the lake [Wonder Lake], without seeing a caribou. My hunting was over. Just after dark I reached Eureka to learn the discouraging news that our horse *Coghlan,* bogging near the lake, and badly 'calked' himself; and also that the crippled horse *Alphonse* that had been left at Eureka, and on which we had depended should anything go wrong, had been sent to Glacier City by the man to whom I had entrusted him.

September 8. This day *Coghlan's* forefoot was so sore that he could not carry a pack, and there was no alternative but to wait until he should sufficiently recover, or to leave behind some of my material or provisions.

The caribou of this region appear to be the same as those that formerly inhabited the Kenai Peninsula, where now they are believed to be extinct. The Kenai species was described by Dr. J. A. Allen under the name *Rangifer stonei.*[*]

When hunting for caribou in early September, 1906, I did not know that during the last days of August most of the caribou of the Toklat region, including the bulls, go north from the Alaska Range to the adjacent treeless country en-

[*] *Rangifer stonei,* Allen, Bull. Am. Museum Nat. Hist., vol. 14, p. 143, May 28, 1901.

tirely outside of the mountain ranges. There they remain not
only during the rut, which begins early in September, but also
throughout the winter and until the following May. During
this time they roam over an area sixty or seventy miles in extent, undoubtedly including within their range the valley of
McKinley River to the region about Muldrow Glacier. When
I was hunting about this glacier in September they had temporarily moved to another part of their fall range. I did not
see a cow caribou east of the Upper West Branch of the
Toklat. West of the Muldrow Glacier the caribou country is
practically outside of the mountain ranges, and here cows remain all the year round, though exceptionally in summer
some go up among the mountains. From early June until about
September first the bulls remain up near the heads of the
rivers, close to the main range, feeding on grass and other
plants during the daytime, and resting at night. Their tracks
show that they enter nearly every canyon, commonly keeping
in the bottoms and valleys, often ranging far up the slopes.
When the velvet begins to fall from their horns, they follow
down the rivers to the country outside the ranges, where they
find and herd the cows. The habits of no other game animal
are so perplexing as those of these caribou—which I hope
some time to discuss.

Back to the Yukon River.

Eureka was practically abandoned, only two or three men remaining. They were well up the creek, intending to spend the winter there. All I found at Eureka was a little village of tents, which for that one season was the scene of vigorous mining activity. After that, only a few men continued to scratch the surface along the creek—probably one or two do so still—but in a short time the locality will be deserted and the moose, reclaiming their own, will reappear in large numbers among the abundant willows of their former feeding grounds. How many times in the great romantic Northland has the history of Eureka been enacted!

Two days in Eureka gave a much needed opportunity to dry all the skins in a cabin. The third day we put a light pack on *Coghlan,* crossed a very boggy stretch of rolling hills to Glacier Creek, and reached Glacier City in the evening. That day's march strongly impressed me with the mighty force and vigor of the pioneers of our race—the men who 'break the wilderness.' Here in a country sealed by snow and ice for nearly nine months of the year, and confronted by difficulties undreamed of by the Kentucky pioneers, these resolute men toiled and conquered. During one fall and winter, after the 'rush' into that region, not only had the whole area for many square miles between Moose and Glacier Creeks been staked out in mining claims, but numerous deep prospect holes had been sunk; work had been done on all the creeks in the vicinity; villages of cabins—'cities,' as they are called in the North—had been built; stores, saloons, horse transportation, and organized distribution of supplies had been established; and winter mail service had been in operation. Karstens had regularly brought in the mail by dog team from Fairbanks, more than a hundred and fifty miles distant.

Among the resolute and hardy characters who have 'broken the wilderness' west of the Mississippi many were the equal —some no doubt the superior—of Daniel Boone, in the very qualities that made him famous. At the time of my visit Alaska thronged with such men—men who accomplished pioneer work of even greater difficulty, though most of their achievements are unrecorded. Some of the communities there established thrive temporarily, but all are dependent on gold. This is rapidly exhausted, and since the land provides no basis for permanent agricultural or industrial development, the people must leave, and their works decay. In many places in the North the food problem is the most vital. In but few of the places where the prospector finds his gold can he live by his rifle—as did the early Kentucky pioneers and the western plainsmen. He has to bring with him the food to sustain life. He does not have to contend with hostile Indians, but he must face and conquer more serious conditions—those of a barren country, intense cold, long winter darkness, and still more, the danger of starvation and disease.

At the time of my visit in September, 1906, Glacier City consisted of thirty or forty cabins, nearly all abandoned. Glacier Creek and other creeks in the vicinity had not 'panned out' well, only a few claims having been, in a limited degree, successful. Nearly all the people had left permanently, but as is the case in all temporary mining camps that fail to produce as anticipated, a few individuals remained hoping that further prospecting might bring better results.

Having been assured that there were many abandoned canoes at Glacier City, we had counted on securing one, but the failure of the camp that summer had driven nearly everybody away. All the canoes had been taken by persons going down the river to the Tanana. Though believing my chance to catch the last steamer on the Yukon was gone, I at once purchased some whipsawed lumber, and we began to construct a boat for ourselves.

The horse *Alphonse* was in a condition that aroused my

indignation. The man who had taken charge of him and prom-
ised to look after him had used him for packing until, through
abuse and lack of feed, he was reduced to skin and bones, and
had to be shot. The man who did this had left the country before my return.

September 10–11. By the evening of September 11, when
the framework of the boat had been completed, two prospectors arrived from down the river with a long poling boat
loaded with provisions. Since they planned to trap and prospect the country beyond Moose Creek, their boat was available. The following morning I succeeded in reducing their
terms to a figure that would permit its purchase. I had given
the horses to Karstens, whose companionship and services had
been in every way so satisfactory. When we shook hands before he started up the creek to take the horses to the Tanana
River, over the mail route trail, I felt as though I were parting
from a good friend.

September 12. This morning we loaded the boat and started
down Glacier Creek.

Billy Taylor, one of the men who later became a member
of Lloyd's party during the ascent of the north ridge of
Denali, came with us. The boat was a heavy, leaky Yukon
poling boat, thirty feet long and very awkward to manage.
The oars, hewed out with an axe, were heavy and badly
shaped; the load was bulky. For fifteen miles Glacier Creek,
then very low, runs in a series of curves and riffles through
which it was extremely difficult to manage the boat, and my
precious material was in constant danger of being lost. The
last ten miles to the junction with Moose Creek at Diamond
City is smoother water, so we propelled the boat with poles.
In going from Glacier City to Diamond City six and a half
hours were required. Thousands of dog salmon were in Glacier Creek, and numerous tracks of black bears were observed
on the bars, but not one track of a grizzly was seen.

Diamond City, similar in size to Glacier City, was deserted,
only one man remaining for the winter.

September 13. After passing a night in an abandoned
cabin, we proceeded down Bearpaw River. Taylor remained

to join a few prospectors who were to follow us. By combined rowing and paddling we descended the river to within three miles of its mouth in nine hours and fifty minutes.

At the junction of Bearpaw and Moose Creeks, the latter discharges the greater volume of water and therefore is the main stream, which meanders in a series of curves for fifty miles to Kantishna River. The Bearpaw is an attractive little river, fairly deep in places, and from one to two hundred feet wide, its current very sluggish, with only an occasional weak riffle on the upper reaches. The numerous shallow bars, except immediately after heavy rains when the river is high, impede the passage of steamboats drawing more than two feet of water. It flows through the vast level swampy country bordering the Kantishna River—a country well covered with timber and abounding in creeks and small lakes. Much tall spruce grows along the banks, and everywhere on both sides big white birches are scattered through the woods.

The trees shut off extended views, but lack of scenery was compensated for by the brilliant colors of the fall foliage. We glided along under a bright sun, surrounded by a wealth of color—and the fall colors of the foliage in the North have always appealed to me much more than those in more southern lands. The frost had already turned both willow and birch leaves yellow, but the alder leaves remained green, as they always do until they shrivel and drop off.

Animal life along the river was scarce. The only mammals seen were an occasional mink gliding along the banks, and numerous red squirrels in the bordering woods. Old moose tracks were often observed on the bars, but bear tracks and beaver cuttings were absent. In this region beaver are not found along the main rivers, but make their dams well back in the woods.

Many flocks of little brown cranes were flying southeast, and several kingfishers, spotted sandpipers, waxwings in flocks, and a few red-breasted mergansers were seen.

September 14–16. We arrived at the Kantishna River in fifty-five minutes; then exactly twenty-five hours of combined rowing and paddling were required to reach the Tanana River.

For a distance of eighteen miles below the Bearpaw the main channel of the Kantishna was not well defined, there being numerous minor channels, several of which are a mile or more in length. This made it difficult to choose the main passage and gain advantage of the swiftest water. The days were clear and beautiful, the air frosty, the nights very cold. There was little to break the monotony of continuous rowing and paddling.

On September 15 I had my last view of Denali, its great dome alone being visible, rising majestically in the heavens. The same morning a black bear was seen well ahead, walking along a bar, but it winded us and ran off before I could get a shot. Hundreds of flocks of migrating cranes were continusually passing over, and I noticed that they maneuvered like those observed the year before on Pelly River. At one point in their flight, each flock, becoming confused, circled higher and higher, until it found the right direction; then assuming the usual wedge formation flew straight away to the southeast. Each flock took exactly the same course.

About twelve or fifteen miles from the Tanana, we suddenly saw a small column of smoke shoot up through the trees on the left bank half a mile ahead. The smoke quickly dissipating, no more was seen. Haydon, thinking it a signal, passed the spot with some anxiety, fearing we should be held up and robbed. But we saw no sign either of fire or man. Two days later, however, a hunchback from Glacier City, who had been successful enough in digging gold to have brought several hundred dollars with him, was rowing alone down the river when, in passing the exact spot where we had seen the smoke, a man stepped out the woods, aimed a rifle and ordered him to row to the shore. Instead of complying, he reached for his own rifle. A second man appeared and both men fired at him and he in turn emptied his magazine at them. His shots, though badly aimed, had the effect of driving them to cover. The shooting undoubtedly prevented them from following his drifting boat. But a bullet had passed through the hunchback's stomach and when his boat touched the opposite bank a few miles farther down, he managed to get out, secure it to the bank, and creep into an abandoned cabin near by. The next day he was found and sent to Fairbanks, where he died. Two men were arrested near the scene of the shooting, and though undoubtedly guilty, and tried on excellent circumstantial evidence, the jury failed to convict and they were released. I have always believed that these men, knowing the hunchback was coming down the river, were waiting to rob him, and that the smoke we saw was a signal to one of them who had been posted on a curve below.

At the mouth of the Kantishna we found a woodchopper who informed us that in a few days another steamer would leave Fairbanks for Dawson, the telegraphic reports of the condition of the Yukon having indicated that the river would remain open for some time.

September 17–20. The next day we rowed thirty-five miles down the Tanana, reached Baker Slough at dark, and then rowed six miles up to the Hot Springs. As there was a telegraph office of the U. S. Signal Corps there, I could keep in touch with the steamers coming down the river. On our way today we passed several Indian camps on the banks of the Tanana, and also several Indians paddling up river in their birchbark canoes. These canoes, very light and cranky, are used by the Indians of the Yukon and Tanana. When going up river the Indians keep in the eddies close to the bank, and by paddling on both sides alternately, make fairly good progress. Small Indian villages are scattered all along the Tanana. At that time the Indians were idle, consuming the season's catch of salmon. With usual improvidence they had already nearly exhausted their salmon, and after a short time would have to go back to their hunting-grounds and kill moose.

We arrived at Baker Hot Springs late at night and I slept in a cabin. The next morning I enjoyed a bountiful breakfast of the hardy vegetables then ripe—cabbages, turnips, beets, and cauliflower. Then, after the luxury of a bath in a large tank from the flowing hot spring water, I put on my civilized clothes, pinched my feet into shoes, and endured the attendant discomforts. Two days later a message came stating that a steamer would pass the Slough the following morning. We at once rowed down to the river and reached it just in time to catch the small boat *Delta,* bound for Tanana. While going down the Slough, I shot and secured a lynx that was sitting on the bank.

September 21–October 9. We arrived at Tanana the morning of September 21 and learned that a steamer would not start up the Yukon for several days. At that time Tanana, with a population of fifty or sixty people, consisted of a single street of log houses—nearly all saloons and gambling houses, but including large supply depots of two commercial companies. An Indian village was situated at the upper end, and Fort Gibbon, a military post, at the lower end. W. R. Rodman, Commercial Agent of the Northern Commercial Company, had in his possession a magnificent pair of interlocked caribou horns which the Indians had found at the head of the Cosna River. With great generosity he gave them to me. The skulls were fairly complete, the horns weatherbeaten. They had evidently become locked by a rotary motion while the bulls were fighting. Without breaking them it was impossible to pull them apart.

September 24 the steamer *Lavelle Young* arrived from Fairbanks and departed the same afternoon for Dawson. It was so crowded with passengers that Haydon and I were packed in a small narrow stateroom in the stern, near the paddle-wheel.

Incidents While Traveling up the Yukon.

I know of no more interesting assemblage than the one that
fills the last outgoing steamer on the Yukon at the end of the
season. The summer's work is over, and since the rivers will
soon freeze there is a final rush to get out of the country. The
crowd on the last steamer is composed of all the diverse human elements of the country and personifies the spirit of
Alaska's far interior—a mixture of capitalists, commercial
men, professional men, laborers, politicians, miners, prospectors, trappers, gamblers, confidence men, musicians, theatrical
and vaudeville men, theatrical women, respectable women of
all classes, and always, in far greater numbers, the several
grades of those unfortunate women who frequent the dance
halls and lower resorts—women more closely identified with
the general life of the community from beginning to end than
any other class of people and also sharing more largely in the
proceeds dug from the ground.

In the cramped quarters of these river steamers the passengers, irrespective of diversity of interests, mingle and elbow
one another in friendly recognition of the limitations of the
situation. Nevertheless, within this democracy the line separating the respected and self-respecting from the less fortunate is subtly drawn. And so, day after day, as the steamer
furrows the opposing current, the whole social life of this
frontier country is mirrored in miniature.

A 'strike' far up the Chandaler River had been reported,
and about twenty hardy miners were on board, with canoes,
dogs, and provisions, all bound for Fort Yukon, where they
were to disembark, wait for winter, and then travel up the
frozen river to sink prospect holes before the ground thawed
out. I learned later that all finally reached their destinations
and made their locations, but the gold did not 'pan out' and

the following season they returned. They had endured endless hardships, incurred debts, and wasted a year in hard work.
Like so many others, another chapter in the history of prospecting in Alaska had been closed.

All the time while going up river the weather was perfect—freezing nights and balmy Indian summer days. The
various elements aboard occupied themselves in conversa-
tion, gambling, card playing, and music. The evenings were
often given to dancing, or the trained talent was called upon
for concerts and vaudeville entertainment. At times, it must
be admitted, some of these elements segregated themselves
from the rest and broke out in unbecoming revelry.

On the fourth day after entering the Yukon flats, a piece
of machinery broke and the boat was tied up for a whole day
for repairs. After steaming on for a few hours, not only did
the machinery break again, but at the same time a cylinder
head was blown into the river. The steamer, totally disabled,
was swung around and tied to a small island. We were under
the Arctic Circle, a hundred and fifty miles from any telegraph station, and provisions were limited. Ice floating by
warned us that the Porcupine River, fifty miles above, was beginning to freeze. The Yukon River always freezes first in
these flats. At Fairbanks there had been rumors that if the
river were reported in good condition, another steamer might
be sent up; so there was nothing to do but wait and trust to
circumstances.

During five uncertain days we remained tied to this island,
the weather growing colder, the quantity of ice in the river
increasing, the provisions becoming more and more reduced.
Under these trying circumstances the gallant spirit of the
Alaskans at once asserted itself. Confronted by a situation so
serious, did they grumble? By no means. Were they panicky
or despondent? Not for a moment. The buoyant, optimistic
spirit of these people, now for several days held in check by the
confines of the boat, seemed to flood over. The occasion was
turned to one of mirth—childish games on the island, more
concerts, more laughter, more good nature, and a closer bond
of good fellowship.

October 1 a steamer came down the river and took a message to the telegraph office at Rampart. The ice was then almost filling the channel. The passengers were offered an opportunity to embark and return down the river, meaning that they might not be able to leave the country before winter. Not one accepted passage; all were willing to take the chance, trusting to the result of the telegraph message, which would inform the company managers of our situation.

Early in the morning of October 3 our uncertainty was relieved by the arrival of the steamboat *Seattle Number 3*. The company had taken the chance and dispatched her on a final trip for Dawson. The boats were soon connected by cables and the powerful engines of the *Seattle Number 3* propelled both against the current.

All ducks and geese had left the Yukon flats and the only birds observed migrating were the little brown cranes. Occasionally ravens were seen. Moose were fairly abundant throughout the flats, where in fall and winter many are killed by Indians. Indians easily travel all over the flats, carrying their light birch canoes overland between the channels.

Above Fort Yukon there was no ice in the river and we made steady progress until the late afternoon of the third day, when something occurred. The *Lavelle Young*—the disabled steamer we had in tow—was a small boat with a passenger capacity of about a hundred and fifty people. All the passenger staterooms were on one deck arranged around the dining room, their windows on the outer deck, the entrance on the inside. The large dining saloon was the only space that could be used between meals as a living or assembly room. The central stateroom was occupied by four criminals en route to the U. S. prison in Seattle. One was a forger, sentenced to two years; another, having committed a serious express robbery of gold bricks, had received a longer sentence. The other two were the noted desperadoes—Thornton and Hendrickson. Both had several times been in prison.

Thornton, having stolen a horse, was captured and placed in the Fairbanks jail. Another man, wearing a mask and a blue parka, had often appeared on the trails between the mining camps and had held up and robbed several of the miners. He was known as the 'blue parka man,' and since Hendrickson, a fugitive from prison at the time, had been seen in the vicinity and as circumstances connected him with these robberies, he was captured and jailed. The U. S. judge being out of the country not to return until late the following summer, Thornton and Hendrickson had been kept in jail awaiting trial on his return.

But their life in the meantime had not been continuously monotonous. Late in the winter, having in some way secured a knife, they had knocked the guard down when he opened the door to bring them food and stabbed him so badly that he survived only as a cripple for life. Both escaped, but some time afterward were retaken. Thornton, before his recapture, attempted suicide by cutting his throat, but was taken to the Fairbanks hospital and later recovered. The judge on his return late in the summer, in order to avoid the retention of the prisoners in the country for another winter, gave each a suspended prison sentence of fifteen years for wounding the guard and breaking jail.

Before they were taken aboard the boat all the prisoners, having been stripped of their clothes, had been thoroughly searched. The stateroom in which they were placed had been carefully searched by the deputy marshal in charge, and everything which he thought might be of use toward assisting an escape had been removed. It was a double stateroom, with three berths, one above another, on each side. The window had been carefully barred with iron and the doorhandle had been taken off, so that the door could be opened only by inserting a key in the lock. The marshal himself always attended to the prisoners' meals, which he handed in to them on plates, with only a spoon to eat with. In addition to the marshal, there were two day guards, one always seated before the door of the stateroom, while the other paced back and forth before the barred window on deck. At night these were relieved by two other guards.

Additional precautions had been taken to prevent any possible attempt at escape on the part of Thornton and Hendrickson. Each was required to wear an 'Oregon Boot.' These were circular disks of iron, weighing thirty pounds each, clamped round the ankle by means of an inside hinge, and secured by a bolt, sunk in a small socket. This was locked by screwing it tightly with a key, inserted in the socket. The key had only a circular opening at one end, which was pushed down over the bolt and turned, the friction holding it tight enough to prevent slipping around the bolt. Iron bars with the ends bent upward were screwed to the sole of one of each of the prisoners' shoes. When the shoe was on, the upturned ends of these bars were attached to the 'Oregon Boot' in such a way as to hold it up off the ankle, so the prisoners could walk for short distances. At night when the prisoners were lying down their shoes were taken off and the iron 'boots' dropped down on the ankles. It was impossible to walk unless this 'boot' was supported by the iron bars attached to the shoe. The only luxuries allowed were cards, pipes, and tobacco.

The two desperadoes, having been closely confined in jail for so long a time, were in weak physical condition. During the trip, most of the passengers had expressed the opinion that the prisoners should be given some relief from their cramped quarters; that they should be allowed to walk about on the island under guard. I often heard passengers ridiculing the close watch that was being maintained over them.

About a hundred miles below Eagle, Nation Creek enters the west side of the Yukon. About twelve miles up this creek were a dozen cabins, occupied by miners who intended to pass the winter working their claims. On the bank of the Yukon, three miles above the mouth of the creek, is Nation City, consisting of three or four cabins and a wood camp. Two of the cabins were occupied by men holding provisions to be taken later by dog team across a trail to the 'diggings' on Nation Creek.

After dark, about 5.30 on the afternoon of October 6, the steamers were tied up to the bank at Nation City, the *Seattle Number 3* on the inside, and the crew immediately began to load them with wood.

Shortly after 6 the dinner gong sounded and in a few moments all the passengers of the *Lavelle Young* were seated around the tables. My seat was opposite that of the marshal, directly in front of the door leading into the prisoners' stateroom. The day guards had just been relieved and one night guard was seated before the door, while the other paced back and forth before the window on the deck. Dinner had been in progress about fifteen minutes when the outside guard suddenly came in, walked rapidly to the marshal, whispered to him, and ran out. The marshal jumped up, pulled his revolver, stepped to the door of the stateroom, quickly inserted a key in the lock, and pointing his revolver ahead, pushed open the door and went in, followed by the inside guard, also with drawn revolver.

Somebody shouted "They have escaped!" and immediately the passengers were thrown into a wild panic. Women screamed, some of them fainted; there was a confused rush in all directions, many going under the tables, others running to their staterooms, some rushing out on deck, while only a few, remaining cool, kept their seats at the table. I noticed that several who had been continually boasting of their bravery were the first to run away.

The marshal and the guard, joined by all the other guards, began to search the steamboats, going through all the staterooms, and inspecting every corner above and below on each boat. But Thornton and Hendrickson *were gone*—only the other two prisoners remained in the stateroom. Both steamers had search-lights; these had been immediately thrown up and down the river bank and against the thick woods bordering it. The captains agreed to hold the steamers until midnight, while volunteers took rifles and went on shore with the marshal to help in the search. Everybody in the country knew the desperate character of Thornton and Hendrickson. The latter, having formerly worked a claim near Nation Creek, was familiar with that part of the country. Two men from Nation City showed singular presence of mind. One took a lantern and started over the trail to warn the miners; the other, an Indian, jumped into his canoe and started down river to warn a camp of Indians fifty miles below.

Not a trace of the escaped prisoners was found. A reward for their capture, dead or alive, was left with an old Montana ex-sheriff who was occupying one of the cabins at Nation City. At midnight we started up river, the marshal and all the guards on board, hoping to get instructions by telegraph at Eagle authorizing further steps to recapture the fugitives. Reaching Eagle, the marshal received instructions from Fairbanks to discharge without pay both outside guards, to employ assistance at Eagle, to return by canoe to Nation, and to retake the escaped prisoners. We arrived in Dawson October 9, where I was obliged to wait four days for a steamer for Whitehorse.

It was learned that Hendrickson while in the jail at Fairbanks had in some way obtained a broken piece of a jeweller's file. This he had inserted in his pipe and smoked a crust around it, so that when the pipe was examined the presence of the file was not suspected. Two small hooks had been left screwed into the wall of the stateroom. The curtain, which had been hung on a thin brass tube about two feet long, through which a wooden rod had been inserted to strengthen it, had been taken away, but the brass rod had been left. Hendrickson, a most ingenious mechanic, having filed off with the tiny file about eight inches of this brass tube, divided it in two pieces. One was flattened out and filed into a small saw; the other was used as a key to unscrew the bolts locking the 'Oregon Boots.' The ceiling of the stateroom, which was only of half-inch board, also contituted the roof of the steamboat. Forward on this roof, near a ladder leading to the forward lower deck, were the officers' quarters.

One of the prisoners had unscrewed a hook from the wall, and lying on his back in the upper berth, had made several adjoining holes through the roof, enabling them to insert the saw. Then at convenient times they had forced the other two prisoners to sit close to the window, obstructing the guard's view, while one sawed above. After each short period of work, both the holes and the incisions made by the saw were filled with soap, which, being white, obliterated evidence of the work and prevented the marshal on his daily inspection from observing it. Finally, a section exactly fifteen inches long and ten inches wide was sawed out of the ceiling but left in place while the prisoners awaited their opportunity.

Learning that the boat was to stop at Nation City, they prepared to escape. Taking out the screws attaching the iron bars to their shoes, they were ready. While the gong was loudly ringing, Hendrickson ripped out the ceiling, and while the other two prisoners backed up against the window, Thornton and Hendrickson climbed up through the hole. Hendrickson, leading the way, descended the ladder and crossing the next boat went ashore. He was followed by Thornton, who when he had descended the ladder and stepped on deck, met the outside guard, but the guard looked at him apparently without recognition. Both prisoners immediately ran into the woods, stumbling in the darkness and going as far back as possible, where they lay shivering, concealed in a thicket, until the steamers left.

The outside guard, who had been pacing back and forth before the window, each time going as far as the forward end of the deck, had suddenly come face to face with Thornton, who had a black beard. The guard was so startled and confused that he did not credit his vision and continued to pace back and forth a couple of times before he realized what he had seen. Then running to the window he saw what had happened and quickly rushed inside to tell the marshal.

On October 11 news reached Dawson that the escaped prisoners had been recaptured. It happened in this way: the marshal, having employed two men, at once started down the river for Nation. The occupants of a roadhouse situated twelve miles above Nation City, and also the miners on Nation Creek, had been warned and were on the lookout. The Montana ex-sheriff also was on the watch. All in that vicinity, hoping to get the reward, were hunting the prisoners.

Thornton and Hendrickson, both in weak physical condition, without warm clothes, blankets, matches, or food, were fugitives in the northern wilderness on the approach of winter, when the temperature at night was already near zero. Cautiously drawing near the cabins on Nation Creek and finding the miners prepared to capture them, they struck across country to the roadhouse, both ill from the effects of the cold and from eating frozen blueberries. The men there recognized them, but being too frightened to capture them, and afraid to keep them out, gave them food and a night's lodging. In the morning Hendrickson and Thornton started down river together but soon separated. Four miles below, Hendrickson saw the Montana ex-sheriff towing a canoe up the bar. The sheriff, on the chance of learning something about the convicts, was on his way to the roadhouse, when suddenly Hendrickson, holding a club, ran to him and ordered him to go back into the canoe and row him across the river, threatening to kill him if he refused and to upset the canoe if he failed to row according to directions. The sheriff at once got into the stern of the canoe, while Hendrickson pushed it out into deep water, at the same time leaping in and taking the oars. Then the sheriff, quickly picking up his rifle, aimed at Hendrickson and compelled him to row back to Nation, where the marshal's men, already arrived, were ready to take him.

The marshal meanwhile was on his way up river when Thornton coming down in the woods saw him. Then Thornton, very ill, deliberately went back to the roadhouse and surrendered. There the marshal took him in charge and later both prisoners were taken back to Eagle, where a small steamer was chartered to carry them to Dawson.

On October 12 I left on the steamer *Dawson* and arrived at Whitehorse four days later. The next day I went by rail to Skagway, and on October 22 boarded the steamer *Jefferson,* which in the afternoon left for Seattle.

Hendrickson and Thornton were aboard under guard. They occupied a stateroom with the door taken off, and a guard watched them day and night. Although both their hands and feet were heavily manacled, the marshal made hourly inspection of the irons. These two desperate men were finally placed in the United States prison on an island near Seattle. A year later both broke out, but were recaptured before escaping from the island. They were immediately transferred to the large Government prison at Leavenworth, Kansas. Thornton has since died, and Hendrickson was discharged February 11, 1920.

On October 24 I left the boat at Ketchikan and spent the next month searching for caribou on the Queen Charlotte Islands.*

That season's experience among the white sheep convinced me that I really knew very little about their habits. I realized that their life history could not be learned without a much longer stay among them and determined to return and devote a year to their study. With this in view I planned to revisit the region, build a substantial cabin just below my old camp on the Toklat, and remain there through the winter, summer, and early fall.

* Results published in 'The Wilderness of the North Pacific Coast Islands,' by Charles Sheldon. Scribner's, 1912.

DENALI

PART II · *1907–1908*

Return to Denali and the Head of Toklat River.

In studying the habits of the white sheep on the northern slopes of the Alaska Range near the great mountain Denali during the summer of 1906, I had been impressed with the inadequacy of observations confined to one season and was convinced that in order to obtain a reasonable knowledge of the life history of these interesting animals the investigation must be extended over the entire year. With this in view, I re-visited the region the following year and remained from July, 1907, until the middle of June, 1908. The observations here recorded therefore cover one complete fall and winter, one spring, and two summers.

Going as before by way of Skagway and Whitehorse and steaming down the Yukon and up the Tanana, I arrived at Fairbanks July 6, 1907. The trip had been uneventful except for the usual vicissitudes of the boat journey on these rivers. Two black bears had been seen—one on a ridgeside near Thirty Mile just below Lake La Barge, the other, a cub on a ridge a mile above Forty Mile. In each case as the steamer passed, the bear fled, quickly seeking cover. It may be of interest to record that during my several boat journeys on the Yukon River between Whitehorse and the delta, and on the Tanana between Fairbanks and its mouth, these two black bears and a lynx were the only game animals observed.

From the time of leaving Whitehorse, June 22, until July 18, when I left Fairbanks, the weather was insufferably hot, the only relief possible being on the decks of the steamer where the air was fanned to a breeze by the speed of the boat.

At Dawson, while delayed a week for a steamer connection, I bought pack outfits for six horses; and at Fairbanks, during a twelve-day layover for the boat to take me up the Kantishna and Bearpaw rivers, I purchased two horses, provisions for a year and other necessary equipment, and also a poling boat thirty feet in length. Nothing had been brought from the States except tea, tobacco, guns, ammunition, collecting material, field glasses, a few books, and other special articles.

Henry Karstens, who had been with me the previous year, was engaged for my entire stay in the country. Jim Wilson of Fairbanks, with his four large mules, was employed to assist in packing the outfit to the headwaters of the Toklat, and Merrifield, formerly a member of the Canadian Northwest Mounted Police, agreed to accompany us temporarily as a packer.

July 18. At Fairbanks, horses, provisions, and baggage were loaded on the small steamer *Luella,* which started down the Tanana about midnight. The Captain had contracted to take my party and five others bound for the Kantishna diggings, with all equipment, to Diamond City at the head of Bearpaw River. Tom Lloyd, who later attained some fame by organizing the first party to reach the north crest of Denali, was among the passengers. The weather had cooled just before the boat left and it rained all the next day and early evening after we entered the Kantishna River. About midnight we were compelled to tie the boat to a bank during a fog that lasted until five in the morning, when we again steamed against the muddy current. At 9.30 we entered Bearpaw River, having experienced little difficulty except at one bar over which the steamer had to be assisted by means of a rope tied to a tree on the bank.

The water in the Bearpaw was low, and we soon found that no apparatus whatever had been provided to help in navigating a shallow river. There was neither block, spar, nor tackle of any kind—not even a steam winch. The rudders were not adapted to the work and the boat had to be tied up for a day while a 'monkey' rudder was constructed. The Captain slept, the mate looked on, while the passengers went ashore and cut a good supply of wood. At midnight we started and after steaming about two miles came to another bar. The Captain said the boat could not pass it and promptly tied up to the bank and again went to sleep for five hours. Although it was then clear to most of us that he had never intended to take us farther than the mouth of the Bearpaw, we went to work and got the boat over. At the next bar we unloaded all the horses, and later, after many unsuccessful attempts, all the freight. The Captain and the mate merely looked on while we toiled, trying to work the winch by hand and maneuvering the boat again and again. At four in the morning we gave it up and decided to take our outfit and provisions in poling boats, leaving the horses to travel along the bank of the river.

One of the passengers, a Mrs. Courtney, who kept a boarding cabin at Glacier City, was returning there with some freight and a fair-sized boat. We arranged to use her boat, which together with our own, heavily loaded, proved sufficient to carry our freight. Mrs. Courtney continued as a passenger, leaving her freight, which she would have to send for later. Karstens and Merrifield each poled a boat, while Wilson and I took the horses overland. A day was required to sort and check the freight and load it in the boats.

At five on the morning of July 24 we started. The weather was again very hot and the mosquitoes were at their maximum *density*—no other word describes their multitudes. I went ahead with an axe, leading a horse, and for the next three days struggled along for fifty miles as I had never struggled with pack horses before. The land was one vast morass, covered with fallen timber and dense underbrush. The horses continually bogged, the mules strayed back, a trail had frequently to be cut, and deep sloughs had to be crossed. The boats, heavily loaded, were poled with difficulty and made about the same progress as we did with the horses.

We were greatly relieved to reach Diamond City, but on starting up the Bearpaw next day found that our worst difficulties were still ahead—for the water was exceedingly low. Owing to this the boat could carry only a very light load, and even so, many hours were consumed in digging passages through the bars. For a few miles we had to relay part of the freight. It was then decided that time would be gained by packing the material from that point to Glacier City, twenty miles away. Meanwhile Karstens and I with our horses and mules would bring up the remainder left at Diamond City. For the next six days we worked long hours. One of the horses was used to haul the boat up against the current, but the labor of continually digging passages through the bars made progress slow. On August 2 we reached Glacier City, at the junction of Glacier Creek with the Bearpaw, and the next day Wilson and Merrifield brought in the final load. At last all our equipment and provisions were assembled at a point beyond which no other difficulty than that of the usual pack horse travel would be encountered.

While working along the river Karstens and I had had no protection against the mosquitoes and upon our arrival at Glacier City our necks and hands were so swollen and bleeding as to cause anxiety. In a day or two however the swelling had gone down and no bad effects followed.

August 4–8. During these five days we took the horses with packs along the exact reverse of the route I had traveled when going out the preceding September. I succeeded in hiring two additional mules that had been in service about the diggings in Glacier Creek, and engaged another man, Young by name, to help in building the cabin. So much time had been lost that no effort could be spared in getting settled in winter quarters. The days were clear and beautiful. The first day we went to the head of Glacier Creek and passed the night in the hospitable cabin of Joe and Fanny Quigley. Quigley was one of those rare honest chivalrous men, found here and there in Alaska, who combined successful individual mining with the traits of a true hunter and an accurate observer of Nature. Fanny, originally from Normandy, was one of the most remarkable women of the Northland, combining with a high degree of efficiency the ability of the white woman and the skill of the Indian woman in all that relates to life in the wilderness. She had come into the country during the rush to Dawson, had followed the gold excitement to Fairbanks, and had then gone on to the Kantishna. She was greatly beloved by all the pioneer men who knew her, each in one way or another having received some kindness from her.

At Eureka we met a young Indian and his sister from a small band, comprising not more than three or four families, belonging to the territory about Minchumina Lake. This boy, like the other men of his band, carried a spear. It consisted of a ten-inch double-edged knife lashed on the end of an eight-foot shaft. I have never known Indians elsewhere in the North to carry spears. This boy and others of the band told me that the purpose was to ward off attacks of bears. They told me also that the spears had been used only "long time ago" when "Indian no shoot Tsawnee" [grizzly bear]. The present custom of carrying a spear, therefore, is merely the perpetuation of a practice useful in the past, but now of no material assistance.

The second day we climbed the ridge dividing Moose Creek from the McKue Fork of the Kantishna, where Denali in all its glory towered above the ragged crestline of snowy summits before us. Descending to the delightful meadow where I had camped the preceding year, I found that the willows had been spreading, and realized that not far in the future the abundant rich grass will be replaced by this shrub. Grazing possibilities must give way to those of browsing, and thus the moose of the region will have a rich area of feed added to their domain.

I tramped ahead of the pack train over ground covered with the luxurious and magnificent flora of the region, then in full bloom. Arctic terns and flocks of Hudsonian curlews flew about; ptarmigan with young continually flushed; the ever-present tree sparrows sang cheerily; flocks of migrating robins passed overhead, and golden eagles soared high and low in the landscape. The chatter of ground squirrels was everywhere heard, and on the third day a fine cross fox with three young (two cross and one red) was seen sitting at its burrow of eight or nine holes, all leading down to the den. Strewn about were the remains of numerous ptarmigan and ground squirrels, and nearly a dozen shrews not yet eaten. Later in the afternoon caribou were seen on the mountainsides, and before going into camp, Merrifield shot one. The next day caribou were plentiful, and the game trails along the mountainsides ushered me into the region of abundant sheep. Ten ewes were perceived lying down on a slope at about the most westerly point where I had observed sheep the previous year.

Delightful reminiscences enriched the pleasure of the five-day tramp among the ridges and valleys of this wonderful Alaska Range, particularly on reaching the neighborhood of my old camp, where so many happy days had been passed. The shelter poles were still up and intact; the year-old horse tracks appeared fresh; my discarded mouse traps were still in good condition, and on the mountain beyond, sheep were discovered in three places.

Later, the pack train arrived. We then proceeded three miles down the river bars to an island of timberline spruces where the new cabin was to be built and I was to establish myself for the winter.

August 8. Since two more trips with the pack horses were necessary to bring in all the provisions, Merrifield and Wilson started back with the pack train early in the morning. I had intended, if grass could be found, to have sufficient hay cut to winter two horses so they could be used early the next spring for a trip to Denali to hunt bears. While Karstens set out to look for hay, Young began to cut the dead spruce trees near by for logs to be used in building the cabin.

Building the Cabin.
Hunting Big Game.
Incredible Abundance of Mice.

The preceding year I had selected this site for my cabin. It was on an ancient level bar on the east side of the Toklat about three miles below my camp of 1906. Here, in the northwest corner of an island of spruce trees, the cabin was to be constructed. Nearby was an old Indian cache, well built and still in a state of preservation good enough for a storehouse for supplies. Drinking water was most convenient, for a fine spring, never freezing except during the coldest winter weather, was only seventy-five feet away, and twenty-five feet farther on a narrow underground channel from the main river broke out of the gravel near the woods, remaining open during the entire winter. Beginning a mile above the woods, a margin of trees bordered the bar at intervals as far as the main Toklat, while on the opposite side of the river a narrow fringe of timber extended to my old camp. No more ideal spot for a timberline cabin could have been found—abundant water only a hundred feet away, spruces large enough to afford protection from the wind, the place surrounded by mountains where sheep were almost always in sight. A grove of straight dead spruces was at hand, providing not only abundant fuel, but also the best of timber with which to construct the cabin. Green timber would have been much less satisfactory, since a cabin of green logs always settles and requires a long time to become sufficiently dry to insure warmth during the winter.

One of the horses purchased at Fairbanks was a dark bay, a very fast well-gaited cattle horse, trained in Oregon and brought into the country the preceding year. He was gentle and intelligent, with strong short-coupled back and good feet, and was equally good as a saddle or a pack animal. I named him *Toklat* and kept him at camp for use throughout the season—until the freeze-up.

After helping cut logs for the cabin I rode *Toklat* up the West Branch for the purpose of observing sheep, caribou, or possible bears, hoping at the same time to kill a sheep conveniently low for easy packing to camp for food. Numerous sheep were where I had seen them the previous year, and caribou were feeding along the lower slopes and on the bars. On leading the horse up the canyon where I had killed two small rams the preceding August, I saw another pair of small rams so high that a bullet sent toward one failed to hit it. I did not return to camp until the evening hour when, after a heavy shower, all the sheep were lying down near the crest-lines.

August 10. The season had been dry and all vegetation was far behind. The stream entering the Toklat near the cabin, and which I called Cabin Creek, has its source in Cabin Divide two miles to the east. Continuing east, the divide dips down to East Fork Toklat, reaching it at a point only four or five miles east of my cabin on the main Toklat. South of the divide is Cabin Peak, while north of it is a high mountain that I named Cabin Divide Mountain—the northern part of which is sometimes referred to as Outside Mountain. Its apparently smooth outlines and rounded summit extend east and west, as do most of the ranges between the forks of the Toklat.

In this region all the mountains, when viewed from even a short distance, appear to have smooth outlines, but in reality are badly broken, as one soon learns when he attempts to tramp over their crests and slopes. Often the slopes on one side present a deceiving evenness while the other side is shattered by a confusion of cliffs and canyons.

Reaching the divide, which consists of rolling green pastures of swelling outlines extending a mile or more between the mountains, ewes and lambs were visible on the slopes on all sides—some lying on the rocks, some feeding, while one walked slowly toward the mountain beyond. A small ram climbed up a precipice and stood looking about for an hour while I watched the others. Finally, the ewes started running

down the slopes, crossing a hundred yards of rolling surface
to a small rocky hill on which they began to feed. In attempting to stalk toward them I witnessed an incident of sheep
habits that later was often repeated. When I had worked to
within three hundred yards of the hill, all were feeding on top
with the watchful actions characteristic of ewes. One old ewe
had kept above the others and was the most alert and watchful
of the band. When the others went out of sight feeding on the
other side, the old ewe remained on top, watching, for twenty
minutes. Then she too disappeared, but only for a few minutes, when she jumped back and again inspected the country
on all sides. This action was repeated again and again for
half an hour. No hunter could have approached nearer than
I was to that hill without being detected. The old ewe was so
nervous that she scarcely fed once. At last she went behind
the top and immediately all the sheep ran to the mountain beyond. She soon caught up with them and all began to feed.
Here they were much less watchful than when on the detached hill; and even the old ewe fed with more indifference
to danger. Any one inexperienced in sheep habits would have
believed this old ewe to be a 'sentinel.' But times too numerous to mention I had seen sheep go out on little detached hills
to feed when no member of the band was more watchful than
another. In this case I had noticed that the younger sheep took
the initiative in running toward the hill and that the old ewe
had followed in the rear. Evidently she had personally experienced danger so that she was constantly on the alert, especially when in an exposed position, as she had been on this
hill.

The sun was low, the sky clear, with not a breeze to disturb
the calm of the rolling green pastures as the various flocks, a
hundred and fifty sheep in all, slowly approached the crests
to lie down for the night.

August 11. Since most of our caribou meat had been consumed I started out on *Toklat* for the purpose of killing some
sheep to provide a supply of food for camp. Intending to hunt
at the head of the Upper East Branch where I had seen rams
the year before, I rode along the flat south of this branch

until I found good grass, then dismounted to give the horse a chance to feed. While looking through my glasses I spied high on the south slopes of Forks Mountain a very light colored grizzly, followed by two very dark cubs. They were climbing the furrowed slopes diagonally and soon passed out of sight. I rode across the channels of the river, tied the horse to a willow near the foot of a 'draw,' and started up a canyon, choosing a route where the wind was favorable for stalking. Having reached a point suitable for an approach in the direction in which the bear had gone, I came near the spot, alertly watching ahead, knowing that at that hour (eleven in the morning) the bear and cubs were probably lying down. A cautious advance of a quarter of a mile over broken slopes had not yielded a sight of them. On reaching a deep V-shaped canyon I paused to view the landscape, which, with the East Branch Range opposite, was particularly impressive. Three caribou were standing below on the bar, one feeding nearby in the meadows. Beyond, the rugged mountains about the upper waters of East Fork Toklat and along Teklanika River were clear and imposing, bringing to mind my experiences there of the previous year.

Scanning the dark precipiced slopes of the opposite side of the canyon I saw a dark object above a high cliff. With the field glasses I recognized the bear, stretched out on her belly asleep, the two little cubs curled up beside her. More surely than any other game animal of the North does the grizzly frequent the upper ranges of the sheep. The canyon was deep and the slope where I stood fell away almost perpendicularly; there was no method of nearer approach except by going below and climbing up in an unfavorable wind. I estimated the distance, with a judgment not then sufficiently experienced, put up my two-hundred-yard sight, and fired. The bear jumped up. I fired again, the bullet striking in a direct line just below her. Rushing toward one of the cubs she cuffed it so that it bawled loudly, then gave a couple of jumps and disappeared over the slope, the cubs following closely.

Descending the canyon and climbing the opposite slope I found no blood sign. The surface being too rocky to record tracks, I continued along the slope, broken by a succession of canyons. Halfway up one of these I saw a large bull caribou standing at rest, head down, in a niche in a cliff. At this season, most of the biggest bulls are solitary and seek rough high spots like this in which to rest. His trail, clearly visible in the finely broken rock of the upper slope, showed that he had come up from below on the smoother slope beyond. His antlers, then in velvet, were magnificent, and I noticed that one tine was slightly broken, and that there was a bulblike swelling on another. After photographing the bull, I left without disturbing him, little suspecting that later his skull and horns would adorn the walls of my home.

Returning to my horse I found him in a state of terror, trembling, stamping, and rushing about at the end of the rope, which fortunately had been securely fastened. A short distance below the spot where he had been tied were the tracks of the bear and her two cubs, showing that they had circled down the slope, passing so close to him that he never quite recovered from the fright. It is significant that there were no blueberries nearer than ten miles, and no salmon nearer than sixty miles. It is perfectly clear that many of the bears of this region do not go for the salmon that ascend the rivers, nor do they feed much, if at all, on berries.

Riding out on the bar of the Upper East Branch I saw the three caribou lying down. While approaching, *Toklat* also saw them, pricked up his ears and attempted to quicken his pace, showing all the eagerness of the well-trained cattle horse for a chase. In order to obtain an August skin of a mature bull I decided to kill one now, and should I also succeed in getting sheep, to leave the bull's carcass for bear bait. When the caribou saw me they jumped up and approached, slightly circling in curiosity until near enough for a shot, which *Toklat* did not mind in the least. One of the bulls was hard hit but continued to walk. I drove him toward the bank until he had climbed over the edge, where another shot killed him. The horse went up and smelled the body without any fright, and stood quietly while I took off the skin.

Proceeding, I soon saw sheep along the slope of West

Branch Mountain, and tying *Toklat,* started to circle upward, noticing before long a few other sheep a mile beyond. These were the slopes on which I had seen so many ewes the year before. Ascending higher, I saw many more near the crest, and several about three miles up on the other side of the river, feeding near the place where I had seen large rams the preceding fall. When I came into view they had climbed well up the slope, reaching a place unfavorable for an approach. I decided therefore to stalk those I had seen beyond on the same slope. It was necessary to cross a canyon and ascend some cliffs to a bench, from the top of which I should be within range. Reaching the bench, I could not see them and knew they must have moved across another canyon. Circling this at the head, and crawling to a selected point, I carefully raised my head and saw two small rams, three ewes, and two lambs about a hundred and fifty yards distant, well bunched near the edge of the canyon. Aiming at the three-year-old ram, I fired and killed him; another shot killed a ewe, and a third was directed toward a smaller ram, which remained standing without a sign of being hit until I approached, when he fell and rolled down the slope. It might be stated here that I have never seen sheep collectively or individually pay the slightest attention to one of their number that was wounded or killed, other than an occasional glance of curiosity.

After dragging the carcasses to a favorable point, I dressed them and spent some time in carrying them down to a place to which *Toklat* could be brought. Then a walk of two miles to the horse and a delightful ride back enabled me to pack them on the saddle and lead him ten miles back to camp, which was reached at midnight. On the way the breezes had died down, the twilight sky was brilliant, and no sounds were heard except the roar of the river, the chatter of ground squirrels, the occasional wing beats of ptarmigan on the bars, and the tramp of *Toklat's* hoofs. In the fading light the new snow on the main Alaska Range shone with a peculiar transparency. Sheep were visible in all directions resting on and near the crests of the mountains, while lower down the bar I saw well ahead the fine old bull caribou already mentioned, and watched him walk across the flat and disappear in another canyon. At midnight it was dark and cold, the camp was silent, the men having gone down the river to cut hay and pass the night. Then came the satisfaction of a bright fire and refreshment before recording in my journal the events of the day.

August 12–17. Now that abundant meat had been provided I spent a week about camp, taking occasional tramps on the mountains. After inspecting the whole adjacent country, Karstens and Young had been able to find and cut only half a ton of hay, so the plan of wintering the horses near the cabin had to be abandoned.

August 13 I tramped over the Geological Survey Divide East, so named because it was the route traveled by Alfred H. Brooks in the original reconnaissance of this country in 1902. This divide runs along the base of a massive broken mountain containing much limestone and rock of various colors, seamed by numerous deep canyons, the extreme north range bordering the forest country of low relief. The divide heads over to the East Fork of the Toklat, and as among all of those between parallel ranges, the creeks heading near the summits flow to Toklat waters. The divide between Outside Mountain and Cabin Divide Mountain is similar in general to Cabin Divide. The year before I had noticed an old camp at the mouth of the creek more than two miles below my cabin. Now visiting it I saw rams' skulls scattered about, and picking up one to examine it found with sudden painful surprise that hornets had made their nest in the brain cavity.

Numerous ewes and lambs were feeding on the slopes on both sides of the summit and I spent a long time watching them. No 'sentinel' was observed and they fed in any direction, with or against the wind. Unnoticed, I climbed a slope until opposite and about four hundred yards away. A fair wind blew from me directly toward them, but not one indicated by any sign that my scent was received. After waiting half an hour I attempted to approach, but they saw me at once and ran diagonally upward along the slope. Their flight attracted the attention of other bands causing them also to walk upward near the crest, constantly looking back for the danger they had not detected. On the summit of the divide was a small lake covering three or four acres, with a green-winged teal and five young swimming on its surface. Teals were frequently observed on the numerous small lakes on the divides and on the rolling country above timber; spotted sandpipers were common, and wandering tattlers occasionally seen about the shores.

The afternoon of August 16 was spent observing sheep. August 17 I rode up to the carcass of the caribou, which as yet nothing had touched. At times during this week I assisted Karstens and Young in constructing the cabin and cut some of the fuel wood for the winter. Also, I trapped mice for specimens.

One of the most astonishing facts of all my experiences in the North—a fact I have never been able to explain—was the incredible abundance of several species of mice this year (1907). They were living both high and low on the mountain crests, and even far out on the river bars, while in 1906 the same little animals had been so scarce that for weeks I had not been able to find any signs of them until finally I caught a few of one species high on the mountain slopes. I have not been able to think of an explanation that would be satisfactory enough even to record as a guess. But the fact remains that in 1907 throughout the entire region west and east from Denali to the Teklanika, and north and south from well outside all the ranges to the main Alaska Range (the region with which I became familiar), the surface was almost everywhere covered with mice. I had only to set traps a few feet out on the bars when in less than half an hour each would contain a mouse which, unless secured immediately, was eaten by others. Those caught on the bars were mostly the then new subspecies of meadow mouse (*Microtus miurus oreas*) with an occasional red-backed mouse (*Evotomys dawsoni*); while those in the woods were mostly *Evotomys* and frequently *Microtus;* and on the slopes above, the lemming (*Lemmus yukonensis*) and several species of *Microtus* (*Microtus drummondi, operarius,* and *xanthognathus*). Both the common

Microtus miurus oreas and the lemmings bred in colonies of five to twelve holes close together, connected underground. I often sat on the bars and watched these meadow mice; they were out all day and very tame. Judging by the stages of development, at least two litters of young had been reared, and by the middle of August the females, both of meadow mice and of lemmings, contained from five to seven embryos each. Sometimes in the same colony I found all three genera—*Microtus, Evotomys,* and *Lemmus.* The meadow mice did not go far from the holes for food, which consisted of grass and seeds. It was very interesting to notice that when an Alaska Canada jay flew near, all suddenly rushed into their holes. Twice I saw a jay dart quickly down, pick up a young meadow mouse and fly to a tree and eat it. Surely the birds of prey and the predatory mammals had abundant food that summer.

August 12. From my cabin at the edge of the woods I looked northwest across the bars and saw on Ram Mountain thirteen rams, including some with large horns. They fed well up on the south slopes about a deep canyon and were in sight at intervals every day for several days. A few mosquitoes, not enough to be annoying, still remained about the woods, and midges had become very abundant. Among the birds, upland plovers were quite abundant on the grassy flats bordering the glacier bars.

August 18. Merrifield and Wilson returned with a relay of provisions and next day started back for Glacier City to bring the remainder of the equipment and supplies for the year. I accompanied them as far as my camp of the previous year, where I set up a small shelter, intending to spend a few days observing sheep, and perhaps kill a bear. That afternoon I rode *Toklat* to the caribou carcass and found a golden eagle feeding on it, but saw no signs of bear. In the evening I felt perfect contentment to be alone in my old camp looking out on the mountains and seeing the sheep climbing upward, while above the summit snowfield the southern sky was brilliantly colored. *Toklat,* hobbled near me without the other horses, was not only lonesome but very timid and nervous, hesitating to feed except when well out on the bars where he could see in all directions.

August 19. In the morning I was awakened early by a ground squirrel that ran back and forth over me in play. After breakfast I rode *Toklat* up the Upper West Branch, where small bands of sheep were on the slopes on both sides of the river. A little farther on a big bull caribou walked down along the foot of Divide Mountain—the big mountain ending the spur that projects from the Main Range between the two upper branches of the Toklat. The horse saw the caribou at a distance and from his actions I judged he mistook it for one of the horses, for he continually attempted to turn toward it until finally I could scarcely restrain him. So I directed his course toward it, hoping to approach near enough for a photograph. But seeing us it ran off, passing close to a small band of sheep. They did not seem in the least concerned about the caribou's state of fright, merely looking at it a moment and then continuing to feed.

I watched the sheep for a long time, and after making tea, again rode on and soon saw the same large band of ewes east of the river that had been there the previous year. Slightly farther on were five bull caribou of fair size standing at rest in the middle of the bar, two with heads down. These were near the point where the branch again forks. On the right is a wide grassy flat, the surface hard and smooth—an ancient bar of the river. I rode near enough to photograph the caribou. When they caught sight of us they began to circle toward us. Seeing that they would come to the flat, I took the rope, enlarged the noose and at the same time tried to restrain *Toklat,* who was dancing with excitement. As I gave chase, the caribou galloped in a curve toward the steep clifflike mountain slope that rises abruptly from the flat. The horse rapidly gained on them and soon I was swinging the noose almost on top of a fine bull, thinking the cliff would prevent them from leaving the flat and thus give me plenty of time to make another attempt, should the noose fail to settle over the bull's head. They were dashing along the foot of the cliffs when, just as I was about to make the throw, all suddenly turned and scrambled up the precipitous slopes, apparently as easily as sheep would have done. The sudden turn of the horse and his abrupt stop almost unseated me. The caribou were soon descending another steep slope two hundred yards to the west and on reaching the bars trotted along down the river until lost to sight.

After recovering from my surprise I rode as far as possible up the fork coming from the east, where I had observed so many ewes the year before. My astonishment was indeed very great to see that the rock spire of Pyramid Mountain, since last I visited it, had almost completely disappeared—a striking illustration of the looseness of the rock and the rapid disintegration of some of the mountains.

August 20–21. For two days I tramped over both the Teklanika* and the Stony Fork divides, the latter being the one on our route to the Toklat. No bear had come to the caribou carcass, but it had been partly eaten and the remainder packed away by wolverines. While observing sheep and caribou on the Teklanika Divide, and examining with the glasses the ridges above the East Fork of the Toklat, I saw a bear— too far away to stalk before dark.

The abundance of mice had brought many marsh hawks to the region; they were constantly in sight flying over the flats and often one might be seen diving down and catching a mouse.

For some time the weather, except for heavy winds blowing from the main range down the valleys, had been most pleasant, with continual bright sunshine and scarcely any rain. From numerous places on the flats, slopes, and crests, Denali in all its magnificence and imposing grandeur reared its massive snowy bulk toward the sky, looming apparently very near although really seventy miles away. It ever dominated the landscape, glorifying that mountain world. So strong and deep were the impressions it produced on me that my journal was almost daily filled with records of the joy of beholding it. The vision can never fade, and the ecstacies produced by such long intimacy with it will linger vividly throughout my life.

* Perhaps Polychrome Pass.

Although there had been no frosts, the mountains were turning brown, and early on the morning of August 21 a wet snow blizzard with heavy wind descended; but the snow that whitened the surface soon melted.

In the afternoon Jim Wilson came riding up, he and Merrifield having arrived at noon with the last loads. I returned with them to the camp.

August 22–24. At last all my provisions and equipment had come. The walls of the cabin had been erected; it remained only to complete the inside, give finishing touches and put things in order, to become settled for the winter.

The following morning Wilson with his four mules started down the Toklat for the Tanana, and Karstens and Young with two mules set out for Glacier City, where they were to cut enough hay to winter the two horses, *Toklat* and *Whistler,* which meanwhile were left with me. Merrifield was to remain until the horses could no longer find feed, then take them to Glacier City.

I found and killed a nice ewe just as the sheep were emerging from a ravine and walking up the slope of a butte. The remaining sheep ran into a canyon surrounded by steep rocky slopes. Not seeing them come out I knew they could not be far ahead and probably were bewildered. Climbing to the summit of the butte, I saw them all standing among some rocks well up on a slope that had not before been visible. Another shot killed a fine dry ewe; then, although not a single sheep had observed me, the others ran upward over the crest. The longer I hunted sheep the more I realized that, as in this stalk, knowledge of the habits and nature of the animals usually assured success in approaching them. I dressed the two ewes and reached the cabin at noon. The horses, which had strayed to a distance, were not brought back in time to go after the meat that afternoon, but next morning we took them up the rough slopes and packed it back to camp.

August 25 was spent observing sheep up the Upper East Branch.

August 27 it rained nearly all day and snowed at night so that by noon the following day eight inches of snow covered the ground. Then nearly all the tree sparrows gathered in small flocks and hopped about on the bare ground under the big spruces. By the next morning the snow, except high on the mountains, had melted and the lower slopes were again brown. Migrating flocks of robins were about; the dwarf birches showed a deep carmine at a distance; some of the willow leaves were yellow, others faded and falling. Autumn had arrived.

August 28. The inside of the cabin was practically completed, the provisions cached, and the equipment conveniently stored.

To the Teklanika Country.
Sheep.
Caribou.
Moose.
Cross Foxes.

The main object of my trip was to study the life history of sheep and incidentally to gather as much information as possible about other mammals. On my tramps I had looked especially for bears, knowing that continued hunting for them would keep me up among the sheep. I had planned therefore to go over to the Teklanika, looking for bears on the way and prepared to spend some time there.

August 29. The horses were packed and taken to my old camp at the Forks, where we were detained two days by rain and thunder storms.

August 31. By noon we were camped in the willows on the East Fork of the Toklat, where it divides in two branches coming from glaciers in the main range. Now that there had been heavy frosts the river was low, easily forded almost anywhere so near its source.

Tramping up the east branch of this fork in the afternoon against a heavy wind I was surprised to see fifteen caribou. Three were small bulls with the velvet already off, standing at rest out on the bar, indifferent to the gale which I could scarcely face. Moose found good feed on this fork of the Toklat and their signs were numerous, but no fresh bear signs were observed.

September 1. Starting early for the head of this same branch, I was accompanied by Merrifield who carried a pick and pan to prospect for gold. The wind blew down the valley so strongly that we could scarcely walk against it. After a climb of two or three hours we were near the head, where the conformation of the mountains formed a funnel-like trough through which the wind, accompanied by cutting hail, drew so fiercely that I did not then attempt to penetrate the narrow passage leading to the glacier.

The caribou were still on the opposite side of the flat and above them were two bands of sheep, several of which were lying down on the bar close to the slope. I noticed two Alaska Canada jays on the bar attempting to fly; they would rise and fly a short distance when the wind would dash them to the ground, and it was not until after several attempts that they finally got under successful flight. A flock of white-tailed ptarmigan near the bar were so tame that Merrifield killed two with a stone. We took shelter in the mouth of a small canyon where tea was made and the ptarmigan broiled on the coals. Merrifield then returned to camp while I walked a short distance up the canyon, which was very rough, with high rocky slopes where marmots were whistling among the crags. Why marmots should inhabit such inhospitable places I could only guess by the supposition that in such places they escaped being dug out by bears. By this time the wind had slackened somewhat and I returned to the river, noticing that most of the sheep were out on the bar. They were feeding and some were lying down, exactly about the tracks we had made when coming up in the morning. I approached to within a hundred yards, directly in the wind, before they saw me, when those on the bar broke into a run for the slopes, though those above merely rose and walked upward.

I then penetrated to the glacier, which occupies an amphitheatre of snowy mountains, but saw no animals, and seeking a sheltered spot, climbed the ridge between the two branches and with the glasses examined the country for bears, without seeing one. Soon a wet snow storm came up, and while walking slowly down the bar I missed the caribou which, as I learned later by observing their tracks, had gone down the flat on a trot, evidently having winded me at a great distance.

September 2. The strong wind of yesterday still roared down the river as I forced myself against it, following the westerly branch, which in general is similar to the other. These two branches are separated by a long grassy ridge rising gradually to the ranges at the heads. I ascended this ridge and walked along it for two or three miles, carefully scanning the country for bears. None were seen. Shortly before reaching the upper end, a band of about forty sheep came in sight running for a quarter of a mile across the flat and stopping to feed slightly above on the slope. I approached to within two hundred feet before they saw me. There were about forty young ewes, two years old or less, and a yearling ram. Only one small ewe was followed by a lamb. I attempted to walk nearer and when one or two began to show slight alarm I paused and photographed them. All looked at me for a few moments and then resumed feeding, some even lying down for a short time. The ewe with the lamb was somewhat more cautious and remained above the others, watching me more closely. Some were badly stained, others less so, the lambs appearing whiter than the others. Some were pawing among the rocks to get at the root of an unidentified plant. One carefully pawed aside the rocks to clear a space in which to double her fore legs under her as she lay down. Seating myself on the dryas of this ancient bar I watched these sheep for an hour. This was the only time in all my experience with sheep that they seemed indifferent to my presence at such a short distance. That one or another kept pausing to watch me between intervals of feeding was the only visible evidence that they saw me. Finally I shouted, again and again, but they only looked at me and continued to feed. I had tramped over a wide area that day, wet and chilled by repeated snow falls, but not a single fresh sign of a bear was observed. At night the frosts were very heavy and each day the snow was lower on the mountain slopes.

September 3. While crossing the summit of the low divide leading to the west branch of the Teklanika we saw five large bull caribou feeding at the foot of the mountain about a quarter of a mile away. Their necks were swelled, and the velvet was either entirely off their horns, or hung in strips. These large bulls had banded and were going outside the ranges for the rut. Almost immediately, when I attempted to walk toward them, they saw me and trotted over a low pass. Heretofore, while the velvet was on their horns, caribou bulls had been reasonably tame, and on seeing me had not at once run off in fright. But, as I learned later, the big bulls become most timid on the approach of the rut.

Descending to the middle or main Teklanika we found the water low and clear. It was full of grayling, which had now run up, the silt caused by the discharging glacier having disappeared, as it always does in September when cold weather prevents rapid melting of the ice. Arriving at my old base camp of 1906 at the Forks, I found all the poles still standing; and the bough bedding seemed fairly fresh. We had but to stretch the silk shelter tent over them, arrange our few provisions and all was ready. Since the frost had destroyed most of the grass, we had put very light packs on the horses, depending mostly on meat for food. After lunch, therefore, I started out to kill some sheep both for food and for bear bait. I had seen so few fresh signs of bears that it was necessary to increase the chances for getting them. Nor had I seen nearly so many sheep along the route from the Toklat as during the year before, the inclement weather having kept them off the more exposed mountain slopes.

When I started north along the river no sheep were in sight, but I knew they could easily be found in more sheltered spots and intended, if possible, to hunt them along the branch opposite where I had killed the bear and cubs the year before. Along the bar were the old tracks of my horses, and also those of a bear that I identified as the very same ones I had observed the year before. These footprints seemed not more than a month old. Proceeding along the meadow land and scanning the broken slopes of Cathedral Mountain, all the events of my stalk for rams the previous year were vividly recalled, and so strong had been the impressions made by the old bear and cubs that I almost felt their presence.

Reaching the edge of the branch I saw, two miles up along the south slope of the outside mountain, three bands of ewes, well separated—a band of ten high up on the slope, one of seven below them, and one of five low down a quarter of a mile nearer the river. The latter band provided just the opportunity wanted to kill sheep in a place easily accessible to horses, and where at the same time the carcasses could be observed from a spot not far from camp.

Descending to the bar, I advanced a mile, hidden from their sight by a high embankment, and crawling out to the centre of the bar behind some willows, studied the situation. The sheep were feeding on an elevated point to which there was no approach without danger of being detected. Yet I saw that if three hundred yards could be gained along the bar I could reach another cut bank and go unseen to a point not too distant for a fair shot. The situation demanded patience, so I waited an hour and a half until all the sheep had disappeared in a hollow; then advanced slowly and watchfully to a bank near which I could move more rapidly until close enough for another inspection. While crawling on the bar I came in sight of the other two bands farther up the slope. The lower of these immediately saw me and ran upward, thus starting the upper band. I waited anxiously, knowing that although a good distance away, they might alarm the sheep I was stalking. But these were not in sight nor did they appear for some time after the others had gone over the crest. In this region sheep, while feeding in exposed places on the extreme outside range, are much wilder than sheep in similar positions on the inside ranges—not because they are hunted by man, for man seldom or never intrudes even on the outside ranges—but probably because wolves are present on the outside range, while they seldom penetrate far inside.

I crept back to the bank, advanced a little farther, and then saw the sheep feeding on willows. Choosing a good point for a shot, two hundred and fifty yards ahead, I managed to reach it and had all five sheep less than a hundred and fifty yards away. The first shot killed a two-year-old ram, and as the remaining sheep jumped about in confusion, two more shots killed a ewe and a lamb, and three more dropped the remaining ewe and lamb. By the time I had dressed four of them it was so nearly dark that I could not at first find the lamb that had fallen out on the bar. While searching for it, it suddenly jumped up and staggered on. Upon my approach it would drop in an attitude of hiding, lying flat with its head and neck stretched forward against the ground. When I was very close it would jump up, stagger ahead, and again attempt to hide. This was repeated several times before I caught it—clearly illustrating the hiding instinct of lambs. I walked back to camp through the darkness as the mists settled on the mountains.

Among my many camps in the North, some were so situated that the firelight danced on the spruces, the sparks mingling with them, while the sound of rushing waters and of the breezes hurrying through the narrow valleys produced a haunting impression of weirdness—a deep sense of the wilderness. The present camp was one in which this effect was strongly pronounced—tempting me to linger long before the radiant fire.

September 4–5. On the morning of September 4 there were six inches of snow on the ground and the storm continued all day, the wet snow melting almost as fast as it fell. Fourteen or fifteen Alaska Canada jays were about camp and it was necessary to snare and destroy many of them in order to save our meat. We did not leave camp until the next morning—a clear beautiful day with six inches of snow still on the ground. This snow revealed the abundance of mice, for their tracks literally covered the bars, meadows, hillsides, and mountains. A much larger track indicated that a fox had passed by close to camp. Three or four golden eagles were seen feeding at the carcasses but the meat had not been damaged and Merrifield packed a ewe and the two lambs on the horses and brought them to camp. I spent the rest of the day near the glaciers at the head of the branch observing numerous but very wild sheep. Lambs were occasionally seen sucking their mothers. Conies were particularly plentiful on the broken rocks at high altitudes.

September 6. A cold night with heavy frost gave promise of good weather, and when I left camp to go up the river the clear sky and crisp air of the morning indicated another fine day. But after an hour a strong wind began to blow, dark clouds rapidly gathered, and the rest of the day was marked by wind and snow flurries. Reaching the bar two miles ahead, up on the slopes of the rolling country west of the river, I saw a cow moose feeding among the willows. I wanted moose meat to bring back to the cabin and here was an opportunity to get it and also to leave part of a carcass where it could be observed from close by my camp. With a strong wind against me it was easy to climb the ridge and undetected reach the spot where the moose was feeding. But when I arrived there and looked, no moose was anywhere visible. Had she departed in any direction I could have seen her, hence I knew she must be lying down in the willows. Seating myself, I scrutinized them with the utmost care and finally saw the tips of her ears just inside the upper edge of the growth. I whistled; the ears at once stiffened erect. A second whistle brought the cow to her feet facing me a hundred and fifty yards away. She fell dead to my shot. She was fat, with a fine long bell; and after dressing her I cut out the fat and the hind quarters which, in two heavy loads, I carried to the bar. The stomach was filled with willow buds and a large quantity of green grass.

While approaching this moose I saw a three-year-old ram walk down a slope and stand behind me, three hundred yards distant, looking at me. For ten minutes he stood directly in my wind with no obstruction between us and I could not observe any indication on his part that he noticed my scent. When I started to walk, he ran off. It was not uncommon to see young rams of that age, or even younger—before the independent nature of the animal had begun to assert itself—thus alone, crossing low rolling country.

The rest of the day was spent near the glacier, where many small bands of sheep were observed, and also a fairly fresh bear track and diggings at almost exactly the same spot where I had killed the bear the previous year.

While returning down the bar late in the afternoon I saw two fine cross foxes galloping along a lower slope not three hundred yards away. It was a fascinating sight to watch these animals quartering up and down, approaching all patches of willow growth, never relaxing a speed evenly maintained, until finally lost to sight. I did not then know that they were hunting ptarmigan. Except in the flight of some birds, no motion has come within my experience that embodies so much grace and ease as that of these northern foxes galloping over the uneven country in search of ptarmigan.

Later, while crossing the bar to get the moose fat, I noticed another cross fox sitting on a small elevation between two channels of the river. As I approached she dived into a burrow, and soon afterward I saw her running up the bar; she had come out of a connecting burrow behind some low willows, where I could not see her until she had gained considerable distance. This successful trick, when I was within shot, seemed to me to display almost more than the traditional fox cunning. Approaching a little nearer I detected the head of a black fox just appearing in some willows; a bullet from my rifle hit the shoulders low enough to prevent it from getting too far down in the hole to be pulled out. It was a pup in fairly good pelage, perfectly black with the exception of here and there a silver-tipped hair, and a white tip on the tail. After carefully examining the skin I felt certain that if I had pulled out the few silver-tipped hairs, as any trapper would have done, this fox would have been as pure 'black' as any fox that had ever been killed.

During my absence Merrifield had been 'panning' for gold on a tributary below camp and reported having seen a bear traveling along the slopes.

September 7. I went up there today, having noticed nothing but eagles and a red fox at the sheep carcasses, and found the bear tracks where Merrifield had reported seeing the animal. Although I followed the tracks as far as possible, and wandered about the whole day in the hope of finding the bear, I did not have the good fortune to see it. The day was snowy and windy and most disagreeable. The snow had not then melted and the sheep, following their usual habits everywhere at such times, came down to feed among the willows. Still, at many other times small bands had been observed feeding indifferently in exposed places, not in the least protected from wind and snow. That night, while we were sitting about the fire, I heard the cry of a lynx about a hundred yards back in the woods. It was a rather low catlike 'meow' somewhat prolonged, and repeated three times. This was the only time in my experience in either the Yukon or Alaska that the voice of a lynx was heard.

September 8. Rain on the 8th practically cleared the snow off the lower country. In the afternoon I started down the bar intending to climb to the summit of Cathedral Mountain in the hope of seeing a bear and also of studying the band of rams which inhabited it. While going down the bars I was interested to observe my own footprints of the previous year, the imprint of every hobnail still marked so clearly that the tracks did not seem over a week old. Climbing up through the canyon where I had seen the rams, I reached the snowfields and wandered all day about the crests without seeing either rams or a bear, although a wide stretch of country was searched through the field glasses. More than ever I was impressed by the beauty of Cathedral Mountain. Never have I seen a mountain of that height more beautiful, with its startling conformation, jagged crests, deep canyons, irregular spurs, and variegated colors. Once while I was sitting on the crest, surrounded by sharp peaks and deep canyons overlooking the windings of the river far below, with numerous little lakes dotting the brown barrens between the timbered border and the mountains beyond, suddenly the sun broke through the clouds and illumined the field of snowy summits. High on a mountain to the west were a hundred ewes and lambs, while just below, a cow moose and its calf were swimming across a shining Alpine lake.

Later I descended to the spot where I had killed the bears and caught the cub. The heap of earth where the bear had buried the sheep carcass was there, but not a sign, not even a piece of bone, of either bear or sheep remained to suggest the tragedy that had taken place there.

September 9. Dawn brought a beautiful clear sunny day, warm notwithstanding the strong wind which, as usual in September, blew down the valleys in the daytime. I was up long before daylight, cooked breakfast, and was soon walking up the bar anticipating a long day about the glaciers. There had been no frost in the night, the wind had not begun to blow at dawn, and everything was still except for the awakening songs of the tree sparrows, the notes of jays, and the croaks of willow ptarmigan. As the glow above the rugged eastern crests cast a rosy light over the landscape, eagles were soaring along the slopes and the silence was often broken by the swishing wing beats of ravens as they flew high above the bar. The river, then very low, sounded only in a faint murmur.

No bear was observed at the moose carcass, the fox burrows had been deserted, and the remains of the black fox had been eaten, not even a bone remaining. Soon the sun, bright and warm, topped the summits and ewes became visible in all directions.

After an enjoyable tramp of three hours I approached the spot where the river forks, just north of the place where I had killed the bear the year before, and where for a hundred yards it flows through a narrow deep canyon. This area I knew to be the home of a band of rams that frequented the south end of the valley. Immediately on rounding the corner I saw five rams with fair horns well up the slope to the left, and six larger rams near the crestline above the canyon. The latter presented an opportunity for a stalk with a chance for a photograph. Before they saw me I managed to circle around and come up on top of a stony ridge where they were walking on the crest. Two went over out of sight while four remained on the skyline just long enough for me to snap my kodak at them, recording a faint impression. At the same time I saw the principal part of the band, fourteen in all, some with very large heads. They were a hundred yards away, across and just above the upper edge of the canyon wall. They had not seen me, and the other rams had departed so quietly that no alarm had been given. A concealing rock was handy and there I remained observing them for over an hour. During that time forty ewes were feeding on the flat just below the glacier at the head of the valley, and three bands of ewes, fifty in all, were on the slopes across the valley.

Since the actions of this band of rams were typical for this season of the year, it is worth while to describe them in some detail. In the band were eight rams with large horns—at least

seven or eight years old—including two very old ones with
horns thoroughly wrinkled, one so old that he had probably
reached the last year or two of his natural life. The other
six varied in age from four to six years. The horns of the
oldest, though badly 'broomed' at the tips, were very large
and heavy, well curved, very dark, and so wrinkled as to present what to me is the supreme development of horn beauty.
All, and particularly the oldest ones, were exceedingly fat, and
when feeding were sluggish, none of them showing the grace
and ease of ewes. All were very badly stained, very much more
so than ewes, rendering them, when on the snow, extremely
conspicuous. While feeding, the individuals scattered, seeming at times to be quite independent of each other. In fact, in-
dividuality and independence of behavior, as compared with
the collective actions of ewes, were the chief traits displayed by
the rams. All were very lazy in feeding, one or another constantly lying down to rest for a short time; then feeding again,
quietly and leisurely, though diligently. Most of them fed
about the walls of the canyon, seeking green food in the niches
of the rocks. When this could not easily be reached, a ram
would circle around and try to push his nose to it; if he failed
he would often, in apparent anger, strike the rocks with his
horns. Continually during his efforts to grasp this green food,
the tip of one horn or the other was scraping the rocks or
pushed hard against them. This is one of the causes of the
horns 'brooming' at the tips.

It was apparent that at this time the rams were so fat that
activity or frequent traveling did not appeal to them. Often
while lying down, one would stretch out his neck and allow the
horns to rest on the ground. This might be for relief from the
weight of the horns, yet quite as frequently I have observed
ewes doing the same thing. While unconscious of danger,
their movements were anything but graceful. Every action
seemed deliberate. The younger ones mostly maintained the
watch, the two older ones seldom looked up, the oldest not at
all, being completely indifferent to everything except feeding
and resting. The old members of the band, in places where
they have fed undisturbed for a long time, seem to depend on

the younger ones to warn them of danger. Those that did look up at short intervals, raised their heads slowly and with such coolness that one might believe they watched with indifference. But by carefully observing them, as I did in this case, one could see that the watch was thorough and constantly maintained in all directions. When a ram strays to a distance from the band he looks about and watches more frequently, but at no time did one act in any way to suggest a 'sentinel.'

At length all passed out of sight beyond the canyon. After allowing sufficient time to elapse, I started through the bottom of the canyon, hoping for a chance to find them in a position to stalk for a photograph. On emerging from the high rugged walls I saw all the rams lying down on the side of a bluff well ahead, and although too far off I made an effort to photograph them. But before I could conceal myself the younger ones saw me and jumping up started to run, followed somewhat indifferently by the older ones. The oldest ram brought up the rear, trotting slowly, scarcely running at all, very reluctant to be disturbed. Nor did he once look back, as all the others did at times. He stopped frequently and was soon joined by a smaller ram, who seemed deliberately to drop behind to remain with him. These very old rams were often accompanied by a younger companion, seemingly a sort of guardian. The rams soon passed out of sight in the broken surface of the basin.

Following their tracks and mounting a ridge I beheld a sublime Alpine scene. High irregularly-carved mountains with serrated crestlines and canyoned slopes enclosed an amphitheatre down either side of which flowed a stream from a small glacier. The upper snowfield shone and sparkled in the sun in strong contrast to the black and red floor of the basin, the bed of a former great glacier. Its bottom, roughly broken by a jumble of intersecting ridges, spotted and streaked with snow, formed a chaos bewildering to the eye.

These gorgeous contrasts of the landscape, combined with such a magnificent view, could not alone have created the impression of perfection had it not been for a complement to crown and complete it. Washington Irving once said that the

Dutch landscape needs the windmill to adorn it, a Spanish landscape increases in loveliness with the ruins of a Moorish castle crowning a height in its midst, while the ornamented scenery of Europe is graced by the village spire, the battlements of a castle, or the turrets of an old family mansion rising above the trees. So too, the wild remote mountain landscape of Alaska needs some evidence of life to perfect it, and the life must be appropriate to a region never inhabited by human beings. Ahead of me, not over three hundred yards distant, a sharp black cone a hundred feet high rose abruptly from the ridge. Crowded closely together in alert attitudes, heads upright, turned in all directions, stood a band of rams, their great horns in harmony with their rugged surroundings, their presence completing the sublimity of the wild scene.

Motionless I stood for a long time but when finally I moved they at once saw me and ran. Reaching the snowfield they broke into single file, the younger rams leading and jumping through the snow until at a safe distance, when they traveled at a walk to a sharply inclined slope, where they again banded closely together and stood watching me. The very old ram trotted only a short distance and on reaching the snow walked slowly, stopping every few moments as if exhausted, not once looking back. When the band stopped he was half a mile in the rear, going still more slowly and stopping to rest more frequently. The other two old rams also soon fell behind the younger ones and walked or trotted, stopping now and then but only once looking back.

While I was searching the basin for a bear, the rams were peacefully lying down in the snow just below the crest. All the bear diggings were several days old—no fresh signs were observed. All the basins along the outside range were covered more or less with bear diggings, evidence that the bears were especially fond of hunting there for ground squirrels, which, perhaps owing to their more shallow burrows, are easier to dig out than in the lower country. Marmots also are more abundant high up near the main range, and occasionally, when one had been careless enough to burrow outside of the rocks, it had been dug out by a bear.

September 10–14. I tramped the mountains and ridges to

the north, inspecting the country about the East Fork of the Teklanika, which is separated from the main Teklanika by the rough mountains behind my camp. The East Fork does not carry so large a volume of water as the main Teklanika, though much larger than the West Fork. It heads in glaciers only a short distance from the basin where I saw the rams the day before. Fresh bear diggings were very scarce, but on that warm windy day sheep, mostly ewes, were observed on all the mountains, some even low on the outside ridges. A few blueberries were still luscious on a ridge eight miles below camp.

A heavy rainstorm kept me about camp for the next two days, giving my feet, which had been somewhat crippled by shoes, a chance to heal sufficiently to permit me to continue tramping. I had watched all the carcasses during this time, but no bear had come to them and I determined never again to kill an animal for bait.

After the violent storm of two days, a heavy frost in the night foretold a perfect day, without clouds or wind. So on September 14 we packed the horses and left camp. While tramping over the divide along the south slopes of Cathedral Mountain, I saw twenty rams, several with large heads, traveling high up on the slope. Holding the horses in a depression I watched them. There were four bands, slightly separated. The one with the oldest rams contained thirteen, all following a trail single file. Three or four three-year-olds wandered slightly above the others. None of the rams were more than seven or eight years old; the one with the largest horns led. The younger rams of this band were as usual more watchful than the older ones. All were going on without pausing to graze, stopping only now and then as new areas came into view, to look upward as well as in other directions. The impressive sight of adult wild rams strung out in single file high on a mountain is not a common one. Here was the band belonging to this particular mountain, the one from which I had killed rams the year before.

At the west end of the mountain where it slopes down to the Toklat, seven or eight rams, three and five years old, were feeding not far up on a smooth grassy slope. They were not much alarmed as we approached with the horses, but one of the small lakes prevented my going near enough to get good photographs. On most of the ranges inhabited by rams, few under five years old are found in the main band of old ones. But on some of these ram mountains, usually adjacent to the main band, were the younger rams, often forty or more. Some of these gradually recruit the band of older ones, while others form special bands, which as they grow older occupy another range.

While we were descending through thick willows not far from the East Fork of the Toklat, a cow moose and two calves, all with long bells, suddenly ran out only a few feet ahead, trotted a short distance, and stopped to gaze at us as we passed. After lunching we turned down the East Fork for about five miles, crossed the ridges to Cabin Divide, and reached the cabin at dark. The East Fork of the Toklat flows through glacier bars similar to those of the main Toklat, but the bars are not so wide and the mountains rise more abruptly. Toward the north this [East] Fork emerges from a high-walled canyon four miles in length.

On that bright sunny day after the storm, sheep were visible on all the mountains in numbers equal to those I had observed while traveling most of this month the year before, but the caribou had left for the country outside the ranges. That day's tramp was delightful because of the great number of sheep peacefully feeding, of near views of rams, of the beauty of the surroundings. The brown background, patched with grass and the sea-green of lichens, was enlivened by the blend of the fall coloring—the yellow of the willow leaves, the carmine of the dwarf birches, the dull crimson of the dryas, and the red of the blueberry bushes. Above were the snowy summits; below, the slopes striated with rocks of many hues.

I had now wandered over all the country traversed the preceding year and the fact most impressed upon me was that the sheep—ewes, lambs, and rams, scattered or in bands—occupied exactly the same areas on the mountains and in about the same numbers, as the year before.

Autumn Days.
Caribou.
Sheep.
Black Fox.

September 15–17. In the night a severe rain-storm descended, continuing for two days, while the third day was blustery and snowy. During this time I could look down the bars through the outside ranges and see clear blue sky and calm weather. Such are the contrasts in weather inside and outside of these mountains.

Most of the grass had been frozen and only a small feed of oats could be allowed the horses, so they were having a hard time. During the storm I was occupied in chopping wood for the winter, clearing brush about the cabin, and in various other minor tasks.

September 18. A cloudless, windless, mild day dawned. At daylight I was walking down the bar on my way to the West Fork of the Toklat (also called Stony Creek). On the west side of the river a mile and a half below the cabin is the mouth of a creek coming down from an easy divide between Ram Mountain and the bordering range directly west of my cabin—the Intermediate Range, I called it. This range or mountain is high with smooth outlines on the east, but is badly broken and rough toward the west. It lies between Ram Mountain and Old Camp Mountain, which is directly behind my camp of the preceding year.

Reaching the creek, I found the old camp of the Geological Survey party under Alfred H. Brooks, which they had occupied August 10, 1902. The date and the names of the members were clearly marked with lead-pencil on a spruce tree where a space had been cleared of bark. I called the divide 'Geological Divide West.' In general it is similar to all the divides of the parallel ranges between the Forks of the Toklat.

On emerging from the narrow belt of spruces, I saw high

on the mountain nine or ten big rams, which, looking from my cabin, I had previously seen at intervals on this part of the mountain. Being now quite near, I watched them for nearly an hour, until at 11.30 they lay down. Then, after a cup of tea, I crossed the divide and soon noticed about twenty small rams low down on the slope near the rolling hills of the divide. Here again were the young rams, less than four years old, adjacent to but not in the same band with the big rams. The conformation offering a fair opportunity for a stalk, I approached to within less than a hundred yards before they saw me, when they immediately crowded together for a moment and then dashed upward—not, however, until I had taken two or three photographs, recording a suggestion of them, although the upward pointing of the kodak caused the slope to appear level. These younger rams are always more nervous than the older ones and watch even more than do the ewes.

I was devoting this day, as in the case of the previous ones, to searching for bears, and was continually scanning the country through the field glasses. A little farther along the divide more very young rams were visible, while ewes were seen in abundance on the Intermediate Range to the south. Just before reaching the West Fork I circled high on the west slopes and traversed their rough areas all the afternoon, with Denali always in view and apparently very near, towering in the sky like a great white dome. At last I climbed over the snowfields of the crest and descended to the bar. Just before reaching it, through my glasses I saw a bear walking across the mouth of the draw south of the cabin. Soon I was plunging across the river, which owing to the warm sun was running high, but it was dark before I reached the spot. I then named this the *Bear Draw* and returned to the cabin. It had been a long arduous tramp and unlucky in that the bear had been seen too late to be followed.

September 19–20. The next two days were very warm, and much of the snow on the mountains had melted. At daylight I hunted in the Bear Draw, and later tramped over all the adjacent country, but saw no sign of the bear. It had not gone out on the bars and the surface elsewhere was not of a character to retain imprints of its feet. The next day, when I went up beyond my old camp over the divide to the West Fork [Stony Creek], there was still no sign of bears. No caribou were within the ranges—only sheep, and they were on all the mountains. A few tree sparrows and now and then a lingering robin were the only birds remaining to remind me of summer.

Merrifield had been cutting dry spruces and hauling them with *Toklat* to the cabin for winter fuel. The poor horses continually came to the cabin and pushed their heads through an open window begging for oats, which we could not give them, as we had to reserve the two or three remaining feeds for hard days when they should begin their return to Glacier City.

September 21. There had been no frost in the night and the day was warm with a strong south wind which in the late afternoon changed to north. I started down river early to look for bears several miles below on the extreme outside slopes of the outside range. Many sheep were on the mountains on both sides. The river soon rose with a good volume of water curling over the rocky bottoms of the channels. Now and for about ten days more, the landscape was one of continual color variations, depending on atmospheric conditions and changing lights as the day progressed, or as the clouds and mists in varying degrees obscured the sun. The earlier carmine of the dwarf birch, the crimson of the dryas, the red of the blueberry bush, and the yellow of the willow, were now all seared to a rich brown. The grass looked parched, like prairie grass in December. All seemed ready for winter. At one hour the mountain slopes would appear uniformly brown, deepening and intensifying the variegated colors of the rocks and making the pale greens, blacks, grays, and reds glow in contrast, creating an aspect both beautiful and austere. At another hour all would be changed to exquisite blends and shades of yellow, brown, and pale green, with patches here and there illuminated to gold. Then, as clouds obscured the sun, the entire color tone might change suddenly to a severe aspect. Thus, during this brief transition period, the colors of the landscape, replacing those of early fall, bring equal joy and inspiration.

It was noon when I had passed outside the range, and after making tea and taking some refreshment I started to climb the slopes of the outside mountain. Soon I was high above the spruces, looking over the vast forested region to the north. After my prolonged and intimate association with the rugged country above timber, the great stretches of spruces extending far away directly below me completed and intensified the feelings aroused by the wilderness—a vague undefinable sense of being a part of these wilds, with unrestrained freedom to wander and enjoy the treasures of emotion they were continually arousing.

No sheep were visible on the outside mountain, and only two small rams high on the slopes across the river. But turning my glasses upon two moving objects on the bar I saw that they were bull caribou. Hastening down and through a narrow strip of spruces, I again saw them, both bulls with fairly large horns, walking up the bar about three-quarters of a mile away. They walked slowly, heads down, now and then pausing a moment for a mouthful of food and then again moving on, one keeping well ahead of the other, never once looking about for danger, while the other maintained a watch, constantly looking behind. I hurried along the east edge of the bar and finally came opposite them and then cautiously advanced parallel with their course, a quarter of a mile away. While thus in sight they continued moving for an hour, and then went into some thick willow brush along the edge of the bar and did not again appear. Crossing the river, I soon went into the willows, and not observing the caribou, slowly advanced until I saw one five hundred yards ahead, just as he was disappearing in the timber. Reaching the spot I followed the tracks of the two bulls, plainly visible on the soft sphagnum moss, indicating that they were feeding on the small patches of lichen scattered about on the ground.

For more than a mile I followed their irregular tracks diagonally upward to the edge of the spruces, when both caribou were observed climbing over a spur near the top of the mountain. They soon passed over the crest and into a ravine where they remained to feed. Circling around the slope to climb against the wind, I stalked upward over a rough surface with dense strips of willows impeding progress. Before reaching the crest of the spur I saw both bulls feeding upward on the slope of the other spur. They fed quietly, seldom looking up, always maintaining a course upward, while I stalked toward them, keeping as much as possible behind low willows. At last the willows became so dense that I could not safely approach nearer. One bull had just reached the crest when, aiming through my two-hundred-yard sight, I fired. He dropped dead and rolled more than a hundred yards down the slope until caught in the willows. Only the horns of the other were then in sight, the body being behind a rock. But after a moment he trotted a little forward and looked down at his dead companion, then continued up on the crest and stood looking about in confusion. I fired and he also dropped and rolled down, stopping not far from the body of the other. Reaching the crest of the spur I rested awhile. The wind had stopped and no sounds were audible save the occasional chatter of a ground squirrel, the chirp of a robin, and the distant roar of the river.

After photographing both animals I carefully dressed them, noting that there was little fat inside their bodies and that their stomachs contained a little grass and a few small plants, but mostly lichen, which was now green. Descending, I reached the bar in the calm of approaching sunset. The landscape colors had softened, the blends changing as the sun lowered until only the mountain crests were illumined, contrasting boldly with the darkening slopes and valley below. Earlier, while the sun was still above the crest and lights and shadows were playing about, I had noticed two miles ahead a very narrow box canyon, presenting the appearance of a wall of rock across the bar. Suddenly a dense mist, resembling a vast cloud of smoke, poured in great volume from the mouth of this canyon, none of it rising above the walls. This cloud soon overspread and buried from sight the east side of the bar and the lower adjacent slopes, while above it all was clear, the slopes and crest catching the full light of the declining sun. The cloud stream kept pouring through the canyon and crept along the bar for several miles, giving a strange and exquisite effect that I had never seen before. But often afterward I saw it in this same spot, though never in any other part of the region. The atmosphere above the canyon is sooner chilled by the surrounding higher mountains than that below, and where the chilled air meets the warm air below, the mist forms quickly.

September 22–23. The morning of the 22d we went down the river with the horses, and leaving them on the bar, carefully skinned the caribou and in two relays brought down the meat, packed it on the horses, and reached the cabin in the afternoon. The tracks of a trotting bull moose crossed the bar a little more than a mile below the cabin. At this time the rut was in full swing and it was most unusual to see moose signs so far up this fork of the Toklat.

The 23d was very warm, the sky clear, and at times light breezes sprang up, shortly to die away leaving the atmosphere calm and serene in the haze that overspread the land. I went up the Geological Divide East, crossed the summit and descended to the East Fork of the Toklat, where I climbed a mountain and tramped about the slopes, all the time looking for signs of bears without seeing any. While crossing the river, two large cow moose were seen feeding among the willows on a slope not a hundred yards distant. No calves were with them. One of the cows was somewhat watchful; the other fed quietly, apparently indifferent to danger. I did not disturb them.

On this fine day, sheep (ewes and lambs) in detached bands were abundant on all the mountains. Some were winding up the slopes; some appeared to be pegged to the steep rocky sides; some were feeding quietly though cautiously on smoother slopes or resting on the rocks; others were resting on the crests and peaks. Again I was impressed with the fact that exceptionally warm weather on a fine day brings the sheep to exposed places where they can be easily observed.

After tramping down the Fork to the canyon, I turned back to the creek that flows down from Cabin Divide and followed it up to the summit. Once, while rounding a curve along the narrow bar. I came suddenly upon four ewes and a lamb, not

more than seventy-five feet distant, feeding close to the foot
of the mountain. I had been walking cautiously and they had
not even suspected me. In my haste to photograph them, I
must have moved the kodak, for neither of the two snapshots
is clearly defined. While the sheep were still unconscious of
my presence I stood motionless in plain sight and gave a whistle. All heads came up and were jerked about in an effort to
locate the source of noise. But they did not see me until I
whistled again, when all fastened on me such a piercing gaze
that I felt almost transfixed by their eyes. For fully five minutes I stood motionless while the sheep remained like statues
watching me—not a movement of their heads could I detect.
Then, as I deliberately moved, all quickly jumped and ran up
the mountain, not stopping until they had passed over the
crest. While looking at me, their stiffened attitudes showed
alarm, but it was my motion that really frightened them.

That day, besides jays, chickadees, ptarmigan and ravens,
I saw tree sparrows, robins, shrikes, and a Wilson snipe.

Now was the period of Indian summer days, occurring at
intervals between those of rain and wind. This day had been
one almost of perfection, the fields of snow on the higher
slopes presenting a contrast that emphasized the warmth and
balminess, while the numerous bands of sheep added an impression of peacefulness. More than all, the haze tempered the
sunlight to a golden tint, softening the colors and giving
vagueness to the outlines of the mountains, causing a feeling
of mystery to pervade the wilderness.

September 24. A very heavy frost during the night foretold the approach of colder weather and warned me that the
horses must be taken out of the region. I had planned to take
them to the outside of the ranges for caribou hunting during
the last days of September, and also to kill six or seven sheep
for a stock of meat for camp while they could be used to carry
it to the cabin. So I left very early in the morning for the
Upper East Branch intending to kill the sheep at a distance
from the cabin. The air was motionless, crisp and sharp
though a dense fog hung low over the country, the clear sky
above giving it a soft bluish tone. Through the mist the ex-

quisite outlines of the spruce tree tops were dimly visible. All about was silence and mystery. As I passed through the half mile of woods and came out on the bars nothing could be seen but the surface immediately near and the blue sky above. I continued on a course undirected by landmarks, and as the sun warmed the atmosphere a brilliant rainbow formed a vast semicircle through the fog. Soon the jagged mountain crests became visible under the sweeping arc, then increased in intensity, while at the same time the snowy crests shining brilliantly in the sunlight appeared as though mysteriously suspended. This impression lasted only until the rainbow colors began to fade and the fog to dispel; then the lower slopes came into view and the fog quickly disappeared leaving the sky cloudless, the sun brightly shining, the landscape sharp and clearly defined.

The two horses were standing motionless out on the bar, enjoying the warmth of the sun. They had been having a hard time and both were growing thin notwithstanding that they were good 'rustlers' and had learned to find all the possible food the region afforded.

As I rounded the point of Divide Mountain and came into the valley of the Upper East Branch a south wind was blowing so strongly that I could scarcely make headway against it. A band of sheep was seen high on the slopes of Divide Mountain and a stalk was planned. Circling around I ascended through a ravine and crossed the slope diagonally upward, passing along low cliffs and through ravines until a selected point was reached near where the sheep had last been seen. They were not visible, but after climbing to another point all were seen lying down a little below me, two hundred yards ahead. At that time I was on an uneven slope, well cushioned with dryas, which enabled me to creep a hundred yards nearer. In spite of the wind I managed to kill five of the sheep, two large dry ewes and three rams two and three years old, all very fat. The eyes of one of the ewes were yellow, those of all the others deep brown—the eyes of the sheep of this region varying between these colors.

The food of the sheep changes with the season. A little

earlier they had fed exclusively on green plants without grass, except the small amount taken incidentally while cropping. But now the stomachs were filled indifferently with several kinds of grass, grass roots, small plants, willow leaves, and an abundance of lichen which was now green.

After dressing the sheep I descended to the bar, made some tea, and went up toward the glaciers, noticing sheep on the mountains on both sides and out on the flats near by. Elsewhere all the sheep were feeding high, as in summer, but up near the main range, now mostly covered with snow, more were coming down on the bars. Although now the pelage of many was cleaner than before, a large number were still badly stained.

While I was proceeding along the bar on the west side of the river, watching the sheep high on the slopes of the East Branch Range, a sight was presented which was not only rare, but fascinating. On the slope just above the bar and directly opposite me, a fox, apparently coal black, suddenly burst into view. He was galloping swiftly along with the easy grace and poetry of motion that delights the eye—his black lustrous coat at times shining in the sun, the white tip of his tail always visible. Slightly upward, then downward, circling back and forth, or speeding away in a straight line, his gallop never relaxed. He was now going straight away, when, approaching a clump of low willows, he veered toward it without a pause until within fifty feet, when with a sudden burst of speed as if pursued, he rushed and plunged with a high leap into the bush. He had not been lost to sight more than five seconds when he sprang out with a ptarmigan in his jaws—the bird almost white in its winter coat. There at the edge of the willows he stopped and ate it, swallowing it in two or three minutes. Then he resumed his hunting gallop until out of sight in the distance. Going to the spot where he had eaten the bird I found only a few of the wing quills remaining.

While returning to the cabin I was interested to find that the willow leaves had already fallen, uncovering the slender branches with well-matured buds, which, with the tips of the twigs, provide the exclusive food of the moose until spring.

September 25–26. These two days were occupied in bringing back the sheep meat, preparing and storing it, and working about the cabin.

North in the Caribou Country.
The Caribou Rut.
Moose Hunting.

September 27 we packed the horses and set out on a caribou hunt in the low country to the north, outside the ranges. Not only did I want to collect a good series of bulls for scientific specimens for the Biological Survey, but also two or three trophies for myself, and a good stock of meat for the five dogs that later would come to the cabin for the winter. Except at the beginning of winter, and then only while traveling, meat must be the only food of the dogs; they consumed the equivalent of a whole caribou every week. To cache a sufficent supply of meat of caribou bulls, which at that time was unfit for man to eat, would save the sheep near the cabin (which otherwise would have to be killed) and would also save much valuable time later.

After traveling steadily for five hours we passed through the last range, where a low connecting ridge juts out to the bar on the east side of the river. Around the corner on a flat, elevated four or five feet above the bar, was a patch of fine large spruces covering two or three acres. Just inside, fifty feet from the bar, where we were sheltered from the wind that was blowing hard, we put up the small open shelter-tent and made camp. This was a delightful spot for a camp—a spring of water near by, plenty of dry spruces for fuel, the ground level and cushioned with spruce needles, and an outlook affording a vast unobstructed sweep across the bar and over the ridges. Directly behind camp rose the ridge leading to the north slopes of the outside mountain; and best of all, the bars here were covered with the wild pea vine, affording excellent food for the horses at a time when all other vegetation had been frost-killed. It was a delight to see the hungry animals immediately begin to graze. Food was so abundant nearby that not once while we occupied that site—Caribou Camp I called it—did they stray more than two hundred yards, always returning to pass the night near the camp-fire.

While lunch was being prepared I climbed the ridge to scan the country through my glasses. Just then two bull caribou came into the field a mile below on the bar, feeding close to an island patch of woods—poplars, willows, and a few spruces. Hastening to camp and seizing my rifle I walked nearly across the bar so that the south wind, which had increased to a gale, would carry my scent off to one side, and then went rapidly down until opposite the woods, which I entered—having now come to a place where the wind was favorable. While walking down the bar the wind had whirled up such clouds of dust that not only could no animal have seen me, but I could not even see the woods. Proceeding cautiously to the farther edge of the trees I saw both caribou walking steadily three hundred yards away. Evidently they had just begun to travel toward the hills. Neither was a very large bull, but the horns of one were very shapely. The wind made my aim so unsteady that five shots were required to kill the two. Hastening back to camp, we brought the horses, measured the largest bull, and took the skins, heads, and meat of both to camp.

Then I climbed a ridge to the east and soon saw a bull with fairly large horns walking toward the woods in which we had made our camp. He was some distance away and I had time to circle and come behind him just as he was about to enter the woods. Since he seemed to be in a direct line between me and the camp I did not fire, fearing the bullet might strike Merrifield. But before I could change position the bull suddenly winded the camp, reared, turned, and ran with great leaps through some scattered spruces and over the ridge, not once giving me a chance for a shot. This caribou acted as all others in this region did when suddenly frightened by scent: between short runs he kept stopping to look back.

September 28. The night was warm and the day dawned cloudless under a bright sun. It was a perfect Indian summer day without haze. At daylight I was outside the woods and about to climb the west ridges when my glasses, turned on the slopes below the north end of Ram Mountain, revealed a herd of caribou. They were above the timber near the foot of the precipitous part of the slopes and so far away that in the dim light their horns could not be seen. Starting across the bar I waded the river, and just before entering the timber caught a glimpse of part of the herd, and though unable to make out their size, could faintly distinguish the horns of a bull among them. The sun came up as soon as I entered the woods, which were on a steeply inclined slope. Willows densely massed among the spruces and the soft deep sphagnum moss rendered progress upward difficult and slow. But finally, picking my way where the timber was more scattered, I was elated to be near enough to see that there were some bulls among the herd. There was no time to scrutinize them for they were feeding actively and steadily moving higher, so it was necessary to quickly study the possibilities of a stalk. Anywhere ahead I would be in plain sight. A slight breeze blew west along the slope, so the only chance to stalk unseen was to circle and approach with the wind. I decided to work Indian fashion against the breeze as far toward them as possible and wait there, trusting that some better opportunity might develop. Crawling over ground wet and boggy, from tree to tree, willow bush to willow bush, hummock to hummock, until within five hundred yards of them, I could safely go no nearer. Here, stretched flat behind a low hummock, I waited and watched. The sun bathed me with a gentle heat, and the sight before me was so interesting that the hour or more in that position gave no subsequent recollection of discomfort or impatience. Here was my opportunity to observe near by, through the glasses, the actions of a band of caribou during the climax of the rut.

In the band were fifteen cows, most of them at the moment lying down, but shortly afterward getting up and feeding. The cows were held together in a herd by an enormous bull with heavy massive horns. When the glasses were turned on those horns my surprise was great to see the broken tine and the bulblike point which positively identified him as the bull

I had seen at rest on the canyon slope of Forks Mountain while looking for the bear I had fired at on August 11! Another bull with magnificent antlers remained below and outside the herd; a third with large horns was nearer the herd, and two smaller bulls were at its edge.

The cows were very watchful and in the manner of sheep kept constantly looking in all directions. The bells of the horses sounding down on the bar were plainly audible and the cows frequently looked in that direction. Once Merrifield fired the shotgun and all the cows turned their heads to look and then unconcernedly began to feed. Their actions when undisturbed by the bulls may be summed up in resting, feeding, and watching. Often, like sheep, their heads while lying at rest were stretched out on the ground. At other times I have seen bulls lying at rest in the same way. I noticed that the cows were as quick to hear all kinds of sounds as the other large wild animals of the region. Under the circumstances, the watchfulness of the cows made an approach as difficult as would have been an approach to a band of sheep—perhaps a little more so, since being taller they could more quickly see objects on uneven ground. All of these cows mildly submitted themselves to the authority of the big bull, seeming to recognize that for the time being they were his exclusive property.

The big bull, though now and then cropping a mouthful, scarcely fed at all. Not once did he watch for danger, nor did he rest. His neck was swelled to large proportions, his mane and throat were white, his body bulky. He presented a very striking appearance as, with horns held slightly back on his swollen neck, he strutted among the cows, caressing them and holding them close together. Several times I observed his generative act, which was similar to that of a domestic bull. A large part of his time was taken up in keeping the two smallest bulls away from the cows. These two bulls were very active, keeping close to the cows and constantly attempting to cut one out or to reach one if it strayed a short distance from the others. The big bull, always quickly detecting such attempts, trotted toward the smaller bull, which at once withdrew, not offering to fight. Yet all the time I watched them the two kept up their efforts to gain a cow, but were always repulsed by the big one, which would at once push his nose against the strayed cow and drive her back into the herd.

The third bull with large horns remained near, but a little farther away than the small ones. Yet several times when the big bull was chasing off one of the smaller ones this bull attempted to approach the herd. It was interesting to notice that whereas the maneuvers of the small bulls caused only an indifferently active interest in the big bull, the attempted approaches of the third bull excited his rage. He would trot toward him, lowering his antlers as he came near, whereat the offending bull would run off at a trot until chased two or three hundred feet. Once when the big bull chased him, after driving him a sufficient distance, he threatened him by stamping his forefeet and shaking his head.

The next largest bull remained below the herd, feeding and watching, seventy-five or more yards distant, not once attempting to approach nearer. Why, I could not understand, for he seemed fully capable of disputing the claim of the big bull to the proprietorship of the cows. At one time the big bull, while chasing another, came quite close to him but neither paid any attention to the other. This bull had a very long mane, which was spotlessly white and at certain angles glistened in the sun, making the whole animal, with his long antlers, a very beautiful sight—especially when posed in an alert watch on the top of a knoll against the mountain background.

I watched the varying scenes of this drama for more than an hour. My attention was so concentrated on the activities of the big bull and the herd that at no time did I scrutinize carefully or comparatively the antlers of this outside bull—the one nearest to me—at least not more than to recognize that they were large and magnificent. My one thought was to kill the big bull, the lord of the herd, this grand animal which previously had stood near me while he was resting on the canyon slope in the rough mountains far to the south. After more than an hour—one of those hours which the wilderness lover seldom has an opportunity to experience—the herd began gradually to feed higher and at last passed out of sight. But the outside bull, although advancing a little in the direction the others were taking, still remained before me, continually watching. Fearing that the herd might move away before I could stalk close enough, I began carefully crawling, always stopping and remaining motionless when the outside bull looked in my direction. I had gained fifty or sixty yards when this bull passed around the slope so far that only his horns remained in sight. At once I arose and walked cautiously but more rapidly. Suddenly one of the small bulls and four cows came trotting back around the slope, followed by the big bull, which soon drove them back, the small bull at the same time circling back higher up. Again I rose and advanced another hundred yards until the outside bull came into full view within easy shot. My course had been so taken that now I was directly against the wind without fear of any of the caribou scenting me.

I crept to within a hundred yards of the outside bull but could not go nearer without being seen. So I waited, stretched flat on the ground. The next fifteen minutes caused me intense anxiety for fear this bull would become frightened, for even though I might kill him, the herd would become alarmed and my chance for the big bull would be gone. Once during this period the horns of a small bull were seen rapidly moving along the slope only a few yards behind the bull that obstructed my stalk, and I knew the big bull was chasing him and that the herd was still near. To my dismay the outside bull began to walk along feeding in a direction where shortly he would receive my scent. Instantly I determined to rise, walk parallel with his course, approach slightly diagonally, and shoot him as soon as he should see me. Then I would run up in sight of the herd, hoping for a chance to kill the leader. With rifle cocked and ready I walked fifteen yards, then paused as the bull looked in another direction. When he resumed feeding, I gained five yards more, getting within seventy-five yards of him. Then up came his head, his eyes fastened on me and instantly his whole body stiffened. At the crack of the rifle he staggered a moment and fell dead.

I had not run far when several of the cows came trotting into sight to see what had happened. On seeing me they at once turned back. Quickly reaching the top of the slope that had concealed the herd, I saw all but two of the cows standing in an attitude of fear about two hundred yards down to the right, the big bull trotting toward them to herd them back. The other two cows were standing not fifty yards ahead of me, looking back at me; the other three bulls were walking off. As I came in sight the big bull saw me, wheeled with a great jump and started trotting directly away. Quickly seating myself, rifle to the shoulder, I followed him with the sight, waiting for him to stop and present a side shot. After going fifty yards he halted, and the dull thud of the bullet sounded as it struck. He staggered a moment and then began to trot. A second shot caused him to move more slowly. At the third he fell dead.

During these shots the third largest bull was trotting away, but stopped as the big bull fell. My first shot hit him, causing him to walk slowly. Following and coming closer I fired two more shots, killing him.

The cows in the meanwhile had come in my wind, when up went all their tails and with great jumps they circled and ran about in confusion. They kept running back and forth, evidently waiting for the bull; then stood near by for a while looking both at their dead leader and at me. They were now so near that I could get some photographs of the herd. Shortly they ran off, circling around the slope, and were soon lost to sight. I had not again noticed the two small bulls and did not afterward see them. My journal records the ecstasies of the moment when, elated by success, the whole surrounding landscape seemed intensified in beauty—the rough face of the great mountain directly behind, the valley of the river below, the rugged ranges extending to the south beyond it, the great spruce forest stretching out in all directions to the north, the Chitsia Range in the distance to the northwest—the whole scene enhanced by the fallen caribou, their horns rising from the ground, their white necks and manes shining under the sun!

The ground over which the big bull had been trotting when shot was a bog. Before reaching him I had almost mired. His legs and parts of his horns were well driven into the mud and it was impossible for me to extricate them and measure him. He had not won the possession of that band of cows without severe fighting and punishment. The end of one of his tines and several parts of the beams of his antlers had been freshly broken, various parts of his body were bruised and bloody, and his legs were gashed and bleeding. A sweet-smelling sickening musky odor emanating from him was so strong that I was almost nauseated. The outside bull, stretched out on the edge of a roll in the surface, was extremely picturesque, his clean dark coat contrasting with the glistening white head, neck and mane, and his fine antlers rising high from the ground. To my agreeable surprise, for the first time since seeing him, I now appreciated that his horns were magnificent. Although somewhat limited as to points they were perfectly symmetrical, one brow tine beautifully developed, and the main beams much longer than those of the big bull. The neck of this bull was not much swelled, his odor though strong was less than that of the big bull; he evidently had not quite reached the climax of his rut. But a fresh cut on his ear demonstrated that he had had at least one collision with some other bull, and I believe that shortly he would have attempted to drive the big bull away from his cows, and with a chance of success.

Knowing that Merrifield must have heard my shots, I went along the slope until the camp was visible and tried to attract his attention by waving, but he did not see me. After photographing both of the bulls I started toward the third, when a big bull was seen approaching, eight hundred yards distant, followed by another; then a cow joined them. I dropped low and they soon came on feeding in a hollow. Unseen by them, I went forward until they next came in sight, four hundred yards away. The leading bull had splendid antlers, those of the other equally fine and seemingly black. These bulls were very watchful and often smelled the ground, indicating that they had been following the band of cows which I had just driven off. They were actively feeding toward me and all I had to do was to lie flat in a good position and wait. When the leading bull came over a rise in the ground a hundred yards away, he at once saw me as I sat with rifle pointed toward him. Quickly he threw up his head and his whole body stiffened with alertness. He was looking intently at me as the shot sounded which killed him. The other bull trotted up in sight and staggered as I fired again, then trotted downward until reaching some willows, where he lay down. The cow had been trotting about bewildered and looking at the bulls until I moved to follow the wounded one, when she galloped off. Another shot finished this bull. Coming nearer, I could scarcely believe what my eyes revealed until I actually felt his handsome antlers. They were in *full velvet,* some of the points still being soft, even bleeding when I pushed the point of a knife into them.

Among the delights of a wilderness hunter are those of skinning and dressing the game high on the mountains. The supreme moments of joy come immediately after the success of a difficult stalk. Then, while this state of exaltation continues, intensifying the beauty of the landscape, comes the fascination of examining the prize. Intense satisfaction merged with feelings of elation sustains one during the labor of taking off the skin to complete the possession of a scientific specimen or trophy. The work is often suspended to smoke a pipeful of tobacco and revel in the scenery, always with the hope of observing other game. The impressions of that bright balmy afternoon, serene and calm while I worked, still linger vividly in my recollection. Several ravens were flying excitedly about, and the warmth of the day invited a swarm of blowflies and other insects to make their last appearance. Numerous conies were bleating back among the broken rock of the mountain side.

It was dark when, after drawing the entrails of all the carcasses, I had taken off the complete skin of one and the capes of four others, besides cutting off the heads and paring the flesh from them. Shouldering the capes and the heads of the first two bulls killed, I struggled downward through the dark woods to the bar and thence to camp. While writing in my journal by firelight, the sky was clear, the air crisp, the stars bright, and not a breath of wind moaned through the spruces or agitated their spired tops.

September 29–30. Early in the morning I heard raindrops pattering on the shelter—the beginning of a heavy southwest gale which with rain and wet snow swept the country all day. We brought in the horses and packed to camp part of the meat and the remaining skin and heads.

Next morning it was snowing and blowing, but the sun soon came out and melted the snow from the lower country. The snowline however, as after other storms, was gradually descending the slopes of the mountains.

While Merrifield made a log cache for the meat, I worked hard all day preparing the skins and skulls. By this time the odor from the skins had become so strong that several times while handling them I was nauseated. The musky, sickening odor, which lasts only during the height of the rut, had permeated the meat and clung to it for three or four months, even after it was frozen, until it was consumed by the dogs. The heads of the three smaller bulls had been badly lacerated, particularly near the burs of the horns, proving that all had been fighting. The one with the horns in the velvet did not show even a scratch. The conclusion was that the cow accompanying the last two bulls had just been separated from some herd. This conclusion seemed justified by the fact that the gashes about the head of the bull with clean horns were freshly bleeding, showing that he had been fighting to obtain her.

In the morning a heavy frost indicated a lowering of temperature during the night, and dense fog hung over the whole country. This was the last day that could be spared for hunting and I hoped to improve it by securing moose meat for winter consumption. I was practically at the upper limit of the moose range of the forested area below, although occasionally one or two animals might stray a few miles farther up this branch of the Toklat. The rut was approaching its end, and under any circumstances moose were not abundant in these upper areas, their range being in the timber farther down.

Just at sunrise I started to climb the higher ridges rising toward the mountain southeast of camp. The air seemed motionless, the silence complete—not even the murmurs of the river half a mile distant being audible. My footsteps on the crisp surface among the spruces and scattered willows sounded sharply as if protesting against the prevailing stillness. The ground was white, the fog so dense that even near objects could be seen but dimly, and the spruces appeared as if delicately draped with gauze. The fog seemed limitless, intensifying the ever-present feeling of mystery. The moisture in the air was rapidly freezing into spicules that fell through the mist, apparently from a clear sky, forming a powdery snow that gathered on the ground and on the dead grass and leaves and clustered about the branches, covering everything with a delicate crystalline frostwork.

Above the mist there was a suggestion of blue sky, while low in the far-away east the blurred sun seemed a huge ball of dull crimson which, as it rose higher, dissolved the mists, making the river bars sparkle like myriads of diamonds and creating patches of rainbow colors that danced in wavy outlines, disappearing and reappearing in the thin vapors through which the trees and ground flashed with a golden glitter. At last all the country as high as the ridgetop was clear and for a short time brilliantly illuminated and glistening; then the warmth destroyed the tiny crystals, leaving the land uniformly white. Never before nor since have I seen atmospheric effects so rapidly changing, so singularly beautiful.

Mist soon settled again over the ridgetops and I had to wait several hours for it to clear enough for hunting. Seating myself and looking out over the bar, I saw a large bull caribou with splendid antlers and striking white mane approach the willows and scattered spruces below me. For a while he continued to feed among them, then lay down to rest on a flat, where he remained for nearly three hours. Later, while hunting along the ridge I saw him rise and disappear.

Wolves, the chief enemy of the caribou, were very abundant here, always hovering about the feeding herd and following them as they roamed, usually in a fairly well-defined circuit. At this time of year the caribou frequent the ridges more than the low country. While the big bull moved about below

me I carefully observed his coloration to see how concealing
it might be as a protection against a wolf—whose eyes are
very much keener than my own. While walking on the frosted
bar more than a mile away his dark body contrasted strongly
with the white background, and at times when the angle was
just right, his white mane flashed in the sun as if displaying
a signal to any animal watching from the ridgetops. He twice
stopped motionless; then he was inconspicuous until he again
began to move. On reaching the rolling country where the
background was white, he was very conspicuous when in motion and sometimes when still, but often blended well with the
environment. When he lay down to rest and remained quiet
he was inconspicuous. But every two or three minutes he
would quickly turn his head to watch, the motion making him
strikingly conspicuous. Later, when the sun had thawed the
frost on the ground, his white mane contrasted so strongly
with the dark background that from many positions he could
instantly be detected. It was obvious that the coloration of the
caribou would not prevent any wolf, hunting along the ridgetops, from quickly perceiving him; in fact, it would attract
his attention.

After the mists had again cleared from the ridge I proceeded, carefully scanning the timbered areas along and below the slopes. The ridgetops were really vast swamps of
'nigger heads' rising up from the water. The snow had filled
the spaces between them almost to a level with their tops, so
that I was continually slipping off into the water, my feet getting such a wetting that they became very cold. Farther up
the ridge wolf tracks appeared here and there among the old
caribou tracks, but no signs of moose. A wind, gentle at first,
began to blow, chasing the mists up the river bars and thus
obscuring the surface, while far across the valley the Chitsia
peaks rose through the clouds, resplendently white in the sunlight. Going down the slope, I kept on to the north in the rolling country, hoping to find a fresh moose track. The wind
soon increased and with it came drifting mists, now obscuring everything, now lifting, so as to interrupt the views. It
was getting late and I was about to set out toward the bars

for camp, which was a long distance away, when, looking at some willows five hundred yards up the slope, I saw the dark body of an animal. Quickly seating myself I watched until its head came in view; it was a cow moose. For half an hour I continued to wait until the expected bull suddenly appeared— a small bull with spike horns.

The two moose fed very quietly, cropping the willow buds, slipping noiselessly through the thick willows, constantly disappearing and suddenly reappearing. They seemed to skulk continually, often raising their heads and looking in all directions. Because of thick willows and the direction of the wind, a successful stalk could not be made directly toward them; therefore, making a wide circle I climbed to a point near the summit opposite them, reaching it just as a heavy cloud of mist blew over and obscured everything. Carefully going toward them for a short distance I waited, though shivering with cold. The mist at last thinned enough to enable me to distinguish blurred objects below and I suddenly saw a dark bulk move among the willows a hundred yards down. The wind came with a blast bringing in dense mists so that everything was blank; and again I waited. The wind stopped, but the mist remained, and though I listened carefully, not a sound could be heard. After fifteen minutes the mist again thinned and the bull moose could be indistinctly seen. Aiming as best I could, the whack of the bullet answered the report; then more mist blew over, concealing the result. For a few moments there was absolute stillness, when again the mist thinned and a blurred bulk suddenly appeared. At the report of the rifle it fell. No sound was audible but the wind, which as the fog rushed in increased and remained while I continued down the steep slope—often slipping and falling, until near the spot where I judged the bull had fallen. After a long search I found the cow, stretched out on her belly with a broken back, yet very much alive. She was small, about a year and a half old. I was about to dispatch her when she drew her ears close down against her head, compressed her lips, and attempted to charge. As I stood near she tried again and again. Her temper was most vicious; often she struck at me with her forefeet. It was finally necessary to stand off and shoot her again. Dressing her took till about dark. I had almost given up finding the bull when I tripped over his spike horn. He was dead. It was a strange sensation to dress him in the darkness, surrounded by fog. This bull and cow were of the same age, probably not having separated since leaving their mother.

After cutting a staff I worked step by step down the rest of the slope to the rolling wooded area below. The wind had ceased but utter darkness, increased by fog, made the task an unpleasant one. For an hour or more I felt my way through bog, willows, and small spruces, guided only by the sound of the river. Suddenly I stepped out of the enveloping mist and found myself on the bar with a wonderful sight before me. The whole bar was covered with a dense low fog, reaching only to my waist, while overhead the stars were shining brilliantly. An arc of northern lights was flashing through the heavens, and the Milky Way seemed doubly illuminated. The thin layer of dense mist clinging so closely to the ground seemed to glow with gentle light, resembling the surface of a vast starlit ocean. Only the white mountain tops, so dimly seen that they appeared very distant, brought back a sense of limitation to the apparently endless expanse of sea.

Another hour's walk brought me to camp and the cheer and warmth of the fire. Merrifield had brought in two more of the caribou and had cached the meat. The only birds seen that day were a few tree sparrows and a gyrfalcon, but while I was writing my journal the thin note of a varied thrush sounded closely in the spruces. This had been a day of new sensations, so impressive that they still linger vividly in my memory.

October 2. The night was much colder and in the morning congealed moisture was rapidly falling through the air, covering the ground like snow and clinging to the trees and other vegetation. A dense fog hung over the country all through the day.

Taking the horses we went up to bring in the remaining caribou, but found that during the night wolves had completely eaten one bull, nothing being left but scattered bones

—even the velvet of the horns having been stripped off. The other bull had been badly mutilated by ravens, but we cut it up and brought it back to camp, intending to go after the moose in the afternoon. The fog however was so dense that I was doubtful about finding them and therefore spent the rest of the day preparing skins and skulls. All vegetation on the bars was badly frozen and the poor horses lingered about the camp-fire, continually coming to the shelter to beg for oats. It was full time for hibernating animals to disappear, and ground squirrels were last seen today.

October 3. It was still colder at daylight when we started with the horses for the moose. The day was clear with alternating clouds and sun. My impressions of the spot where the carcasses lay were vague indeed, and after a long search I was about to give it up when still farther along the ridge we noticed two ravens hovering about some spruces. Going there the moose were quickly found, the skins taken off, the meat cut up and brought back to camp. The stomachs contained only willow buds and some of the terminal twigs unavoidably taken while cropping off the buds—the exclusive food of the moose until new vegetation sprouts in the spring.

After lunch, when all the meat had been put in the cache, we packed the horses and traveled back to the cabin, reaching it by dark. The exquisite effects of the landscape through which we traveled while going up the river will never be forgotten. Evidently the night atmosphere had been heavily laden with moisture, for in the morning the thin frost spicules were still falling. The ground was white, all vegetation seemed crystallized with over half an inch of transparent covering, in myriad forms. The willows and spruces were draped in gauzy lace in an infinite variety of patterns. Under a clouded sky the willow flats and spruce-covered slopes would appear overlaid with foam; while when the sun broke through, the patches caught by its rays would shine with sparkling brilliancy; and again, when the clouds had passed from under the sun, the whole country would glitter. It was too cold for melting and all day until the sun was low the passing clouds brought continual new effects. Never before had any wilderness revealed itself to me clothed in such daintily exquisite garb, and I can never hope to experience such beauteous effects again.

During our absence from the cabin the lowest temperature registered was plus 10 degrees Fahrenheit, but undoubtedly down in the caribou country where we had camped it had been much colder. I did not then know that on this day the long winter had begun.

Beginning of Winter.
A Bear Hunt.
Storing Habit of Jays.

October 4–6. A snowstorm continued all of the 4th, eight inches of snow having fallen by night. For the last time I saw a robin. The final departure of these birds was coincident with the extinction of fall—the beginning of winter. October 5 the sun broke through the clouds and Merrifield left with the horses for Glacier. My good horse *Toklat* had gone. Gentle, intelligent, ambitious, fast and well gaited under the saddle, and an admirable pack horse, he had become a camp pet and I was so attached to him that a feeling of loneliness came over me as soon as he had gone. Snow again fell in the afternoon and continued through the next day, leaving fourteen inches on the ground.

During these three days I was busy preparing and drying the skins, putting the cabin in order and, most important, chopping and splitting a good supply of firewood.

October 7. Everything had been arranged satisfactorily before the morning of October 7, which was a perfect, clear, calm day, the thermometer a degree below zero. Shortly after daylight I was tramping up the bar. Alone in that remote section of the Alaskan wilderness, I had a strange feeling of complete possession of these wilds. What a change in the aspect of the country since my last tramp in the same direction! The brown colors were now replaced by white—the intense white of fresh spotless snow—that on the mountain crests appearing positively brilliant in its purity. The snow mantle, high and low, except on the mountain cliffs, completely covered the surface. No breeze had ruffled it. The spruce trees were loaded with it, as were most of the willows.

Not far from the cabin were numerous tracks of a snow-

167

shoe rabbit which had come up to the cabin woods. That year
these rabbits were very scarce, though occasionally throughout the winter one would come to the cabin woods and attempt
to install itself, feeding on the abundant willows. But, whenever rabbit tracks in the snow were observed, the following
night or the next, the hoots of a great horned owl near by
would be heard. Then no fresh tracks could be found in the
woods and none leading from them. Never had I observed
the destructiveness of this owl so clearly as in the case of
these rabbits throughout that winter.

As I tramped along, twelve rams were in their usual place
high up on Ram Mountain, just starting to travel single file,
wading through the snow or jumping where it was deep. Occasionally they would stop, paw away the snow, and feed. On
another mountain I saw from a distance the spotted surface
where sheep had fed.

As I went on, the landscape confused me. Everything was
white, the old landmarks were buried, and only familiar cliffs
and peaks reminded me of the country I had known. Wolverine tracks were seen crossing to the east side of the bar, and
when well over near the west side, I saw a lynx walk across
the entrance to the Bear Draw.

Following up a canyon south of Old Camp Mountain and
climbing to the top of the divide without finding bear tracks,
I retraced my steps and went back over the bar to the tracks
of the lynx already seen. Just within the narrow border of
spruce trees the lynx had sat down in the snow near a brush
pile. Rabbit tracks led into the pile and on the other side
fresher tracks showed that the animal had emerged on a run.
The lynx had not caught it, nor had it followed, for its trail
led in another direction.

On the way back to the cabin the tracks of a wolverine
showed that it had entered the willows and traveled well concealed close to a high cutbank until reaching my trail in the
woods, which it had followed for a short distance and then
turned off.

That day the note of the varied thrush was heard for the
last time; a mallard duck and a few flocks of redpolls were

seen, and now and then were heard the sweet notes of Alaska pine grosbeaks.

October 8. I had trapped numerous mice before, mostly meadow mice (*Microtus*) and red-backed mice (*Evotomys*) and now and then a shrew. Yesterday, the whole surface of the woods and parts of the bars had been checkered with their trails. Now, numbers of both these mice, and also shrews, began to invade the cabin. Thus far, mostly females had been caught and it was some time before the males were commonly taken. Every morning from ten to fifteen were found in traps set inside the cabin. The shrews were especially cannibalistic and it was seldom that more than three of four of the mice or shrews in the traps each morning were not eaten or badly mutilated. Every night about fifteen traps were set on the floor, and as soon as the candle was blown out and I had wrapped myself in my robe, they would begin to snap. One night the fifteen traps all snapped in less than half an hour, and after I rose and reset them, they soon began snapping again. Almost every night mice ran over me or played about on top of me and had to be driven away before I could sleep. The thin grating sound made by the shrews in chewing other shrews or mice in the traps was heard almost nightly before I slept.

This was another beautiful day. The morning was spent in chopping wood and developing photographs. In the afternoon I went out on the bar to look for sheep and soon saw twenty high up on the mountain slopes. They, unlike the large majority, were fairly clean, but their color, because of the light staining of their pelage, presented a strong contrast to the white snow. Their trails and the patches of ground where they had pawed away the snow served to locate them.

October 9. The trail of a fox crossing the bar was noticed; also numerous trails of mice leading off at least a mile diagonally across it. They had lived on the bar through the summer and were now making for higher land.

The river had begun to 'glacier,' as it is called in this country—signifying that where the stream runs slowly, it freezes, causing overflows, diversions, and new channels, which in turn

freeze, and so on. As the weather becomes colder new channels constantly spread and overflow until the resulting ice cap
not only overspreads the whole bar but in places, before
spring, attains a depth of more than twenty feet.

In the strip of woods were the tracks of a few rabbits,
many weasels and red squirrels, and the trail of a lynx. When
I reached the divide, the tracks of the rams that were accustomed to feed on Ram Mountain were seen, but the animals
themselves were not visible.

I was about to start across the divide when my eye caught
the motion of a dark object on the snow not far under
the crest near which the rams were usually seen. Through
the field glasses I saw that it was a grizzly bear hard at
work digging in the snow up near the rugged peak. How
to stalk it was a puzzle. My rubber shoe packs were slippery, making it extremely dangerous to climb the steep slopes
—for the ground beneath the snow was icy. The wind was
unfavorable for any possible approach; therefore it seemed
best to watch the bear, hoping it might finally move to a
better position. It was digging out mice, and now and then
a ground squirrel. The mice had made tunnels under the snow
leading from their holes. The bear, evidently scenting a mouse
in a tunnel, would plunge its nose into the snow, its snout
ploughing through, often as far as ten feet, until the mouse
had gone down into its hole in the ground; then the bear would
dig it out and catch it with a paw. When the bear's face came
out all covered with snow it looked like a white mask. Then
the bear would walk about, often tossing its head to sniff the
breezes until another mouse was scented, or the burrow of a
ground squirrel was found. Twice I saw it dig out ground
squirrels, in one case taking twenty minutes, in the other, half
an hour. While digging it would often sit and pant like a dog,
frequently pausing to toss its head for hostile scents, but not
once did it look for danger.

The bear was brown and very fat, its belly protruding, and
the snow clinging densely to the fur of the legs and under
parts gave it a most grotesque appearance. From a distance
of less than six hundred yards I tried to estimate its relative

size, and every attempt forced the conclusion that it was a "big bear." Its high fore-shoulders, fat condition, and long fur, all made it look "big" and I felt certain that it must be a large male.

After a couple of hours the bear started north along the slope and it was my turn to climb, in the hope that by following its trail a good shot might be had. The route lay upward through a dense growth of low willows for four hundred yards to the open ground. By holding on to the willows I struggled up, and coming out in a hollow saw the bear directly above very near the crest. It had circled upward and back directly above where it had first been seen. Such irregular actions of feeding bears make their stalking interesting and full of excitement. One can never tell which way they may turn, or where, after being lost to sight, they may reappear.

The bear suddenly scented a mouse and dug it out, and soon afterward scented a ground squirrel and began digging. It was about in a position where it might scent me, so I began to approach directly toward it in plain sight. Nearby on my left was a canyon, but the slope upward toward the bear was so steep, and the slippery soles of my shoes offered such scant foothold that, even by using the butt of my rifle as a staff, I kept slipping and falling. By steadily climbing a point was finally reached only three hundred yards below the bear, which had not once looked away from its digging. The slope was so steep I could scarcely stand. The bear suddenly threw up its head, ran a few feet upward and turned to look; I knew it had scented me. While putting up my three-hundred-yard sight I slipped and fell but kept from sliding down by pushing the rifle butt in the ground. As quickly as possible I worked to a position on my knees, raised my rifle, and with unsteady aim, fired. The bear jumped and ran at full speed diagonally down the slope and was soon lost to sight. My position was too precarious to permit swinging the rifle and firing a second shot. Struggling up to its trail I could find no blood. To my surprise the tracks were small—positively not those of a 'big' grizzly. After conscientiously taking every precaution to estimate its size, as clearly observed from a reasonable distance,

I had been deceived. The traditional grizzly, that of most hunters' and observers' tales, seen but not killed and measured, is usually a 'big' one. All my experience with grizzly bears has led me to one positive conclusion: lack of confidence in any estimate of size not based upon measurement by steel tape.

I followed the trail, and for the first time since the snow, looked out attentively over the white landscape, which, previously so familiar, was now bewildering, inhospitable, and strange. The bear had continued to run downward around the slope to the timber, where some blood was seen. It had kept just inside the woods for a mile and then had climbed to the densest strip of willows well above, where the slope was very steep, pushing through them for a mile and a half, and always keeping concealed. Now and then a drop of blood induced me to follow persistently. It was getting late; a heavy fog had drifted in, and the willows were so dense and the snow so deep that I could scarcely struggle along. Above the willows the trail led diagonally upward for another mile, crossing in and out of small canyons until a deep narrow rugged one was reached, where the bear had turned and followed directly up the frozen stream—leaving an occasional drop of blood. While tramping upward enclosed by the canyon walls I realized that darkness was approaching. The fog had become dense and heavy flakes of snow began to fall. Having at last ascended to where the canyon head appeared to end against surrounding cliffs I peered through the mist hoping to see the bear, but was disappointed. Keeping on to the very head of the canyon the trail was seen in the snow between two ledges, still leading upward toward the peak. The snow was then falling heavily, it was almost dark, and I had to abandon the search. Descending, and passing through the timber in darkness, I stopped to build a fire and make tea before tramping back to the cabin in the blizzard that was then sweeping over the glacier bars. The strange experience of following the bear along the steep mountainside, through snow and dense willows and then up the dark narrow canyon through fog and falling snow, always eagerly anticipating a sight of the animal ahead, and then the return through the darkness of the woods as the blasts of wind whirled the snow along the bars—all impressed me with the joy and the desolation of this northern wilderness.

October 10. Four inches of snow fell today even while the sun was dimly visible. Late in the afternoon I walked through the cabin woods to the south end. The spruces, still retaining the earlier snow, were now completely wrapped in soft white mantles. These dense northern spruces present a variety of forms—most of them symmetrically pointed, others broadly or irregularly rounded. Some were encircled by snow wreaths in parallel circles or wound with white ascending spirals, while others were covered with snow in irregular masses. The snow was so light and powdery that it scarcely seemed to add weight to the branches, giving the trees the appearance of being covered with foam of purest white.

Through the woods were snowy vistas—on one side the snow fields on the broad bar; on the other, the rolling white ridges, while all around were the encircling snowy mountains.

October 11. Snow fell lightly all day, accumulating more heavily on the trees. The green spruces were partly frozen, the ground about half frozen. In the morning I chopped and split wood, both green and dry. It was necessary to go some distance to fell the trees, so I had to pack them in on my back and then chop them in lengths of eight or ten inches and split the pieces rather small for the stove. Wood in these camp stoves is consumed very rapidly and it was necessary to lay up a large supply in order to be well provided in case an accident should at any time prevent me from chopping. That morning an accident that might have been serious did occur, for while splitting a length of green spruce, a piece flew up and struck me just above the outer edge of the right eye, cutting a gash to the bone. Feeling thankful that the eye itself had not been injured I bound up the wound with surgical tape, and afterward was not inconvenienced by it except that for a while the spot was sensitive to cold. When the bandage was removed two weeks later, the cut had completely healed.

The woods about the cabin were silent except for the Alaska

Canada jays. They were delightful cheery companions during the weeks that I remained alone, and in fact during the whole winter while the cabin was occupied.

Early in August, shortly after we reached the spot where the cabin was to be constructed, two or three of the jays appeared, and when fresh meat was brought in, others kept coming until nine in all remained about the place. Here was an opportunity to observe these interesting birds, so rather than destroy them I decided to endure the continual annoyance of their thefts. This necessitated much extra work in the way of carefully sealing the caches and protecting meat and other provisions, and also the skins and skulls of specimens. They became more and more familiar while Merrifield was there with me, until, after about three weeks, some of them would alight on my hand and grasp meat held in my fingers. Soon all would thus take meat or bread or any other food from my fingers whenever I went out of the cabin to feed them.

When I repeated a series of short whistles, all would immediately fly toward me, alight on my head, shoulders, and hands, and even quarrel while picking the food. It was not long before some of them were always sitting in the trees near the cabin waiting for my appearance, and whistling would quickly summon all the others. Before long, a series of whistles anywhere in the cabin woods would call them, and if I held my hand as if food were to be offered, they would alight on me. Often, after hearing the whistles, some would come and alight on me without the suggestion of offering food. I could quietly stroke any of them without evidence of dislike on their part, and four of them did not in the least resent being handled.

After Merrifield left and I was alone in the cabin the jays became still more familiar and seemed to adjust their mode of living to one that depended almost exclusively on me. They were completely dominated by one persistent, insatiable passion—that of *strong* food. Should meat, dough, bread, or any cooked food except fruit, be placed in a spot accessible to them, they would at once begin to pick off pieces and store them on branches, crotches, or pieces of bark, returning immediately to repeat the operation. Like ants they would keep at it during the day until all was cached. They carried the food to any nearby tree, occasionally to a stump, more rarely a high thick willow bush. Usually they stored in trees that were close by, but sometimes as far as a hundred yards from the cabin. Often they would later re-store the food in another tree. While persistently hiding various kinds of food, they were most attracted by meat. When fresh meat was brought to camp they attacked it with frenzy, never once pausing in seizing, picking, flying, and storing, over and over again, so long as the meat was left within reach.

The food was stored carelessly, particularly when a quantity stimulated their activities. Often the pieces fell from the branches nearly as fast as stored. When a quantity was before them they stored blindly, immediately forgetting where they had put it. Many times they were seen searching for the stored pieces. Seldom did they stop to eat any food offered them; they only took it, flew to a tree and deposited it. Later they would search and find some of it and eat it. When only a small quantity was given, they placed it more carefully and better remembered where they had located it. After continuously watching them throughout the fall and winter, it seemed evident that notwithstanding the abundance of food, they were light feeders.

By vigorous pecking they could cut solidly frozen meat and carry it off piece by piece. This they accomplished by pecking into it until they could grasp a piece firmly with their bills and hold it, when by rapidly fluttering their wings, they pulled it loose. Their most interesting habit, which was frequently witnessed during the winter, was that of catching shrews and occasionally mice, as they ran over the snow. A jay would suddenly dart downward, strike a shrew with its beak, and instantly seize it with the bill and fly off to store it. So far as I could observe, the blow with the beak killed or stunned the shrews, but more than once I have seen a mouse struggling between the mandibles of a flying bird, which after alighting on a tree held it with the feet while giving a few rapid pecks to kill it; then the jay would fly to another tree and leave it.

Thus the Alaska jays, besides owls, hawks, wolves, foxes, bears, wolverines, weasels, martens, and lynxes, prey on shrews and mice in winter—probably also in summer. If the white winter pelage of rabbits and lemmings and the white plumage of ptarmigans were caused by the necessity for a protective coloring, why should not the same cause have produced a similar color in mice and shrews during the winter when they have to escape the same and even more enemies.*

The jays that visited the cabin had now adjusted their habits somewhat to my own routine. At daylight they would all perch on trees close to the swinging window of the cabin, below which stood the eating table. One, which I named Nellie, would stand on the outside window-sill. As soon as they saw me move inside the cabin all would fly to a tree just outside the window, its branches coming close to it. Some would join Nellie on the window-sill. Often they would peck at the window-pane. When breakfast was on the table they would become excited. Taking my seat I would watch them for a few moments until their impatience so resembled begging that I could not resist slightly opening the window. But I had long before learned to place some food on a plate close to the sill rather than risk their flying too far in. At once they would come in and begin the storing operation, and would clean off the plate before the window was closed. After breakfast the window was opened and food held in my hands. Quickly all would enter and alight on me. Two would take food from my hand, the others waiting; then there would be a scramble for the hand, sometimes a little fighting, until two others took possession of my fingers and seized the food. When these flew off, they would be replaced by two others. Occasionally three jays at once secured foothold, but usually when two were on my hand they would fight off the others. Usually when two jays were there the others waited patiently until the two flew off to store the food they had taken. Often the window was opened, permitting the jays

---

* [In most parts of the vast areas inhabited by meadow mice and shrews, these animals do not run much on exposed surfaces but are protected by runways, vegetation, and other cover.—C. H. M.]

to come in and search the cabin. Their keen eyes immediately spied any food scattered about and they quickly carried it out to store.

The activities of all the jays, even when engaged in the excitement of storing, ceased at dusk, and they flew into the trees to pass the night. During the middle hours of the day they usually became listless, sometimes ceasing work altogether for an hour or two. When the weather was extremely cold and they were perched on the limbs of trees they always kept their feathers fluffed out, so when I looked out of the cabin window in the morning, I could always judge whether or not the temperature was low by observing whether their feathers were fluffed or compressed against their bodies.

In the morning I worked at odd tasks about the cabin, labeling specimens, recording and filing photographic films, preparing yeast bread, and so on. In the afternoon I usually took the shotgun and walked through the woods where the spruces with their dense foliage and snow mantles had thus far shielded the ground immediately underneath so it was still bare. These trees had developed in a great variety of forms, some very irregular, some spired, others with the branches holding their width well to the tops. On all these trees the lower limbs spread out close to the ground. The forms of the spruces here are much the same as in other forests of interior Alaska near timberline.

No tracks of animals or birds were visible, all were keeping close during the snowfall. When I stopped to listen, not a sound was audible except the far-off dull roar of the river. Once, when pausing for a moment, I faintly heard in the distance a mysterious sound new to these regions, and as it approached recognized the wingbeats of wild fowl. Looking up, I saw three snow geese flying southward toward the main range. Occasionally a jay's note sounded from the trees, and once I heard the sweet notes of pine grosbeaks flying by. Near the cabin a woodpecker's tapping sounded, and an Alaska three-toed woodpecker was shot for a specimen and put in the cache to freeze until I could prepare its skin.

Winter Neighbors of the Wilderness.

October 12. The day was clear and calm, the sun bright, the thermometer about 10 degrees above zero all day. I was soon tramping up the bars. The snow on the flats was about eighteen inches deep; that on the trees had accumulated and presented a still more wintry impression than the day before. The mountains were all white, no wind having yet blown the snow off the exposed places. Across the river a band of rams was feeding at the exact spot where I had fired at the bear; and by following some trails with the glasses I saw a band of fifteen ewes on a mountain leading downward from the highest peak, east of the cabin. Seven ewes were feeding, two lying down, on the mountain behind my old camp, and twenty or thirty more were easily visible on the mountain across the Upper East Branch, while at the same time about twenty small rams were on the east slopes of Divide Mountain. Five of these rams later came down and fed for a while on the bar. Most of the sheep seen that day were high on the mountains in the same places in which they were usually seen during summer and fall. Their trails on the fresh snow indicated their movements—where they had been feeding and where resting. Everywhere they had pawed away snow to reach the vegetation beneath.

This afforded a fine opportunity to observe the contrast in color of these northern white sheep against the background of snow before the winds had scattered it on the mountain slopes. Their stained pelage rendered them very conspicuous against a background exclusively of snow, and when in such spots it was extremely easy to detect them. But when at some distance and near the stunted willows they were hard to see. Their dirty pelage caused them to blend with the exposed

178

rocks and bare patches where they had scraped away the snow.

Throughout the winter and spring the possibilities of observing the snow trails of sheep, caribou, moose, and bears, were carefully noted. When one looks along the mountain slopes, even when inspecting them through good field glasses, or when from an elevation he looks over the snow of the level country below and fails to see the trail of an animal where it should be easily visible, he is likely to conclude hastily that no large animal has walked over the surface in view. But more experience in observing snow trails of these animals will teach him that he might not be looking from the right angle to see a trail that from another point of view would be plainly visible. A trail is often invisible when it runs parallel to the observer's course, and also when viewed from certain angles, particularly when it crosses uneven surfaces, partially windswept, of snow and bare ground. Therefore, before concluding that snow trails are absent, it is wise to continue scanning the surface from different elevations.

Nearer the main range the fresh tracks of two or three foxes indicated the presence of these beautiful animals, the trail of one showing his search for mice, his tracks passing around nearly all the clumps of willows, both on the bars and along the lower slopes.

By the time I had returned nearer the cabin the snow had become everywhere dotted with small holes made by mice. Thousands of them had tunneled under it, coming at intervals to the surface, but merely exposing a hole—not coming out to travel on top. There had been none of these holes in the morning. Throughout the winter the mouse holes were anywhere characteristic marks on the snow. Usually the mice, mostly *Evotomys* and *Microtus,* did not emerge from them, using them merely as lookouts. Here and there however, amid the numerous holes, a few had come out and made runways between them.

October 13. Morning temperature minus 7. The increased cold, though clear and calm, convinced me that it really was winter. In the morning I developed kodak films and chopped wood and in the afternoon walked through the woods up to the Bear Draw. The day before, several flocks of redpolls had been flying high, continually uttering their attractive notes, which closely resemble those of the goldfinch. This day they were more abundant although most of them passed over, going toward the east, while a few occasionally loitered for a short time near the tops of the spruces. During all the rest of October and well into November they daily passed in flocks and their notes, continually uttered, added a characteristic sound to the impressions of that period. But a still sweeter and more plaintive bird song—that of the pine grosbeaks passing overhead—sounded frequently each day, also bringing joy. Often the eye was delighted by the sight of these beautiful birds the males of which are carmine or red, as they paused to feed, keeping low in the spruces and willows. All were migrating south. A ptarmigan in white plumage was seen in the woods, also a grouse, which I shot and skinned.

Now the snow began to reveal the animal life of the woods. The mice had made regular trails between their holes and about the willow clumps and bases of the spruces; red squirrels had traveled between the trees; an occasional weasel had tracked all about the woods; and not far from the cabin a rabbit from across the bar had so tracked up a small area that one might be led to believe there had been many of them.

On this day for the first time I walked with the long snowshoes. I had two pairs of snowshoes: one about six feet long for use in the deeper snow of the woods and lower country; the other, three-and-a-half feet long, for use above timber and for climbing, and also when breaking trail ahead of the dogs. The snow in the woods was twelve inches deep, not quite enough for good snowshoeing.

Also for the first time, owing perhaps to lower temperature, a new atmospheric effect was noticed. Across the river bar well toward the other side, air waves were dancing like heat waves in summer.

October 14. A light snow fell all day, which I spent chopping, doing odd jobs about the cabin, and reading. The number of books brought was necessarily few. Besides a work on ornithology and the first issue taken from the press of Sumner's *Folkways,* I had in small flexible leather Shakespeare's plays and some of Ben Jonson's; the poems of Chaucer, Keats, Wordsworth, Tennyson, and Matthew Arnold; the essays of Montaigne, Lamb, Adrian, and some of Ruskin, and a selection of other English essayists. Since I was to live surrounded by natural phenomena, I had hoped that some of Ruskin's descriptive passages might arouse in me a deeper appreciation of landscape and sky in that magnificent country where the effects were on a scale that Ruskin had never observed. And yet, while admiring the brilliancy of his descriptions, they did not give rise to a single emotion or inspiration corresponding to my own feelings as aroused by the manifestations of Nature about me.

October 15. The meat of the sheep I had killed in September was hung outside on poles nailed between trees, where it was carefully surrounded by gunnysacks to protect it from the jays. It was slightly spoiled and therefore kept for the dogs, while I set out to kill another for our own use. The day was perfect—a clear sky, and no wind. The river was roaring through snow banks and shallow ice gorges, setting a limit on the direction I could go, for I could not cross it without wading. I hoped, however, that an ice bridge could be found above, so a start on snowshoes was made, but it was soon apparent that all the water was open and hence it was necessary to follow up Bear Draw over a low divide to the south, halfway up, leading to the divide pastures across the ridges directly behind the cabin.

It may be well to describe here the physiological effects experienced immediately after the first zero weather. It produced in me a continuous state of exhilaration similar to the effect of champagne, but without any disturbing influence on the brain; also a surprising bodily resistance to cold, except in some of the extremities—hands, feet, nose, cheeks, and ears. Apparently my wind was improved, for without losing breath I could climb or run in a way that in warmer temperature earlier in the season would have been impossible. To this increased physical energy, which continued until the following April, I attribute the mental exhilaration that makes existence and activity in the winter of the northern wilderness a continuous joy and inspiration.

For a long time I continued to wear the same clothing that had been worn since August—light undershirt and gauze drawers reaching to the knees, light gabardine trousers and a buckskin shirt. In my rucksack I always carried a squirrel-skinned parka for use in wind when high in the mountains, or when inactive without a fire. No hat was worn either in summer or winter, but eartabs, made from thick socks, were secured about my head with tape, and even during the cold winds of winter no sensation of cold was experienced in my head (where the growth of hair was scant). The object of this experiment—to increase the growth of hair— was not successful. A pair of silk gloves with moosehide mittens drawn over them kept my hands warm during the entire winter. The silk gloves were necessary to protect the hands temporarily while shooting or doing other momentary jobs that required the use of the fingers. The mittens were joined by a soft cord passed over the back of the neck so they would remain suspended when my hands were uncovered for any purpose. Except when snowshoeing in moccasins, rubber shoe packs and three pairs of socks were worn. Late in November my summer underclothing was replaced by that of heavy wool, the buckskin shirt by a thick flannel one, the trousers by woolen ones; these served well for clothing during the whole winter. Invariably in winter, except when not exercising, a white drill parka was worn over my shirt.

By the middle of October rabbit tracks had become more abundant in the woods, and the holes and tracks of mice seemed to cover the whole lower country and reach well up the mountains. Flocks of singing redpolls kept passing over; the notes of jays sounded here and there wherever there were spruces; willow ptarmigan were often seen among the willows, mostly above timberline though common below; and occasional ravens flew about, usually keeping high near the mountain crests.

When I reached the upper snowfield of the divide, Denali, seemingly very near, was almost shining in the heavens. The snow was deeper here and it seemed strange though pleasant to speed along over it without annoyance from the uneven ground to which I had been accustomed while tramping before the snow came. An old moose track or two on the snow showed that at times during the rut a bull had passed over the divide, which was the southern limit of moose tracks on this branch of the Toklat—though it is quite possible that occasionally a moose may have wandered a mile or more farther south in the spruces on the other side of the river.

Crossing to the north side of the divide I soon saw sheep tracks. Several ewes and lambs had been working about the divide and along the slopes. They had traveled high, using their summer trails, and had scattered to feed, digging away the snow, particularly about willows. Finally, after I had tramped to the lower end and then back along Cabin Divide Mountain, three sheep, apparently ewes, were seen near the head of Cabin Creek, where if one was killed it could be conveniently taken down the creek bed to the cabin. Going up the slope and carefully working along I finally reached a point a hundred and fifty yards below, where I shot the ewe, which came rolling down almost to the creek. I was surprised then to see the other two suddenly come in sight, but after a look down at the falling sheep they ran upward and disappeared. They were lambs, their apparent size, owing to the long pelage, having prevented me from recognizing them from a distance, unaided by field glasses.

While dressing the ewe my hands were kept from freezing by plunging them every few moments inside the warm body —the only way in which one can dress or skin large game during very low temperature. The stomach was full and contained dry grass, dryas and other small plants, willow shoots, and lichen. The udder was somewhat reduced, but still full of milk. Shouldering the ewe and struggling down the creek for more than two miles to the cabin, my first long tramp on snowshoes was completed.

On this day it was noticeable that during clear weather at

low temperature one is likely to be deceived by the apparent nearness of the mountains—exactly as on our own western plains.

October 17. Early in the morning I tramped down the river seeking a place to cross. New channels were forming and spreading over the bar, here and there dammed by the ice, causing overflows, which in turn were freezing, as elsewhere described. After much winding about I reached the main channel and after an hour's search found a temporary ice bridge. It was a hazardous crossing, for the main channel, compressed and narrowed by the side ice, had greatly deepened the water so that the rapids had increased to a torrent.

About a mile below I saw a wolverine track and followed it, interested to observe the manner in which the animal traveled. The trail showed that it always kept as much as possible in concealment. The tracks, wherever possible, were in willows close to the cut bank of the river, where they continued for some distance until leading out to the river. Failing to find a place to cross, the wolverine had returned in its tracks and gone directly into the woods.

Since I could not cross for another five miles I returned through the snow, which though not deep enough for snowshoeing was still deep enough to make unpleasant tramping —for the crust just failed to hold, and nothing is more tiresome than breaking through at every step. There was not so much snow below the cabin as above, for the mountains were more windswept.

For the first time that season two fairly large rams were seen on the outside mountain, lying down just below the crest. This part of the mountain, up to that time, had been the feeding ground for the ewes—rams had never occupied it. There were plenty of trails below the rams, indicating that the ewes had been feeding among the willows. The bar was covered with mouse trails, many of which showed that mice had been caught between the new channels of the river. Numerous mice must thus be lost every winter while the river is 'glaciering.' During the summer and fall they occupy the bars wherever willows grow, and breed there. Evidently most of them remain until driven out by the overflows, when they attempt to cross to higher ground. If they suddenly find themselves hemmed in between newly formed channels, they must perish, for thick ice soon spreads over the places where they have been living and it is doubtful if they could swim the continuous rapids.

On my return it required a long time to find another crossing but finally it was accomplished, almost opposite the cabin, though not without wetting my feet and freezing my rubber shoe packs.

At the cabin I found that a red squirrel had been cutting my meat and was still at it. I shot him. There were six red squirrels about the woods near by and I had intended to observe them through the winter. But since they had discovered the cache and had become destructive it was necessary to kill all but one. This one was driven away so often that he finally became wary. Female shrews were now invading the cabin and three or four were caught in the traps every night. The shrews were more cannibalistic than the mice and destroyed nearly all the mice trapped in the cabin. They kept coming in for a few weeks until finally so many were killed that they became scarce.

No ground squirrels had been observed since October 2, nor were any bear tracks seen since I wounded the bear on October 9—evidently all were hibernating.

October 18–21. During these four days, between intervals of tramping back on the divide and wandering in the woods, I chopped wood and performed tasks about the cabin. These included repairing the stove, propping up the side of the cabin, trying out moose and caribou fat, making shelves for the cache and platforms between trees for storing trophies and specimens, and hewing boards from a spruce tree for a bunk. The bottom of my bed was a moose skin stretched and nailed on six-inch hewn boards. On this were placed two sheep skins sewn together and covered with horse blankets. No warmer mattress could have been devised, and while sleeping in the cabin throughout the winter I needed only an old caribou skin weighing eight pounds—purchased the year before from Indians at Fork Yukon for ten dollars.

The ewe had been butchered and carved into steaks, roasts, and chops. All the cuts had been placed on shelves in the outside cache and were solidly frozen. For cooking it was only necessary to bring one into the cabin, where it slowly thawed. But it was disappointing to find that the season for delicious mutton had passed. Soon after the cold sets in and the sheep begin to feed on frozen grasses and other small plants and willow buds and dry leaves, the meat loses its flavor and is not nearly so good as winter caribou, and much less desirable than moose meat, which in the northern wilderness takes the place of beef the year round. Besides, sheep fat becomes slightly rancid by intense freezing so it was customary to cut it off before cooking the mutton. From the latter part of June to early October the meat of the mountain sheep, to my taste, is the choicest in flavor of all game. That of a three-year-old dry ewe in August brings joy to the epicure. But in the North, after October, one should if possible obtain a supply of moose meat for a steady diet—but unfortunately I did not learn this until later.

One of the jays, named Nellie, which had become very tame, flew into the cabin, and catching sight of a piece of fat used as bait on a mouse trap, darted at it and was caught, though not seriously hurt. After being liberated, she did not seem frightened and soon began to fly about the cabin seeking food. She finally claimed the outside window-sill as her exclusive property and continually sat there, always pecking at the window and waiting for it to be opened. She was obviously gratified to receive food, although she never ate it, but always flew to a tree to store it.

Hudsonian chickadees were constantly about the cabin. No other bird resident of the North so endears itself to a lover of birds as does this sociable friendly little creature. It is thoroughly confiding and seems almost completely to lack fear of man. It is always in motion, flitting about the branches of spruce and willow trees. When walking in the woods, if I paused to listen, a movement in the branches of a spruce near by would catch my eye and one or more chickadees would be discovered among the branches, hunting through the needles, clinging from any angle, and often suspended from the outer side of a twig, ever restlessly seeking food. Soon one would see me and seeming to disguise its approach by continuing the search for food, it would come down low within a few feet and suddenly greet me with its sweet plaintive though rather wheezy *chickadee-dee-dee*. The others would gather round in curiosity and loiter about me as if really enjoying my company. All through the season it was an undiminished joy to fall in with these little birds. I was always sure of their welcome and attention. Like the jays, they seemed indifferent to cold, but unlike those birds the chickadees were active about the trees during the severest storms of winter. The jays were interesting to watch and study, and their companionship enlivened the solitude. But the chickadees aroused affection, they went straight to the heart.

Ravens were encountered flying about the woods and although one or two discovered the food possibilities near the cabin, unlike the jays, not one attempted to meddle. Often one would perch on a nearby limb and after watching with a greedy look both the cabin and me as I moved about, would apparently go to sleep. If it attempted to come too near, all the jays would immediately attack and drive it off.

Sometimes at dusk a great horned owl was heard hooting, and the next day, as already stated, no fresh rabbit tracks were to be found. That year rabbits were very scarce, but all through the winter one would occasionally come into the cabin woods and make its home under some log or brush heap. But *always* within a day or two the hooting of the owl would be heard and the rabbit would disappear. This clearly substantiates the deadly reputation of these owls. What countless numbers of rabbits they must consume each winter!

On October 21 an Alaska three-toed woodpecker and a Rocky Mountain creeper were collected in the woods, the creeper being the only one observed. Flocks of redpolls still kept migrating over the woods without stopping, moving in an easterly direction.

The sheep, all ewes and lambs, were feeding about their accustomed places on the mountains east of the cabin, but for a week I had not seen rams on Sheldon Mountain. They had scattered and moved.

For two days winds swept over the mountains, baring the exposed slopes and piling the snow into deep drifts in the ravines, hollows and other sheltered places. The snow was like fine dry powder, very light and easily blown through the air by even light breezes. The finely triturated character of the snow in this region should be understood by any one interested in winter life in the North. Throughout the winter, with rare exceptions, the constant cold prevents it from becoming damp, and when compressed it freezes hard, almost like ice. A snowshoe trail made by passing once and returning will be hard enough on the following morning to hold dogs pulling a sled. After one passes over it two or three times on snowshoes it will be hard enough to hold a man without them, and will remain so during the rest of the winter and early spring. As the snow increases in depth, the pressure packs it so that light breezes do not lift it, but if the wind blows hard, clouds of fine particles fill the air.

The winds had again changed the landscape. Instead of the uniform white blanket covering the trees and ground, the trees were now bare, contrasting with the whites and browns of the surrounding mountainsides. The grandeur of the mountains was stern and austere—still beautiful though causing a feeling of desolation. Although I was conscious of an increasing desire to be out among them, to enjoy the freedom and sense of possession of the whole wild region and its animal life, the desolation of it all served to intensify the satisfaction of returning to my little cabin home, where I always received the excited welcome of the jays and found warmth and food, reading, and healthful sleep.

October 22–24. For several days the air seemed quite warm with the thermometer well above zero. I tramped over the divide along the outside mountains, also near the crests of the Bear Draw and up the bars to the point of the mountain at the Forks, but could not cross the river until later, when ice bridges would be formed. My tramping therefore was limited to the east side. Few sheep were observed, a fact showing that they had not yet moved toward the outside ranges.

On October 22 my journal contains the first recorded impression of the winter skies, then beginning to display the glory of colors that continued all winter, even though the sun remained below the crests all through the day—as it did now. The clouds and sky on the west were rich golden, while the heavy banks to the east were deep pink, merging on the south with forbidding gray clouds that hung over the main range beneath a sky of cold steel blue. As the sun sank lower and the gold in the western sky faded, the clouds above became pink while those in the east grew dark. Soon the western horizon retained only an exquisite glow as a background to the snowy mountain skyline.

That day a jay had somehow entered the cache and was pinned down in a mouse trap. It was quite badly hurt and could not stand on its feet, so I put it in a corner of the cabin for the night. In the morning it was sitting on the floor, its feathers fluffed out. Two others were perched on the window-sill outside waiting for some sign of activity within. When the fire was made and the cabin warmed up, I cooked and ate breakfast; then the jay began to hop about the floor, apparently none the worse for the accident. Suddenly it flew up to the table and finding plenty of food at once became excited, filled its throat with rice, and began to look for a place to store it. At first it flew about perplexed, then deposited its mouthful in my rucksack on the floor. The next load it dropped into a pail, the next into a folded caribou skin, and another in the pile of split wood near the stove. Finally cleaning up the table, having deposited food in convenient spots all over the cabin, it began to look for a place to get out, often alighting on my head, shoulder or hand. It kept chirping in curiosity at the strange surroundings, but showed not the slightest fear; and finally when let out the window, it soon came back and perched on the sill.

During the summer, one of the sights of the North that had always impressed me was a fringe of spruce trees against

the skyline. Now however the dark spruce tops were silhouetted against the white snowfields of the slopes, their forms
clearly outlined, decorating the landscape. For four days the
wind had blown, sweeping the slopes and bars and deepening
the drifts.

My cabin was now ready for winter. I had made a large
baking of bread, developed films, and prepared many specimens.

October 25. A heavy wind from the south blew all day
and continued the next day, though then much warmer.

October 26. The bars were blown so bare that while
tramping up the Upper East Branch I could almost avoid the
snow. I was then facing the wind to watch sheep, knowing
they would be there in greater numbers than below.

Flocks of redpolls, flying eastward, were particularly numerous, and the notes of pine grosbeaks, which were usually
migrating southward in pairs, sounded frequently along the
edge of the woods.

Soon after passing the Bear Draw I saw a dark object
moving across the pasture slopes between the strips of
spruces. The glasses showed it to be a wolverine—the first I
had ever seen. At times, plunging in the deep snowdrifts of
the hollows, it almost disappeared; but it kept running, with
the awkward gait of a small bear, which it resembled, and
continued for three hundred yards, to enter the next spruces,
where it was lost to view.

At the Forks, six fairly large rams were seen on the
south slopes of Old Camp Mountain—the first observed on
that mountain. Recalling the rams seen for the first time on
the outside mountain, and the absence of the band from their
usual place on Sheldon Mountain, it seemed clear that the
rams had begun to widen their range; and in passing around
the point at the Forks, about thirty ewes and a few small
rams were seen two hundred yards out on the flat, near the
foot of Divide Mountain. They soon became alarmed and ran
for the mountain, where from a high point they watched me
while I crossed the river on an ice bridge. Well up on the
slopes, they remained resting or feeding all the afternoon.

As I proceeded, many places were noticed where ewes had fed on the flat close to the mountains. It was clear that now more frequently than formerly they were coming up the branches to the willows on the flats. From a point overlooking the slopes of Polychrome Mountain I saw another band a couple of miles away.

Turning into the spruces I found a beautiful sheltered spot near which I had tied the horse *Toklat* when the bear frightened him. Here, protected from the wind, I built a fire and made tea. After about an hour I came out on the bar, faced the wind, and started up the branch, but the sheep had gone out of sight. By this time I knew pretty well the several sheep bands and their mountain trails, and also their favorite spots for feeding. Knowing exactly where they should be found, it was seldom that their movements, when feeding undisturbed, could not be anticipated. About three miles up the branch I saw a band high up near the crest, just where I knew they would be. There were thirty ewes and a small ram or two, but no large ram was near, the rut having not yet begun.

The sun was low as I retraced my steps and came around Divide Mountain, facing a golden sky. On the skyline were several sheep which, observed through the field glasses, seemed fairly to shine against the brilliantly glowing background. At the Forks the wind was dead, not even a faint breeze disturbing the calm. The reflected rays of the setting sun had changed the dark crestline of Old Camp Mountain to deep indigo blue in exquisite contrast to the snow below and the black of the lower slopes. Color soon fairly poured into the sky—rich pink in the west, with lighter tints north and south. As I paused to enjoy them, at the moment of highest colors there appeared on the very crest of Old Camp Mountain five large rams, their horns sharply silhouetted against the glorious sky, their bodies apparently submerged in the dark blue of the crestline. To the south the colors deepened above the clear blue near the white crests of the main range while pinks and salmons merged throughout the western horizon, contrasting with the sombre gray of the east. Then all the rocks and bare slopes took on a deep chocolate, changing to gray as darkness began to settle, leaving only the outlines of the mountains visible.

October 27–29. These three days were occupied in developing films, preparing specimens, and wandering about the woods and over the mountains to the east.

October 30. Early morning temperature 17 degrees below zero. After a difficult crossing of the river, that was then spreading in several channels—each freezing and forcing the water into a new one—I went far down its course. Three or four rams, having crossed over from Sheldon Mountain (as indicated by the snow), were feeding and resting near the crest of the outside mountain. The fresh trail of a wolverine, concealed inside the willows, followed the same course as when last observed and then entered the woods. Just after passing through the canyon I saw a fine cow moose and calf watching me from some scattered spruces about a hundred yards distant on the opposite bank of the river. Evidently they had heard me approach. They could easily have been shot, and later, when I realized the luxury of moose meat in winter, the omission was regretted. Instantly they stepped back into thicker spruces and later emerged a quarter of a mile above and disappeared over a ridge. The sight of moose among the spruces always gives an added charm—the consciousness of the presence of a noble form of wild life. There is something mysterious about the moose—something evoking a sense of creatures of the long past. To see one skulking in remote wilderness depths arouses primitive emotions difficult to analyze.

Well below, a few rabbit tracks were on the bars, and also the trail of another wolverine, showing an effort at concealment. On my return the mist hung low, hiding the surface, while above, the great mountains seemed suspended in the atmosphere.

October 31. Increasing cold indicated that winter had thoroughly settled over the country, and a light snow falling through thin mists in a temperature of 24 degrees below zero ended the month of October. Today I put on moosehide moccasins; with one or two exceptions they were not discarded until spring. The month of October gave me my first experience of the approach of the northern winter. No impressions seem so closely associated with remote wildernesses or linger so vividly in the memory, as those of characteristic sounds. In summer the commonest and most vivid sounds are the chatter of ground squirrels, the whistle of marmots, the songs of tree sparrows, thrushes, and other small birds, the croak of ravens, the murmur or roar of the river rapids, and the moaning of the sweeping currents; while in October are heard the joyful notes of the redpolls and the plaintive song of the pine grosbeaks—the redpolls first coming in numbers to the upper country, the grosbeaks passing through on their way south.

November 1–2. Early morning temperature 26 degrees below zero on both days. These two days were cold, calm, and cloudless—the kind of winter days that bring intense exhilaration and joy to one who tramps among the mountains to observe the wild animals and birds and to read the records of animal life on the snow. On November 1 the smaller snowshoes were used. Several bands of ewes were seen feeding high on the mountains, and for the first time ewes were seen on Old Camp Mountain, a fact showing that all the sheep were widening their feeding range. At two different points I saw wolverine tracks and discovered a fox track along the bars near the Forks. Everywhere in the ravines where willows grew could be found tracks of ptarmigan.

The next day, the long snowshoes were worn and a visit was made to the creek flowing down from Cabin Divide. Not very far up, the trail of a wolverine was crossed, and shortly afterward, that of a fox. Near the head of the Fork, well up on the slope, were two small rams, a ewe, and a lamb. It was a fine sensation to sweep up over the snow of the creek bed where during the summer I had so often toiled among rough rocks and precipitous slopes; while now, instead of stumbling among the nigger-heads, I could glide smoothly over the deep snowdrifts. Soon four fair-sized rams were seen on the slopes to the south, the largest, six or seven years old. They were very alert, although they did not seem to feed very actively. Their trail led down Cabin Divide Mountain to the level area of the divide, which they crossed in single file by a series of jumps, each ram jumping exactly in the tracks of the one ahead, so that the trail looked like one made by a single heavy animal. A rabbit track passed over the divide leading to some stunted willows, where I was surprised to see a jay so far above the timber.

Well down toward the lower end of the divide were seven ewes. Advancing toward them in the expectation of continuing on to the East Fork of the Toklat, and while exhilarated by the pleasure of making such easy progress, I came to a deep snowdrift where the entire webbing of the right snowshoe gave way completely; and while struggling to extricate my leg from the snow, the left likewise broke through. The webbing made by the Indians is usually too weak to withstand the rough work given snowshoes by heavy white men, but until this accident I had not realized it. After freeing myself from the snowshoes my troubles began. The snow was so light that I sank in it up to my neck. It was with great difficulty that, using the snowshoe for a spade, I began to dig a path—this being apparently the only method by which I could get through the fifty feet of drift to higher ground, where the snow was not so deep. It required three hours of cold hard discouraging work to reach a point where by exhausting effort it was possible to wade without digging. Later it was necessary to struggle up the slope and circle all the drifts back to the head of the creek. It was long after dark and my progress was discouraging until I reached the spruces, where I made a large fire and some tea. Then I gradually worked downward along the sides of the creek and reached the cabin at midnight.

November 3. Early morning temperature 30 degrees below zero. Though colder after a light snowfall at night, the day was as fair as the previous one. On the small snowshoes I walked rapidly up river on the trail broken two days before. A wolverine had crossed this trail and struck off over the bar. Ahead, at dawn, was a magnificent sky, the sun then not rising until about ten in the morning. Hastening along opposite Old Camp Mountain, intending to go up the Upper West Branch, I saw six rams just below the crest, evidently those that had been loitering there before. When I came closer to the mountain, three of them were seen to have big horns—one, extra fine horns.

On such a day and so near my old camp I could not resist an attempt to secure the best ram for a trophy, and at once planned a stalk. As an aid in climbing icy mountains my rucksack contained a pair of iron creepers that could be strapped over the moccasins. After going up through the deep snow of the woods, I planted the snowshoes at the edge, put on the creepers, and waded up a steep ravine to the left, well hidden from the rams. Then, after crossing diagonally a steep icy slope, the crest was passed and a way was found along the crags on the other side until opposite the rams. Carefully creeping over the top I saw them about four hundred yards down to my left; three were feeding, the others lying down. The big one, his horns glittering black against the snow, was standing motionless, looking downward. All around and in the distance were the snow-covered mountains, the rock pinnacles and spires standing out sharply in dark contrasts, with here and there white icy slopes glittering in the sun, while the valleys below seemed one great blanket of endless white. A sharp wind blowing from the north made it necessary for me to keep constantly rubbing my nose to prevent it from freezing. Slowly and carefully descending through a hollow until at a selected point, I crept through the snow and stood up with rifle ready. The rams were only a hundred yards distant, all feeding and entirely unsuspicious. Carefully aiming at the big one, I pressed the trigger, but without result. A second effort and the bolt still failed to respond. Then, dropping back out of sight, I found that the lock was so frozen that it was hopeless to try to make it work.

I stalked back in my tracks as carefully as I had approached, rounded the crest, descended to my snowshoes, and then followed my trail to the bar. Looking up I saw the rams still feeding and pawing the snow near the same spot, the big one little realizing that he owed his life to a temperature 30 degrees below zero. On another slope well up the branch could be seen twenty sheep, but it was too late to cross over there to inspect them. Clouds and mists were settling about the main range, fog was beginning to stream upward through the distant canyon to the south, and a stinging wind was lashing my face as I continued toward the cabin. Looking back, I beheld two clear-cut magnificent rainbows extending in complete parallel arcs across the sky, the western ends of both resting on Old Camp Mountain. Through their colors the rams could be dimly seen, while beyond, under the middle of the arcs, the white peaks of the main range were visible, apparently suspended above the mists, as noted on another occasion.

Before the cabin was reached all was dense fog; snow had begun to fall and the sky became dark—the bright cheerful day replaced by grim desolation. At the cabin the rifle was carefully cleaned and the lock put in boiling water to remove every particle of grease. This is always necessary in the extreme cold of the North, but later it was found that without any grease on the bolt the friction was sufficient at times to cause a misfire. The bolt was wiped with a rag greased with vaseline and gave no further trouble during the winter.

Visitors at the Cabin.
Ram Hunting.

November 4–5. Morning temperatures 29 degrees and 36 degrees below zero. The morning of November 4 was occupied in baking bread, repairing snowshoes, developing films, and preparing specimens of small mammals. About three in the afternoon a strange sound out on the bar led me to the edge of the woods, when I was surprised to see two dog teams approaching. One was driven by Merrifield, the other by Rice, a prospector spending the winter at Glacier. They had come for two purposes: to tell me that there would be nobody in Glacier to take care of the horses, and that Merrifield, who was soon to leave for Fairbanks, had better take the horses there for the winter. To this I consented, knowing that in the spring Karstens could go out and bring them back. They came especially to get loads of sheep meat, and furthermore, Merrifield had obligated himself to obtain the head of a ram for some one in Glacier. Since I did not want my sheep above the cabin disturbed by anybody except myself, they were glad to agree to get their sheep on the outside mountain.

The delightful solitude of the wilderness I had been enjoying was thus suddenly broken; nine active dogs were tied outside the cabin, and the jays at once disappeared. As host, it was necessary for me to provide meat for the dogs, and also at once to cook a large quantity for the men. Rice, who had not eaten fresh meat for several months, promptly consumed a whole fryingpan-full, and about two hours later cooked and ate an equal amount again, and before going to bed finished a third meal.

The next day both left early to hunt sheep while I remained about the cabin to watch the dogs and prepare a good meal for the men—to be ready on their return. Once, two dogs be-

197

gan to fight and I brought them into the cabin and tied them
well apart. When I was out for a short time, one broke loose
and ate a whole slab of bacon, which unfortunately had been
left within reach. Later in the afternoon through the field
glasses I saw two wolverines running down the south slope
from the crest of Cabin Divide Mountain.

When Rice came in he reported that he had not found any
sheep. He was soon followed by Merrifield, who had seen some
on the outside mountain too far away to go for them. He had
come directly over the crest of Cabin Divide Mountain at
about the time I had seen the wolverines. This explains what
I had not at first understood—why wolverines should be on
the crests, where there was no food unless they were able to
kill a sheep.

November 6. Morning temperature 32 degrees below zero.
I had prepared plenty of food for both dogs and men, and
while Merrifield and Rice again went to the outside mountain,
I went up the river hoping to get the ram that Merrifield
wanted and also perhaps a second one to replenish my stock of
meat, which was rapidly being exhausted. It was a fine calm
day. A rabbit had come across the bar and entered the woods,
and numerous tracks of weasels were everywhere, particularly
about the mouse holes. Near the top of Forks Mountain were
two ewes and three lambs, and two large rams were climbing
the slope toward them. They had just traveled from Old
Camp Mountain across the bar. When they reached the ewes
one of them suddenly mounted a ewe, and then without further attention both rams climbed diagonally along the slope
and passed over the crest. This was the first positive sign of
the rut that had been observed. Since the latter part of October the ram bands had broken up and the rams had been
traveling about visiting mountains where they had not been
seen before. But up to that time they had not joined the ewes.
The rut was now in its initial stage, here and there a ewe being in condition for service.

Approaching Divide Mountain I soon saw a large band of
sheep—more than seventy-five—well up on the west side.
Among them were three rams, two of which were about five

years old. I watched them for a while, but since the rams paid no attention to the ewes, keeping apart in the manner of younger rams in summer, there was no evidence that rut activities were taking place. Such a band of ewes had not before been observed on the north end of Divide Mountain—which usually was the feeding ground of young rams. It seemed clear that this band was an aggregation of smaller bands that the increased snowfall had driven out of the main range. It proved interesting to observe carefully this band of ewes. Their actions indicated that it was composed of six independent groups, each of which, while all were more or less together, kept in such close association and displayed such mutual independence, that there could be no doubt that the large band was an assemblage of smaller ones. Nothing suggesting a 'sentinel' was observed at any time among them.

I decided to kill, if possible, the larger ram, so circled around the bar to the east slope, put on my creepers, slung the snowshoes on my back, and gradually ascended to the crest. It was warmer up there than on the bar below. The sheep were a few hundred yards lower down, all actively pawing the snow and feeding. The sun was below the horizon, the sky was filled with glorious colors, and rich gold surrounded the summit of Denali. I carefully worked down to within a hundred and fifty yards of the sheep and then, crawling over a slight elevation, had them all in sight—not one suspicious of danger, although some of the ewes displayed their usual caution. After a few moments the ram offered a good target; he fell to my shot and rolled downward. The others looked up toward me intently, although some turned their heads in the direction of the rolling ram. So long as I remained motionless none recognized me, but when I moved quickly, aiming at the other ram, all started running and shortly disappeared in a canyon.

While I was photographing and dressing the ram the bleat of a cony sounded among the broken rocks nearby—a reminder of summer days. The ram had unusually yellow eyes. Its stomach contained lichen and a variety of grass and other small plants, some of them quite green. It was dark long before the cabin was reached. Here I found Karstens with his five dogs, having that afternoon arrived from Fairbanks after a trying trip, owing to lack of snow in the lower country. During the day Merrifield had killed five ewes, including three lambs, but Rice had experienced another blank day. That night the dogs consumed all my surplus meat except enough reserved for ourselves to last a day or two.

November 7–8. On the morning of November 7 the temperature registered 34 degrees below zero. Merrifield went with a dog team to bring in the sheep he had killed, while Rice and I went up to Divide Mountain with another dog team to fetch the ram. The dogs and sled were taken up the slope to the carcass. The skin was taken off and the meat loaded on the sled and brought back. I was surprised to find that the neck, head, and flesh on the back of the ram were still warm, although the nose, eyes, and exposed flesh were frozen.

On November 8 Merrifield and Rice started early for Glacier while I went out to try to kill a ram for a scientific specimen, which also would replenish our meat supply. I had discovered that for five dogs the meat of an average sheep provided only two meals.

Going up the bar, I saw some sheep on the north slope of the mountain on the south side of Bear Draw. They soon passed out of sight, but shortly two rams appeared, which from a distance seemed of fair size. After studying the ground and planning a stalk, I followed up the creek, crossed a slope and reached a point well behind the spur on which they had been sighted. The temperature was about zero, but the exertion of climbing caused me to perspire freely—even though I was wearing summer underclothing covered only by a flannel shirt and parka. The atmosphere suggested that of a November Indian summer day in northern New England, and yet the state of continual exhilaration was maintained. Leaving the snowshoes at the foot of the spur, I found enough bare patches for climbing without creepers. Finally reaching the crest of the spur near its junction with the mountain, I carefully, step by step, walked across to inspect the other side.

The sun was bright and the landscape indeed inspiring, but

the crust was so weak that my feet broke through, making so much noise that it was necessary to proceed very slowly. Finding neither sheep nor tracks it was clear that the sheep must be feeding close below me. Working cautiously downward to a point where an advance of a few feet would bring the lower slope in sight, I resisted the temptation to hurry and look until my breath had been recovered. Then, creeping upward and slowly raising my head, I discovered a ewe and lamb fifty yards below. Both were pawing away the snow and feeding, but no other sheep were in sight. So long as they were there my advance was cut off. But if they realized their danger and ran directly down they could not be seen by the sheep that were just below. So I rose a little higher and waited a moment, and then sat up motionless in plain sight. The lamb saw me and stood rigidly gazing at me, while the ewe continued feeding. After a moment the lamb jerked its head upward, immediately attracting the attention of the ewe, which then looked up and saw me. Both stood gazing at me for a few seconds, then the ewe turned and, followed by the lamb, ran down the slope.

Waiting a few minutes but hearing no sound, I crept another hundred feet downward and rising slowly saw a ram and several ewes, with a larger ram to their left, a hundred and fifty yards below. The ram fell motionless to my shot, all the others dashing downward, crossing the creek and climbing Cabin Peak.

The ram was a handsome five-year-old, with slightly stained pelage, though cleaner now than at other times of the year. The pelages of all the sheep were cleanest in early November, after which they began to get badly stained.

The air seemed balmy, and while the ram lay there in the snow I sat near and smoked my pipe. The view extended down the Toklat and across the forested areas below to the Chitsea Peak fifty miles away, while to the west Denali loomed up glowing in the sun, with all its crusted snowfields glistening. Then the descending sun threw vast shadows that appeared deep blue on the eastern slopes.

I took off the skin of the ram, cut off the head, cut off all

fat and tallow, and dressed the carcass. The stomach contained almost exclusively grass, including a few green plants.
Putting skin, skull, and fat in my rucksack I took the snowshoes and broke a trail diagonally to the cabin woods.

Rams now were certainly more in evidence with the ewes,
though in this band no signs of the active rut had been observed.

November 9–10. On the morning of November 9 I was
very much surprised to find that although the thermometer
was below zero, rain and sleet were falling; this continued at
intervals until noon.

After lunch we hitched the dogs to a small sled and went
for the ram. When we came in sight of it a smaller ram was
standing above it, evidently the other one I had seen the day
before. He watched us coming up the slope and as we approached the creek he walked upward among the cliffs, where
he stood for a while before retreating out of sight. As we were
crossing the ice of the creek bed all the dogs suddenly stopped,
threw up their heads, and held their noses pointing up the
Draw. Looking in that direction through my field glasses I
saw several sheep high on a slope a mile and a half distant.
The wind was blowing down the Draw and the dogs had
caught the scent.

Three ravens were standing around the carcass and had
cleaned one side to the bone. Attaching a rope to it, we told
the dogs to "mush" and they hauled it down the slope to the
sled. We were soon back in the cabin and because of a heavy
southwest wind remained there all the next day.

November 11. At this date daylight came at seven in the
morning; one could first see rifle sights at eight; the sun
showed a little above the mountain crests about ten, remaining for two hours before setting; at 3.30 in the afternoon it
was too dark to see rifle sights, and at 4.30 it was dark. I have
often been asked how one adjusts himself to these shorter
hours. Since the days shortened gradually I naturally retired
earlier and rose later, thus sleeping longer hours. When I
tramped for the day I did not take lunch, but was satisfied
with a good breakfast and one later meal. My habits were

unconsciously adjusted to the advancing winter hours of daylight, exactly the same as one so adjusts in the United States.

Karstens hitched the dogs to the large sled and started down to bring back a load of caribou meat for the dogs. I went up Bear Draw and crossed over the divide between the Bear Draw ranges and Cabin Peak, and then circled down the rolling pastures of Cabin Divide. When the thermometer was only slightly above zero it was uncomfortably warm while walking, and while climbing I perspired too freely. This called for extra caution whenever I stopped, even for a short time, because in that northern atmosphere a chill quickly succeeds inactivity. It was a beautiful clear day, but because of the height of the intervening mountains the sun was not seen. Redpolls in fewer numbers were still making music in the air, and shortly after I left the cabin the notes of a single pine grosbeak were heard—the first since October 26 and the last of the season.

On top of Cabin Peak were twelve ewes and lambs, which of late had traveled toward the ranges to the north. They were nearing the foot of Cabin Divide Mountain when I came around, and seeing me they quickly ran up the slope until all stood on the skyline, where the sun's rays caught them and made them almost shine against the deep blue sky beyond. A gyrfalcon sailed by; fox and weasel tracks on the snow revealed their mouse hunting; and mouse holes and tracks were everywhere.

On the East Fork of the Toklat were tracks of a few sheep that had crossed to the north and then turned back, traveling on the snow and ice of the creek bed. Reaching the pastures again, I faced a wonderful glowing sky, at first all fiery, then crimson, changing to deep pink and salmon, and merging into lighter colors above. With this loveliness before me I tramped for an hour, until looking down I could see the dark spruces spreading like a soft blackish mantle over the austere white of the lower slopes. It was dark when I came down the creek, and as I went out on the bars the moon was rising through the mist over the main range, the peaks below appearing like shadowy forms and giving rise to the mystic feelings that are ever aroused by silver moonlight.

November 12–13. These two days were spent about the cabin. New webbing was put on the snowshoes, and trees were cut for another cache, and also for kennels for the dogs. A sled with 300 pounds of caribou meat stood near. The jays flew about frantically and continually tried to alight on it. But the pure Malamute dog, *Silas,* stood by all day guarding it, driving off each jay that attempted to touch it. The second day he became tired of his self-imposed task and all the jays attacked the meat, never once ceasing to pick and store during the hours of daylight. By this time they were rapidly becoming accustomed to the dogs, who paid no attention whatever to them.

November 14–15. Feeling that it was necessary, if I were to study the beginning of the rut of the sheep, to have a camp nearer the main bands, I loaded the sled with a small tent (six by six feet), a very small sheet-iron stove, my caribou skin robe, and a few provisions, which the dogs rapidly pulled to the spruces on the slope below my old camp. Here were several dead trees for wood, and after we had cleared away the snow and put up the tent, Karstens took the dogs back to the cabin. I chopped and split a good supply of wood, cut boughs for a bed, melted snow for water, and arranged the camp for occupancy. The ice then extended clear across the bars and here and there the river was breaking out and overflowing, then again quickly freezing, forcing the water to find outlets somewhere else. The ice was daily becoming thicker. That night the moonlight beautified the whole region, the bars fairly glistened, and the mountains, towering around them, seemed like great silent silvery walls.

It was steadily growing colder as I tramped for two hours up the Upper West Branch in a mist so dense that I could not see anything. When it cleared, twenty-two ewes and lambs were visible high on the slopes to the west, accompanied by a four-year-old ram, which occasionally paid attention to one of them, but at other times fed along with the others. Near the head of the branch no signs of sheep were evident, but a few fox tracks and those of a wolverine appeared along the bar. This was five miles beyond any timber and the wolverine tracks were not found below, so it was clear that the animal had been among the mountains near the main range. Its trail came down one mountain and led up another.

While returning to camp, I faced on the north a most exquisite sky of colors not before noticed. Far below, the bars and lower slopes of the outside range were covered by a bank of dense mist. The mountains above were deep blue and purple, the background of sky clear blue, streaked by layers of delicate clouds surrounding the mountains in wreaths—the lowest pinkish, the next soft sea green, then one of deep blue, and finally one of faint pink, gradually merging into the dull gray of the sky above. The whole sky faintly caught the glow of the sun through the mists.

On Forks Mountain were two small bands of ewes, and shortly after, while walking around Divide Mountain, I heard conies. A heavy wind blew in such dense mists that I had to return to the tent, not reaching it till long after dark.

November 16. With a wondrous dawning sky before me I hastened toward the Upper East Branch, facing clouds of golden glory over the main range, the crests of which were lighted by the sun below. Sheep were soon visible on the slopes of Polychrome Mountain and I started toward them on the crust, which had been thoroughly windswept. There were fifteen ewes and lambs, accompanied by a small ram, and soon all lay down. It was clear that on the windswept slopes these sheep must have obtained a good amount of feed during the two hours after daylight, otherwise they would not have rested during the short day. I kept on against a strong head wind to the head of the branch which flows from the largest glacier of the East Fork of the Toklat. Near the head were eleven ewes and lambs, and all the sheep trails were very high, indicating that the animals were moving northward.

As I walked through the narrow outlet at the very head of the mountain-engirdled basin all the peaks and rugged crests were capped with pink and golden clouds, while the glacier seemed to shine blue. The sun soon set, the sky colors intensified, and for three hours I walked back beholding the glory of the colored horizon about the crags, peaks and snowfields of the windswept mountains. Before I reached the tent, the moonlight began to stream through the clouds over the crests to the east, causing a silvery glow that constantly intensified until the moon itself appeared over the summits, bathing both mountains and valleys with its soft lovely light. During that winter, when I spent so much time among these magnificent mountains and valleys, beholding the ever-changing glory of the skies, my enjoyment led to the hope that the reality of these Nature paintings, so beyond the imagination of artists, might some day be caught on canvas.

Today I had been on snowshoes for twelve hours without resting, but although a little tired on reaching the camp, as soon as I had eaten some meat and rice and drunk a cup of tea, my fatigue disappeared.

November 17. I went up the creek clear over the divide leading to the head of the West Fork of the Toklat (also called Stony Creek). Both fox and wolverine tracks were along the creek and the divide. I could not imagine why the wolverine had gone there any more than I could why one should have been near the head of the branches so far beyond the timber. Following the tracks I could see no evidence of mouse hunting, but the trail continued without interruption. Evidently the animal was making for some definite point beyond. On the mountain to the south I saw a five-year-old ram traveling. Farther along on the same mountain was a band of ewes and lambs resting high, and well above them a four-year ram, also resting. On the very summit, six hundred yards from these sheep, was a six-year-old ram lying down against the skyline. All sheep now were very high and all were extremely watchful, looking both up and down. As before, I saw no evidence of 'sentinels.' The rams were clearly traveling, either singly, in pairs, or sometimes three together. All the ram bands of the region were thus split up, each member going on a hunt for ewes, which were just entering the period of rut.

Although I was wearing a white parka it was very noticeable how quickly sheep could see me from a long distance and how quickly, at this season, they became nervous or frightened. All were more restless now—neither their actions nor movements were normal. Returning over my morning's trail I noticed the track of a ram that had come down the slope and crossed the bar to my tracks, following them for a few feet without crossing and then turning back up the slope. By long experience I knew that sheep pay no attention to the trail of a man—its odor not in the least frightening them—so I concluded that the ram had seen my trail from up the slope, and thinking it was that of other sheep, had come down with the idea of following it.

The Sheep Rut.

November 18. Last night, when I reached the tent, the wind was increasing; this morning it was snowing and a thin mist covered the mountains. Since I had found so few sheep in this upper country I started back very early to go below to the outside range, where I could observe the movements of sheep and at the same time get some caribou, both for dog food and for specimens in November pelage. While proceeding down the bars I met Karstens coming up with the dogs, and after asking him to pack up the camp material and take it back to the cabin, I continued against wind and snow. I felt no cold, but surrounded by mountains only faintly visible through the mists, and with fine snow whirling and drifting all about me, experienced a sensation of peculiar loneliness. Once when the mist lifted for a short time, looking through the glasses I saw up Bear Draw, in the exact spot where I had killed the last ram, a fairly large band of sheep. As I traveled toward them through the deep snow of the creek bed the mist thickened and they appeared like dark bulks almost black against the snow. Crossing through the woods I finally reached a spot so near that I could distinctly see them all. There were about forty ewes and lambs, two apparently large rams and two smaller ones. The mist on the glasses prevented a clear definition of the horns, but although blurred, they looked large. I saw at once that before me was a scene of the beginning of the active rut, the initial stage of which had been noted on November 6, and which continued till the middle of December.

The ewes were herded by the two large rams. The band fed continually, many of the ewes evidently not yet being in season. The two big rams always remained close together, con-

208

tinually working among the ewes, now smelling them, now one or the other serving one with a quick mount. Both would often smell the same ewe at the same time, and once one of the rams served a ewe while the other stood by his side. These two rams fed but little, yet now and then one would lower his head and crop a few mouthfuls. The two younger rams mingled as part of the ewe band, now and then smelling a ewe, and once one of them served one. Not once did any of the four rams show any sign of jealousy or pugnacity—in fact in the activities of the two large rams there seemed to exist a friendly partnership. Often the ewes would advance, when at once these two rams separated from the band and stood together, their heads pushed well forward, until the last ewe had gone on. Then they would bring up the rear and again go among the ewes. All the ewes acted leisurely and unconcerned. Those in season often urinated; then one or both of the large rams went to the spot and smelled it. Occasionally a big ram would suddenly extend his head forward, his horns resting on his outstretched neck, his nose elevated, and trot directly to a ewe to pay attention to her for a few minutes. During all the time I watched them there was one ewe and lamb that remained well apart from the others, undoubtedly not members of any of the ewe groups that composed this band. The rams paid no attention to her and she followed the band, always keeping well on its outskirts.

At last the sheep began to walk more rapidly upward, feeding as they went, and finally they began to go toward the trail that ran south just under the mountain crest. The two rams waited side by side carefully watching the ewes until all were ahead, when they followed, still keeping abreast of one another. The ewe and lamb remained at one side, somewhat behind, although they followed in the direction the band was taking. When the ewes in the lead reached the trail they walked on it for a short distance and began to feed. I decided to shoot the larger ram and hurried through the scattered spruces and willows at the foot of the slope for half a mile, and before climbing selected a point from which I could see the sheep when they came along. Nearly all were strung out single file on the trail, each group slightly separated from the others. Often while they loitered and fed, another group would close up. After the ewes of the last group reached the trail, all lay down, and the four rams behind, after watching them a moment, lay down also. The two smaller rams soon rose, walked forward, and joined the ewes. At this time the single ewe and lamb remained standing close behind the rams.

Soon all the sheep were in motion, and while climbing I could see the various groups strung along at intervals for a quarter of a mile, all slowly traveling without feeding. Although the way was steep and rough and the surface icy, I finally reached a rock fifty yards below the trail and lay down behind it. Through the light mist and falling snow could dimly be seen the fringe of forest, the bars below and the mountains beyond. Whirlwinds of snow were continually swept along the slopes, the wind howled among the rocks and roared along the cliffs. Soon the first ewes came, directly in the trail, seeming so close that I scarcely dared breathe. For half an hour others continued to follow. They advanced on a walk where the snow was light, but jumped through it where it was deep. When I had counted forty-two, including the foreign ewe and lamb, I watched over the leveled rifle for the appearance of the rams. My interest was intense. At first only the horns were visible; then the heads and bodies emerged and my rifle was brought up to aim. At this short distance, to my disappointment, I saw that the horns of the largest ram were not so large as they had seemed when observed through the mist. They were compact and well curled, but had not grown for more than six years. The rifle was lowered, and the rams strutted by proudly with extended necks and soon disappeared. Not one had even suspected my near presence. I descended and reached the cabin after dark.

November 19–21. Temperatures 7 degrees to 13 degrees below. November 19 was spent preparing for a trip below to the caribou range. Roughlocks were put on the snowshoes. These are triangular bars lashed below the forward bar of the snowshoe, enabling one to walk on steep slopes without slipping. While we were working, two of the dogs got in a fight and one was so badly bitten in the leg that a start could not be made for another two days. November 21 I started south to watch the sheep and while going up the bars over the new snow, noticed that there were practically no mouse holes, all the mice having left for the woods. It was a very clear day, but a biting wind from the north kept stinging my face.

Soon some sheep were seen on Forks Mountain, too far away to distinguish them, and shortly a single ram appeared on Old Camp Mountain. He was traveling and looking about, evidently searching for ewes. As I came a little nearer to the sheep, a ewe was seen lying down on the corner peak of the mountain, indifferent to her complete exposure to the cold. Below her were three more ewes, a lamb, and a good ram. The only possible stalk was an ascent at a point hidden by cliffs, but on reaching it the overflowing river cut off my advance so that I had to walk out in sight of the sheep. Seeing me they ran, the ram continually turning back to watch me.

I then went around by Divide Mountain and saw the whole band that I had stalked three days before, high on the mountains near Teklanika Divide. In two days they had completely circled the slopes to that point, a fact that indicated their feeding range during this time. The sun was well below the horizon when I started back, the wind had ceased and complete quiet reigned; not even the sound of the river running under the ice could be heard. Only the creaking of my snowshoes broke the stillness. Denali, rising in a brilliant golden sky, was before me; the north sky was banked with clouds of purest pink, deepening above to the dark blue of the ether; and later, the gold behind Denali was replaced by crimson. Some of the snow on the spruce forest fringe had frozen and white ice was clinging to the branches. The full moon came over the mountains and the light poured over the forest, making the trees glitter and sparkle as if studded with diamonds. For three miles I walked along the bars through this lovely moonlight scene.

Dog Sledding.
Caribou Hunting.
Unidentified Monuments.

November 22. Morning temperature 18 below zero. On a calm cloudless day we started at dawn, the dogs pulling the large sled that contained the small tent, robes, and a few provisions. The team was a good one, five dogs thoroughly trained in all varieties of work. The leader, *Nigger,* was a large black dog of mixed collie, mastiff, and native blood. He usually kept well to his work, setting a good pace on smooth trails and pulling hard in deep snow or on hills. He was obedient to the word signals—*mush,* meaning start; *gee,* turn right; *haw,* turn left; and *whoa,* stop. He always kept well in the trail and was intelligent in picking a route while off a trail, which was more commonly the way we traveled. He could not however be classed as one of the expert leaders often found among the dog teams of the North. *Bones* was always hitched behind him—a very large strong dog of Malamute blood with a mixed strain of the setter. He was a perfect dog for the place, of great pulling strength which he always used to the limit. Both *Nigger* and *Bones* had been so addicted to fighting that they had been castrated. This, while it very much reduced their combative tendency, did not seem in any way to reduce their strength or ambition. Behind *Nigger* and *Bones* came *Silas,* a pure Malamute, a natural-born sled dog, the most interesting one of the team. He was powerful, always willing to work, never shirked, never did more than his share. His traits and natural actions were wolflike, yet he was thoroughly domesticated and a perfect companion for man in the northern winter climate. If any of the other dogs disputed his rule he was always ready to fight, yet occasionally *Bones* would close with him and if permitted might have conquered.

During the whole season *Silas* never had to be punished. Behind him came *Jimmie,* a mongrel with native blood predominating; then *Sailor,* of native and mastiff blood, always next to the sled. Both *Jimmie* and *Sailor* were strong and capable, but neither had intelligence and both were inclined to shirk, so they received most of the whippings. We had two sleds, a large one on which six hundred pounds could be loaded, and a small Yukon sled for use in lighter work. When on a good trail or on ice, the driver guided the sled by the handlebars behind, but when the trail was rough, or while breaking through snow, he guided by holding a gee-pole in front, just behind the dogs.

Karstens had the reputation of being one of the best dog drivers in the North. He always took the best of care of his dogs, taking no end of trouble to prepare ample food, and arranging the best available spots for them to rest. He always insisted however on their strict attention to work and never permitted one to shirk. In case of failure on the part of any dog the discipline was severe. While on a trip they were generally chained to trees at night, and spruce boughs were always cut for their beds. None of them ever seemed to feel the cold; they would wade long distances through overflows on the ice without apparent discomfort, but on leaving the water would at once lie down and with their teeth clean the ice off their feet and legs.

It has been found by long experience in Alaska that dogs can do the best work if a good amount of cereal is added to their food. Rice and bacon have proved perhaps the best food, yet dried king salmon may be equally good, although more bulky to haul. We had a fair supply of rice and stale bacon that was used on long trips, to last to destination. Usually meat was given them, but they did not work so well on that as an exclusive diet. While at the cabin the meat was cooked, but when out working, it was often given raw. The five dogs together would consume an average caribou a week.

On this trip the load was not heavy and the dogs trotted along while we ran behind, but on reaching areas of ice we would sit on the sled, and the dogs seemed to take positive delight in quickening the pace. Since we were likely to have to pass through overflows we wore Eskimo mukluks obtained from Nome. These were made of sealskin, extending to the knees, and were waterproof.

In the canyon a fresh wolverine track was seen following the same course that I had noted on two previous occasions. Farther down, toward the north end of Sheldon Mountain, a small ram was seen traversing the slope by himself. After passing the caribou camp we turned up through the woods toward the spot where the moose had been killed. In places where the snow was deep I went ahead on snowshoes to break a trail for the dogs.

As we approached the ridge four moose were seen slowly walking single file among the short willows near the top. A cow followed by a calf was leading, then came another cow followed by a small bull. All cropped the willow buds until they heard Karstens shouting at the dogs a quarter of a mile away. Then, without looking around, they began to trot and kept on until some scattered spruces were reached, where they hid behind the trees and looked downward, trying to locate the source of the noise. We continued over the rough ground for fifty yards but apparently they did not see us until Karstens again yelled at the dogs, when they trotted away faster than before and soon passed out of sight. We quartered upward and on reaching the top saw the moose walking and feeding on the flats about two miles south. All had conspicuous bells, and the calf at that distance looked almost as large as the cows.

The sun set as we started along the foothills to the east, leaving the sky full of color. Below, the forested areas appeared limitless, giving as always the impression of the mystery of the wilderness. On the foothills bordering the north base of the outside mountain there was a good crust. The dogs easily pulled the sled and progress was rapid. For a while the upper half of Denali loomed up against a sky suggesting molten red iron, with vast banks of clouds glowing pink above it. Adjacent skies were fiery here, yellow there, and golden elsewhere, while rich colors extended all around the horizon—

pink, sea green, salmon, amethyst, and hues of exquisite blue.

Fox tracks were abundant over all this country, a rabbit had now and then wandered up the slopes, wolverine tracks were common, and everywhere the snow was dotted with mouse holes. We crossed two ravines filled with scattered spruces and found fresh moose tracks in each, showing that the animals were near by. But I did not intend to shoot here, as I hoped later to hunt especially for them nearer the foot of Denali. Just before dark about fifty caribou were seen several miles below on the flats.

It was long after dark when we reached the last draw near the East Fork of the Toklat and stopped at the upper limit of spruces, pitched the tent, tethered the dogs under the trees, and cooked dinner. While thus traveling together, as soon as a spot was selected for camp (if possible near a dead spruce) Karstens set up the tent after having cleaned away the snow with a snowshoe, while I took the axe, chopped down a dead spruce tree, cut it in eight-inch lengths, and split them in pieces suitable for the small stove. By the time the tent was up, wood was ready for a fire—always the first thing needed. Then, when possible, boughs were cut for our bedding and that of the dogs. A large pan was always carried for cooking dog food—rice and bacon, or rice and meat—and this was put on the stove as soon as our own meal had been cooked. Karstens had a robe of wolf skin and I one of coon skin. When camping together we slept on the wolf robe and pulled the coon robe over us. Kindling and shavings were always laid by the stove at night so a fire could be started quickly in the morning. It required only ten or fifteen minutes to warm the little six-foot tent in the coldest weather.

November 23. On this beautiful clear day the temperature rose from 11 degrees below to 10 above zero. Before daylight I was well up at the foot of the mountain, having seen numerous tracks of lynx, wolverine, and fox. Directing the glasses along the crest a single sheep was seen, and turning them toward the flats about four miles below, several small bands of caribou came into the field. At once I started toward them, and proceeding along the hills bordering the draw, saw six or seven caribou in an open space between strips of spruces two and a half miles below the camp. Entering the woods I was obliged to circle for a mile to get in a favorable wind before reaching the spot selected for an approach. The snowshoes breaking through the thin crust made so much noise that I took them off; but even then, though carefully forcing each toe through the crust, I had great difficulty in wading through the deep snow without noise. Soon the caribou could be seen in an open space but too far off to risk a shot, so I went back in the woods, circled, and finally reached the edge of the trees opposite them and two hundred yards distant. Before me were seven caribou, all without horns except one with very small ones. All appeared to be cows except the one with horns, which looked like a very small bull. They were digging away the snow and feeding on the lichen below.

After trying two photographs, I selected the largest cow and it fell to the shot, the others trotting a short distance to the edge of the woods, where they stopped to look. After another shot, aimed at the one with horns, all trotted into the woods out of sight. The dead caribou proved to be a bull that had recently shed its horns—the pedicels still slightly bloody. After dressing it I took up the trail of the others and found the one with horns dead about a mile below. The stomachs of both contained lichen and a few willow buds. In several places caribou tracks had been seen about the willows, but it was a surprise to learn that these animals really do eat a small quantity of willow—exclusive winter food of the moose. Camp was reached some time after dark. While in the woods I noticed that the snow had been trodden down around a small spruce tree that had been freshly rubbed naked and broken by the horns of a caribou bull. Is it possible that the bulls do this to loosen their horns for the purpose of more easily casting them?

There had been a peculiar haze all day, but the upper half of Denali was always visible, though faint and shadowy in a sky of brilliant gold.

November 24. Minimum temperature 15 degrees below. It was cloudy and misty when we took the dogs to the carcasses of the caribou killed yesterday; they were soon loaded on the sled and taken back to camp by Karstens. I went on toward the lower country and soon sighted caribou on the flats four or five miles below; they were the remnants of the small band I had stalked the day before, three miles farther west. Their trail showed that after the shooting they had gone only a short distance before scattering out to feed, removing the snow in patches three feet or more square until the lichen was exposed. I walked rapidly toward the lower bands, four in all, widely separated, with five to eight caribou in each. In one band of seven was one with long horns that seemed surely a bull. In two of the bands none had horns, but I knew they were bulls that had shed their antlers.

Before approaching the horned bull I saw the entire band lie down on a flat, where any possibility of stalking seemed doubtful. The only chance was through half an acre of scattered spruces that reached to within four hundred yards of them. So, after circling, I entered the spruces and advanced to the tree nearest the animals. The crust was very light, and the snow deep. Taking off the snowshoes I crept by degrees toward them for a hundred and fifty yards, where, rather than risk detection, I carefully cleared a space in the snow and sat with rifle ready for a shot. The 'bull' was resting with his head and horns stretched out on the snow. There was no wind. I whistled, but not one of the band noticed it. Again and again I whistled as loud as possible, but could detect no motion suggesting that any one of them paid the least attention to it. Then I began shouting, but still there was no response, although the noise must have been clearly audible to them. The indifference of these caribou is still a mystery. Sound sleep would not be a reasonable explanation. Finally, after I continued shouting, one turned its head in my direction, but that was all; it paid no further attention. Then I waved a mitten in a semicircle, yelling at the same time. This had the desired effect, for the one looking at me jumped up at once and all the others quickly came to their feet. The animal with the horns fell at the shot, the others trotted a few feet and stopped. Then I fired and killed another. As the others began to trot away a third shot brought back the thud of a striking bullet, but all kept on until out of sight.

The nearest dead one, a small bull without horns, was dressed; then, turning to the one with horns, my surprise was great to find *a large cow* with horns fifty-one inches in length! After photographing her, while the thermometer was more than 10 degrees below zero, I took off the entire skin and cut off the head. The only way I could prevent the skin from freezing, immediately after separating it from the flesh, was to keep putting it back against the body. The stomachs of both animals contained lichens exclusively. Although the fog had then settled densely and darkness was rapidly approaching, I took up the trail of the wounded caribou and followed to where it had lain down; but it had arisen and traveled on. By this time it was completely dark and the fog was so dense that I could not even see the ground.

Taking a course that, as best I could judge, would lead me toward camp, I started back to tramp upward over the nine intervening miles of bald rolling hills. For the whole distance the surface was hummocky, irregular, and full of deep hollows filled with snow. Since I could not see the ground, the walking on snowshoes was difficult and fatiguing. I constantly stumbled or fell. Enshrouded in thick fog, my strange sensations during that cold night tramp through the mysterious darkness will never be forgotten. It was necessary to move slowly and feel my steps, uncertain of the course, doubtful of the point I might finally reach. There was no motion in the air, and no sound was heard but the creaking of the snowshoes. I felt that I was a mere speck in the inky blackness of the ghostly vapor that enveloped me; the sense of complete loneliness was vivid, there was not even a consciousness that I was gaining distance. I pushed on and on, buried in mystery, my single purpose being to repeat each advancing footstep and avoid falling. After struggling on for several hours, it was a great relief to find the trail made by the dogs and sled. This soon led into the spruces where the fog, for a reason I cannot understand, was less dense. It was then only a quarter of a mile to camp. I have never experienced a more pleasing sight than that of the dimly lighted tent in which Karstens had left the candle burning while he slept.

November 25–26. Temperatures 16 to 20 degrees below. Karstens had shot three willow ptarmigan, which we consumed for breakfast. The meat of this bird, even throughout the winter, was tender and delicious, resembling that of the ruffed grouse. Its winter food here consists exclusively of willow buds. The sky was slightly overcast, but the air was clear, and while we were following the sled dogs along the trail, the tracks of a fox indicated that it had begun to run toward the dead caribou. It followed an irregular course beside the trail, always keeping on a crust hard enough to avoid breaking through. While approaching the carcass I saw the fox, a red one, running away, and three ravens feeding on the frozen entrails. All the carcasses were frozen solid.

While Karstens rested, I went to look for the wounded caribou and for three miles followed the tracks of the band it had joined, until convinced that it had not been sufficiently injured to cause it to separate or straggle behind. Two miles beyond was a band of fourteen cows, all with horns, and several miles farther, a band of forty or fifty more. Returning, I followed the dogs, which were struggling ahead pulling the heavy load.

The next day being so foggy that nothing could be observed at any distance, traps were set for mice and weasels, and one or two for foxes. A Nelson downy woodpecker was shot in the woods. This species was common in the timber all winter, particularly in the lower country. The afternoon was spent tramping below in the woods, studying tracks to find out what the caribou had been doing. They had browsed on willows, but in this upper area the crust was so hard that the bands had merely passed through in searching for places where it was easier to dig down to lichens. It is possible that had the snow been soft they might not have browsed on willows; nevertheless I observed willow browsing in many places below, where there was no crust. A few rabbit tracks were about, and for a short distance a wolverine had followed my trail of three days before. Visiting a few traps on my return, three red-backed mice and one shrew were found in them.

November 27. Morning temperature 22 degrees below. This morning four red-backed mice, two shrews, and a lemming were in the traps. There were literally millions of mouse holes in the snow, and while about many of the holes there was dung, still there was no evidence that the mice had traveled much on the surface between the holes. Often the heads of the mice were seen just pushed out of the holes, but when I was observed they were quickly withdrawn.

The morning was so misty that I did not start out until it cleared, about eleven, when I went east on the ridge to look for caribou. One had crossed the ridge early that morning, but no other signs were found on these upper hills and ridges; still, through the glasses several bands were seen far down on the flats. Returning to the foot of the mountain, I found the light waves so active that all objects observed through the glasses were blurred, so that sheep, if any had been there, could not have been detected. Today the mirage was present, but of varying strength; at times some objects appeared enlarged; at other times low mountains were reflected, later fading away.

November 28. During the night the thermometer had registered 12 below, yet at daylight a warm wind was blowing from the south and the mercury stood just at freezing. I was soon tramping rapidly toward the lower country, while the wind whirled great quantities of snow close along the ground, filling the hollows with deep drifts. Reaching an elevation, before going down to the more level ground, I saw a band of caribou five miles away on the flats. As I started toward them, another band appeared, coming from the southwest. They were traveling single file without feeding, evidently just entering this feeding area. Changing my course I went to intercept the incoming band.

While I was crossing a small ravine filled with scattered willows, three willow ptarmigan flushed, and flying out a short distance alighted on the snow, where they remained motionless. They blended with the color of the snow so well that I had to scrutinize the ground carefully to see them. Their attitudes and actions indicated consciousness of the concealing

quality of their immaculately white plumage, which is so pure
that it adds real beauty to the inhospitable desolation of the
snowfields. A snowy owl with much gray in its plumage sat
motionless on a hummock, but it saw me and flew before I
had approached nearer than a few hundred yards. It did not
go far before alighting, and remained in one spot as long as
I was in sight.

Finally I came near enough to the caribou to observe them
closely as they continued walking in single file without stopping. There were fourteen in all—eight bulls without antlers,
and six cows with horns of varying length, none very long.
One cow had lost the right horn. Three of the caribou were
so white as to contrast strongly with the others—in fact, at
a distance they appeared pure white. Concealed by the un-
evenness of the ground I allowed this band to pass, and then
proceeded toward the larger band still two or three miles
away. They all disappeared in a ravine, but coming closer I
saw the tips of a horn or two, and as they did not move, I
knew the caribou were lying down. This indifference when
resting concealed is in striking contrast to the resting habits
of sheep, for sheep would surely have selected a position
where they would have had a good outlook. Yet I have often
seen caribou resting in a manner similar to that of sheep.

As I was approaching this band they arose and began
to feed, for I could see many horns in motion. When within
two hundred yards of them, four came in plain sight on my
left and saw me before I could assume a motionless attitude.
They looked intently at me and then trotted down in the
ravine. This action seemed to alarm the whole band, for all,
about thirty, immediately trotted into sight. They apparently
knew my exact position, for as soon as they came in sight
they looked directly at me—all except a few calves with short
spike horns; these kept galloping about chasing each other in
play. Soon a few of the old ones began to walk away, but after
going a short distance stopped again to look The others stood
gazing at me while I snapped the kodak. Then I advanced
with the kodak forward, pressing the bulb twice more before
they became agitated with curiosity, when they began to move

back and forth until about half of the band started walking to the left while the others went directly ahead.

Knowing that those advancing to the left would soon receive my scent, wafted by the gentle breeze blowing in that direction, I carefully watched the effect. And sure enough, when they arrived at about the spot I had anticipated, up went their tails and off they galloped at great speed up the gentle slopes to the top of a hill. The other half of the band galloped toward them and as the two divisions closed together, clouds of snow flew up in all directions. Reaching the hilltop they stopped and looked back a moment and then disappeared. Hurrying on, I saw them about half a mile distant, walking toward and not far from the newly arrived band of fourteen, with which they mixed indifferently, all stopping to feed as if nothing had happened. Although I watched them for some time through the glasses no signs of nervousness on their part could be detected, nor did any of them seem more than ordinarily watchful.

All about, throughout these lower areas where the crust was thin or absent, the holes dug by caribou while feeding were so numerous that the snow was densely pitted. These diggings varied in age according to the coming and going of the bands.

In this band of thirty all were horned cows and calves, and three of them had antlers fully as large and as long as those of the cow killed three days before. Three of the cows were almost white, the others varying greatly—some very dark, others much lighter. It was late, and turning back I faced a sky aglow with gold and pink. On my way up the gradual incline over the drifted hummocky snow on the flat an occasional wolverine trail was passed, and now and then in the willow ravines a single rabbit track and the signs of ermine in their search for mice, while everywhere ptarmigan had been running among the willows. Another band of twenty caribou was approaching single file from the southwest, and when nearer, several of them were seen to be bulls without horns, the others cows—the horns of one very large. Shortly afterward I found in the snow a single large antler of a bull, that appeared to have been recently shed. Six ravens were feeding on the remains of the caribou I had killed, but no mammal tracks were about them. Camp was reached long after dark.

November 29. I left the tent at daylight in a fog, hoping it would clear so I could climb the mountain and observe the sheep. In the upper part of the 'draw,' brown leaves still clung to the willows, adding a pretty bit of color to the bleak surroundings. Two or three foxes had been mousing about close to the mountain slopes, but none had been caught in the traps Karstens had set for them. Several snowy owls were observed sitting on hummocks watching for mice, all as wild as the one seen the day before. As the air cleared, a gyrfalcon appeared sailing along the crest, and six or seven ptarmigan were running among the nearby willows. It seemed clear that the foxes had been looking for ptarmigan since there were but few mouse holes so high on the slope. Turning the glasses toward the lower country, I saw the band of caribou stalked the previous day, now greatly increased in numbers, feeding about the same area; and two or three small bands were traveling toward them from the southwest. As I reached the crest of a high spur, a cloud quickly blew over the mountain and I experienced the strange sensation of being suspended high in the mist. After waiting nearly an hour the fog thickened, so I was forced to descend blindly and reached the tent just at dark, when the whole country was densely buried in mist.

November 30. The morning dawned cloudless, and Karstens and I were soon tramping toward the mountain. Approaching the head of the draw we saw a red fox nosing about for mice. Soon it lay down, coiling itself on a little knoll. Descending into a hollow I had a good cover until very near, but when I cautiously stepped in sight with rifle ready, the fox had gone and was soon seen running up a ridge at some distance. It had undoubtedly winded me. Several snowy owls were observed—all very wild, not permitting an approach near enough for a shot. Karstens remained to look after his traps while I climbed the spur that leads up to the main mountain. Proceeding a short distance along its crest I found a low monument of rocks five feet high, and a little farther on a second, both made by piling large rocks on a boulder. A careful search failed to reveal records of any kind. A man who had been there hunting caribou three years previously told Karstens that he had seen these monuments, but Indians whom I interviewed later said they knew nothing about them. It is likely that they had been there a long time, perhaps made by Indians, yet no one that I knew in the whole country had ever seen Indian signs like them.

While standing near the monuments I saw eleven ewes and two small rams on the crest of the main mountain. These rams kept chasing the ewes together, keeping them herded. Lower on the same spur I saw a two-year-old ram and two ewes. They were feeding near me on the opposite side, not a hundred yards away, when a fine five-year-old ram came toward them. He saw me first, as I was moving, and at once turned and walked off about four hundred yards, then stood on the brink of the canyon and watched me for a long time. When I again moved, he ran, disappearing in the canyon and followed by the two ewes and the small ram.

The ascent to the crest was steep and rough, but finally I reached the top and looked off to the north, where the vast mysterious wildness of bleak snow barrens succeeded by dark forests stretched away in rolling uneven outlines until lost to vision. To the east were jumbled, rough, precipiced mountains, while bewildering peaks and ranges led to the snowy ranges on the south, and these in turn swept westward in immaculate whiteness culminating in Denali.

CHAPTER 21

Battles of the Big Rams.
Hunting Old Rams.

Scattered along the eastern crests were five ewe bands varying in numbers from five to sixteen, and with them were some lambs and very small rams. Four old rams of good age were visiting them, each independently of the other. The rut was active. Often two bucks would rut in the same band, but friendly relations were always maintained. They were not more than a quarter of a mile away, all in plain sight on the wide level crest. Concealing myself behind a rock, with the sea of mountains before me and with brilliant exquisitely colored skies above, I observed through the glasses the interesting actions of these beautiful northern animals while engaged in perpetuating their kind—which I hope will forever bring joy to those who shall be fortunate enough to see them where Nature has provided such a wondrously beautiful habitat.

The rut was active and four rams of good age kept serving the ewes in all the bands. Each ram served only one or two ewes in a band and then went on to the next. After leaving one band, a ram would both walk and trot toward another. Sometimes, while walking or trotting, the head was held in a natural position, at other times it was extended forward, the neck stretched straight out, the horns apparently resting on it. In one case two rams served ewes at the same time in the same band. One ewe was served twice at different times by different rams. None of the rams fed at all during the hour they were observed, but one or the other frequently walked off to one side and stood looking at the ewes, sometimes with head stretched out, sometimes with head held back and neck swelled out. After a while he would again visit the ewes.

But the undisturbed friendly possession of the ewes by these rams was soon to be disputed, for from afar along the crest came a single ram with large horns, much larger than those of the rams present, head drawn back, neck swelled, walking with springy steps in a majestic strut. None of the active rams noticed him. Straight toward them he came, nearer and nearer, without quickening his pace or changing his attitude. With intense interest I watched him and also the band he was approaching. One of the rams, having just served a ewe, appeared to take no notice whatever of the approaching rival, which then was within twenty feet and had not yet changed either gait or attitude. When he had advanced five feet more I detected the first sign that the smaller ram had seen him, for, as if he had been watching the approaching ram all the time and had been planning to meet him, he suddenly backed off and slightly lowered his head. At the same time the other also slightly lowered his head. They rushed at each other at speed, lowering their heads still more as their horns met squarely, butting together with a sharp knock. The smaller ram was knocked backward and a little sidewise, but recovering at once, both backed about fifteen feet and again rushed together. This time the smaller ram was pushed well back, vanquished. He quickly turned and trotted down the slope, the larger ram trotting after him to the edge.

During this battle all the other sheep—ewes and rams— merely looked on quite indifferently. Then the conqueror trotted back, smelled a ewe and served her, and immediately started walking toward the next band in leisurely fashion, maintaining the same attitude as that in which he had first approached. The ewes of the first band quietly resumed feeding, without apparent interest in the events about to follow.

As the big ram approached the second band, the smaller ram near the ewes simply looked at him without assuming any attitude of defense. The big ram walked straight toward him. At fifteen feet down went both heads and they rushed together. The sound of the shock was louder than before and I could see no advantage gained by either. Quickly backing, they again came together, and still again. Apparently no advantage was gained, but after both had backed and faced each other there was a pause. It was a short pause, followed by another rush. At the crash, the smaller ram was thrown back, after which he trotted off down the slope. The victor did not follow. He stood for a few moments quietly looking at the ewes; then stretched out his neck, elevated his nostrils, and maintained this position for at least five minutes. Then turning he walked toward the third band a hundred yards farther on, in my direction. There was no ram in this band of five. On reaching it, without preliminaries, he served a ewe; then at once turned and walked toward a fourth band of twelve, in which was one active ram. All the ewes stood between this ram and the approaching one and at first looked at him indifferently as they went on feeding. The ram with them also looked casually at the oncoming big one, occasionally turning his head and looking in other directions. He was the largest of the four rams that had been working among the ewes— about seven years old I judged. He seemed as large and heavy as the one coming to contest his rights and was the first of the four to show any early evidence of a combative spirit on the approach of a rival. When the newcomer was a hundred feet distant the younger ram walked around the ewes and faced him, head back, muscles apparently tense, and twice stamped a forefoot. The rival proudly strutted on, showing no sign of excitement, no hesitation, approaching as if no obstacle stood between him and the ewes.

I watched intently. When they were twenty feet apart, as if the fight had been previously arranged, both rams lowered their heads, rushed, and came together with a glancing blow, passing each other. The knock re-echoed from a pinnacle to the left. Turning almost instantly, both backed and this time struck squarely with a loud but duller sound than before, neither gaining any advantage. Again backing and again butting, the result was the same, though the larger ram seemed to be pushed a bit to one side. After this, both backed and stood facing each other. Then for a few minutes both seemed to relax and I thought they would not resume fighting. But the younger one made a motion and again both lowered their heads and came squarely together, striking so fiercely that both were pushed upward on their hind legs, the younger al-

most falling over backward. As they separated, they stood a
moment close together; then the younger walked away and
slowly went down the slope out of sight.

During the battle the ewes of the various bands either
looked on indifferently or continued feeding. When the vic-
tory had been gained the fourth ram left his band and walked
over the slope in the direction taken by the last vanquished
ram. The victor was thus left the undisputed master of all
the ewes. He merely stood near the band, without any attempt to mingle or to resume activities. He was not a hundred yards away from me, and through the glasses I saw
that a large piece had been freshly chipped off his left horn
and the whole end splintered. For a long time, until the light
had dulled, the victor stood in proud restful attitude, while
the ewes fed. Then one of the bands farther on walked down
the slope; the others fed in that direction and soon all passed
out of sight, the victor bringing up the rear of the last band.
His horns were close-curled, very massive, well wrinkled; he
was of good age and his head would have made a fine trophy.
After they had passed out of sight I saw, about a mile ahead,
the two defeated rams walking together in single file.

It was late, the daylight nearly gone, so I sought a ravine
and holding the butt of my rifle as a brake, began to slide
swiftly down the soft snow, the momentum increasing until
I was halfway down, when I saw a canyon directly below.
Becoming alarmed, I held the rifle butt so as to swerve to a
bare slope on one side, but was badly scratched before I could
stop. It was dark before I reached the foot of the slope, where
fortunately finding my snowshoes I followed my trail back to
the tent.

December 1–2. These two days were cloudy and windy.
Karstens took two sled loads of meat to the cache at the caribou camp and I put out many small traps for mice and brought
in the large ones, none of which had deceived the foxes—they
had walked all around them. The mice (*Microtus* and *Evotomys*) and the shrews (*Sorex*) were very abundant everywhere, and lemmings on the low ridges. Many of each species were taken in the traps but the majority had been eaten

by others. High on the ridge, shrews were trapped among
the lemmings. Lemmings travel between their holes much
more than do the mice; they were usually found in colonies, a
hundred holes sometimes close together, and the animals were
frequently seen running between them.

One afternoon was devoted to observing the snowy owls,
which, just outside of the high ranges, were very abundant.
The greatest numbers seemed to remain on the sloping and
rolling ground along the base of the mountain. While fairly
plentiful they were not so often noted below in the more level
country where, judging by the holes in the snow, mice were
less abundant.

I saw perhaps forty or fifty snowy owls that afternoon—
many gray of various shades, some very dark, a few very
white. All were wild and I was not successful in approaching close enough to kill one with the shotgun. All sat motionless, either on a hummock or a surface elevation, their heads
constantly revolving as they watched for mice. Though I
observed them carefully I did not see one attempt to capture
a mouse. They constantly changed position; after having sat
long enough in one place to convince themselves that no mice
were likely to appear, they would move on. One or another
was always on the wing. While sitting, viewed from most
angles, they were quite inconspicuous unless seen against a
skyline. Yet at times, from other angles, they were easily
seen. In flight they are difficult to follow with the eye as they
keep close to the snow-covered ground and constantly twist
and turn at sharp angles, quickly becoming lost among the
rolls of the surface. I did not see any of them fly far before
alighting to watch for mice. Inside the ranges they were
scarce, and up near my cabin and beyond were seldom seen.

Looking down from the tops of the ridges I saw many
more caribou on the flats than at any time before. There
were perhaps two hundred in all, in bands of varying size,
scattered not far apart, feeding nearer the forks of the East
Branch of the Toklat, but too far for me to go to watch them.

Karstens had spent several weeks in this camp the previous
winter, hunting caribou for market, and had carefully ob-

served them. At that time there had been little crust near the mountain and most of the caribou had seemed to feed up there. For seven or eight days none would be observed; then bands of varying size would begin to arrive from the southwest and feed for a day or two, after which they would move on to the east. At times Karstens counted as many as five hundred in this area. They came on an average about every nine days, and were always accompanied by a few wolves, which, although not often seen, were heard howling at night. While I was in the region I neither saw nor heard wolves.

From such information as I could gather from others who had been to the eastward in winter, this band of caribou traveled regularly at intervals, just outside the ranges, going east not far beyond the Teklanika River and returning in a circle near the timber, which they often penetrated, crossing the Toklat above the Forks and swinging over the hills. Their route crossed Moose Creek near its head and continued to near the foot of Muldrow Glacier, where they turned back close to the outward-bound route, thus completing the circuit.

After the rut, this method of traveling was continued all winter. The route varied slightly according to the depth of snow and condition of the crust. These were undoubtedly the caribou I had seen scattered about within the ranges during the summer. Later I found their routes and the limits of their travels toward the west, but did not follow them to the east. They were ever restless and on the move.

December 3. On this date dawn came at 8.40 and rifle sights could not be seen after 2.30 P. M. Having camped so close to the mountain we had not seen the sun since leaving the cabin. At dawn everything was packed on top of a load of meat and we started through a fog which hung in a thin layer over the ground, while the sky above was clear and full of beautiful colors, much softened when seen through the mist. The winds had drifted the snow in billows on these rolling hills so that the whole surface resembled a vast sea of white choppy waves. We, as well as the dogs, were soon covered with a thick coating of filmy frost, presenting the appearance of moving snow creatures.

Just before dark we reached the cabin, where we were greeted excitedly by the jays, which immediately fluttered all over me and then began to peck at the meat on the sled. When it began to darken, the jays flew to the trees for the night, two roosting close by the cabin window. After having been cramped in the little tent, the cabin seemed a palace. It was soon delightfully warm, several candles gave it cheer, a hearty meal was cooked, and we luxuriated long before tumbling into our bunks. The thermometer at the cabin recorded 26 degrees below zero, four degrees lower than the temperature at our tent outside the range.

December 4–5. It snowed all day, and the following day a mist hung low over all the country. I devoted the time to an examination of the woods, preparing specimens and photographs, assisting in the construction of dog kennels, and in attempting to find sheep, which the fog prevented. A few redpolls were still flying over the woods. Fresh rabbit tracks were noticed one day, but not again, as a great horned owl had appeared. A wolverine had passed through the woods a few days before, proceeding south for a short distance along the edge of the bar, and had then turned up along the slopes. Every nine or ten days during the winteer the tracks of a wolverine took this course. Tracks of another, at about the same interval, passed on the same course through the lower canyon. A third had a regular course up near the forks, and a fourth, one up through the divide west to Bog Hill. From these four trails that I had the opportunity to observe I inferred that it was quite possible that wolverines travel regular routes through the winter. Since these wolverine tracks always led up the bare mountain slopes I could never follow them far enough to determine the distance covered. It seemed probable that they extended ten or more miles, passing directly over the intervening ranges. By this time the cabin jays had become so tame that, when perched low on the trees, I could, without frightening them, stroke two of them.

December 6–7. The 6th was a clear day and at dawn I was off to secure, if possible, a good ram for a trophy. In addition to a few fall and winter specimens for the Biological Sur-

vey, I wanted four trophies in winter and spring pelage
for myself, each illustrating a different type of horn. Several sheep were observed on Intermediate Mountain, and
from opposite Bear Draw eight or nine ewes were seen on
the summit of Cabin Peak, with a ram of fair size standing
near but outside the band. At times it would trot about and
look off as if something were approaching. When near the
summit of the Draw I saw, up on the slopes of the south side,
two good rams and two ewes, all feeding close together. Not
far away a ewe appeared, running, followed by a ram with
splendid large horns; he soon caught up and served her. Then
another big ram came around a slope and going up to the
same ewe smelled her, while the other stood close by without
showing any objection. Two or three other rams and a few
ewes were feeding near but only this ewe received special attention. Two of the rams I recognized by their horns as having belonged to the band I had observed during the fall, and
it was certain that all were members of the same band.

I decided to stalk them and if possible kill the largest.
Rapidly snowshoeing in a diagonal course up through the
spruces and climbing around the slope, I crept forward but
found all the sheep in places where it was not possible to approach them. Therefore I waited in the hope that they might
move to some point where a stalk might be possible. Before
I had been there long the wind increased, squalls successively
whirled around picking up the snow in clouds that filled the
air. Except at intervals between squalls, I could see nothing, but presently caught a glimpse of all the sheep ascending,
led by the big ram. The ewes were next behind and were followed by the other rams. I knew they were going up to shelter and that soon they could look down and see me, so I rapidly
descended and returned to the cabin.

When exposed to snow squalls the bolt of my rifle always
filled with the fine particles of snow, so that evening I made
a band to protect it and afterward always carried it in my
rucksack. This was the only fault of the bolt action rifle that
was discovered during the winter.

At this period the sun, or probably its reflection, like the dim globe of a setting sun, came only just above the horizon of the mountain crests for an hour each day, giving five hours of daylight, which most of the time was sufficient to admit of taking successful photographs. Before daylight next morning I was well up the bar and soon saw three or four sheep near the spot where they had been observed the day before. One was a ram, but there was not enough light to enable me to see the size of his horns. Following my course of the previous day, I was ready to plan a stalk, should large rams be found with the others.

In passing through the woods I saw seven or eight beautiful white ptarmigan, not fifteen feet away, hide behind a spruce tree; they flushed while I was maneuvering to photograph them. Emerging from the trees I scanned the west slopes of the mountain leading to the forks. High up near the crest was a ram with splendid horns, slowly walking along the upper sheep trail, so familiar to me, toward the Bear Draw. He continually stopped to feed. The rugged and craggy west slopes of this mountain, furrowed by deep canyons and gorges, were twice divided by long and wide canyons extending up to amphitheaters near the crests, which were extremely jagged and bordered by many precipices. I planned a climb to the foot of a cliff near the trail, where I could watch the face of the mountain and at the same time intercept the ram should he continue, as seemed likely, to the Bear Draw.

After ascending the slope, I took off my snowshoes, stuck them in the snow, put on my creepers and zigzagged slowly upward to the last hundred yards, where the incline was very steep and icy, with deep snowbanks that might slide. Using my rifle as a staff, at times jamming the butt into the crust to make footholes for my steps, I finally reached the last snowbank below the icy cliff. Here I hesitated, fearing the snow would slide under my weight, but finally made the attempt and crossed upward to the rocks that had been selected as a waiting place. Here the surface was windswept and the footing secure. Putting on my squirrel-skin parka to insure warmth, and lighting my pipe, I took position and waited.

Fortunately, from this point the view was free along the west face of the mountain and around the slopes of the Bear Draw. The scene was inspiring: Directly ahead, in the direction of the big ram, were steep slopes with rough out-jutting spurs and canyons filled with snow or with walls bared by slides. To the left were the north slopes, equally rough, leading to the amphitheater of mountains surrounding the Bear Draw, some bare and windswept, others white, the rolling area of the basin contrasting with the severe surroundings. Below were the wide ice-capped bars, flanked by the fringe of timber, while above, the crests of Old Camp Mountain were touched with sunlight that made them glow. Beyond, across a sea of summits, the domed bulk of Denali, fringed with gold, loomed in the heavens. Behind were the outside mountains, their crests shining white in the sun's rays, while the cabin woods seemed like a dark island set in a sea of snow. Below, in the pastures leading to the cabin woods, a fox was careering in a hunt for mice, the grace and charm of his movements pleasing my senses during the hour he was in view. On Cabin Peak were a few ewes and lambs peacefully feeding about the very summit, while below, not far to my left, were all the ewes seen there the day before. But the largest rams were absent, leaving only two very small ones and an old one. The old ram carried a type of horns that I coveted, for they were very short, compact, and closely curled. He paid exclusive attention to the same ewe, often chasing her for long distances and closely following wherever she went. Finally he moved away a little and began to feed quietly. Later, a few of the ewes separated from the others and traveled up the slopes to the east, apparently forming an independent little band.

With these sights in view I waited with keen interest and joy until the sun sank below the horizon.

All this time I had kept an eye on the approaching big ram, catching frequent glimpses of him as he gradually came toward me along the sheep trail. He would appear over the crest of a spur, then disappear, only to reappear still nearer. Often he remained a long time feeding in a small canyon; at other times he loitered in plain sight on open spaces. A slight wind was gently blowing from me in his direction, but I did not feel that this would necessarily alarm him, for the slopes were rough and the eddies and currents of air uncertain. When he passed near the point where I had watched the large band passing through the mist and snowstorm on November 18, I recalled the contrast with this day of glory and color. During the two hours that I remained waiting he kept coming nearer, always pausing on the crest of each spur to look carefully, sometimes up, sometimes down, and even behind. Finally he descended into the last canyon between us. Then came moments of doubt and suspense for I knew that the trail divided, one branch leading directly to me, the other farther down, out of sight behind a precipice. Should he take that one, the outcome would be in doubt. Waiting anxiously, a glimpse of his horns showed that he had taken the lower trail. Having foreseen this contingency I hastened down to the east far enough to have the trail below within shot. The risk of the descent was forgotten in the eagerness of the chase, but I was quickly reminded of the danger by slipping, and only saved myself by using the butt of the rifle.

Reaching the selected point I waited, lying flat. But when, after a sufficient time, no ram appeared on the trail, I was perplexed. Suddenly his horns came in sight above, at the very spot I had but recently left. He had turned from the lower trail to the upper one. Quickly he rose into full sight and stood alert against the skyline, neck swelled, horns held a little back and tipped to one side. Then he turned his head and looked directly at me, his eyes seeming to pierce me. Never shall I forget the sight of that lordly ram standing rigid and alert below the rocky cliffs and jagged crests, with Denali beyond, majestic and magnificent against a sky painted with glowing colors.

My rifle shot echoed from the mountain walls; the ram jumped, staggered a moment, recovered himself, took two bounds upward and sank in his tracks.

When he stood at the spot where I had been waiting so long, why did he not wind my presence and run instead of merely looking about? He was only a hundred and fifty yards away.

As soon as I knew he was dead I walked a short distance around the slope and saw the ewes and the ram with compact horns. They were feeding quietly, apparently not having been frightened by the echoes of the shot. The ram stood a little apart broadside, presenting a well-defined target. He appeared to be nearly six hundred yards away; nevertheless I decided to try a shot at him—a risk I have rarely taken at such a distance. Aiming well above him I pulled the trigger. He ran somewhat wildly for a few yards, and vanished behind the point of a spur. At the same time all the ewes rushed up over the crest. He did not reappear and I thought he might have been hit.

While working my way up to the dead ram the wind increased, the snow began to whirl and the cold became penetrating. After photographing the ram, I cut away a large cake of snow beneath him, stamped down the rest, and carefully lowered him into the depression so he would not roll down the mountain while I was taking off his cape and head. The horns were large and massive, with ten rings, and were freshly chipped at the tips, the end of the right one having been cracked and slightly splintered. He carried evidence of recent combats: two flesh wounds on the face, one on the cheek, and a cut below the left eye. His face was very dirty and his long silky winter coat was stained brownish. The lachrymal glands were greatly enlarged, the areas around the eyes much swollen, the testes enlarged, and a strong odor emanated from the body. Heavy balls of ice were attached to both dew claws, and the slits between the cloven hoofs were heavily wedged with ice, indicating that he had crossed an overflow on the bar. The iris was yellow, the nose and lips dull blackish gray.

As I worked on the ram in clouds of drifting snow a jay suddenly came flying up from the distant woods and attempted to alight on the body, but quickly departed when I waved at it. After separating the ram's cape from the neck I cut off the head and examined the stomach, which contained exclusively grass, some of it green at the roots.

Lynx Killing Sheep.

December 8. An overcast sky shed a gloom over the country early in the morning as I tramped up the bars hoping to find the second ram shot at the day before. On the way I saw a raven flying down into the canyon in which the ram had disappeared, and while going up Bear Draw saw several others flying about the same spot, so I knew the ram was dead.

Ahead was Cabin Peak, with its smooth northern slopes partly windswept, its broken south face falling to the creek bed. This side is almost perpendicular and so eroded that little is left but a series of craggy cliffs irregularly furrowed with narrow shallow V-shaped gullies. When I came near the mountain three sheep were seen feeding low on the smooth incline near the cliffs. One was recognized as the smallest ram in the band seen the day before. When within a hundred yards, they passed around on the cliffs out of sight. Here, I thought, might be an opportunity to walk quickly along the face of the cliff and photograph them at close range. Slinging the rifle on my back and holding the camera ready, I advanced slowly and cautiously. Then I stepped up on an elevation in order to locate the sheep, which I knew had not suspected my presence. But they were nowhere in sight and, after advancing another hundred yards without seeing them, I thought they were probably in one of the steep gullies. When fifty yards farther on, my eyes caught a white object on the snow in the creek bed at the foot of the cliffs about ninety yards ahead. On looking through the glasses my surprise was great, for pressed into the snow was an apparently dead sheep, its head covered with blood, and crouched beside it was a lynx, intently watching me. I pushed the kodak into its case

237

and unslung the rifle, while the lynx ran a hundred feet up the creek and disappeared among the crags. Hurrying forward, I saw it climb among the rocks with easy agility and again disappear. Reaching a point opposite where it had last been seen I carefully scrutinized the crags and finally spied it standing on the edge of a cliff, looking down at me. Its color and markings caused it to blend almost completely with the rocks. It was at least a hundred and fifty yards above me, and in order to improve the chance of hitting it, I slowly moved back across the creek to a high sloping bank where, reclining against a snowdrift and with elbow on my knees, I could obtain a good rest for an aim. The lynx remained motionless, but at the shot dropped over the cliff, bounding and rolling until it fell over a small precipice into a gully, down which it slid swiftly to the creek bed. The bullet had struck it in the neck.

Picking up the lynx I carried it over to the sheep, coiled it as nearly as possible in the position in which it had first been seen, and photographed it. On examining the sheep I was shocked to find the head completely covered with bloody foam, and warm blood still streaming from the eyes. It lay as though dead, the forelegs doubled under and the head pushed into the snow. Grasping a horn, I lifted the head, when to my horror the poor animal struggled up on its forefeet, tottered a moment, and sank to its knees. I quickly dispatched it. Both eyes had been completely gouged out, and surrounding them were deep gashes. The signs in the snow were unmistakable, revealing exactly what had happened only a few moments before I came to witness the end of this horrible tragedy. At great risk I scaled the rocks three hundred feet up to the point where the attack had been made.

The lynx had come down from above, its tracks showing that it had crept along, crossing ravines, crouching on a rock or in the snow, all the time watching the sheep. It finally lay in wait on a jutting ledge over a gully about six feet deep. The sheep—a young ram—had fed along unconscious of danger, and as it stepped into the gully just below the lynx, the lynx had leapt onto the centre of its back, fastening its teeth above and below the left eye, both rows sinking with a firm grip well into the bone. The ram had struggled down the gulch, endeavoring without success to throw off its enemy. The snow in the hollow was churned and bloody, and here and there on the rocks at the sides were patches of blood, where the ram had struck its head. Then, where it had slid and struggled downward for three hundred feet to the creek bed, the snow for a space twenty-five feet square was trampled and bloody. The ram had been thrown several times during the struggle and undoubtedly the lynx had kept chewing about its left eye. It was evident that the lynx at one time had lost its hold on the left eye and had then fastened its teeth about the right eye, which had been completely bitten out—though the gouged space about it was not so large as that about the left. The left ear was entirely torn off. Finally the ram, from shock, loss of blood, and exhaustion, had sunk down in the position where I found it, and where it would shortly have died.

A careful examination of the ram revealed that only claw punctures were on the skin. Of these, there were eleven a little below and behind the left ear, all close together; there were three just below the right shoulder, four deep ones an inch to the right of the spine in the middle of the back, and three ten inches farther back, just to the left of the spine. The flesh under these punctures showed that the claws had been more or less buried in it. It was evident therefore that the lynx had landed on the back of the ram and buried its left fore claws in the neck below and behind the left ear, its right fore claws just below the right shoulder, its right hind claws in the middle of the back, and its left hind claws in the small of the back. Thus fastened to the back of the ram, with its teeth deeply embedded around the left eye, it had kept a death grip while the ram struggled downward. About the right eye and along the right side of the jaw the skin was full of perforations, showing that the lynx had fastened its claws there while chewing out the eye. Except about the eyes the ram bore no evidence of a tooth mark.

Only the forefeet of the lynx were bloody, but removal of the skin showed a bad bruise on the right haunch, and examination of the skull showed that the squamosal arm of the right zygomatic arch was fractured, evidently a result of striking against the rocks. The lynx was a male, weighing twenty pounds; the ram was about twenty months old and weighed 115 pounds.

On reflection I realized that at that time of year an attack on the eyes is practically the only method by which a lynx could kill a sheep. The hair on the neck of the ram was four inches long and so thick that it would suffocate an animal with such small jaws as those of a lynx, should it attempt to bite through at any point other than the throat. And a lynx could not get a throat hold, so the eyes present the only vulnerable spots and they can only be reached from the back.

After taking a series of photographs and skinning the lynx I went up the canyon and found the other ram. The ravens had picked out the eyes and bored through the walls to the fat of the belly. It was a fine buck with seven rings on its horns; these were particularly interesting as representing the narrow short compact type, a specimen of which I had greatly desired. Taking off its cape and head, I hurried back to the cabin, reaching it after dark.

December 9–13. After a careful examination and study of the skins and bodies of the ram and lynx, the following four days were given to observing the rut of the sheep. Watching the rams among the ewes I often witnessed many short battles, all single combats. Friendly rams remained among the ewes, serving them indifferently. The fights always occurred when stranger rams attempted to enter the bands. At times new rams intruded among the ewes and shared their privileges without apparent objection on the part of rams already with the band. My observations during the rut led to the conclusion that most, if not all, combats among rams at this period are between members of bands occupying different areas during the summer. Rams that have run together in the same band, although they may separate and perhaps travel widely, do not fight when they meet seeking ewes at the rutting time. In fact, twice I recognized rams joining a ewe band that already was being served by rams (one in

one case, three in another) of the same band, and no antagonism was shown.

It was clear also that not all the ewes were in season at the
same time. From early November until January new ewes
kept entering their period and the rams were constantly traveling to find those that were receptive. At this time the sheep
kept high on the mountains, on windswept slopes, and were
utterly indifferent to cold and wind. All through the winter
I saw bands resting in spots exposed to heavy winds.

Moose Hunting at Base of Denali.

December 13. Morning temperature 23 degrees below. In the afternoon we started with sled and dogs for Denali, where it was hoped some fine moose might be obtained. The tent was pitched in the spruces above my old camp, and being higher, the view over the flats and surrounding mountains was practically unobstructed. The snow was deep, and the moon, almost full, poured its light over the bars, making the mountains glow and the frosted trees sparkle. On our first evening the little tent was faintly illuminated by candle-light; the sparks shot up out of the small stovepipe, the dogs were chained, each to a tree, and complete silence reigned. The day had been cold, clear, and in the low country perfectly calm, but above, about the crests, the snow was driving in clouds on a high south wind. The thermometer had registered 20 degrees below zero when we arrived at 2.30, but at eight in the evening a light south wind began to blow and the temperature soon rose to 18 above. The winds blowing at a high altitude during the day had been the precursor of a warm wave.

December 14. Morning temperature 20 degrees below. We started at daylight against a strong south wind which continued all day, making traveling unpleasant. We were retracing our usual course to the foot of the Muldrow Glacier,* the large sled carrying a load of 400 pounds. I went ahead, treading down the deep snow with the smaller snowshoes, to break a trail on which the dogs might more easily follow. There is much misconception about the realities of traveling by dog sled. On well-packed trails, where the snow has been beaten

---

* It was not until 1910 that the Lloyd party penetrated the ranges to this region and informed the world of the course of this great glacier.

down and frozen, as on level ground and rivers, the sled if not too heavily loaded is easy to keep on the trail by holding the handle bars; and the dogs, after they have started the sled and gained some momentum, go along easily, walking fast, often trotting. Under such conditions, and when it is not storming, dog-sledding is simple and delightful. On the glare ice of overflows and rivers the dogs trot merrily along without effort, and the driver, if not too cold, stands or sits on the sled cheerily shouting encouragement to the dogs, who respond to the exhilaration and joy of such travel. But in the woods or on uneven, hilly, rough, or mountainous country without trails, sledding is quite another matter—it is hard work for both driver and dogs. In order to steer, the driver holds the gee pole ahead of the sled, which on rough ground is difficult to hold in its course, and the dogs merely keep low and pull hard. Such driving is nothing less than heavy freighting —equivalent to freighting with horses over rough lumber roads.

Often we had to unhitch the dogs and ease the sled down steep banks or slopes, and in order to climb the hills were obliged to lighten the load and make a double trip. It was not cold, but the wind whirled clouds of snow about, affording little chance to view the surrounding mountains. After passing the foot of the slope opposite the spot where I had shot the bear in August, 1906, I saw my staff still standing in the 'nigger head' where I had left it before starting to make the stalk. After we had double-tripped over Bog Hill it became clear that we could not make the expected destination before dark, so I hastened ahead down the creek to a spot in the willows near one of my old camps. Here such dry wood as would be necessary was gathered, a space in the snow was dug for the tent, willow brush was cut and thrown on the ground for a bed, and then, although it was dark, I started back to meet Karstens. Returning more than an hour later, we pitched the tent and soon had the fire going. Water was still running in the creek below thick ice, so we did not have to melt snow.

December 15. The day was clear and calm but uncomfortably warm for traveling (thermometer 23 degrees above).

We pulled across the bars to the head of the canyon and in an hour and a half covered the six miles through it. An occasional raven, several ptarmigan, and the tracks of fox and wolverine were the only signs of life seen during these two days. Below the canyon was much open water and the almost continuous overflows made the deep snow mere slush. We put on mukluks and drove the dogs ahead as they pulled and strained to overcome the difficulties of this increasingly heavy work. We were overtaken by dark with the open creek between us and the fringe of timber on the other side, while on our side there were not even willows. The slush continued, and the dogs were exhausted, but we had to force them ahead as it was necessary to cross in order to find fuel for a fire and dry our legs, which were very wet. Besides, the temperature was falling. After a time the dogs became so exhausted that all lay down in the water, and it was only by whipping them that they could be forced to struggle on. But we had to continue. After two hours of this I feared they might give out completely and leave us in a serious position. Finally however we found an ice bridge and the dogs, when headed across it, almost bounded forward toward the poplars and willows a hundred yards beyond. Arriving, they all dropped down and curled up in the harness. Karstens vigorously cleared away the snow and put up the tent by the light of a pile of brush I had cut and fired. I chopped wood for the stove and soon we were warm and the teakettle was boiling. When I went out and unharnessed the dogs, what was my surprise to see them run around in the snow, chasing each other in play without showing fatigue from their long exhausting work of the day. Their vitality was almost beyond belief.

December 16. Shortly after leaving in the morning we reached smooth ice on which, for three miles, the dogs trotted. This was followed by deep snow through which trail breaking was heavy work. As we turned into the woods leading up the valley of McKinley Fork the depth of the snow increased and we pulled through it until nearly dark, when we made a good camp with plenty of wood among the hospitable spruces. Denali, great and majestic, loomed ahead in the moonlight.

For two days we had been traveling in near view of the whole range, surmounted by richly colored skies.

December 17. I shall always remember vividly this day's travel of eight miles or more up the bars of McKinley Fork to the limit of spruces at the lower end of the dead moraine of Peters Glacier. It was calm, with patches of clouds above in the deep blue sky. Directly ahead was Denali, surrounded by an amphitheater of lower peaks, and with lofty ranges sweeping away on both sides. Such a view is so overpowering and sublime that words cannot describe it. And now with the heavens a glory of color, the greatest of word artists could scarcely hope to convey more than a suggestion of the depth and intensity of its impressiveness. It was before us all day, and under varying lights for many days thereafter. I am glad that my journal is filled with records of it because neither memory nor imagination could bring back its magnitude, nor my emotions in beholding it.

Groups of heavy clouds hovered along the crests of the entire range, all highly colored and gold fringed when touched by the sun. Some were of varying shades of gold, yellow, pink, and crimson, all deepening with the sinking of the sun, while at the same time the vast snowfields took on a reflected rosy hue; and clouds forming about Denali appeared like vast camp-fires succeeding one another in the spaces beyond. These extraordinary colors filled two-thirds of the horizon—the shades, tones and tints ever changing, the glowing cloud banks ever reconstructing in new forms. And Denali, 'The High One,' towering above the other snow-clad peaks of the southern horizon, lifted itself up into the resplendent heavens.

Straight ahead for five hours we traveled along the middle of the wide ice-capped bars of the river, which was now mostly open and rushing with a subdued roar between walls of ice twelve or fifteen feet high. We were enclosed in a forest of dark spruces, their tops presenting an irregularly spired outline against the horizon below and the snowfields of the higher slopes beyond. We were in a remote wilderness and felt that we were then in the presence of animal life hidden in the nearby spruces. A few rabbit tracks led from the

woods over the bars, which also were crossed by numerous
weasel tracks. Once all the dogs of the team pointed their
noses to the west, stopped for a moment, and then jumped
against the harness trying to bolt in that direction. It became
so difficult to keep them on the course that the whip had to be
applied to prevent their turning toward the scent, which
evidently was that of a cow moose and her calf whose fresh
tracks crossed the bar near by. Farther on, the fresh tracks of
two caribou crossed the bars, and still farther up, those of a
whole band. A wolverine had traveled up the bar the night
before, and numerous ptarmigan were seen near the edges of
the woods.

Before dark we pulled up a steep bank at the upper end of
the trees at the terminus of the moraine, its hummocky snow-
covered surface extending in billowy outlines to the great
mountain. Here were the tent poles of a camp made by Judge
Wickersham, the first man to attempt to climb Denali. Abundant dry spruces surrounded it and the open river was near.
Quickly our tent was set up, a fire started, and preparations
made to pass the night. Denali, although six miles distant,
seemed almost above us.

December 18. Dog feed for only three meals remained,
so it was necessary at once to secure meat of some kind before specializing on moose with large horns. By daylight I
had crossed the river on an ice bridge just above camp, bound
for the west ridges where caribou might be found. In starting, as I stepped out of the tent, a flock of little chickadees
greeted me, two or three ravens flew by, and some ptarmigan
were clucking near. It was warm, fairly clear, and a light
breeze from the southwest determined me to hunt in that direction. On reaching the ridges I found caribou trails in the
snow, and the tracks everywhere showed that at times these
animals fed there. All through the woods I noticed trees rubbed
clear of bark by the horns of moose or caribou. I tramped in a
southwest direction all day without seeing an animal of any
kind, or any fresh tracks except those of the wolverine,
though ptarmigan were numerous. The snow was deep, filling the gullies and hollows, and there was little crust.

I can never forget this day, when I first viewed from an elevation the wild expanse of country buried under the winter snow. The skies about Denali were radiant with glory, the invisible sun filling the clear distant heaven with a golden background for the richly colored clouds that hung over the range. The western horizon was completely filled with a heavy bank of superimposed strata of different shades of pink, a color phenomenon I had never before witnessed and could not understand. It was like a solid rainbow of richly contrasted shades of pink stretched across the western horizon and walled high into the sky. When there later in December and in January a similar phenomenon was of frequent occurrence. The majesty of these stupendous mountains with their gorgeous skies, brilliantly colored clouds, and dark coniferous forests certainly cannot be surpassed in wondrous beauty anywhere in the world.

The north face of Denali, owing to frequent snow-slides, presented numerous spaces of bare black rock. At this time there was little snow on the upper reaches of its glacier cap, as shown by its deep blue color. The wide forest stretching away to the south at times seemed black, while the area of Lake Minchumina to the northwest stood out white. The great moraine and the bordering outside ranges were white variegated by areas of exposed rock—yet all was so softened under the colored skies that there was no feeling of desolation. So intense was my joy in these surroundings that it gave me a feeling of detachment from the world—the senses overpowered by the beauty and glory before me.

December 19. Morning temperature 15 degrees above. With some anxiety I started for the east ridges in the hope of securing meat for camp. The day was calm and warm, with fairly clear skies, the temperature gradually lowering in the afternoon. Having to pass through a wide strip of woods where the snow was very deep I used the long snowshoes, and climbing a high ridge reached the fields so familiar to me— recalling my experience there with caribou the year before, when the slopes were green. Now all was white, buried under deep snow; and since no wind stronger than a breeze had swept the surface, the depth was fairly even. From the crest, which was much higher than any point reached the day before, Denali rose before me under tinted clouds and skies, with the same bank of color in the west. In the distance far over the black forest I could see the Nuchusala Mountains at the right of Lake Minchumina, and much farther to the left the Sischu range beyond the Kuskoquim, their crests touched by the sunlight and shining white above the black surrounding forests. Here and there the low sun behind the great range sent its rays through passes in the mountains, and later I often had the joy of beholding many of the peaks tipped by its light.

Keeping along the crest of the ridge I continually scanned the country below but saw only old caribou tracks, and going south, I looked among the willows at the head of a branch of Grayling Creek, which came down through the valley just east of the ridge. It was about a mile wide in places and dense willows standing in three feet of snow extended over large areas well up toward its head. Seeing nothing in that direction, I returned and was continuing north somewhat below my camp, when well below and two hundred yards out in the willows, my eye caught a dark spot, which the glasses soon revealed to be a moose without horns, lying down. Going ahead to a more favorable point, I suddenly saw another moose, one with large horns, rise up and begin cropping the willows. In studying a possible approach I was much puzzled to find a way to keep out of sight and at the same time approach against the gentle breeze that was blowing down the creek. After selecting a route in a wide circle that would bring me quartering in a favorable wind, I went back out of sight; then going over the top I gradually worked downward, often sliding over steep snowbanks where in order to get out again I was obliged temporarily to take off the snowshoes. At last, reaching a selected point, I looked over and saw both moose, still distant, quietly feeding—the one with horns, very dark, the one without horns, quite brown. The snow was so deep and the snowshoes so noisy that I felt great anxiety as to the result. After approaching so near that the noise might be heard, I proceeded most carefully, one step at a time, always letting the pressure of my weight bear slowly on the snowshoe to avoid the creaking. Often in plain sight, it was necessary to stoop and watch for opportunities to advance unseen; yet by degrees I was getting nearer and the animals were still unsuspicious. Finally, in order to gain the last hundred yards to a point where I would be within shot, the greatest caution and patience were needed to avoid noise or movement when the game might be facing in my direction. At first I tried to advance without snowshoes, but finding it impossible to pass the hollows, I had to put them on again and work along a step at a time.

The breeze had ceased, no sounds were audible, when suddenly the rolling thunderous roar of an avalanche reverberated along the valley.

The last fifty yards were behind a concealing knoll. I do not know how long it took to accomplish that distance, but at last, coming to the top, I slowly raised my head only to find no moose in sight. Dropping down and thrusting my snowshoes ahead, I slowly rose to my full height and then saw the horns of the moose among the willows, and close by a dark bulk which I knew was the other moose. Both were lying down. Cocking the rifle I advanced a few feet to the edge of the knoll, when the bull with horns, nearly two hundred yards away, heard me. Instantly turning his head toward me he sprang to his feet, his side well exposed. The other moose rose almost at the same time, but I fired before the bull with horns again moved. He dropped in his tracks in a manner that meant immediate death. The other started off, attempting to trot, but each foot sank deeply in the snow. A bullet through his right hind quarter caused him to totter a moment. He then tried to go forward but could not get through the snow, and lay down. As I approached, he struggled up and tried again, but could not start and again lay down, remaining until I had crossed the creek and was very near. Then he rose and faced me. Taking my kodak I walked up within twenty feet, when he attempted to rush at me and even gained a few feet; then stood, ears laid close, lips compressed and moving, his dark eyes snapping viciously. I dared not go nearer, but after a couple of exposures with the camera, finished him with a bullet in his heart.

The colors of the heavens about Denali had deepened, and it is doubtful if ever before had moose been stalked and killed by a sportsman under such radiant skies and in the midst of such a glorious landscape—though in the future no doubt these noble animals will often be viewed under Denali and beneath December skies.

The last bull was very large and his horns had apparently been shed within two weeks. His skull made a worthy specimen for the Biological Survey. The other moose was very dark, his horns well proportioned, the blades large with a spread of fifty-nine inches. Neither animal had a 'bell,' but instead, a thick oval appendage ten inches long hanging about six inches down from the throat.

After photographing them I took off my snowshoes, cleared away the snow, and removed the cape and head of the dark moose. It was cold work and before it was finished the moon had risen and was throwing its soft light on Denali. After hanging the cape on the willows, I gralloched the other one and then built a large fire to dry my hands and arms, which had been bared during the skinning; I then smoked my pipe while contemplating with joy the experiences of the day and the mystery of great Denali illumined by the moonlight. Then came the return tramp over the ridge to camp, where at nine o'clock I arrived with a small burden of meat. The dogs had been howling and on my arrival jumped about me in joyful anticipation. They had long before detected the odors that told them what had happened. Each was immediately given a piece of liver, and Karstens was made happy by knowing that dog food in abundance was now assured.

December 20. This morning we took the dog team over the ridge to the dead moose, loaded the sled with both heads, the complete skin of the brown one, and the other skin, together with as much meat as possible, and returned.

While skinning the moose I noticed a small ram and three ewes low down on the ridge close to the mountain on the east side of the valley, where the snow was very deep. The sheep seemed much agitated, running back and forth through the snow and continually looking back, watching the mountain. Two ravens also had discovered us and while we were working kept flying about in great excitement. At camp we stretched the green moose hide across the bunk Karstens had constructed and thus for the rest of the time had a warm sleeping couch.

It has been asserted that an animal never falls dead in its tracks from a heart shot, yet my bullet struck the dark moose low in the shoulder, smashed it, tore through the upper part of the heart and the opposite ribs, and lay under the skin well mushroomed but not at all shattered. This moose dropped dead without even a struggle. Both animals were mature and very large, the brown one the larger and older. They had little fat but the meat was richer and more tender than that of any moose I have ever tasted. The food in their stomachs consisted exclusively of willow buds.

December 22–23. During the early morning a light snow was falling, and while Karstens took the dogs to bring another load of meat, I built a high cache, on which the meat was placed. Two jays found it and immediately began to pick at it, continuing until dark.

After cutting the meat off one of the skulls I started directly west to break a trail over the succession of ridges to the next valley, five or six miles away, which I wanted to examine, hoping that later a moose with extra large horns might be killed there.

The snow was deep on these ridges and between some of them were small ponds now frozen and buried. Old tracks of foxes and wolverines were much in evidence. Denali, surrounded with radiant skies and seen through a lightly falling snow, was on my left. Finally, looking down from the top of the last ridge I saw the line of spruces bordering the river which, smaller than McKinley Fork, emerged from Peters Glacier through a narrow gap at the east corner of the mountain. The valley was covered with willows and from its centre rose an isolated hill.

Two moose were seen walking up the river a mile to the south, and after traveling in that direction about an equal distance along the high ridge bordering the valley, I saw that a third moose had joined them. Only one of the three had horns, and they did not look very large. Two miles farther south were three more moose feeding in the willows, but since it was nearly dark and their horns could not be distinguished, I retraced my steps, beating down the trail to camp.

Because of a dense fog lasting all day on December 23, I remained in the tent and completed the preparation of the moose cape for a trophy. After ten o'clock in the morning the cold rapidly increased so that by dark, when the fog had lifted, the thermometer had fallen twenty degrees. It rose somewhat, however, during the night. At this date the first indication of dawn came at 7.30 A. M.; at 2.15 P. M. it was too dark to see rifle sights, and at 3.15 it was dark.

December 24. Karstens left very early for Glacier City, to spend Christmas and a few days with the miners there. The day was calm and clear and I tramped rapidly over my trail to the west valley, reaching it in about two hours. Many mice had crossed it during the night, and a fox and a wolverine had been near it. In this region, where the snow was everywhere deep on the ridges and slopes, the mice did not bring their holes to the surface as they did in the Toklat country; but among the willows on the flats their holes were abundant.

In about two hours I reached the valley and soon saw a hornless moose feeding at the base of the mountain, three or four miles to the south; then three others, a mile nearer. Descending, I crossed an ice bridge over the river, proceeded diagonally across the flat and climbed the ridge, where the animals could be more clearly observed. While climbing, a beautiful snowy owl flew from a hummock on the ridge top long before I approached it. I was within plain sight of the three moose; they were lying down and none of them had horns. But half a mile to their left a bull with large horns was feeding. After circling the ridge and coming nearer, I saw still another bull, his head obscured by the willows. Since the horns of the first one looked very large, I planned a stalk and descended to the river bottom where I could advance under cover of the willows. After crossing the river I had not gone far before five more bull moose suddenly came into view not two hundred yards away, all quietly browsing among the willows. They had just arisen from resting. Only one had horns and these were small.

Their presence added greatly to the difficulty of stalking the bull ahead, and to avoid alarming them it was necessary for me to withdraw some distance and circle around far beyond. At last I reached a thick clump of willows on a swell in the surface, within a hundred and fifty yards of the bull. After carefully creeping up, I rose with rifle cocked. There, broadside to me, was the big bull, feeding without suspicion; but his horns were not so large as those of the bull I had already killed. Near him were seven hornless bulls just up from resting; and a hundred yards to the left were three more, only one of which had horns, and those small.

Unfortunately my kodak failed to work, as a film of ice had formed over the lens. Lowering my rifle I stood motionless watching the moose as they slowly moved about, cropping the tops of the willows. While advancing I had noticed that the bull with large horns at times stood still with his head hanging down in the attitude common to bull caribou at rest. All the bulls were large and their bells were oval-oblong; many of them were dark, others more brownish.

Finally I deliberately walked forward. As soon as one saw me in motion, all immediately turned their heads toward me for a moment and quickly trotted away toward Denali, about two miles ahead. The two bulls with horns brought up the rear as the others, in irregular formation, awkwardly plunged through the snow, advancing zigzag, their forefeet always sinking deep through the soft crust, their hind feet apparently not breaking through. Every hundred yards they would stop for a moment and then resume flight. But when they reached the base of Denali they scattered out and began to feed among the open patches of low willows—not very plentiful so near the mountain.

It was long after dark when I reached the tent. Again

alone in this magnificent region, I enjoyed a sense of complete isolation with nothing to disturb my undisputed possession of it. The constant subdued roar of the river beneath its ice walls and the continual thunder of the avalanches on Denali, reverberating through the cold air, were the only noises that broke the winter solitude.

December 25. Morning temperature 29 degrees below. A heavy fog that hung low in the morning did not lift until ten, and when I had climbed the east ridges, it descended again and became so dense that I could see only a short distance in any direction.

After I had returned to the tent, two prospectors who had come to the lower McKinley River to stake some claims suddenly appeared through the mist. They had met Karstens the day before and had come to get a supply of meat. Taking a load from the cache they soon departed.

December 26. Morning terperature 31 degrees below. It was my purpose to spend this day about the base of Denali. Fog hung low when I rose before daylight, and although it continued, I started up the river bed. On the snow-covered moraine wolverine tracks were everywhere abundant, and old moose tracks were plentiful among the stunted willows along the river and elsewhere for three miles above the timber. After proceeding four miles I found myself above the fog. Denali, immaculately clear, towered above me, its lower slopes crossed by a thin band of pink vapor, the sky above it pink, yellow, gold, crimson, of ever-changing color tones. Conies were bleating all about on the moraine, and willow ptarmigan were abundant. A chickadee flttted among the uppermost willows, and old tracks of a small band of sheep, coming from the outside mountain to the west, crossed the moraine toward the eastern foothills.

Great avalanches continually kept falling with crashing sounds that rolled among the outside ranges. The river near the glacier was open and the murmur of its current was audible though subdued. The whole vast north face of Denali was mutilated by avalanches, exposing the underlying black rock. The great mountain rose above me desolate, magnificent, overpowering. The lower ranges were white, while below, nothing could be seen but the fog, which took on the appearance of thick clouds. I felt, as never before, completely alone in the presence of this mighty mountain; no words can describe my feelings.

That evening in the little tent I was absorbed in vivid memories of the Christmas days of happy childhood.

December 27. Temperature 32 degrees below.

A blanket of mist indicating low temperature hovered over the country, yet it was not so dense as to discourage me from setting out at daylight to climb the east ridges. When I left the tent before dawn the aurora was brilliantly flashing, the long shafts of light highly illumined through the mist. Soon after arriving on top and looking below, my eyes caught a large dark object on the slope a hundred feet above the willow flats. It was a hornless bull, his bulk looming big and black through the mist. For some time he stood as if merely meditating among the snowfields, his form somewhat indistinct, though magnified in the mist, giving a mysterious impression—a feeling of the presence of an animal of a prehistoric age. No sound disturbed the stillness, the atmosphere was motionless, the painted skies around Denali reflected delicate colors in the haze below. The bull, two hundred yards away, and I, stood motionless—the only evidences of life in that vast panorama of winter landscape. Then he slowly walked down to feed among the willows, passing within a hundred feet of the spot where the two moose had been killed some time before, but not seeming in the least to notice the signs of the tragedy or the trails of men and dogs; yet he was more watchful, much more so, than were the two bulls seen there before. Among the willows he became indistinct, and as the vapors thickened he gradually faded to invisibility, leaving only a vivid impression.

The fog now obscured everything, obliging me to return. The remainder of the day was spent putting out mouse traps and preparing specimens of red-backed mice that had already been caught. Two jays had been picking away the meat in the cache to such an extent that it became necessary to destroy them. One or two ravens were always about but apparently they did not dare, even during my absence, to touch the meat.

December 28. Morning temperature 33 degrees below. An almost imperceptible breeze had completely cleared the fog when early in the morning I started over the east ridge, hoping to go far beyond to investigate the willow flats in that direction. Just before I reached the top, six rock ptarmigan flushed from some low willows and flying about a hundred yards plunged into the soft snow, where they remained motionless. They were invisible until I had advanced to within twenty-five yards. Some were half buried in the snow and did not move until I was within ten yards, when they flew off and disappeared.

Looking down from the top of the ridge I saw on the other side, a mile and a half away, the bull I had seen the previous day. He was already alarmed and was throwing his nose about in an effort to locate the direction of the scent that was warning him of danger. He immediately began to climb the slope, then turned and trotted along the side, plunging through the snow and stopping every few minutes to look across the flat in my direction. Finally he turned upward, climbed the ridge crest, and disappeared over it. It was interesting thus to observe the long distance, even in the cold of winter, at which a moose could detect and become alarmed by the odor of man.

December 29–31. These three days were cold (temperatures 38 degrees to 35 degrees below) and the night mist, dispelled at dawn, left the atmosphere clear and calm. The same glorious colors painted the skies, intensifying the splendor of Denali; and each night the sky was highly illumined with the radiance of brilliant auroras. Putting on my fur parka I would go outside the tent and watch the moving dancing paths of auroral splendor as they flashed across the star-sparkled heavens. Often the lights circled from north to south and sinking behind Denali, faintly illuminated it. Great streamers and ribbons were thrown out, some curving back, some with light green or mauve fringes bordering the opalescent tints of the main display.

While tramping during these intensely cold days, my nose continually froze, each day becoming more tender and sensitive from the constant rubbing to thaw it out. Otherwise I felt no cold while in motion but realized that exercise must be continued. Every day during the hours of daylight I tramped over different areas among the ridges to the northeast. Many old tracks of moose and caribou were seen, but not one of these animals. On December 31, when I reached the tent after dark, Karstens and the dogs were there. That day the skies about Denali had been full of richly colored clouds, and the year died as the heavens were flashing with auroral fire.

Hunting at North Base of Denali.
Antics of Caribou at Sight of Trail.
Lynx and Raven.
Another Sheep Killed by Lynx.

January 1, 1908. Morning temperature 37 degrees below. At daylight I started over the west ridges. The sky was clear, the trail frozen hard, while with snowshoes on my back I walked rapidly, the sharp crackling sound of my footsteps indicating the intenseness of the cold.

Not far from camp was the track of a bull moose that had crossed the trail on a walk and a little farther on had returned on a trot, evidently having scented the camp and rushed back in fright toward the timber. The fresh track of a wolverine crossed the snowshoe trail and was followed for some distance by that of a fox. Ptarmigan abounded near the willows, and later another track of a wolverine was observed, and also tracks of two foxes, while weasel tracks were everywhere among the willows on the flat. Looking north from the crest of a high ridge I saw a large band of caribou three miles beyond, on a ridge near the flats; and, reaching the top of the last ridge, saw two or three fresh moose tracks leading down the slopes, and discovered the caribou, then far to the north, traveling in the direction of my trail. No moose being visible among the large areas of willows below, I descended and crossed to a low isolated ridge in the middle of the flat, noticing on the way that many moose had crossed my old snowshoe trail without becoming alarmed—the scent probably having vanished from it by that time.

From the crest of this ridge I was able to see new areas of willows when suddenly four moose came in sight. One seemed to have large horns. Leaving snowshoes and rucksack, I crept forward through the deep snow against a light but piercing wind—sufficient however to freeze my nose and chill me quickly. Moving cautiously to a low willow bush within two hundred yards of the animals and looking through the glasses I was greatly disappointed to see that the largest horns did not exceed those of the bull already killed. Two of the other bulls had very small horns, and one, the largest of the four and somewhat lighter in color, had no horns at all. All were feeding without suspicion, although now and then one would carelessly look about.

Creeping back to where my rucksack had been left I went below out of sight and jumped about to warm myself and rub my frozen nose. Then, taking the kodak, I again crept forward. Three of the moose were still feeding, the one with the large horns lying down. To avoid disturbing them, I had to move slowly, even stopping at times. Because of this inactivity I became colder and colder and my nose froze again. Having crawled so long through the snow I was so chilled that I began to feel numb and could not attempt the slow task of creeping nearer, as would have been easily possible in warmer weather. With kodak ready I advanced fifteen or twenty yards before the bull that had been lying down jumped up and faced me—he being the first to become alarmed. Pointing the kodak I pressed the release and even had time to take another exposure before the three trotted off toward the base of Denali, a mile ahead, where they began to feed quietly as if they somehow felt secure in the protection of the great mountain.

As I hurried back on my trail it was long before the chilling effect of the stalk gave way to more active circulation— in fact, not until after the exertion of climbing the first ridge. While returning I found that the caribou had approached close to my trail but had not crossed it. They had followed close beside it for fifty yards and then had swung out in a wide circle among the hills. Their tracks on the snow showed that the trail must have created confusion among them, for some had traveled directly in it a short distance and then had jumped out and run for a short distance. All had trotted back and forth near it and many had run beside it.

After crossing a couple of ridges I saw the caribou, forty or fifty in number—all cows with small horns—directly approaching the trail about two hundred yards ahead. They advanced without hesitation to within twenty yards of it and stopped, apparently looking at it. Then, with seeming restlessness, a few walked forward, extending their noses to better catch the scent, and stepping cautiously as if trying to avoid breaking through a crust on deep snow—though the snow was so soft that they sank eight or more inches at every step. Those in front stopped four or five feet from the trail, all straining their necks forward, trying to smell it. Those behind walked about with curiosity. One cautiously stepped on the trail and after slowly letting one foot down to rest in it, suddenly jumped back six or seven feet and ran back to the rest of the band, all then trotting short distances back and forth or in circles. A few walked up to the trail and jumped or trotted back, only to approach again and repeat the same maneuvers. When all had come close to it the confusion became so great that I could not recall all the movements to record in my journal. One advanced thirty feet by a series of diagonal leaps, each seven or eight feet in length. Another galloped forty or fifty yards close along the trail and then wheeled and circled back to the others. Some were very cautious, repeatedly creeping up to it and slowly backing away. The calves simply trotted or walked aimlessly for short distances in any direction, keeping near the others. Two jumped into the trail and galloped a few yards directly in it, then, bounding out, stood motionless for a few moments to watch the others. One sprang clear across the trail and quickly turning, jumped back again.

These and many other maneuvers continued for ten or fifteen minutes, giving the impression that at first the caribou were confused by curiosity rather than by alarm, and then that they were merely playing with the trail and the faint scent of my tracks, as if in sport. Finally one started, leading close along the trail, repeatedly stretching its neck and smelling, with its nose held close to it. Then the rest began to follow, some leaping about, others making short dashes along it—all acting as if they were following a well-marked line which, although it stimulated them to play, must not be crossed. As they passed out of sight over a low ridge I followed and noticed where they, before I saw them, had approached the trail, played about it and then retired in a wide circle to approach it again at the point where I had watched them. Arriving on a ridge I saw the last of the band going over another high ridge a short distance ahead, and so hurried along. On top, the trail turned to the right, going a little below the crest directly toward Denali.

When I reached the top, not fifty yards ahead and a little below, the whole band was standing close together, all looking directly at me, having heard my approaching footsteps. There they stood in the snowfields of the ridges where the rosy hues of the sky were reflected on the snow, and behind them towered the stupendous background of Denali. During such moments, if one loves the wild sublimity of the mountains and the presence of wild game animals, he feels profoundly the haunting mystery and isolation of the deep recesses of the unknown wilderness and is consumed by a happiness so intense that not even the imagination of a poetic genius could adequately express it.

The caribou, after five or six minutes, began to quarter toward the left, now and then stopping to look at me, and then continued to circle until the gentle breeze gave them my scent, when they galloped in fright over another ridge. These were the only caribou I saw that winter about Denali. It was long after dark when I reached the tent and enjoyed the warmth of the little stove. The sights and experiences of New Year's Day of 1908 can never fade from memory.

January 2. Morning temperature 31 degrees below. This evening a note in my journal states that the day had been much warmer. Throughout the winter I found that when the thermometer was 35 degrees or more below zero there was a distinct sense of cold that called for caution. Between 20 and 30 degrees below it was delightful and I felt exhilarated while tramping, and even perspired freely when running or climbing. Temperatures between 30 and 35 degrees below caused no inconvenience when the wind was not blowing. In fact, the winter cold, if one is properly protected at the extremities, is pleasant until it falls below −35 degrees.

Karstens went out to set traps for both foxes and mice, while I again went over the east ridge, still hoping that a moose with great horns might be found. A very fresh lynx track crossed the snowshoe trail, and when on the ridge toward the spot where the moose had been killed, I noticed that two or three moose had trotted over it from points above my camp. Evidently they had come from the west, well up the glacial moraine, and had been frightened by the scent of our camp. As I later learned, they had not even paused in the east valley, but had continued across and over another ridge. From this and other experiences it became clear to me that after being frightened by scent, moose go much farther without stopping than when frightened by sight.

On two occasions I had seen a raven sitting on a rock on the side of the slope opposite where the entrails of the moose were left, and now I noticed it on the rock picking at something, evidently a piece of frozen meat it had carried there. Suddenly I saw a lynx crossing my trail near the bed of the river not far from the remains of the moose. The raven left its post, flew over the willows near the offal and after twice swooping down at the lynx, which evidently was about to begin a meal, flew a little beyond and disappeared among the willows, quickly rising again with something in its beak which it carried back to its perch on the rock. I interpreted this to signify that the lynx was feeding at the nearer entrails, while the raven flew beyond to those of the other moose. I hurried down into the willows near enough to see the spot where the lynx had been, but evidently it had heard me and had withdrawn. As I stood motionless, the raven came flying over me, and circling to a point two hundred feet below the entrails, swooped down, quickly rose, and twice more circled and swooped at the same spot, after which it flew back and perched on the rock. I then knew that the raven had pointed out the location of the lynx. Cautiously moving a few feet to the right I saw his ears in the exact spot indicated by the raven and then was able to make out his head. Aiming just below it I fired and the head disappeared. The raven, as the shot sounded, was flying directly over me and continued without pausing, going directly to the lynx and swooping at it, then returned to its post. The lynx was still sitting, its head a little lower, the bullet having creased its neck. It was soon dispatched.

The only reason I had been able to get this lynx was that the raven had clearly indicated its position. I reflected on the possibility of constructing a story exploiting the intelligence of the raven, had this experience fallen to one of the imaginative nature writers! It might have been claimed that by flying over me the raven had first fixed my attention on itself, and then had indicated the position of the lynx, knowing that by thus making it possible for me to kill him I might rid it of the animal that was keeping it away from its food supply and devouring it himself. But unfortunately for that theory I had noticed lynx trails from several directions leading to the entrails, and recalled having previously seen the raven swooping down near the entrails and acting in the same manner as today. It had merely flown over me, as ravens often do when approached near a carcass on which they are feeding. It had swooped at the lynx, as probably it had been accustomed to do whenever one had approached the entrails. Once I saw a raven swoop at a bear sleeping near a carcass high on a mountainside. This day the raven had merely been acting in its customary way.

The lynx was a fine mature male weighing about twenty pounds. Like all lynxes I have killed in the North, it was infested with fleas. Putting it in the rucksack, I returned to the tent.

January 3. Temperature 23 degrees below. Several redbacked and meadow mice and a few shrews were found in the traps. The morning was so mild that I felt uncomfortably warm while climbing the east ridge. In one place I almost stepped on two rock ptarmigan that had remained motionless in the snow. In the shade of early morning or evening it was almost impossible for a man to see ptarmigan unless they were moving on the snow, yet I doubt not that a fox could easily locate them by scent, or perhaps even by sight.

From the top of the ridge I swept the opposite slopes with

my field glasses. The day was exceptionally clear, and I saw a lynx feeding on something whitish which I thought could only be a sheep. Immediately descending I crossed through some willows, and looking again saw plainly the carcass of a sheep. The lynx, having already seen me, was curled alongside of it looking in my direction. It remained motionless in that position all the time I was crossing the flat and until I had started the ascent. But before I was within shot it ran along the slope to the left and disappeared in a gully filled with willows.

Reaching the carcass of the sheep I found the whole tragedy written on the snow and made a most careful examination of the record, following tracks and signs in all directions. The slope, which was very steep, was covered with ten or fifteen inches of snow. Exactly a hundred and fifty paces above the carcass a mass of rock rising abruptly from a canyon projected six feet above the slope. The lynx, concealed just below the rim of the canyon, had crept back and forth for a hundred feet, many times squatting, watching the approach of two sheep. At first they came single file directly toward the canyon and a little above the rock where the lynx had lain in wait. But when a hundred feet away from the canyon they turned diagonally downward toward the rock, and then, slightly separating, descended abreast. The lynx, still concealed below the canyon edge, had crept—quickly no doubt—to the rock up which he had moved from the inner side, and there lay waiting to pounce on the passing sheep. At exactly eight feet from the rock the sheep had turned downward and descended eighteen feet, when the lynx leaped off the rock and, bounding down to the nearest sheep, sprang on its back and fastened its teeth around the left eye. Neither of the sheep had started to run before the lynx sprang; then the uninjured one ran downward and joined three others that had been feeding a hundred yards away. All four then ran out on the last spur. It was on this spur that Karstens and I had seen a ram and three ewes in an agitated state on December 20, and it seems almost certain that the lynx had made the attack only a short time before we had sighted them.

The snow indicated that after the lynx had sprung upon her back, the ewe had slid downward for fifty yards to a place where the incline was less steep, and for the next hundred yards had slid or struggled back and forth irregularly to the point where I found her. Here had been a desperate struggle, as shown by the marks of the lynx's feet on the snow. From the point of attack to where the ewe finally fell not a single mark indicated that the lynx's feet had touched the snow; this is my reason for inferring so positively that it had sprung on her back and remained there. The snow for the entire distance of the struggle was spattered with blood.

The ewe was in her second year, weighing I should judge between a hundred and thirty and a hundred and fifty pounds. The whole side of the frozen carcass had been eaten away as far as the neck, which as yet was untouched. The head was pressed into the snow, the left eye was completely gouged out deep into the bone of the skull, the left ear also was included in the area that had been chewed off. Neither the right eye, right ear, nor right side of the face were scratched, the skin on that side not showing even a claw mark. But the skin on the left side of the head was well punctured by the claws, indicating that after the ewe had fallen, the lynx had grasped the face with its fore paws in order to gnaw deeper into the eye. Evidently it had been lying near the carcass for several days, as shown by a circular bed in the snow worn down to the moss. The lynx had made numerous tracks up and down the canyon and also high along the mountain slope to the south.

The little band of five sheep, including the victim, had come over the Peters Glacier, having made the trail seen on December 20, and after crossing the ridges, had traversed the flat and ascended the mountain, circling around above the head of the canyon. It is likely that the lynx had seen them approaching and had remained on the slope watching for an opportunity to make a kill.

After taking off the head of the ewe and putting it in my rucksack I climbed around the north face of the mountain and descended into the next creek, a branch of the Clearwater, well enclosed in an amphitheater of rough snow-covered mountains. Here a dark snowy owl was sitting on a rock well up a slope, appearing lonely indeed in such a retired recess—yet the mere presence of life in such a spot added cheer to the cold desolation. A wolverine's trail followed down another slope, and I was greatly surprised to see the tracks of a single rabbit coming directly down from the peak. Following it, I saw where the rabbit had gone up another slope to some willows high on the side. The willows on the higher slopes were all very stunted and probably for this reason it was convenient for rabbits to reach up and feed on their tips. No other explanation would account for the presence of rabbits in such remote high places. Weasel tracks and also those of a fox were about, but since no track of a moose was found I turned back. It was dusk when I crossed the flats, but looking back, the lynx was again seen feeding on the carcass and I at once turned, climbing up a gully until opposite, when it became so dark that I had to advance to within twenty-five feet of the sheep before I could see it. The lynx was not there. It was dark when I had again descended to the flats, but my trail to the tent was easy to follow.

January 4–6. On the morning of January 4 Karstens took some steel traps to set by the entrails of the moose and about the sheep carcass, while I went over the west ridges and carefully examined all the willow flats without seeing a moose. Four moose, however, had come down from the east slopes and traveled for some distance in my snowshoe trail. This showed quite conclusively that moose are not frightened by the trail of man after the scent has disappeared.

On January 5 Karstens and I went to examine the traps. While descending to the flat I saw the lynx again feeding at the sheep carcass. He suddenly rose and ran upward, apparently in fright. At the same time we saw a wolverine running toward the dead sheep, thus explaining the sudden departure of the lynx—for evidently the relation of a lynx to a wolverine is one of fear. The wolverine kept on to the carcass and began vigorously tearing it and feeding on it, every little while throwing up its head to look about, probably for the purpose of detecting a possible intruder. We thought every moment that he would get into one of our traps, and finally, judging from the way he seemed to struggle, believed he was caught. Descending, we had crossed over the flats when the wolverine, still a mile and a half away, saw us and at once ran upward. Though often pausing to look at us he kept on to some cliffs just below the top, where he disappeared in a crevice. Wild indeed was this wolverine!

As we approached the sheep we saw the lynx sitting quietly two hundred yards above, looking down at us. Advancing a little farther we saw him slowly crouch down on the snow, in which attitude he remained until we reached the traps, when he sneaked off to a canyon on the left.

Both traps had been sprung. After resetting them I climbed to search for the wolverine and found that he had entered a narrow crevice in the cliffs, doubtless leading to his den, for his tracks led in from all directions.

A gyrfalcon was soaring about the mountain crests, often standing out in relief against Denali and the brilliant skies, adding life to the glory of the view. A few conies were heard, and high on the ridges very small shrews were common and some were in the traps; but nothing had been near the entrails of the moose.

When returning over the ridge I looked back and saw the lynx walking across the slope toward the carcass, but he had not reached it before the darkness obscured him. Verily, neither man nor wolverine could keep him from the prey he had fairly won by his swift fierce attack. The next day, owing to this trait of persistence, he stepped into one of my traps and was held fast. As we approached he lay back in fighting attitude, and at the moment of greatest anger, as I was photographing him, his ears lay flat, his eyes seemed to enlarge, and he tried to spring at me. He was a fine male lynx weighing as near as we could judge twenty-two or twenty-three pounds. I took off his skin while Karstens reset the traps in the hope of catching the wolverine.

By this time the atmosphere had become too hazy to see clearly for any distance, and we returned to the tent.

January 7. Half an inch of snow fell during the night, and on the east ridges the higher temperature had brought out more mice, for on the fresh snow their tracks were now abundant everywhere. There were also a few trails of lemmings, but nothing was in any of the steel traps.

I started across the flat intending to climb high and wander about the mountains to the east. Although the day was cloudy, Denali was clear, and there were colorful vistas of radiant sky. Passing the sheep carcass I circled upward to the very peak, 6,000 feet high, right against the northeast shoulder of Denali.

Donning my parka I spent a long time enjoying the vast panorama—the great white stretches of the Alaska Range on either side, the limitless forests of black spruce to the north, the mountains above illumined by the sun as its light found paths through the changing clouds.

I saw no signs of sheep or moose except the trail of the fated sheep that had crossed toward the watching lynx.

During my stay, no fewer than four great avalanches thundered down the face of Denali, starting as mighty moving masses perhaps fifteen thousand feet above me, and obscured by clouds of snow as they rapidly gained momentum, accompanied by an increasing roar until they finally crashed between the mountain walls. From the far side of the northeast shoulder of the great mountain came more frequently the deep rumblings of distant avalanches that were devastating the slopes above Muldrow Glacier—further evidences of the destructive operation of colossal forces.

January 8–9. A dense fog covered the whole country, yet we went east to examine the traps, returning as the fog became sufficiently transparent to permit views of the rich but not clearly defined colors of the sky. Nothing was in the traps this day or the next, when Karstens visited them, while I went to the west without seeing a single moose or caribou.

January 10. Morning temperature 26 degrees below. Being anxious to get back among the sheep I decided to spend only three more days in this region before returning to my cabin on the Toklat—one for a final visit to the base of Denali, one for a tramp to the willow flats on the west, the third for packing and breaking camp. The day was clear and the air sharp as I walked up the moraine over my trail, now frozen so hard that snowshoes were not necessary. In fact, after once the trails had been traveled, snowshoes were not needed on any of them. At the end of the trail the snowshoes were put on and I struggled up and down over the uneven moraine to the very base of Denali. Here were tracks of a cony and one of a lynx, the latter so fresh that the animal must have passed just before I appeared. Ptarmigan tracks were numerous everywhere but I did not see any of the birds.

While at the foot of the mountain three avalanches came down—one merely a large area of snow sliding down the glacier toward the west and transforming itself into great volumes of snow clouds, accompanied by a dull muffled roar. Practically all the ice of the glacier blanketing the north slope of Denali was clear deep blue, its snow covering having slid down the almost perpendicular slopes.

After wandering about searching without success for signs of sheep, I returned and tried several photographs from a point where Denali just filled the finder of the kodak, then paused longer to indulge in the delight of viewing the great mountain against its background of richly colored sky and clouds. Below it the vast black forest swept away, the white surface of Lake Minchumina conspicuous in its midst, the crests of the mountain beyond and those of the ranges about Moose Creek all glistening white in the rays of the low hanging sun, which reached them through paths in the ranges. As I watched the colors change and deepen, a great mass of pink clouds of surpassing loveliness settled over the western crest of Denali. I shall never again view this mountain in winter, with its skies of exquisite color, but those who do in the future may perhaps realize the depth of my feelings.

January 11. Temperature 20 below. At daylight I was crossing the west ridges with a feeling of sadness, for it was my last tramp under Denali, The High One. The day was cloudless, without a breath of wind—ideal for photography— and the temperature was perfect for enjoyment. At the high-

est point on the ridges I used two films, including panoramic
views of the great upheaval of mountains before me, hoping
thus to preserve a suggestion of the scene. But alas! All the
negatives of this trip, though sufficiently clear, fail completely
to convey any adequate impression—in fact hardly a suggestion—of the vast mountain world about me. It must be left
to others with more suitable cameras and a better knowledge of mountain photography to give the world correct pic-
tures of these landscapes.

From the top of the ridge near the river flats four hornless moose—one large bull and three small ones—were seen
walking across to the timber, while on the crest I noticed
fresh fox tracks and a snowy owl. Then, well up in the flats
toward Denali I spied two more moose lying down in the willows. Descending and advancing out of sight until opposite
them, I climbed up again, and looking over saw that they were
very large hornless bulls, now up and feeding. After wandering over the flats, careful not to disturb them and without
finding signs of others, I returned. It was early evening, the
sky colors were changing and a fine half moon was mounting higher and higher above the eastern peaks of the foothills. Yellow gold changing to crimson suffused Denali; to
the west was a solid layer of pink; and to the north, above
the sun-tipped peaks and crests, the horizon took on purple
tones. Every day the sunlight was playing lower on the mountains and the sky colors were becoming more yellow.

Reaching camp, I found Karstens back with all the traps.
The sagacious wolverine had not again approached the carcass. What a contrast to the less suspicious lynx! In this region animals have not been trapped except by one man, who
one winter set a few fox traps eight miles below. It is outside the trapping area of the few Indians about Lake Minchumina; no Indian signs whatever were in evidence. Yet
here the wolverine and the lynx display exactly the same degree of caution that is characteristic of their kind in regions
that have been trapped for many years—suggesting that much
knowledge may be gained of the traits of animals by observing the effects of long-continued trapping. No animals of the

North have been so much and so successfully trapped as the marten and the lynx. Yet, after many years of excessive trapping, they continue to walk into traps almost without suspicion. On the other hand, no animals in these regions have been less trapped than the wolf and the wolverine, yet both are so cautious that it is difficult to capture either. Martens and lynxes do not become educated to caution; wolves, foxes, and wolverines are inherently cautious. Animals that are most preyed upon, like rabbits, mice, and squirrels, walk into traps indifferently; some animals that prey upon them but are not themselves in danger from natural enemies, avoid traps with much intelligence. I believe that the causes of these differences lie so far back in the race history of these animals that they cannot now be determined.

A strange fact observed after shooting the lynx near the remains of the moose was that no raven was seen near them again so long as we were there. A possible explanation may be that ravens may have been killed by poisoned baits put out by some of the few men in the Kantishna region.

January 12. The last day in this camp was occupied in preparing and packing specimens and arranging for our departure. It was now clear that the older moose, those having the largest horns, had shed them before my arrival, although most of the hunters with whom I had discussed the matter had told me that moose do not shed their horns until well along in January. This was another confirmation of many experiences in the North, namely, that it was necessary to learn by personal observation the facts in regard to the life histories of boreal animals.

At the north base of Denali neither rabbits (with one exception), squirrels, cow moose, nor any birds except those mentioned, were observed in the area of my hunting. That winter, and probably every winter, Denali and the adjoining high unbroken Alaska Range on either side, shelter the adjacent region on the north from wind. The snow therefore lies deep, and one must go several miles east or west to find windswept surfaces. For this reason sheep rarely feed there, and caribou seldom attempt it. Both go east or west, where the surface is more exposed to wind. Moose however come up from the timbered regions to crop the willows wherever they grow, except high on the mountain slopes.

When Denali National Park shall be made easy of access, with accommodations and facilities for travel, including a comfortable lodge at the foot of the moraine of Peters Glacier —as surely it will be—it is not difficult to anticipate the enjoyment and inspiration visitors will receive. They wll be overwhelmed by the sublime views of Nature's stupendous upheaval, as so many have been by the Grand Canyon of the Colorado, Nature's great excavation. And it may be added that no one can realize the greatest glory of Denali until he shall behold it in December or early January, the period when the sun is lowest, when the sky radiances reach their greatest intensification and deepest coloring. Thus to view Denali towering in a sky of unimagined splendor evokes a state of supreme exaltation.

Back to the Toklat Cabin.

January 13–19. On January 13, a beautiful clear day, with Denali looming up in a yellow golden sky and the clouds to the east showing a rosy blush, we gave word to the dogs and started down the broken trail. After going a mile a cow moose and calf were seen feeding among the willows only two hundred feet ahead, but they saw the dogs and trotted back into the woods. Fresh moose tracks crossed the bars, and at one point the fresh tracks of a band of caribou. We crossed the Muldrow Branch as a cow and calf moose trotted away to the left; then continued over the ridges, across the lake, and down Moose Creek to the little mining camp of Eureka, where the night was spent at the cabin of Aleck Mitchell. On starting I ran ahead of the dogs continuously for eight miles and suffered therefrom. To start abruptly on such a run before first walking some distance was most unwise, resulting in severe pains in the groins that returned for three days whenever I attempted to travel. The next morning three hours were required to reach the cabin of Tom Lloyd at the head of Glen Creek. Lloyd, with Charley McGonigle, Billy Taylor, and one or two others, was prospecting a mining claim near the crest of a high ridge behind the cabin. There we remained for three days—until I was in better condition to travel.

Later, Lloyd organized the party, including McGonigle, Taylor, and Pete Anderson, which made the ascent of the north peak of Denali. McGonigle turned back just before reaching the summit of the north crest, but Taylor and Anderson kept on and planted a flagstaff on it. This feat, successfully achieved by these hardy Alaskans, untrained and inexperienced in technical Alpine work, was one of the most remarkable mountain climbs ever achieved. The summits they

had always had in view were those of the north ridge of
Denali, which they believed to be the highest, and they wanted
to fly the flag from a point where it might be seen from the
north side. Had they so wished, with a little more effort they
could have reached the highest point of the mountain, which
is on the other ridge.

From the crest of the high ridge behind Lloyd's cabin extended a magnificent unobstructed view, reaching along the
Alaska Range east and west of Denali. While standing there
with Tom Lloyd, I told him of the double ridge summit and
of the great ice fall descending easterly from the basin between them; and asserted my belief that if no technical difficulties should be found below the upper areas, the great
mountain could be climbed from the ridge bordering the north
side of the glacier. This was the ridge up which it was later
found possible to make the ascent. At that time no one had
suspected the course of the Muldrow Glacier or had identified it with the ice fall I had observed. However, I believe
that the plan later conceived by Lloyd was wholly independent
of what I had casually told him, and that he had probably
forgotten all about it.

Willow ptarmigan and redpolls were abundant throughout
these ridges, and I saw both a hairy and a downy woodpecker.
On January 17 we pulled out from Glen Creek, crossed over
into the spruce timber, through which we traveled a mile,
then another mile over a divide to Willow Creek and three
miles to its head, then to Myrtle Creek and down to Clearwater, the western tributary of the Toklat. Here we met
Burns, a trapper more than sixty years old, who had a cabin
above, near a mining claim. Burns was one of those men, at
that time frequently met in the North, who had been so long
alone, isolated in the woods, that the presence of others seemed
to annoy, rather than please, him. He had already reached the
stage of hallucinations—a fate of so many who have lived
similar lives.

After a while we camped; and the following day reached the
Toklat and followed it up stream for several miles until just
before dark, when we pitched the tent. It had snowed heavily

all day, so we were unable to keep the trail; the river was high and there were continuous heavy overflows.

By two in the afternoon of January 19 we reached my cabin. When we entered the woods, the jays flew about greatly excited, and as I held out my hand two of them immediately alighted on it. I soon brought a supply of meat, but instead of eating the small pieces offered, they only seized them and flew off to store them.

The self-registering thermometer left at the cabin recorded 37 degrees below zero, the lowest during our absence. After the dogs had been fed and the cabin heated, it seemed more like a home than many homes in civilization to which I had returned after an absence in the wilderness.

That day the sun was up just above the crests of the main ranges for more than two hours.

January 20–21. Minimum temperatures 35 degrees and 34 degrees below zero. At daylight on January 20 I went up the river to observe the sheep. The recent snow was still on the mountain slopes, all the bars were white, the ice extended all the way across and in places was lifted up to a height of seven or eight feet. Owing to the pressure of the dammed waters below, it was continually cracking with a sound like that of a rifle shot.

High on the slopes on the south side of Bear Draw were about thirty ewes and a three-year-old ram; no large ram was near them. They were feeding and resting, and their coats were exceedingly dirty. No sheep were observed on the mountains beyond, and no tracks except those of mice on the new snow.

While examining the high Indian cache the next day, I found that during our absence the lips and noses of all my caribou scalps and skins stored there had been completely eaten off either by the jays or the red squirrels, and that numerous mice had tunneled through the moss between the cabin logs and had destroyed much meat.

January 22–23. Minimum temperatures 25 degrees and 12 degrees below zero. I went up the creek leading to the divide near Sheldon Mountain and traveled well over on the other side. Only four sheep were to be seen; they were high up and too far distant to show the sex. There was also a fairly fresh moose track, and that of a lynx crossing it. The high cascade falling from the cliffs of the canyon on the south side of Sheldon Mountain was frozen for several hundred feet up from the bottom, presenting a fine contrast to the dark rugged canyon walls.

A heavy wind blowing all the next day swept off much snow from the mountain slopes. I remained at the cabin, developing films, washing clothes, and attending to other necessary chores.

January 24–25. Fresh meat was again needed as the fat on our supply had become rancid, rendering it unfit for use except as dog food.

At daylight I started up the river. The sky was clear and the air calm below, but the upper slopes were harassed by a violent wind, great clouds of drifting and whirling snow obscuring the crests. Such high winds were frequent during the winter months and always signified that later in the day they would descend and blow strongly over the lower slopes.

Three inches of snow had fallen during the night, but in the early morning no tracks were observed except those of a lynx that had come out of the Bear Draw, and those of numerous ptarmigan among the willows on either side of the creek. Shortly after starting up this draw and not far below Cabin Peak I saw two ewes, each with a lamb almost as large as its mother; and near the point where I had killed the big ram on December 7 was a band of twenty or thirty ewes.

While perfectly calm along the bed of the creek and for some distance up the slope, the higher parts of the mountain were swept by such a violent wind that I could scarcely climb against it, and the fine snow particles driven into my eyes almost blinded me. Finally, reaching the rocks on the south side some distance below the peak, I crept out on the slope and saw that the ewes had moved to a still higher position and could not be approached without taking alarm. There was no alternative except to descend, go up nearer the head of the draw, and circle upward around the mountain.

Then followed a sheep stalk that gave me new experiences in

winter hunting. When I reached the peak after a couple of hours, the blasts of wind struck me with such force that I could not keep my footing and was obliged to crawl on my knees to a point where I could look over. But except at short intervals, when the wind slackened and the snow ceased whirling, I could see nothing. Finally I caught a momentary glimpse of the sheep a hundred yards below on the right, when the snow cloud again enveloped me and obscured everything. Taking a seat facing the wind, with rifle ready for a shot, at one moment I was completely isolated in whirling snow, the next, I could see below the clear calm country of ice bars, snow, and bordering forests. Near by, the mountain crests presented a wild aspect—the snow clouds driven by the hurricane streaming swiftly along the summits, and on some of the larger peaks forming whirlwinds of revolving vapors. Try as I could, there was at first no clear interval long enough to permit a bead on one of the sheep; they continued to feed quietly, indifferent to wind and snow. Again and again I made the attempt without success, becoming so chilled that it was doubtful whether I could remain in that position much longer. At last the opportunity came for a quick aim and fire. The sheep dropped in its tracks; the three others ran off. Soon a lamb came back over the top, and seeing me, remained at a good distance, hovering around until I stood up, when it ran over the other side of the peak.

Working my way down to the dead ewe, I found her at the head of a long steep snowslide that continued to the foot of the slope. Taking her horns under my right arm and holding the snowshoes lashed together as a brake, I sat down and slid smoothly, with increasing momentum, until in a few moments the more level ground at the foot of the slide was reached. Here the sheep was dressed and found to be fairly fat. Her pelage was extremely dirty, and both horns were cracked perpendicularly near the butt—the right for two inches on the outside, the left for five inches. No cause for this was evident unless, either in play or by accident, they had struck against a rock. One was blunted at the tip. I have seen horns of ewes broomed at the tips quite as frequently as among the rams. She was a three-year-old ewe and her udder still contained a good supply of milk. At that time and for another month, lambs though able to take care of themselves often suckle their mothers. This act seemed to annoy the ewes, who would only permit it for very short periods. Her stomach contained mostly grass, with some lichen and a fair proportion of various plants, some of which were still green.

Tying a red handkerchief on a willow stick planted near the carcass and looking across the draw, I saw a red fox running along the base of the mountain. Evidently it had seen me.

The wind had now descended to the lower country and was blowing fiercely as I pushed against it to the woods. The cabin was reached not long before dark, but Karstens at once hitched the dogs to the light sled and started for the sheep. In fifty minutes he was back.

Although the thermometer registered below zero during the night, the following day was recorded in my journal as "warm and springlike." It was so mild all day that while tramping I did not even cover my hands. The morning was calm and the mountains, having been swept by the wind, were bare in places, appearing striped. So mild and still was the atmosphere as almost to forebode a thunderstorm. The main range ahead was overcast with deep purple, the sun was obscured by a pure pink cloud, the skies were gorgeous. The ice on the bars was swelling and breaking with loud cracking reports that echoed from the mountain walls.

It was delightful to loiter along, searching for sheep through the field glasses and reading the fresh signs of animal activities on the snow, which the day before had shown no evidences of wild life. Mice had been running all about and many tiny tracks led out on the bars, turning back after reaching the ice. Weasel tracks also were common. Ptarmigan were everywhere among the willows and several of them expressed premature springlike joy by stretching their wings and strutting over the snow. At Bear Draw a wolverine had come from the narrow strip of woods to the south and followed my trail of the previous day. Near the Forks, thirteen sheep—ewes, lambs, and a three-year-old ram—were quietly feeding along the crest of Forks Mountain. As usual, a wind was blowing down the Upper East Branch, where several small bands of ewes were seen high on the mountains. Retracing my steps, I entered the second canyon below the Forks —a narrow gorge cutting through high rugged slopes broken by lofty cliffs, turreted and weathered in fantastic shapes. The deep canyon was dark within, but looking down between the walls I could see the river bars and Old Camp Mountain. At the head of the canyon was a high peak illuminated by the sunlight. Thus the gloom of my course upward, both ahead and behind, was relieved by areas sparkling with light.

When I had climbed up toward the head of the canyon, eleven ewes suddenly appeared on the peak and stood motionless in bold relief against a rich lavender skyline. The bright sunlight on their white coats magnified their size and seemed to lift their bodies above the surface so that they appeared suspended against the sky—a picture still vivid before me.

At this time the big rams were no longer with the ewes; these were scattered in small bands, always feeding high on the mountains. No sheep tracks were on the bars or lower slopes and there were no signs to indicate that sheep were browsing among the willows.

Open Water at the Toklat Cutoff.
Mallards and Ouzels Wintering There.
Minchumina Indians.
Return to the Cabin.
Silver Fox.

January 26. The first summer I entered this region I had been told that all through the winter numerous mallard ducks remained on the open water of the Toklat about fifty miles below my cabin. Wishing to test the accuracy of these reports Karstens and I started with dogs and a small sled loaded with robes and provisions sufficient for five or six days. We pushed along easily over stretches of clear ice, but with difficulty through overflows and deep snow. The day was warm and here and there bands of mist stretched across the wide river bars. No animal tracks were observed on the bars.

Near the mouth of Clearwater Creek we saw smoke among the trees, and driving the dogs in, found a small camp, with Sam Means—an interesting character, one of the peculiar products of the North—seated near a fire, melting snow to make tea. For a number of years he had wandered about Alaska, usually alone, sometimes thinking he was prospecting, but often traveling merely to gratify a desire to see new regions, where he could support himself and his dogs on game. He roamed with three dogs, a small sled, bits of flour, rice, tea, and sugar, while a fur robe, an axe, and a strip of canvas provided him with shelter. He was then journeying for the purpose, as he had convinced himself, of obtaining photographs in the hope that he might be invited to give an exhibition at the proposed Seattle-Alaskan Exposition.

After lunching with him we started and had not gone far when I saw a hawk owl—the only one observed during the entire winter. From there on, the snow was much deeper and progress was very slow, yet by dark when we camped, we had covered twenty-seven miles.

January 27. A warm day for winter: minimum temperature 18 degrees above. After six hours of travel we reached the open water of the Toklat at a place called the Cutoff— the beginning of an old Indian trail from the Toklat to the Nenana River. It was the trail always used in passing to and from the Kantishna mining district. On that reach of the Toklat the bars are very wide. The only animal tracks seen were those of a cross fox, which ran for a while ahead of us, always keeping at a safe distance from a possible rifle shot. Just before reaching the Cutoff we saw an Indian walking ahead carrying his rifle; he was returning from an unsuccessful moose hunt. We pulled up on the bank among the tents of half a dozen families of Indians from Minchumina Lake, who were encamped there. Immediately both men and women ran out of their tents to drive away their dogs, which were threatening those of our own team; and I noticed several little children, almost naked, come out and stand in the snow with bare feet.

During the whole winter, even in the coldest weather, there is always open water on the Toklat from that point downstream for four or five miles. There are several channels, all open. This place marks the upper end of the salmon run and the water was filled with dead salmon and their eggs. They supply food for ducks all winter. On our arrival, a flock of about thirty ducks had circled and flown down the river. The water was strongly bubbling up through the gravel, indicating an underground flow.

The dogs were taken into an old abandoned cabin, where we passed the night. Each dog seemed thoroughly cowed and when unharnessed they all immediately withdrew under the old bunks, from which it was difficult to entice them, even with food. They knew only too well that they were in a hostile camp and that should one venture outside, an attack from the Indian dogs would be the immediate result.

January 28. At dawn I stepped out of the cabin, shotgun in hand, hoping to collect some ducks. The snow hung heavy on the trees, and on the ground it was two or three feet deep. Not a breeze rustled the branches; the forest betokened the dead of winter. The Indians were still asleep in their tents, which, set in the spruces, stood out against the snow-covered bars. Walking through the tents to the bank of the river I beheld Denali in full view in the distance, with streaks of red shooting through the sky over its summit. Several ravens were flying about picking up pieces of salmon that the dogs had dragged out of the water, and eight or nine of the dogs themselves were feeding on the rotting fish along the bars. From the forest on all sides came the notes of the redpolls. But what surprised me most in this region of winter cold was to hear along the open water the beautiful prolonged warbling song of a small bird, seemingly a symbol of spring. Several small flocks of ducks were flying back and forth, but the sweet bird song first claimed my attention and I determined to find the songster that was pouring forth such music among ice and snow. As I advanced to the river bank, the music seemed to issue from directly beneath me in the ice gorge, through which the waters swiftly flowed. Cautiously stepping to the edge, I spied a water ouzel sitting on a projection of ice close to the water. Others were in the frosted willows nearby, and still others on and about the ice.

Vapors then began to rise from the ice gorges as if steam were pouring forth, yet the waters that flowed near the level of the ice were clear. Some distance ahead was a large eddying pool formed by a sharp curve of the river, where I could see a few ducks diving for salmon flesh. There the open water was close to shore and the willows afforded concealment, enabling me to creep close enough to shoot a fine male mallard. At the report, other mallards arose all along the river, flying and circling in all directions around the bars. Farther down stream I concealed myself behind a willow bush until a flock of a dozen came flying by, when with two shots I got another male and a female. Then for some time I watched the ducks that were continually flying along the river, and others diving in the water. In all I counted about a hundred mallards, but these must have been only a small part of those feeding along the entire stretch of open water. All the ducks were very wild.

Mallards are known to have passed the entire winter along this stretch since 1904, a fact told me by trappers who occupied a cabin here during that winter, and by the Kantishna miners, who since that time have passed every winter here. Karstens has killed mallards here in two successive winters and has found several with frozen toes—in some cases the toes had dropped off entirely. The Indians told me that these ducks had always been there in winter, and later I collected the following reliable records of mallards wintering in Alaska: fifteen or sixteen had wintered for several years in open water at the head of the salmon run on Moose Creek, not far from Glacier City; a considerable number had wintered below Gulkana Lake in the outlet that flows into Copper River; and a few in the open water of a small tributary of Tanana River just below the mouth of the Delta. Probably there are many other places in the interior of Alaska where mallards pass the winter, despite temperatures sometimes falling to 60 degrees below zero, Fahrenheit.

After collecting a water ouzel I returned to the cabin. It was nearly eleven in the morning, but not one Indian was awake. Shortly afterward, however, they began to bestir themselves. After skinning my birds, I spent the remainder of the day and the evening with the Indians. Five families and three unattached individuals were encamped here, all from Lake Minchumina. They represented nearly all the survivors of this tribe, which at one time was large and powerful. These Indians had been to Nenana, where they had remained for some time with the Mission Indians who made that point, near the Mission buildings, their headquarters. The Minchuminas had brought their year's catch of furs and on the trail had met the Nenana Indians, who induced them to trade their furs for tin crosses and other worthless trinkets obtained at Nenana.

These few families were now returning to Lake Minchumina with practically no food supplies except small quantities of flour and tea. They had been obliged to remain here until a moose could be killed for food, their dogs meanwhile feeding on dead salmon. One of the Indians had killed a small cow

moose a week before, but before our arrival it had been completely consumed.

Each family had a tent, a small stove, and plenty of blankets and clothing. The women cut all the wood, and only two
of the men seemed to hunt. These had put out a few traps
and that morning had caught a wolverine. Two of the boys
went out for a short distance in the woods looking for rabbits, which were very scarce that year, most of them having
died. Rabbits were at the periodical minimum. Not one of the
seven men in the party was vigorous and all seemed indifferent to the precarious condition they were in, nor did any
of them attempt active hunting.

They were very friendly with me. I gave them tobacco and
such sugar as could be spared, and spent the evening in the
tent of the chief, where all except the children crowded in.

One could speak a few words of English. He told me that
their name for Mount McKinley is "Denali, The High One,"
and that Mount Foraker is "Sultana, The Women or Wife."
I could gather little information from them about the animals,
probably because there was no interpreter for a free conversa-
tion. Why these Indians preferred to remain there with little
food, rather than travel a short distance up the river where
caribou were abundant, was hard to understand. I purchased
from them several pairs of moccasins, a pair of snowshoes,
and a handsome parka made of ground squirrel skins fringed
with squirrel tails and strips of mountain sheep skin.

January 29–31. We followed our trail back for two days,
seeing on the bars tracks of two lynxes, a fox, and a rabbit.
Reaching the cabin before dark, we found Burns, a trapper,
awaiting us. He had just tramped over from his cabin, and
failing to get any sheep had followed our trail. The thermometer left at the cabin recorded +4 as the lowest temperature during our absence; this was five degrees higher
than the lowest at the Cutoff. Burns left next morning, and
I remained about the cabin all day.

February 1. As our stock of meat was running low and
I wanted a ram with large horns for a February trophy, I
started up river to hunt. The day was cloudless, calm and

warm, the outlines of all the mountain crests were sharply
defined in the clear atmosphere, and it was delightful to be
hunting here where familiarity with the landscapes intensified, rather than diminished, my admiration for them. As I
passed up the creek of Bear Draw two flocks of ptarmigan
were feeding along the banks, and a fresh fox track led up
into the basin. Before reaching the head I turned up to the
left around Cabin Peak and came over near the foot of the
slopes leading to Cabin Divide.

At this season rams were not in their summer and fall
haunts, but might be found anywhere on any part of the
mountains. It was not long before I spied four about a mile
ahead, high on a spur. Climbing as high was practicable
for snowshoes, I had picked my way along the rough face for
half a mile, when suddenly all four rams came in sight against
the skyline of the summit crest, all clearly outlined in alert attitudes, looking over the bleak country below. One had horns
large enough for a trophy. Watching an opportunity, I
dropped out of sight in a canyon and started to climb the steep
incline of crusted snow on the other side, but notwithstanding
the roughlocks on the snowshoes, I began to slip backward
and only saved myself from a dangerous fall by jamming the
butt of my rifle into the snow.

The rams, having apparently satisfied themselves that there
was no danger below, descended to feed in a canyon leading
down from the crest. As the last one disappeared I hastened
forward to a point where the noise of the snowshoes on the
crust might reach them. Then slowly, step by step, I approached a small ravine that separated me from the spur
above the rams. In the bottom the drifts were deep, and the
snow very soft; and after crossing it I found the crust so thin
that I could not dispense with the snowshoes. With all the caution I could command I worked up to the crest, and then, rifle
ready, slowly rose—to find no rams in sight. But I had seen
enough to know exactly where they were—in a small hollow
not far to the right. An advance of only twenty feet would
bring me to a point from which they could be seen. In spite of
redoubled caution, now and then the crust would break and

make a faint noise. Reaching the point, I cautiously rose and saw them standing close together, not seventy-five yards away, heads up, all looking directly at me. They had heard me, and on my appearance dashed for the opposite slope, only a few feet distant. Quickly dropping to my knees I held the rifle ready for a bead on the big ram, which then was so mixed with the others that I could not cover him. He ran fifty yards upward, then stopped a moment to look back, and again turned to go—but it was too late, for I had his hind quarter well covered with the sight and fired instantly. He stopped and staggered—and I knew he was mine. The three others stopped and stood for a moment looking down at the leader, then quickly turned and ran over the crest.

The ram soon fell, kicked once or twice, and died. He had fine evenly shaped horns with seven rings. His coat was thick and long, quite dirty, the hair so loose it could easily be pulled out in handfuls. I sat for a while to smoke my pipe and gaze over the panorama of snow-covered ranges. Low on the slopes of Cabin Divide Mountain ten or twelve ewes were in sight, feeding.

After photographing the ram I took off the scalp and head and examined the stomach; it contained grass, various small plants, lichens, and many willow buds. When about to go, I noticed a red fox on the snow about three hundred yards away; it was standing motionless looking up at me. Seating myself, I tried a shot. At the report it made a high leap and ran at full speed for some distance along the mountainside and stopped. Turning my glasses I saw that the bullet had at least touched its foreleg, which it was licking. Then it ran on, apparently without the leg being disabled; yet it would stop every little while to lick the wound. It was dark by the time I had descended Cabin Creek and reached the cabin.

February 2–8. During these seven days the minimum temperatures ranged from 19 to 3 degrees below zero. After piloting Karstens with the dog sled to the ram's carcass I went over the mountains to East Fork, noticing but few sheep. On returning to the cabin I found Sam Means there, intending to start the following day for East Fork with the hope of photographing rams.

The weather, except when the wind was strong, was clear and fiercely cold. At this date dawn came at 6.30, rifle sights could be seen from 7.30 in the morning until 3.45 in the afternoon, and it was dark at 4.30. The sun remained above the horizon a considerable time, the days were lengthening fast. Though at times the sky colors were still rich and beautiful, the period of prolonged, intensified colors had passed.

There were now very few mouse holes in the snow, weasel tracks were less numerous, but fox tracks were more plentiful than at any time during the winter. A rabbit or two had come to the woods, followed as usual by owls, so their tracks were not observed again. The explanation would seem to be that because the woods are surrounded by ice or snow, the owls could easily see the trails and so locate the rabbits. Across the river, and below, where the strip of woods was continuous, the owls did not have such an easy time.

The jays kept amusing me by their continued intimacy, but they and the dogs were completely indifferent to each other. The single red squirrel I had left alive had his nest of leaves, twigs, spruce needles and bark in a spruce tree about two hundred yards from the cabin. He never came near the cabin, but when the temperature was not very low he ran about the woods, from tree to tree, and we often heard him chattering. Near his nest, in a receptacle of limbs growing densely near the tree trunk, he had stored more than a bushel of dried fungi, and at the foot of the tree had accumulated a large heap of them. All were a small species of *Russula*. These, together with the seeds of the spruce cones, provided his food all winter. When the temperature was low he remained in the nest. At no time did I observe his tracks more than two hundred yards away. He was not at all timid and I often stood and watched him eating a fungus as he sat on a limb not two feet above my head.

Wolverine tracks appeared in the vicinity of the cabin every eight or nine days, each leading somewhere up the mountain slopes. From this it seemed obvious that wolverines travel periodically over given routes. Except for jays, ravens, willow ptarmigan, an occasional snowy owl on the divides, and a few chickadees sometimes seen in the woods, bird life was practically absent.

During this week I wandered over the mountains watching the sheep, which were traveling widely and actively in order to maintain themselves on the poor food of the bare slopes. Karstens accompanied me one day to the outside mountain divide for the purpose of hauling down the hay that had been cut in the fall, and while loading it we heard several faint rifle shots in the mountains. The winter market hunters were there, and the following day Karstens saw numerous tracks of ewes and lambs that had been driven across the divide. February 7 and 8 Karstens went to haul back a load of meat from the caribou cache in which we had stored it, but found that wolverines had long been at work there and had packed off practically all the meat. This was a serious disappointment, for it meant that more meat must be provided for the dogs. Karstens visited the camp of the market hunters and found four men with sixteen dogs. They had been camped near the base of the outside mountain for some time and had killed a large number of ewes and lambs.

February 9. Early in the morning as I was going up the river a fine silver fox came into view. It was trotting along the lower slope of Cabin Peak, stopping frequently to look for mice, and soon passed out of sight. Several small bands of ewes were seen high about Bear Draw. The winds had now cleared so much snow off the mountains that I decided to climb the summits at the head of the Draw and devote the day to observing sheep from the crests. It might be mentioned here that for a long time I had noticed everywhere among these mountains that the winds had blown down great quantities of sheep dung, scattering it everywhere on the snow below—even as far as half a mile out on the level places. During the summer, therefore, over numerous wide areas at the foot of the mountains, quantities of dung would be observed that might lead one to conclude that sheep had been accustomed to feed there.

When high up on the slopes I made a long stalk in order to photograph a band of ewes, but though near enough for an

exposure, they did not show in the negative. I had been close
to them and in the wind for at least ten minutes without their
showing alarm, but finally they became uneasy and were
watching for me when I came in sight. Then at once they ran
up over the crest—evidently having scented me before I appeared. It was so warm on the crests that I did not even wear
gloves.

High up in the mountain world I proceeded, climbing peak
after peak, constantly coming into new areas of rugged canyons, precipitous slopes, high picturesque cliffs, and wide
scenic basins. The sea of peaks and shaggy crests extended to
Denali, whose great bulk rose up into the clouds. Many ewe
bands were seen, and now and then a few rams, some with
good horns. Playing about the divides were three foxes, and
ravens were flying along the crests. Ravens were so often seen
passing along the summits that I was perplexed to know why
they should fly so high in winter. Today I saw one alight
near a peak and pick up a small object, which it carried in its
beak to another peak, where it alighted and ate it. This object
appeared to be about an inch in diameter and looked like a
white snowball. I could not imagine what it was unless it might
be the frosted dung of a wolverine or lynx, the only animals
likely to have been on the crests in winter.

Returning to the cabin, I found Sam Means there with the
head of a good ram, which he wanted me to prepare for him.
He had also a live mature female wolverine which he had
caught in a trap set at the ram's carcass. We built a shelter for
the wolverine outside the cabin and chained it there. Three of
its toes on one forefoot were somewhat injured by the trap,
but this did not seem to trouble it. It weighed twenty-one
pounds.

February 10. In the morning, after preparing Means'
trophy, I climbed up to the wide pastures near Cabin Peak
in the hope of again seeing the silver fox. Looking from a
little hill, it was not long before I spied a black spot in the centre of the area, and turning my glasses on it saw that it was
the silver fox, curled up asleep with its tail folded over its
head. Hoping that later it might begin to search for mice and

approach close enough for a shot, I crept to a willow bush and waited, well concealed. My patience was not rewarded, for it soon became too dark to see the rifle sights, so I carefully withdrew, leaving the fox still sleeping. It had chosen a safe spot, out in the open, where it could not be approached without being disturbed.

February 11. Means left early, while Karstens was setting out to bring back a load of hay. Taking three traps I hurried up toward the meadows to lay out tempting, though dangerous, bait for the fox. At daylight it was calm, but long before the slopes were reached the wind had increased to a gale. Reaching the lower end of the pastures, I lifted a thin piece of crust in a clump of willows, set a trap, and after replacing the crust, scattered pieces of ptarmigan and feathers about; then set another trap.

The peaks about Bear Draw caught the wind and sent it whirling downward to join the gale blowing over the exposed pastures. Every few moments great snow-laden whirlwinds swept over the surface, completely obscuring even the ground at my feet. Tying a mitten over the muzzle of the rifle and wrapping my parka about the lock, I faced the whirling snow, scarcely able to make headway against it. I had not gone far, when during a lull in the gale I saw the silver fox trotting along the foot of Cabin Peak, half a mile away. But in a moment the snow again enveloped me, and I realized that only by a series of advances while the whirling snow clouds were concealing me could I reach a point where a shot might be possible. Starting forward while the snow filled the air, and lying down when it ceased for a few moments, I advanced very slowly, and the fine snow entered every possible opening in my clothing. Nevertheless it was intensely exciting. At times the fox was seen galloping downward, again standing motionless; at other times trotting diagonally toward me, only to be obliterated by the snow-whirls and to reappear well up on the slopes. But at last I came within three hundred yards of the area in which he had been hunting, and noticing a willow bush a little farther on, concealed myself behind it and waited, shivering with cold. It was keenly interesting to see so near, between the periods of snow-whirls, Alaska's choicest animal running, skipping, trotting, or sitting and watching for the abundant mice. Once he ran so far that I became discouraged, thinking it would not be possible to endure the cold much longer. Later he turned and ran toward some willows and I regretted that I had not continued on to that point. Finally, just as a snow cloud was obscuring the fox, I saw him turn on the run and head directly toward me. There followed moments of eager anticipation until the whirling snow cleared, when directly below me a hundred and fifty yards to the right I saw him sitting on a hummock, intently watching the ground. My rifle had been cleared for a shot, and suppressing my shivering as best I could, I aimed and fired. The fox sprang in the air with a cry, leaped forward six feet and fell dead— having been struck low in the chest.

He was a fine mature male of steel-gray color, his pelage thoroughly prime and immaculately clean. He was a better prize than I had realized when trying so eagerly to get him. After taking a photograph and filling the wound with snow, I put him in my rucksack and returned to the cabin.

A Captive Wolverine.
Guests at the Cabin.
Quigley's Experience with a Lynx.

February 12–14. On February 12, after passing the day setting fox traps and wandering about, I had a fall in the cabin, injuring a leg so that for a couple of days little tramping could be undertaken.

It proved interesting to observe the traits of the wolverine chained in the small log house we had constructed for her. At first she was very savage and when approached would growl; then as I came nearer she would make a whistling chatter. If I went too close she would spring at me. She was always alert and watchful of the dogs, though they paid no attention to her. The first night she ravenously ate meat and another night consumed the entire carcass of the fox. She ate solidly frozen meat without any difficulty, displaying decided skill in her method of turning and tearing it in the direction of the grain. After a couple of days she came forward when I approached with a piece of meat, growling slightly but without any of the fierceness previously displayed. She was continually active, particularly early in the morning, walking back and forth and tugging at the chain. When lying down on her back she assumed grotesque attitudes. Most interesting were her cleanly habits. Very timid at first, she evacuated in a corner of the little shelter and immediately afterward picked up some of the hay on the floor with her teeth and carefully laid it over the excrement, and then pawed over it such material as she could reach, covering it completely. After that she always went outside to evacuate, each time attempting to cover it.

The reputation of the wolverine for robbing caches and the baits of traps, and even for eating fur animals caught in traps, is well deserved. It persists in these habits, and because of its great strength does much damage to caches and deadfalls. Wolverines have been known to carry off animals caught in traps, with the traps attached. But many descriptions of these annoying habits are not limited to exploits along the trap line but include tales of thieving, malicious destruction of property, the soiling of food, and even the carrying off of empty traps. Reliable proof of such statements has not been forthcoming, and in view of my own observations and inquiries in the North I am disposed to regard them as products of the imagination.

Late in the afternoon of February 13 the four market hunters, with all their dogs, came to my cabin. They had killed more than twenty ewes and lambs, but since they had been there for some time their dogs had consumed so many that after all they did not have the desired loads of meat to take back to Fairbanks—and they had frightened most of the sheep from the accessible parts of the outside mountain. For this reason they decided to spend some time up the river beyond my cabin to kill more sheep. Naturally I was deeply disappointed to hear that my sheep, which I had been so carefully observing, were to be disturbed by vigorous market hunting, but could do nothing to prevent it. In the evening however, when the men had heard me discuss the habits of the sheep, outlining the various bands I had been watching, they realized that their hunting would put an end to my opportunities. Showing a fine spirit, they at once decided to return and hunt caribou in the lower country. Before going they gave me the skull of a choice male lynx, killed by one of their dogs. They had found the animal feeding on the carcass of a sheep they had killed, and as they approached it, their dogs rushed forward. The lynx jumped on a rock and stood at bay, but one of the dogs seized it by the neck and killed it. None of the other four dogs had attempted to touch it.

February 15. This morning we found that the wolverine had gone, having twisted off its chain. On my appearance the dogs ran to the woodpile, when the wolverine, which had crawled in there, betrayed herself by growling. As breakfast had just been prepared we sat down to eat, thinking the dogs would prevent her from attempting to escape—at least for the time being. But in a few moments we heard a commotion and dashing out saw the wolverine running over the snow, followed by all the dogs. After going seventy-five yards she went up a tree, climbing to the very top. She climbed so easily, in the manner of a coon, that no one seeing her could doubt that wolverines are accustomed to climbing trees. Karstens brought the axe and felled the tree. The wolverine, not at all hurt, again started to run, almost surrounded by the dogs, none of which cared to tackle her until *Sailor* attempted to seize her. She immediately threw herself on her back, assuming a fighting attitude. We drove *Sailor* away and again she ran, but after going a short distance, climbed another tree. Felling that one we pinned her down with poles—though she fought savagely with teeth, legs, and claws—and succeeded in putting the chain on her, though she bit it viciously. After we had secured her she calmed down, acting as she had before her escape.

This evening Joe and Fanny Quigley arrived, with three dogs, having come from Glacier Creek to get a load of sheep meat.

February 16–21. These five days were mild, with a stiff south wind, except one day when it blew strongly from the south. Three times I went out with the Quigleys for sheep, and once Quigley went alone. Although sheep were seen and stalked, none were killed. A couple of spruce grouse that had come up into the cabin woods were killed and eaten and the flavor was very good, the usual spruce-tainted taste of the flesh not being apparent.

February 22. Minimum temperature 22 degrees above. On this day I went hunting with Mrs. Quigley and after an arduous mountain climb, which she made as easily as any man, we came close to a band of thirty-four sheep; but her rifle missed fire twice, and then she missed them running. While we were climbing over the irregular surface the sheep had kept moving through ravines and hollows so that, had it not been for a raven, it would have been difficult to keep them located. But wherever they went. the raven kept flying over them and circling, as if to keep us informed of the exact spot where they could be found. I had often watched ravens acting in a similar way with a band of traveling sheep when no attempt to stalk them was being made.

Quigley, like ourselves, had not succeeded in killing any sheep.

February 23. Today we all went up the river. From the Forks several bands of sheep were visible in different directions, all feeding very high. Redpolls had begun to pass through the upper country, as on this day I heard them for the first time since early winter. Mrs. Quigley and I went a short distance up the Upper East Branch, where a band of rams was seen near the crest of the north end of Polychrome Mountain. After carefully studying the possible approaches we started a long and interesting stalk, once sitting still for an hour before we could move unseen. Most of the sheep were young rams, but two had fair horns. They finally went in among some cliffs where they could not be seen from above, so we descended diagonally and finally came to a point where all were in plain sight, leisurely feeding only a hundred and fifty yards away. After Mrs. Quigley's first shot they began to run upward and continued to run while she fired several times, until they passed over the crest. None of the shots had taken effect and we returned to the cabin to find that the others also had been unsuccessful.

February 24 and 25. While Karstens and I went out to set traps the Quigleys again hunted without success. The following day, while they were hunting elsewhere, I went back over Cabin Divide to watch the sheep and among others saw two good rams feeding high on the range to the south. Ewes and lambs were on the other ranges. Taking a good position I watched all the sheep for a couple of hours, until fog began to settle, when I returned. At one time the two rams lay down, one facing down, the other up, both continually keeping a close watch. In fact these rams were extremely cautious, probably because they had been driven off the outside mountain by the market hunters.

During his visit Joe Quigley told me of an unusual experience with a female lynx—as unusual as it is reliable, and therefore worthy of record.

Early one morning, when going along his trap line near Glacier Creek, he saw the fresh tracks of a lynx. While returning over the same trail late in the afternoon he saw a lynx near the same point. It was crouching, facing the trail and about fifteen feet away. As he passed, it watched him without moving. Continuing on for a short distance he cut a willow club and started back, keeping in the trail until opposite the lynx, when he turned and slowly began to approach it. The lynx began to growl, and as Quigley came nearer, it growled continuously, at the same time gradually rising on its fore legs. When within six feet of it he raised his club to strike, and as he took a step nearer, the lynx sprang into some low willows and ran circling to a point two or three hundred feet down the creek behind him. As it ran Quigley threw his club but missed it. Picking up the club, he saw that the lynx had jumped up on a steep bank, where it remained watching while he approached to within thirty or forty feet. The lynx was about eight feet up the bank, which was too precipitous for Quigley to climb within striking distance, so he decided to go a little nearer and then run swiftly across the ice in order to gain sufficient momentum to enable him to jump high enough to reach it with the club. He did so, and as he jumped upward with the club held ready to strike, the lynx, which until that moment had remained crouching motionless, though continually growling, sprang directly at him. Quickly swinging the club he struck the lynx on the head while it was in mid-air, stunning it completely. The skull of this lynx is now in the collection of the Biological Survey in Washington.

February 26–28. These three days we were confined to the cabin by a continuous heavy snow blizzard. Twice I attempted to go up the river to see what the sheep were doing under such severe weather conditions, but snow so filled the air that I could not see in any direction. During these blizzards I wandered about the woods and was surprised to notice chickadees feeding among the spruces, completely indifferent to wind and whirling snow. The jays kept pretty well under cover of the dense branches, but now and then one would venture out for pieces of food they had stored in the trees.

February 29. Since all the meat for the dogs had been consumed, it was necessary that sheep should be immediately obtained. Karstens and the Quigleys went up the river with a dog team, while I started up Cabin Creek to get a ram or two near East Fork, at a sufficient distance from the locality where I had been continually observing the sheep. It was a perfect day, without wind, the sun shining brightly in a cloudless sky. Ten or twelve inches of snow had fallen, covering everything with immaculate white except where the winds had swept it off. Deep drifts filled the hollows, ravines, and surfaces that were sheltered from the winds, and great perpendicular drift banks lined the sides of the canyons. In passing through the thin strip of woods, I noticed a rabbit track followed by that of a lynx; ptarmigan tracks and those of weasels were abundant, but there was no evidence of mice on the surface of the snow.

Three or four small bands of ewes were feeding high on the mountains bordering both sides of the divide, and all stood watching me as I snowshoed by and passed out of sight down the creek flowing to East Fork. A couple of miles down I turned up a small branch flowing from the south between high rugged mountains bordering East Fork, and was soon traveling up the bottom of a canyon where every bend brought new sights of the jagged rocky inclines by which I was surrounded. A beautiful white snowy owl flew down from a mountain crest and suddenly floating across the canyon alighted on a high black rock jutting out from a cliff. There it sat watching me with curiosity as I passed almost below it.

A short distance farther on I saw a fine ram on a sharp peak above, the sunlight exaggerating the whiteness of his coat in contrast to the darkness of the rock on which he stood. He saw me at once and being at a safe distance, looked down and watched me for a few moments before jumping back and disappearing. He carried good horns, though not quite large enough to tempt me to a stalk.

The canyon in leading up through mountains became rougher and narrower, its high perpendicular walls closing in almost to the point of meeting. Here the snow must have been twenty or thirty feet deep, and the narrow snowshoes sank a foot or more at every step.

Emerging from the box canyon, I was surrounded by rock-walled slopes and high peaks, many of which were buried under deep snow. Not far below the summit were six rams, one with good horns, quietly pawing away the snow and feeding.

Sticking my snowshoes in the snow and strapping on my creepers I began the ascent of a mountain to the left, from the peak of which I could get a good shot across a canyon at the rams, then just below the opposite rim. I slowly toiled upward, struggling through deep snow and over precipitous icy slopes, now and then creeping to the canyon edge to peer at the sheep, which continued to feed in about the same spot. Reaching the top, I walked carefully to the foot of the peak—an almost sheer rock projecting twenty-five feet above the crest. With redoubled caution, step by step I ascended, pausing just below the summit. The sun was shining brilliantly, not a cloud was in the sky, and no sound broke the stillness of the mountain world about me. To the left loomed range after range between the East Fork and the Teklanika—a vast sea of peaks, some icy and glittering—while before me were high snow-covered summits.

Creeping upward a few feet more and turning my legs forward, I slowly rose to a sitting position, rifle cocked and ready. The rams were still there, about two hundred yards away, slowly feeding on the steep irregular slope broken by rock slides and crags, and wholly unsuspicious. The one with the large horns began to walk away in such a position that it was doubtful if he would turn and expose himself broadside. Therefore I quickly fired, and heard the bullet strike. The others ran up over the crest, but before reaching it one with smaller horns paused a moment to look back. After my shot he staggered and then trotted in my direction. The big ram had risen and after two more shots struggled down the canyon, where he fell and died. The smaller one was then running near the top when, struck by another bullet, he turned, ran a few feet downward, and fell dead.

After photographing the two rams I dressed both, took off the scalp and head of the larger, put the head in my rucksack, and returned to the Divide and thence to the cabin.

The Quigleys came back with two ewes and a yearling ram, quite delighted with this supply of sheep meat to take to their mining cabin. They had seen plenty of sheep and the fresh track of a wolf, the first that had come into the upper country since I had been there.

March 1. While Karstens took the dogs up my trail to bring back the sheep, and the Quigleys again hunted up river, I tramped over the Geological Divide West and entered the canyon of Sheldon Mountain to see if the rams that during the spring and summer frequent that region had returned. Finding no signs of them I came back to the cabin, soon followed by the Quigleys, who had not succeeded in getting more sheep. Later, Karstens returned with the carcasses of the two rams.

March 2. The Quigleys left for their cabin on Glacier Creek early in the morning. They had been delightful guests and I had greatly enjoyed their visit. I went up river to observe the sheep and more particularly to see if there was any evidence that the wolf was hunting them, but found none.

It was another beautiful day, the sun so bright that it was difficult to realize that only a short time before I had been tramping this region in the shadowy light of the low winter sun.

Several fresh weasel tracks were about the woods, a couple of rabbits were now there, and a lynx had been sneaking about trying to capture them. At the point of Forks Mountain I saw a well-marked trail coming down to the bar from high among the rocks. It had been made by a wolverine, which had traveled back and forth on it. Marks on the snow, both in the trail and alongside of it, showed that the wolverine had dragged some heavy bulk down the mountain and across the bar. Here and there the snow was stained with blood and marked with the hair of sheep. The wolverine tracks had sunk so far into the snow, and the depressions alongside the trail were so deep that it was clear that very large pieces of sheep carcass must have been pulled along. The trail led up over a fairly steep bank on the other side of the bar, where it seemed incredible that so small an animal could have dragged objects of such weight through the deep soft snow.

The trail continued about a hundred yards into the woods, and there in a hollow under the spruce trees the wolverine had eaten the sheep. Numerous pieces of skin and bones, and frozen grass from the paunch, remained; also several large frozen balls of solid meat that had been gnawed into globular shapes. The snow all about was tramped down hard, and in two places there were deep circular spaces where the wolverine had curled up and slept. Evidently a small sheep, wounded two days before by Quigley, had either died or been killed by the wolverine high up on Forks Mountain, at least a mile and a half from the spot to which the animal had dragged it.

Trappers have told me that wolverines take meat from caches and carry it to a distance before eating it, and I was glad to confirm this by my own observation. Judging by the great quantity of feces the wolverine had continually evacuated, it must have consumed an incredible amount of meat in a short time—as my captive wolverine had done. Few writers have realized this extraordinary voracity and capacity of the wolverine, and for that reason the theft of great quantities of food from caches has been attributed to motives other than those of hunger. Obviously there are good grounds for the name 'glutton' early bestowed on this animal.

I waited at the spot for two hours hoping the wolverine might return, but it did not, and when I went to the bar and looked high up on the mountain slope I saw it running and watched it through the field glasses. It acted as if hunting for mice, running from place to place and nosing about the ground. It would often turn on its back and chew and scratch near the base of its tail, a practice in which my captive wolverine was constantly indulging, evidently to relieve itching. Reaching the mountain crest, it sat on its haunches and looked below for a long time before passing out of sight.

During the remainder of the day I watched two or three bands of sheep, and then returned to the cabin. Redpolls were now frequent about the woods and willow ptarmigan seemed to be more abundant everywhere, the storms evidently having driven them down from the higher reaches of willows. The Canada jays were as friendly as usual and one even flew down beside my wolverine and fearlessly picked up a piece of meat.

The captive wolverine was now quite tame. She was ceaselessly active, walking back and forth at the end of the chain, and whenever I came near she jumped forward to beg for meat, always consuming quickly all within reach. She possessed keen quick sight, and many tests proved that her power of scent was as strong as that of a wolf. She had no fear of the dogs, and they paid no attention to her. Her intelligence was of a high order. She would carefully avoid any strange object placed near her, such as a small box, a piece of cloth, or an axe head, never approaching it without suspicion and caution, and never touching it. Her fear of strange objects was exactly like that of wolves, one of which, when in Mexico, I had kept in captivity from birth. This trait of avoiding strange objects seems to be inborn in both and accounts for the difficulty in enticing either a wolf or a wolverine to step into a trap. My wolverine had tried so persistently to bite off her chain that she had broken two of her canine teeth; still she never gave up the attempt. She would quietly take meat from my hand and seemed to have lost fear of me, yet would not permit me to put my hand on her.

March 3–4. March 3 was passed in the mountains watching several bands of sheep. The following day, after leaving a large supply of meat with the wolverine, Karstens and I packed the sled and with the dogs pulled up to my old camp, behind which in the woods we set up the small tent and built a cache. It snowed heavily all day, and while chopping wood I looked across the bar at the foot of Forks Mountain, where a trap for foxes had been set over the entrails of a sheep, and saw a dark animal moving. Quickly getting the glasses I plainly saw a wolverine and every moment expected to see it get caught in the trap. But although it circled the spot several times, it avoided the trap and eventually turned and climbed the cliffs and was last seen running along the crest. Repeated observations demonstrated that the wolverine is completely at home among the mountain crags.

In this region the lynx, the wolverine, and the grizzly bear are the three animals that wander at ease in the woods—in the rolling country above timber, and in the rough mountains— although the lynx does not frequent the higher parts so much as do the others.

March 5. Another warm day—minimum temperature 24 degrees above. I had come to this camp for several purposes: to trap foxes, which were more abundant here than below; possibly to observe wolves, which had made their appearance recently; to watch sheep, where they were most abundant; and to kill a fine ram in March pelage for a trophy. This place, where I had first explored and enjoyed the region, was endeared to me, and the broad views of the bars and mountains brought back memories of former happy experiences.

Taking three fox traps to Upper East Branch I noticed a couple of bands of ewes feeding high on Polychrome Mountain and a few on Divide Mountain. One trap was set at the point, and another at the upper end of Divide Mountain near the little lake where a rough saddle makes over to Upper West Branch. High up were thirty ewes and lambs lying down, with several small rams near by, while adjoining these were four larger rams feeding—one with fine spiral horns, and another, which accompanied him, with horns having a very wide spread. The contrast of the two types was so striking that I determined to spare no efforts to collect them both. Since there was then no chance for a stalk because of the position of the ewes, I went on for some distance and set the other trap. When I returned many of the ewes were feeding, while the rams were lying down. I then climbed to the saddle, the deep snow in the creek bed making progress very slow, but when I reached the top the rams were just going over the crest and the ewes soon followed until none were in sight.

It was apparent that the four large rams were independent

of the ewes, and also that the pair with the contrasting horns were independent of the other two, having joined them temporarily. Taking off the snowshoes and putting on the creepers, I toiled upward to the crest at the thead of Ram Canyon, where the wild disorder of the variously colored rock below alternating with ice and snow seemed more desolate even than in summer.

The route toward the sheep was very rugged, and there was not time to attempt it before dark. The sheep had been pawing away snow to get their food, and it was evident that they had not occupied this part of the mountain more than a day. Wishing to avoid the risk of disturbing sheep that were not well settled in a feeding area, I returned to the tent.

At this time all the sheep kept very high on the mountains. Ice and snow, even in rough precipitous places, never seemed in the least to impede their traveling, for they ranged the mountains with as much ease as in summer. All were very dirty, some extremely so.

A fox had dug all about one of Karstens' traps but had not touched the snow close to it. Both willow ptarmigan and redpolls were abundant everywhere among the willows.

March 6. Just after daylight I noticed an animal in the trap where I had seen the wolverine at the Forks. Hastening over there we found a female lynx securely gripped in the trap. She had attempted to dig down to the bait, which was covered with snow and could not have been detected except by scent. This contradicts an assertion often made that all members of the cat tribe hunt or locate their food *exclusively by sight.* The lynx remained squatted, apparently asleep, and seemed wholly indifferent to our approach. Karstens shot her with the .22 rifle. She was in a half-starved condition and fleas were swarming on her skin.

Continuing on, I found that nothing had been near my first trap, but that a fox had circled all about the second, not at any time coming nearer than ten feet. Nothing had been near the third trap.

Circling cautiously out on the bar I saw three of the large rams, including the coveted pair, well ahead, feeding high on the mountain not far from where they were yesterday. I could discover no safe approach and therefore waited a long time until they had worked upward to a point to which, possibly, a stalk might be made. Not far from them were four small rams feeding independently, and I was certain that the ewes must be somewhere near.

When independent bands of sheep are thus feeding near each other, stalking becomes very difficult. I put on the creepers and after a long arduous climb over very rough slopes reached the crest. Cautiously peering over, at first I saw no sheep, but at length, about a third of a mile ahead, the desired rams were seen lying down on the sharp summit of a high projecting peak, both facing in my direction. Their bodies were quite inconspicuous, but their horns were sharply defined against the skyline. The contrast between the two types of horns was so marked that my eagerness to possess them increased, yet I could see no possible chance of stalking them without disturbing the other sheep, which by their actions would give the alarm. For two hours I remained there, until it was too late for a stalk that day, but the rams did not rise and I knew it would be wise to descend before other sheep might detect me. It was late when I reached the bar, but still, through the glasses, the rams could be seen resting in the same spot. It may be mentioned here that throughout the winter, during the short hours of daylight, the sheep were obliged to fill their stomachs quickly, for even then they rested as much during the day as they do in summer.

March 7. Snow fell all day and at times it was foggy, but I was out early hoping to find the rams in a place where they might be approached. A fox had pawed away the snow, exposing the edge of my second trap, but had not attempted to get the bait under it. Four small rams were seen feeding about the tracks I had made the day before. The coveted rams were feeding slightly below the peak on which they had last rested. They were separated a little, but each frequently looked at the other. For two hours I watched them, between shifting fogs, until dense fog settled over the mountains, the snow fell more heavily, and the skies darkened.

Karstens, returning from a trip to the cabin for dog food, reported that my wolverine had again broken its chain and escaped. He had put out a number of fox traps, but thus far had caught nothing. One of the traps had been dug under and the bait taken, but had not been sprung. He also reported a fresh wolf track on the divide to the west, showing that the wolf whose track was seen by Quigley the last day of February (or another one) was now ranging over the mountains.

March 8. A light snow was falling as I crossed the flat. Three hundred yards away, on Divide Mountain, a red fox was hunting mice. It had followed my trail ignoring the traps except the second one. This it had sprung, digging away the snow without attempting to touch the bait.

The pair of rams with the fine horns were still feeding near the same place though somewhat lower, and I was able to select a good route for the approach. Not long afterward, however, they moved upward and stood for a long time looking down the bars, then continued without pausing and disappeared. Hurrying down the slope I watched them until they joined a band of four smaller rams, and all six continued to the massive limestone mountain near the main range. The tracks showed that the four smaller rams had that morning descended Polychrome Mountain and crossed the bars. They were a new band working toward their summer range on the limestone mountain. Walking three miles up the bar to near its head I could see no sheep anywhere, and it was then too late to climb among the peaks to search them out.

Returning to the east side of the bar I put out a poisoned bait at the foot of the Teklanika Divide at a point where a large wolverine regularly passed. We had not been successful in trapping this animal, and to make sure of at least one good specimen for the Biological Survey I felt obliged to resort to poison. A strong wind accompanied by a rapid fall in temperature caused my nose to freeze several times before camp was reached.

*Dangerous Stalk for Rams
on Polychrome Mountain.
The Coveted Rams Killed.
Wolves.*

March 9. While climbing the mountains the past few days I had been uncomfortable because of warmer weather. It was a delight therefore to start out in the snapping cold, with the accompanying feeling of exhilaration. Several foxes had been running about and I noticed that one pair had kept together, ranging the lower slopes, always on the run. They were probably hunting ptarmigan. A large wolverine had eaten the poisoned bait and signs on the snow indicated that it had been very sick, yet it had gone upward toward Polychrome Mountain. I followed its trail and was disappointed to lose it among some bare areas high among the canyoned slopes. Two bands of ewes were near when I descended, quickly frightening them. Going up the bar a couple of miles, I saw five rams —three with splendid heads—quite low near the saddle of Divide Mountain. They were in a position where they could easily have been stalked, but as neither of the coveted pair was among them I kept on. The day was perfect, clear and calm, and the mountains were white and glistening in the bright sunlight—none of the fresh snow having yet been swept off. High on the slopes of the limestone mountain the two rams were seen, though too far off for me to distinguish their horns. Crossing to the west side of the bar I hastened forward, finding that they were the pair I was seeking, and in a position entirely favorable for a stalk, although so high that a long time would be necessary to accomplish it. Hurrying on for another mile I passed up a canyon and began a long dangerous climb. After three hours I had circled the slope to a point near the place where the rams had last been seen feeding.

306

The place was entirely in view but no rams were there.
Working slowly around the craggy precipitous slope until satisfied that they had departed, I sat down to think the matter over.
Suddenly two sheep appeared on the bar directly below me and
my glasses revealed the pair I was stalking. They were soon
joined by a yearling ram. The large ram with the close spiral
led, the other two following and watching alertly in all directions. They stopped across the bar at the foot of Polychrome
Mountain and began to feed. I was in plain sight high on the
slope, but dared not move and had to remain for two hours,
until they started upward on the rough slopes, giving me a
chance to descend without alarming them. It was a long way
and by the time I reached the bar it was too late to attempt
to find them, then hidden high among the crags. In order to
avoid the possibility of allowing them to see me, I waited
until dark before starting back to the tent. It had been fascinating to sit high on the mountain on this fine clear day and
watch the various bands of sheep. Conies were abundant also,
and their constant bleating had been the only sound breaking
the silence of the mountain world.

Day after day while attempting to approach these two rams
my desire to get them had increased. Great care had been
taken to keep my presence concealed from them and from the
other sheep near by, yet now that they had crossed the Polychrome Mountain it was doubtful whether they could again
be found. I had not previously seen this wide-horned ram and
thought that probably he belonged to a band occupying a
feeding area well back in the rough jumble of mountains between Polychrome and the East Fork of the Toklat—a section I had not attempted to investigate. Like all the sheep, he
and his companion were now working back to the feeding
grounds they had occupied for seven months.

My snowshoe trail was well beaten for most of the way
back, but hastening along it in the dark it was three hours
before the camp was reached. There were now about eleven
hours of daylight in which rifle sights could be seen.

March 10. The hunt for the two rams continued during
another perfect day, without breeze or clouds, and the snow-

shoes creaked and squeaked as I sped along exhilarated by the sharp cold air. From a point three miles up the Upper East Branch, the glasses revealed a band of sheep on the mountainside near the limestone peak, where I had attempted to stalk the rams the day before. Recognizing the possibility that they might have recrossed the bar to join these sheep, I thought it wise to take no chances and therefore tramped the mile across the bar in order to approach the area under cover of the slopes and at the same time keep watch of Polychrome Mountain. I had not gone a mile before the pair of rams were seen quietly feeding near the crest of the mountain, where they had last been seen the day before, and in a spot splendidly located for a favorable stalk. Recrossing the bar and advancing a couple of miles I turned diagonally up the lower slope, leaving my snowshoes at the foot of the bluffs.

After putting on the creepers and pulling the straps extra tight, I began the ascent through great snowdrifts where it was most exhausting to force a way, and then up over icy slopes to the top of the bluffs. I remembered that when I had reached this spot in summer the continual chatter of ground squirrels filled the air, while now only the occasional bleat of a cony broke the stillness. I had gone but a short distance along the level top of the bluffs when the two rams walked out in plain sight on the farther brink of a canyon, and after looking about for a few moments, started upward, stopping now and then to crop a mouthful of food. I lay motionless on my side watching them. They kept ascending and finally walked faster, with a steady gait, and passed over the crest. I knew they had started for other ranges and that my only chance to get them was to continue following as long as daylight lasted. It was then noon and I rested while eating a good-sized piece of bread, at the same time watching the ewe bands high on the slopes across the bar. Although at that hour the temperature was about 10 below zero, the sun seemed to pour down delightful warmth.

I attacked the steep rocky mountainside and worked upward, now struggling through a canyon, now through snow and broken rock until near the top, where the shale rose

almost sheer for twenty feet with a perpendicular rim rock
six feet high forming the crest. When studying the ascent
from below no better spot had appeared, yet here I paused
some time before attempting it. Then, with rifle on my back
and digging the ends of the creepers in the shale while holding
on as best I could with gloved hands, I crawled up to the rock
and found it loose and disintegrating. I had taken two steps
up by jamming the toes of the creepers between protruding
pebbles and holding on with bare hands, and was placing my
third foothold when the pebble on which my creeper was resting fell, and the stone I was grasping above began to loosen.
The slope fell so precipitously for a thousand feet that I could
not jump back without falling and dashing downward. After
a moment of fearful suspense I managed to change my handhold, and by a scramble, succeeded in getting a good grip on
the rim, where I held firmly as the rocks under my feet gave
way. Drawing my body up, with elbows over the rim, I lifted
myself up, swung one knee on the edge, and was soon on top.
The sense of serious danger had been so strong and the exertion so great that I rested awhile to recover.

I walked to the point where the rams had disappeared and
saw sections of their trail on the snow, passing over spur
after spur toward the ranges that flank the divide of the East
Fork of the Toklat. I followed their tracks, now and then
pausing to view new areas of rough mountains—the silence
unbroken save by the bleats of the conies. The canyons were
deep, some more than a thousand feet. Passing over one spur
and descending a deep canyon, I climbed over another spur as
high as the mountain crest; and so kept toiling up and down,
often losing the trail on the bare spaces and consuming time
in regaining it. After tramping over three spurs I could see
the trail ahead crossing a very rough country and leading to
a basin at the source of a tributary of East Fork. Three more
canyons and spurs were passed before I reached the crest of
a mountain leading out at right angles from the main range.
Then I saw the two rams three-quarters of a mile below,
quietly feeding near the bottom of a basin, where the ground
appeared checkered from the holes they had made in pawing

away the snow. They were in a splendid place for a stalk, and my eagerness was intense as I dropped back below the crest and descended diagonally over the crusted snowbanks to the bottom of a canyon, where I slid rapidly downward to a point opposite them. Then began an ascent of three hundred feet on hard crust, where it was impossible to avoid making a noise. Pausing below the crest, with rifle ready but fearful that the rams, now within easy shot, had heard my footsteps, I crept forward and slowly arose. What was my dismay to behold them out of range on the crest of a lower ridge and taking a course back toward Polychrome Mountain!

There was nothing to do but take up the trail and again follow it. The rams were steadily traveling, keeping well ahead, always out of sight. Up over a mountain I climbed and then down, up again and through rough canyons, passing three high spurs and coming to the brink of a vast basin with walls almost perpendicular, separating the last spur from Polychrome Mountain. The rams had descended into it and had gone directly up the icy rock of the other side—how, I can never know. I saw them just below the crest, nearly opposite me. They stood in sharp outline against a golden sky, and going down on the other side, passed out of sight.

In order to reach the mountain I had to travel a long distance on the crest of the spur, broken by sharp crags and spired peaks. The sheep trail wound around on dangerous slopes, yet I was able to keep on it. Nearer the mountain the surface was less broken and here a large band of sheep had entered the trail, probably two days before. I was surprised to see a wolverine track following it—made apparently just after the sheep had passed. It is not improbable that the animal was following and hunting the sheep.

I reached the crest of Polychrome Mountain three miles north of where I had earlier ascended it, and half a mile south of the point where the rams had disappeared. Pushing along on the narrow rim, broken by fantastic pinnacles, I picked up the trail of the rams and cautiously followed to a peak rising from the crest, which I ascended and peered over. There, about three hundred and fifty yards ahead, was another sharp peak on the summit of which stood both rams, looking directly at me. Their alert attitude indicated clearly that they had seen me; they knew I was following them. The sight was impressive, but I was deeply disappointed at the thought that my long hunt would probably end in failure. They quickly turned and went below the peak. I followed, still going as cautiously and noiselessly as possible, and mounted the peak they had been standing on. They were watching from another peak about the same distance ahead, both looking at me as my head rose inch by inch into the line of vision. After a moment they turned and disappeared. The peak they were on was near the north end of the mountain and was the culmination of a great buttress that jutted well out from the crest, from which high cliffs on three sides fell away to precipitous slopes below. I realized at once that the rams might reach parts of the cliffs inaccessible to man and hide there, safe from sight or approach.

With renewed hope however I went forward, cautiously climbing the peak, and found that their tracks were not visible either in the snow beyond, or anywhere below. It was evident that they were hiding on the cliffs; and after a short inspection I concluded they were on the north side. But finding no approach on that side, I turned and carefully inspected the south side. At first I tried to work forward near the crest, but was blocked by a smooth wall. Then, a little lower down, another possible route was attempted. It was very cold, my hands were numb, the sun had been down for a long time and darkness was at hand. Step by step I worked along the cliff, finding footholds or handholds among loose and doubtful rocks, with a perpendicular wall falling two hundred feet below me. With forced disregard of the danger of returning in darkness, I kept on till within twenty feet of the end, where the other side could be seen. I was making some noise when I reached it and before looking over paused to compose myself. It was too dark to see through the peep sight of the rifle, so I put up the open sight. The silence was complete; the slopes below were indistinct; the mountain crests were shadowy forms in the vast space leading to Denali—the great summit alone illumined by the sun.

Creeping upward and pushing my rifle forward, I slowly raised my head. There, only a hundred feet along the cliff and thirty feet below the top, were the two rams. They were lying side by side on a rock shelf jutting out from the wall, their breasts at the very edge, more than a hundred feet of sheer space below. They had heard me and both were looking at me as my eyes reached the line of sight. The picture of these wild rams left an impression that will ever remain. My rifle quickly covered the nearest ram—the one with the close spiral—and as the report echoed and re-echoed, he stretched out convulsed, while the other sprang to his feet. Before he could run I fired again and he also dropped, but slowly rose again. At another shot he fell over the edge at the exact instant the other did; both shooting down through the air together, bounding as they struck the slope below, and continuing downward *for three thousand feet*—their course marked by the snow that was tossed up like patches of vapor.

There was no time to rest, smoke my pipe, or enjoy the landscape, for though in a state of highly wrought exhilaration I instantly realized the seriousness of the situation— caught in the dark on the side of a cliff, with the cold of night rapidly increasing. I started back for a few feet in a very faint light, hoping to find some spot where I could sit, and if necessary remain all night. My squirrel-skin parka in the rucksack might possibly prevent me from freezing. I did find a spot, a very small one, and after putting on the parka, took my position. When my body was warm I began to feel for loose rocks, with the idea of placing them below me so that in case of being overcome with sleep, I would not slide downward, but could not find any. After a while the sky in the east began to brighten, then moonlight touched some of the rocks on the crest, reviving hope that later it might light the cliff sufficiently for me to leave. An hour passed, a fine half-moon rose in the clear sky, the snowfields were illumined between the black shadowy spaces, and light shone directly on the cliff.

My legs and feet were cold, but after stamping to start the

circulation, and with rifle slung on my back, I moved step by step, often securing footholds in the dark spaces by feeling, and gradually arrived at a place I did not believe it possible to cross in the faint light. But a few feet below was a rift in the cliff lighted by the moon and showing a snow slope descending at a very sharp incline. After some hesitation I let myself down and found a hard crust. Unslinging the rifle and using it to make footholes in the hard snow, I worked down to the bed of the canyon. Now that I was in the snow my relief was intense, for I knew that if necessary I could make a snow house and probably keep from freezing. The canyon about a hundred feet below was walled on both sides, and working my way through the narrow space I found the snow sloping smoothly almost to the foot of the mountain. Still holding the rifle as a brake I sat down and slid rapidly, in a short time reaching a gentle slope close to the spot where the tumbling rams had landed. The joy and relief of that moonlight slide through the steep canyon, after the experiences of that day, can never be repeated.

At the spot where I had stopped was a smooth path in the snow, apparently made by some object sliding from the side of the canyon. Going up the opposite side I found the rams, their horns uninjured, the snow matted in their coats and glistening under the moon. Returning, I had not gone more than twenty feet down the smooth incline when I came upon a large male wolverine, frozen stiff. He was the one that had taken my poisoned bait the day before. After crossing the slope for two miles and just before reaching the cliffs a thousand feet above, he had died and rolled down.

I was too elated to mind the tramp of two miles to recover my snowshoes, or the longer tramp back to the tent, where the cheer of tea, food, and warmth awaited me. That was my last hunt for sheep in the northern wilderness. The heads of these two rams now hang on my walls, constantly reminding me of the experiences of that day.

March 11. During the night a fox had ventured close to the tent. In the morning while driving the dog team around the point of Divide Mountain on the way to the big rams

killed last evening we saw four small rams crossing the bar
to Forks Mountain. They were at last going to their accustomed summer feeding ground, where they would remain until
fall. Reaching the spot where the old rams with the coveted
horns had fallen I photographed them and took off the heads
and scalps. The horns of both were excellent specimens, one
having eight rings and measuring 12¾ inches in circumference, 37¾ in length, and 23¾ from tip to tip; the other, six
rings, measuring 12⅝ inches in circumference, 32⅜ in length,
and 31 from tip to tip. The dogs pulled all the meat to the
sled, on which it was loaded and hauled to camp.

The wolverine, a fine male specimen, weighed 36 pounds.
His total length was 43⅝ inches, tail 8⁹⁄₁₆ inches, hind foot
7½, height 15¾. His stomach contained the feathers of
ptarmigan and the remains, including two tails, of ground
squirrels. It does not seem possible that a wolverine could at
this season dig out a ground squirrel, which would imply that
an occasional squirrel had broken its hibernation and had
come to the surface, where it had been captured.

March 12–13. Minimum temperatures −22 degrees, −33
degrees. Clear weather continued for the next five days, while
the temperature remained low. Yet in the sunlight it was a
joy to be out among the mountains. On March 12 a pine grosbeak, the last migrating bird to leave in the fall, was the first
to arrive in the cold spring. Its sweet notes sounding in the
woods near the tent, like those of the water ouzel, seemed in-
consistent with the environment. Willow ptarmigan, an occasional jay, redpolls, and chickadees were about the woods
here, with now and then a downy woodpecker among the willows; while here and there, usually quite high, was a snowy
owl. Foxes were very active, running all over the upper country. Karstens caught three in two days, but I did not succeed
in getting any in my traps. A few red squirrels chattered
in the trees, but most of the mice and shrews kept under the
snow.

March 14–15. Minimum temperatures −25 degrees, −19
degrees. On March 14 a strong wind swept the mountain
slopes, which resumed their usual winter appearance of snow

and ice intermingled with bare areas. While crossing the flats I came upon a fresh wolf track and followed it. The wolf had struck the trail of a small sheep that had descended Divide Mountain and crossed the bars, and had followed it on the run up Forks Mountain. There he had turned and gone back to Divide Mountain, climbing fairly high and passing around the slope. Finally, seeing three ewes feeding about seventy-five yards below, he had crept a few yards and dashed toward them. His running tracks approached them to within about a hundred feet and then turned diagonally upward. The sheep had escaped by rushing toward a craggy place a hundred and fifty yards above. He had failed to catch them, although he chased them nearly to the rocks.

At the saddle the wolf had gone over to the west side of Divide Mountain and there dashed down at a single sheep in exactly the same way, with the same result. Then he had crossed the bar and gone over the slopes of the bordering mountain, where there were but few sheep. This had happened early in the morning. Another wolf had hunted in a similar way over by Old Camp Mountain and its method of pursuit by dashing down on the sheep from above was exactly the same. In all, I carefully observed nine records, plainly written on the snow, where these two wolves had thus tried to catch sheep. Doubtless they had made several other attempts. Except in the case of the wolf that had crossed the flat following the sheep trail, I saw no signs of any other method of hunting.

There was no evidence that a wolf had caught a sheep, but all the sheep in these areas had become badly frightened and most of them kept very high. It was only for two days that wolves had come as far east as Divide Mountain; most of the time for about two weeks they had hunted along the divide toward Clearwater Creek, where there were but few sheep. Although neither Karstens nor I saw these wolves, the snow revealed their movements, showing that they had traveled widely toward the west. These were the only wolf tracks observed by me inside these mountain ranges. I believe nearly all the wolves remained in the lower country following the caribou outside the ranges, and that these two were attracted here by the killing and wounding of sheep on the outside mountain by the market hunters. We could not entice them into traps.

At this time I noticed that the ewes were slightly swollen with lambs. Occasionally a last season's lamb, still conspicuously small and nursing, was running with its mother. Such lambs must have been born in June or even in early July.

March 16. Minimum temperature −23 degrees. While going over the Teklanika Divide today I found the burrow of a fox near some willows, with well-beaten trails leading out in all directions. It had kept the hole open by constantly digging away the snow, and had dug all about for mice. I was surprised to see fresh tracks of a flock of ptarmigan in the low willows within a few feet of the burrow!

Not very high on the east end of Forks Mountain was a band of twelve rams, some with large horns—one with very big ones. After a long stalk I peered over a knoll and found them all lying down, some with their necks stretched out, the heads resting on the ground on one horn. After arranging my kodak I slowly arose, but they quickly saw me and ran upward among the rocks, where some of them paused to look back. They were rather distant, but not too far to show on the film. They ran up and bunched on the very peak, their forms and horns clearly silhouetted, presenting the most magnificent of all animal sights on mountains—rams standing motionless and alert on the skyline.

A large band of ewes was on the slopes to the east; in fact, many of the sheep had gone there since they were disturbed by the wolf. A wolf frightens sheep more than does any other animal, principally for the reason that he continually chases them. Other enemies capture them by stealth.

March 17–19. Minimum temperatures −23 degrees, −24 degrees, −19 degrees. During these three days I traveled in the mountains, watching the sheep and following the wolf tracks. Several wolverines were about, and foxes continued numerous, though none got into my traps. Karstens caught a fine cross fox, thus completing a nice series for the Biological Survey. He had also found the claws of a wolverine in one of his traps.

The sheep bands were loosely formed; they had not yet consolidated for the summer, but were still obliged to travel actively for food. Yet the various independent small bands, which later would make up the larger ones, were all the time working near each other—that is, feeding in the same localities.

On March 19 I gathered in my traps and returned to the cabin. On approaching it I whistled and all the jays flew about me in great excitement, some alighting on my head and shoulders.

During my absence the thermometer at the cabin had recorded a temperature of 41 degrees below zero—eight degrees lower than the lowest recorded by a similar thermometer outside my tent four miles above.

March 20–25. On three of these six days there were heavy snowstorms. Much work remained to be done. I had to prepare specimens, skin all the foxes, which now were solidly frozen, develop photograph films, and chop and split a large supply of wood. Karstens was to leave as soon as possible for Nenana, taking a full sled load of trophies and natural history material. Then he must go to Fairbanks and bring back the horse *Toklat*, which would be needed in May to pack supplies to the base of Denali, where spring bear hunting might be most interesting. Time was found however to make several trips about the woods, and one back over Cabin Divide.

At five one afternoon the temperature was 12 degrees below zero; then a strong warm wind sprang up from the south and at the end of an hour, when it ceased, the thermometer registered 20 degrees above—but immediately lowered again, falling to 12 degrees below before morning. Such winds, occasional all through the winter, were quite warm within the mountains near the main range, but below, outside the ranges, were very cold.

During this week some of the jays began to sing. Their song was a beautiful prolonged warble of rising and falling inflection, modulated in tone and repeated more and more frequently each day. Many redpolls were flying over, and occasionally the sweet note of a pine grosbeak sounded among the snow-laden spruces.

March 26. The day was clear and warm when Karstens with dogs and sled set out for Nenana and Fairbanks. I was soon out for a tramp up through Bear Draw, over the narrow divide, and among the ranges bordering Cabin Divide. The country was immaculately white, broken only by the exposed rock on the mountains. A few small bands of sheep were seen, nearly all traveling to find areas of lighter snow.

Ptarmigan were numerous below, but the only mammal tracks observed were those of a lynx, a wolverine, and a few weasels. In the evening there was a wonderful yellow sky, followed after dark by a brilliant display of northern lights.

On returning to the cabin I missed the dogs, which all winter had greeted me with demonstrations of joy. One of them, *Silas,* possessed traits of a kind to enlist strong affection; and all had been so interesting that I had become very fond of them. It was a long time before I could accustom myself to their absence.

March 27–29. On March 27 there was a light fall of snow. I set a trap for a lynx at the edge of Bear Draw, where the ptarmigan were very numerous.

The pelages of both the mice and the shrews caught in our traps were now in prime condition and the testes of the shrews were much enlarged.

Complete enjoyment of the wilderness needs periods of solitude. And in the silence since the departure of my companion, the feeling of undisturbed freedom gave me the happiness I have always realized when thus living alone.

A heavy blizzard continued during the next two days and great quantities of snow poured over the country. I wandered through the woods in three feet of snow, where some of the drifts were five or six feet deep. A couple of rabbits were there, and three or four flocks of ptarmigan. Chickadees fed about the trees regardless of the storm, while the Canada jays sitting on limbs close to the tree trunks were continually singing. One of them sprang a mouse trap, the wire striking its head. I brought it into the cabin in a dazed condition, and after marking it by clipping a few of the tail feathers, put it down on my couch. After two hours it revived, hopped about the floor, and began to fly from place to place, picking up food and storing it in the cabin. Then I let it out.

March 30–31. On March 30 there was a heavy wind, and snow fell all the afternoon. When I fed the jays the one that had been injured seemed too stiff and sore to fly down from the low limb on which it was sitting, but leaned forward and took food from my hand.

A lynx in my trap was brought back to the cabin. While taking off its skin I caught a hundred and twenty-six fleas as they crawled to the tips of the hairs. These were only a portion of the swarm, the rest remaining in the fur.

The last day of March I passed among the mountains, watching a few bands of sheep. Most of the foxes of this immediate region seemed to range above the Forks, as their tracks were not often seen below. While returning I found the tracks of my escaped wolverine, not only near the cabin, but also for a short distance following my trail made in the morning. Noticing a rabbit track in the woods I followed it to the upturned roots of a tree, where the animal was sitting in a well-protected position. It was collected for a specimen.

Tramping and Hunting from the Cabin.
Wolverine.
Lynx and White Rabbits.
Ground Squirrels.
Early Birds.
First Grizzly of Spring.

April 1–4. On the first of April a dense fog hung over the country. The day was mild and calm and mystery pervaded the woods, causing a sense of pleasant loneliness. The spruces were draped with hoary frost, thickest on the north side, where it was woven about the branches in delicate textures. Redpolls were abundant in the woods, and it was pleasant to hear through the fog the sweet notes of pine grosbeaks.

Although I could see only a few feet in any direction, I walked through Bear Draw without finding anything in the traps, and returning, followed the various trails of the escaped wolverine near the cabin. She had buried in the snow many pieces of meat, the remainder of the stock left her, and the night before had dug up two of them. In burying food she had followed the usual practice of wolverines, a habit, like that of the jays, of storing food for future use. This, in addition to their gluttonous capacity, explains why, when they rob caches, they carry away such surprising quantities of food. It is likely also that this storing instinct induces them at times to pack away other articles—especially those that retain the odor of food.

On April 2 it snowed nearly all day. The wolverine had sprung and overturned the trap set for her, and had eaten all the rabbit flesh under and about it. Many ptarmigan were in the woods, all very wild, as they always were immediately after storms, and at other times when among the trees. I shot one for the larder; its crop was full of willow buds—the exclusive food of these birds in winter.

On April 3 the snow continued to fall most of the day. The

wolverine had again sprung my trap. I followed her trail to the upturned roots of a dead tree near the end of the woods and heard her growl. Digging away the snow I could see her collar and a few inches of chain on her neck. She was shot and her skull preserved for a specimen.

Going to Bear Draw I watched a band of sheep. They were very active, pawing away snow in search of feed and restlessly moving over considerable distances.

April 4 seemed very cold and snow fell abundantly until dark.

April 5. Temperature — 16 degrees. April was clear, cold, and calm. Yet, while I was tramping over Cabin Divide at noon, the sun was almost hot. Turning down the other side I went up through the box canyon to the place where I had killed the rams on February 29 and saw a few sheep which, protected from the wind, had evidently remained feeding there.

Before the sun's rays had warmed the surface, the new snowfields were very white and fresh—showing only a few uncovered rocks. But now, owing to the warmer sun and changed atmospheric conditions, the rocks and cliffs everywhere were overspread with thin delicate frostings in exquisite patterns that sparkled in the sunlight, producing one of the most beautiful effects I have seen among the mountains. Aside from a sheep and a fox track I saw no signs of life except ptarmigan, which had now returned to the willows in high places—as high on the mountains as willows grow.

April 6 and 7. On April 6 when leaving camp I saw a man approaching from the bar below. He was a prospector named Capps, from Glacier Creek, who with two companions was camped on the Clearwater. They had come to get some meat but were unable to find any. They had followed my old snowshoe trail hoping to find my cabin. Soon the others came and all spent the night with me. Since they were not hunters and did not want to attempt any more mountain climbing for sheep, they decided after talking with me to go down the river and try for caribou.

Bread baking occupied the next morning, and in the afternoon I crossed the mountains near Bear Draw, but saw no sheep or other sign of animal life. A heavy north wind and a driving snowstorm had caused the game to seek shelter.

April 8–10. April 8 was bright and clear. Reaching the Forks in the morning, I saw a lynx high on the bluffs of Forks Mountain; it had seen me and had started to run. Evidently it had gone to the crags for no other purpose than to hunt sheep. It appeared again high on the mountainside below some cliffs and saw me as I came in sight, and while I stood motionless, it crept forward a little way and then crouched and remained there watching me. When I moved again it ran swiftly along the slope and soon was lost to sight.

Only a few sheep were on Divide Mountain, and only two small bands in sight on Polychrome Mountain.

Above the bluffs of Forks Mountain I saw a flock of snow buntings; and a golden eagle was soaring high above a huge nest that had been conspicuous on the cliffs ever since I had become familiar with the features of the mountain. These were positive signs of spring.

After returning to the cabin I looked out on the bars and saw a man about a mile below, groping about and using his rifle as a staff. Observing that he was going irregularly in small circles and believing he was in trouble, perhaps ill, I hastened to him and found it was Capps. He was completely snow blind, his eyes badly inflamed and exceedingly painful. While hunting caribou below the outside mountain the glare had suddenly affected his eyes so he could scarcely hold them open. He had started for my cabin but by the time I saw him was quite helpless and did not know where he was. I brought him to the cabin, put him in Karstens' bunk and tried to relieve his pain by applying bandages of hot water, but he suffered intensely all through the night.

The next day (April 9) I remained at the cabin with him. A jay found in one of the mouse traps set under a spruce far from the cabin was so badly wounded that I had to kill it. In the afternoon Karstens returned with my horse *Toklat*, accompanied by his favorite dog *Silas*—the other dogs being left at Nenana. He had met Merrifield hauling a sled load of material for Nenana and so had been saved the trip to Fairbanks to get the horse.

April 10 was a clear warm day, the first that seemed really springlike. Tramping through the woods and back over Cabin Peak, I watched a couple of bands of sheep. Redpolls were now very numerous, and I saw two of the jays darting at a hawk owl on the top of a spruce tree. But the most interesting event of the day was the discovery of the first ground squirrel of spring. While crossing the flat east of the woods I heard its chatter and soon saw it run a short distance and dive into its hole.

April 11–18. Beginning on April 10 the sky was clear for eight days, but a heavy wind blew each day except on the 11th. It now became dark about 7.15 P. M. and dawned at 3 A. M. On the high mountain slopes exposed to the sun the snow melted slightly, but elsewhere showed no evidence of thawing. While tramping in places sheltered from the wind the sun felt hot and I did not wear gloves.

On April 12 Capps left the cabin. We put up a tent to shelter the horse and built a railing in front of the hay stack so he could feed without scattering the hay.

For a long time I had been watching the jays, trying to locate a nest, but without success. The foliage of the spruces was so dense as easily to conceal a nest, and except when I called the jays to feed, they kept away in the woods. Now and then one was seen sitting on a limb preening its feathers. Only a few ground squirrels came out, as they were still obliged to dig up through the snow.

The slight crust was not hard enough to prevent the ptarmigan from leaving footprints. Many measurements were made of their stride (from front toe to front toe) , and it was surprising to find the average between 12 and 14 inches— rarely shortening under 12 inches. One day a lynx track was followed through the woods and back over the ridges, until lost on the bare slopes. It led to the willow patches where there were ptarmigan tracks, and the snow showed that the lynx had often crouched, evidently with the idea of capturing a ptarmigan. Owing to the winds, the sheep did not feed so

boldly on the exposed slopes, and now all the ewes were heavy
with lambs. On April 14 I observed snowbirds and redpolls,
but few other birds were seen. Mouse tracks, however, again
became very abundant and a large number of traps were set
in order to collect specimens in spring pelage.

April 19. All day a warm wind blew strongly from the
south and everywhere the snow began to melt. Several lemmings, red-backed mice, meadow mice, a shrew, and a large
ground squirrel were caught in traps set in the woods. All,
particularly the ground squirrel, were remarkably fat, and
the testicles of the males were much swollen, although as yet
there was no evidence of embryos in the females. The stomachs of all contained green material.

In the afternoon nine ewes and lambs were seen toward the
head of Bear Draw, all feeding high on broken rock slopes
where vegetation was scanty. Practically all the old long hair
about the face and heads of the sheep was shed, only here and
there tufts remaining.

The most surprising observation was the complete absence
of ravens. During early winter they had been abundant, but
for some time I had noticed a progressive scarcity,* and now
all had disappeared—nor was one observed afterward so long
as I remained in that part of the country. Later, the probable
cause of their disappearance was learned. At Nenana two
trappers who had spent the winter thirty miles to the eastward of my cabin told me that during March they had put out
lines of poisoned bait for foxes, covering all that section of
the mountains, with one line reaching almost to the East
Fork of the Toklat. Strychnin in small balls of tallow had
been scattered along their snowshoe trails. They said that
nearly 200 ravens had been found dead from the poison, and
that they had not been successful in poisoning the foxes until
after the ravens had been practically exterminated. Then
they killed more than sixty foxes, including seven fine silver
grays.

April 21. The warm wind continued, the snow again
showed evidence of melting, and on the mountain slopes I

---

* Last mentioned on February 9, 1908.

first noticed that it was slightly settling. The mouse traps were well filled, and in one I regretted to find a dead jay. Lemmings were so abundant that several were caught in traps set at holes grouped within a few feet of each other, as well as specimens of *Microtus* and *Evotomys*. To avoid killing the jays, the traps were carefully concealed.

A pair of ptarmigan were seen in the woods, the female still white, the male beginning to turn—the neck, throat, and sides of head already dark brown, the comb quite red. They were very tame, acting quite differently from those I had seen in the woods during the past month. Ground squirrels were digging out of the snow very rapidly in the timber, but on the open slopes above only a few had come out. They seemed fatter than when they began to hibernate in the fall, and their claws were long and sharp.

In the afternoon I tramped back over the mountains to see the sheep and noticed several bands of ewes, all feeding among the broken rock well toward the crests, particularly where the snow had recently melted. Now the ewes fed only a short time before lying down to rest. Through the glasses they could be seen pawing a great deal among the rocks, even where there was no snow.

Since April 19 or 20, beginning about seven each evening and continuing about twenty minutes there had been a wonderful pink sky all around the horizon except to the west. It resembled the colors of the winter skies, yet seemed softer.

There was no sign of grass or green vegetation anywhere on the bare slopes, yet I wrote in my journal that it seemed like the verge of spring.

Toklat, my horse, surely felt lonesome. When I was outside the cabin he followed me about, and when inside preparing specimens by an open window, he would stand close to it by the hour and watch me. When I left for a tramp he could follow only a short distance where the trails were hard, and where the snow was too soft to bear his weight he seemed to regret parting.

April 22. The day was clear, the sun hot, and the snow melted more rapidly. Three jays were found dead in the traps, so I removed them all from the woods and set them back on the slopes east of the cabin. Great horned owls were now more frequent in the timber of the upper country, hooting every evening either in the cabin woods or in those across the bar, probably attracted by the abundance of mice.

Sam Means arrived with his three dogs from Fairbanks en route for the foot of Denali, where he was going to take photographs.

April 23–25. The south wind continued for two days, which were occupied in preparing specimens of mammals, attending to traps, and tramping to observe sheep. April 24 was the day when the snow softened sufficiently to invite all the ground squirrels to come out, for the woods suddenly became alive with them and they were running abundantly all over the flats and adjacent areas. Ptarmigan were observed in pairs; the cocks were beginning to be demonstrative with the females, and their heads were now dark brown. April 25 was a warm clear day and the mice were even more in evidence running over the snow. The sheep still kept high among the broken rocks, scarcely any appearing on the lower slopes. Very few birds had arrived—so far as observed—but it is likely that many had passed over this upper region.

April 26. The day was beautifully clear and calm with congenial warmth in the air, bringing joy as I tramped up Cabin Creek and over the divide to the East Fork of the Toklat. Here and there was now exposed the top of a 'nigger head' and I dreaded the approaching time when instead of sailing freely over the surface on snowshoes, I must again struggle on foot through the boggy uneven ground.

The welcome song of a tree sparrow greeted my ears, and a pair were seen feeding low in the willows. Afterward they seemed quiet and kept concealed among the bushes. The croaking of ptarmigan was frequently heard. They were now in pairs and very numerous. The cocks with combs erect kept strutting about the females and chasing them, and some of the hens were beginning to change to a darker color, particularly about the head and neck. A moth, flying close to the snow of the creek bed, indicated the awakening of the insect

world. Ground squirrels were everywhere except on the deep
snow of the divide. Their constant chatter, even in the midst
of snowfields, signified the arrival of spring. But the most
interesting sight was that of thousands and thousands of lemmings running everywhere high and low over the snow. Sitting up, running, chasing each other, hurrying from hole to
hole, they were everywhere; never before have I been in the
presence of so much wild life, small as it was. Some meadow
mice (*Microtus*) were among them, but neither red-backed
mice nor shrews. Golden eagles were soaring across the snowfields, and three large rams with splendid horns were feeding
high among the broken rocks near the crests bordering the
south side of the divide.

Arriving at the Upper East Branch I made tea in the open
for the first time since October, and while enjoying the rest,
saw twelve rams—some with extraordinarily fine horns—not
far away but high on the rough rocky slope of the mountain
across the Fork. I noticed, as had been observed several times
recently, that they had been pawing among the broken rock
where there was no snow. While watching them my eye
caught a movement a hundred yards from them on the same
level, and the glasses revealed a lynx. It was creeping along
a rock and after stopping a moment continued toward them
for twenty feet to another rock. Then it carefully crept up
the rock and slowly raised its head—just enough to watch
them. There it remained for twenty minutes while the rams
fed about the same spot, constantly keeping a careful watch
in all directions. They then moved away and finally the last
passed out of sight. The lynx at once hurried diagonally upward in their direction, moving in a rapid crouching walk and
rising to full height every few feet to look ahead, yet keeping
on until near the crest when it again crept up a rock and
slowly lifting its head, looked for a moment; then stood at
full height and looked again. Not seeing the sheep it descended, crept slowly along the crest, and disappeared on the
other side. I crossed the river, went up a narrow canyon and
after climbing to the spot where the lynx had last been seen,
walked far along the crest but did not again see either the

lynx or the rams. At a distance were several bands of ewes all feeding among broken rocks, and over the divide still other bands were seen, resting for the night.

While descending the ridges leading down to the Cabin Woods I heard a thin chatter and saw a lemming trying to dig down through the crust. But the crust was too hard and instead of running, it turned and faced me, chattering. As I stepped a little nearer it assumed a fierce attitude and rushed at me, again chattering in rage. When I stooped and extended my hand it rushed at me again and again and would have bitten my fingers had not my hand been quickly withdrawn. It never stopped chattering; its fury increased as I teased it. It would not run. It was a fine male so I saved it for a specimen. That day I saw several northern shrikes, and on the divide a very dark snowy owl flying low often dipped down to grasp a mouse, after which it would alight on a hummock and eat it.

Arriving near the cabin I found the traps full of lemmings and containing also a few meadow mice (*Microtus*). It was seldom now that a red-backed mouse (*Evotomys*) or a shrew was caught in the traps. While they were abundant in winter, they were not much in evidence after March. Two more of the jays were dead in the traps and it was not long before the others met the same fate—for they seemed to find the baited traps at any distance. Their strange companionship became only an interesting memory. They had not endeared themselves to me, for their chief characteristic had been greed.

That day I realized that my plan to hunt bears about Denali could not be fulfilled. The season would be over before enough vegetation would grow to support the horse—and the horse was necessary to pack equipment and provisions.

April 27 and 28. During these two days a strong south wind blew again. April 28 was so warm that there was a genuine thaw, the snow becoming very wet.

Besides preparing specimens of mammals I observed several bands of ewes, all continuing to feed high among the rocks. They were rapidly shedding their winter coats, presenting a ragged appearance as if patched with long hair.

Lynxes were common in the timber, judging from the number of their tracks, but I could discover no evidence that they were hunting mice; and mice were so abundant that if the lynxes had eaten them to any extent they must have been well fed. On the contrary, all the lynxes that I examined were in a very starved condition.

In this region rabbits had been scarce in 1906, and the year 1907 was the maximum of their periodic scarcity. Yet that year lynxes were common throughout the region, as all with whom I discussed the subject agreed. The generally accepted theory that the abundance or scarcity of lynxes corresponds with the abundance or scarcity of rabbits, did not prove to be a fact.*

April 29. Early in the morning the ruby-crowned kinglets were pouring out their full volume of song in the woods; bluebottle flies and a small black fly were abundant, and a spider was seen crawling over the snow. Later in the day the first junco was observed—it was quietly feeding in the low willows on a high mountain slope. The snow had so melted on the ice covering the bars that for the first time I could walk on it without snowshoes. Small streams were pouring down all the ravines, and the mountains were assuming a vertically striated aspect owing to the melting of the snow along the gulches.

The day was spent among the mountains near the Forks

---

* The fact of the periodic increase and decrease of the northern lynx and the white rabbit, and the additional fact that in general terms the abundance or scarcity of the lynx is dependent on the abundance or scarcity of the rabbit, have been known for generations to the northern tribes of Alaska and Canada, and have been commented on by various early writers. In the case of the rabbit the decrease is due to disease; in the case of the lynx, to starvation augmented by defective reproduction.

During 1907, in the region immediately north of the Alaska Range, rabbits were at their minimum while lynxes were still abundant—though in a starving condition. And Sheldon's discovery that lynxes were then killing sheep is significant in the same connection. In other words, during the year of greatest scarcity of rabbits, lynxes were still fairly plentiful but were having great difficulty in securing food. They were emaciated and in no condition to withstand the winter, and furthermore were so enfeebled that the survivors must have been in no condition for breeding. The year of greatest scarcity of the lynx therefore would not coincide exactly with the rabbit minimum but would occur the following year.—C. H. M.

watching the sheep, which still fed high on the bare areas. A golden eagle was on her nest on the cliffs at the Forks. She did not leave until I looked down on her from above, when she flew over the crests. There were two eggs in the nest. At considerable risk I worked along the cliffs to a point from which I obtained a photograph showing the nest and eggs, the slopes of Divide Mountain, and the north end of Polychrome Mountain. Above the cliffs I saw a dead meadow mouse about three feet up from the ground, transfixed on the sharp point of a broken willow. It was not mutilated in any way and must have been placed there by a shrike.

April 30–May 1. On the morning of the last day of April juncos were in the woods, and numerous ruby-crowned kinglets were singing their loud warbling notes. One ever marvels that such rich songs can issue from the throats of such tiny birds. Now the insect world seemed alive, though as yet there was no green vegetation; still, a mosquito was seen flying over two feet of snow.

Down the river, where the snow was melting faster than near camp, more water was in the creeks, and streams were dashing down the slopes. The ice of the main river, for the first time, was beginning to sink in its channel.

Two bands of sheep were observed, both feeding high, and a pair of short-eared owls, soaring.

Heretofore all the ground squirrels captured were males, but today I caught a female; she contained no embryos. These squirrels were now all out, high and low. The males came out first, the females later. Judging by the actions of the males, which were chasing the females and running rather long distances to different holes, they were beginning to breed.

May 1 was a very windy day but I went out and watched a few sheep, and noticed several short-eared owls, all flying high.

May 2. May 2 was so beautiful and clear that I started for Bear Draw intending to climb the mountains at its head to obtain a series of photographs. At this time the landscape was more striking than at any other time of the year—all the mountains were exquisitely beautiful. The snow on the slopes

most exposed to the sun had melted, leaving them striped.
The rock colors were fresh and rich, the south slopes in places
so bare as to appear only narrowly streaked with white. The
whole landscape was full of contrasts.

This was the first day since fall that it was practicable to
go without snowshoes. There were sheep on the mountains
about Bear Draw as I climbed up over the broken rock slopes
near the head of the highest peak of the south crest.

Here all the glories of the region were visible—in the west
the great Denali rising in unbroken white; nearer by a circular panorama of mountains, canyons, rivers, and valleys—
a vast area of contrasting colors, now more beautiful than
I had ever beheld it. After taking numerous photographs I sat
for a long time to enjoy the scene. I had tramped over it more
than any one else and knew recesses that no other white man
had ever seen; and because of having wandered so much alone
in it I felt associated with it by an intimacy that almost made
me a part of it. My sense of mental proprietorship in that
region is still strong.

May 3. Careful attention was given the tracks of sheep,
caribou, and horses made last fall and now uncovered by the
melting of the snow. Many of them looked so fresh that they
seemed only a few days old.

During the previous two weeks I had daily watched for
signs of bears, knowing that at any time they might come
forth from their winter sleep. In fact, I had been directing my
tramps in the hope of seeing their well-known trails on the
snow slopes. But as yet there had been no evidence that a bear
was anywhere in the country.

On May 3 I tramped up the Upper East Branch and spent
a good part of the morning locating the sheep bands seen the
day before. This was mainly for the purpose of observing the
distance they had traveled in search of new feeding areas, for
at this time they were moving about more actively than in
early April. Starting from the west face of Forks Mountain
a band of twenty ewes had gone over to near Polychrome
Pass; a band of six that had been in Bear Draw the day before were now beyond the twenty; and still farther on were

eleven fine rams near the area where they would spend the summer. Other small bands had not moved far during the past twenty-four hours.

By noon I had gone some distance up the Upper East Branch and there made tea and passed the lunch hour. Under the bright sun the colors of Polychrome Mountain were particularly rich—so beautiful indeed that I was tempted to linger where I could continually behold them.

While lunching I saw the first robin observed this spring, also some rosy finches, and the first butterfly. Then, going a little farther and crossing the bar, I saw two large bands of sheep feeding near the crest, and began to climb, hoping to stalk close enough to see what kind of vegetation they were eating. Before going far the track of a small bear was found on a patch of snow. Climbing to a good lookout I remained for some time watching the slopes, but seeing no bear, returned down the Branch and climbed some high bluffs leading over to East Fork Divide.

Before starting over the Divide I sat down and with the field glasses carefully inspected the mountains. On examining a steep slope, I was rewarded by seeing a small light-colored grizzly. It was indulging in the most grotesque play imaginable, while not a hundred yards above it were more than thirty ewes quietly feeding, all completely indifferent to its near presence. The bear was repeatedly turning somersaults, rolling a few feet down the slope, and running short distances upward. Often it would lie on its back, throw up all four feet and attempt to strike them together. These antics continued for ten minutes or more, while only one of the sheep—a yearling lamb—looked directly at it. The others maintained their usual watch, apparently taking no interest in the bear.

The bear then went at a half-gallop down a canyon leading to the viscera of a sheep previously killed there, and I started toward it against a favorable wind. After descending and climbing out of the canyon I could not see any sign of the bear and went on for some distance before seeing it. It was running at great speed up the steep slope and on reaching the rougher crags, passed out of sight in the canyon. Climbing high and gradually working upward to within three hundred yards of the cliffs from which the wolverine had fallen, I sat down to search the slopes with the glasses, but failed to see the bear. Then, glancing over the cliffs with my naked eyes, I noticed a dark object on a ledge near the upper edge of the cliffs. It was the bear, lying flat on its belly with fore legs stretched forward, its head resting on them. Less than seventy-five yards above it were the sheep, still feeding where they were before.

Through the glasses I saw that the bear was watching me, and just as I was bringing up my rifle, it sprang up and ran. Three shots missed, but while it was still rushing along the slope a fourth shot caused it to stop a moment to seize its left fore leg; then quickly whirling, it ran again, and my fifth shot missed. At the sound of the rifle the sheep ran upward to the crest. The bear disappeared in a canyon and I hurried forward and found its trail. There was a little blood, but the tracks showed that the leg was not broken. Going out on a spur, through the glass I saw the bear half a mile away, still running diagonally upward at the same speed. Every hundred yards or so it stopped a moment, apparently to lick its wounded leg. I watched it at intervals till it passed over the crest a mile and a half beyond.

Returning to the remains of the sheep I carefully studied the record on the snow. About two days before, as near as could be judged, the bear had come from the direction of East Fork Divide and had fed on the viscera. Apparently it had visited them three times and had consumed most of them; and each time, after satisfying its appetite, it had climbed half a mile to the cliffs, where it had rested between meals. I saw it descend after its play. It went directly to the carcasses and, discovering my track, made a few hours before, at once ran upward. It was then that I saw it. It was a young bear, probably a female, and must have been a light feeder. I returned to the cabin with an elated feeling, for the bear season was at hand!

Abundance and Antics of Short-Eared Owls.
Grizzly Bears.

May 4. Early in the morning of May 4 the melodious song of a fox sparrow sounded near by, and going out I collected the bird for a specimen. For a week or more many of these sparrows migrated through the cabin woods, but none remained. Another charming bird, the Gambel sparrow, was also first observed. Its song, which soon sounded in all parts of the region, became in May and early June my sweetest association of bear hunting days.

The day was fine and clear and I hastened down the river and along the outside mountains, but not seeing any bear signs, returned late in the afternoon.

The evening was calm, and taking the shotgun I went back on the ridges to collect a couple of short-eared owls. Lying motionless, flat on my back, on the uneven surface among the tufts of grass, only a short time was required to secure two for specimens as they flew by close to the ground, hunting lemmings. For the next two weeks these owls were exceedingly abundant all over the region, high and low. All were paired, and many hundreds of pairs were there. At times ten or fifteen pairs soared high in the air, near enough together to resemble a flock. While some hunted more or less all through the day, they were most active after six in the evening, both hunting and soaring in easy graceful flight. Even when hunting, the birds of a pair usually remained close together; if they became separated it was only a very short time before they rejoined each other. While hunting the abundant lemmings they flew swiftly close to the ground, now and then merely dipping to grasp one, the act scarcely causing any interruption of the flight. But immediately after picking one up, the owl would alight on a hummock or shrubby tree and quickly eat it—the mate meanwhile circling near until it resumed its hunting flight. The birds of a pair often chased each other and circled in play, then alighted to rest on the ground or on a willow or stunted spruce in the open.

They constantly soared high, not gliding calmly like eagles, hawks, and vultures, but soaring with wings extended for a few moments, then flapping again, meanwhile uttering a rather rapid succession of low hoots that became fainter according to the distance. This habit of soaring in pairs was noted all through the night. At times the owls reached such an altitude that they looked like mere specks in the sky, but even from this height their low hoots could be heard. While soaring aloft, every little while one would dive perpendicularly for twenty feet or more, at the time of descent quickly flapping its wings and making a peculiar noise, which has been described as a shrill barking call, like the *ki-yi* of a small dog—a fair imitation. After repeated and careful observation I was convinced that it was made by the rapid wing beats while diving. Often single birds soared high, and while thus alone the hooting was continuous. Most of the dives were made by single birds, which in many instances were later joined by their mates. Whenever an owl was shot, its mate soared high above me, continually hooting and diving for about an hour. The peculiar actions of the owls at this season are doubtless a part of the mating maneuvers, and I suspect that the habit of hooting when on the wing is a means of keeping in touch with one another.

The great abundance of the owls did not continue after the middle of May, yet some remained throughout the summer.

On calm evenings while delicately tinted clouds hovered over the higher mountains it was delightful to sit on the ridge and watch the performances of these owls.

At dusk when complete silence reigned over the snowy expanse, suddenly a full thrush song, loud and sustained, broke the mysterious calm. It was that of a robin perched on the spire of a high spruce, its voice having a metallic ring much more pronounced than my recollection of it farther south.

Thus to hear it in the snowy wilds gave an impression of the bird entirely different from that gained in more domestic surroundings. From that time on, and from high on the mountains to the lowest valleys, the music of the robin was among the most common, most friendly, and most welcome of the forest songs.

May 5. This was a day of beautiful cloud effects, different from any I had seen before. I was out early searching for bears between the main Toklat and the head of Stony Creek. Twelve or fourteen fine rams were on Sheldon Mountain, having returned to their summer feeding areas, and several ewe bands were in Bear Draw and on Forks Mountain. Going up the bar I reached the creek that comes down the north slopes of Old Camp Mountain, and following it westerly to and over the divide to Stony Creek, had much difficulty ascending the canyons because of deep snow and overflows; but on the ridges the 'nigger heads' were still hard and the walking fairly good. The snow up there was so deeply crusted that it held my weight—a great advantage except for the fact that the bears would not break through to leave conspicuous trails.

Sheep were in sight on all sides as I reached the divide and carefully inspected the areas toward the west. Many rosy finches and snowflakes were migrating by that point, and ptarmigan were much in evidence. Walking up the crest of a spur connecting with Old Camp Mountain, I climbed nearly to the summit and sat down to watch for bears. Light gusts of wind irregularly swept by. Masses of changing clouds, some dark and gloomy, obscured the skies; rainbows arched across some of the cloud-filled spaces; heavy hail squalls descended, but only for a few moments; while here and there the sun broke through, illuminating spots on the slopes and producing contrasts of light and gloom. Intermediate Mountain, near by to the north, was mostly bare, exposing its characteristic black surface; to the west were the ranges at the head of Moose Creek; to the northeast, the snowy tips of the Teklanika Ranges. Directly below me the face of Old Camp Mountain was scarred by canyons, cliffs, buttes and deep ravines; the south slopes of the outside mountains were partly bare; the ice cap of the bar stood in white relief between the dark bordering strips of timber. Each divide and basin was covered with a white cloud that appeared like an island suspended amid the mountains and gave off occasional streamers that reached upward to the crests, while wisps of vapor hung in patches on the slopes. I felt that I had never before seen such exquisite displays and contrasts of mountain landscape.

Numerous sheep were near. No fewer than seven bands, aggregating more than seventy sheep, were feeding or resting on the north slopes of Intermediate Mountain. There were thirteen a few hundred yards below, and more than forty strung along the slopes of Old Camp Mountain. The winter coats were nearly shed. All the mature ewes were swollen with young and rested more than usual, their necks stretched out on the ground. They appeared to feed exclusively by pawing away the gravel or broken rock.

For a long time, high on this mountain, and with all these sheep before me, I waited and watched for a bear. At seven in the evening, not having seen any sign, I decided to return. The sun was low in the clear western sky, the breezes had died down, complete calm prevailed.

I had descended some distance and gone out on a spur when a patch of color five hundred yards away attracted my attention. Turning the glasses, I recognized the back of a bear. Selecting a point a hundred and fifty yards above it from which a good shot could be obtained, only a moment was required to plan a stalk. Cautiously going back and climbing up I reached the spur and then began a careful descent, step by step. Had I attempted to follow the crest of the spur I would have been in plain sight of the bear most of the time, therefore I was obliged to keep on the steep slope just below the crest. It was all broken rock, necessitating extra caution. Once, peering over, I saw the bear stretched on its belly, its head between its fore legs, soundly sleeping, with a fine large cub curled up asleep beside it. Creeping back, I redoubled my caution, often sitting down and arranging the broken rock

for a noiseless footstep. Finally a low jutting cliff stopped
my descent and it was necessary to creep up to the summit
and descend abruptly for fifty feet in plain sight in order to
reach the spot selected for a shot. With rifle ready and eyes
on the sleeping bears, I worked downward. The silence was
broken only by the croaking of cock ptarmigan flying along
the slopes, and the subdued murmur of the creek beneath the
deep snow. The whole mountain panorama before me was
sharp and clear under the setting sun, now just above the
horizon. High in this mountain recess the bears peacefully
slept, while step by step I descended slowly toward them.
There was not a breath of wind.

When I had come within five feet of the selected point,
confident that I had not made the faintest noise, the old bear
suddenly rose and looked downward, her ears pricked up.
Instantly I sat down, with the sight of the rifle covering her
forequarters, and fired. She grabbed her side, turned around
once, and fell a few feet below the crest. The cub jumped up,
began bawling, and followed her. She immediately recovered,
ran back to the crest, turned and came running directly toward me, but with difficulty for her mouth was open and she
was breathing heavily, evidently badly wounded. With rifle
ready I waited, intending to shoot when she reached a point
fifty feet below me. The cub had followed, soon passing her
and keeping well ahead. She did not go more than a hundred
yards before she stopped, turned, and with ears cocked forward looked intently downward across the canyon. She still
thought the danger was in the opposite direction. At another
shot she fell dead on the edge of the crest.

The cub, then at the foot of a steep rocky pitch where I
could not see it, suddenly emerged not four feet from me;
I could have touched it with the rifle. It turned, looked down
at its mother, and stood for two or three minutes bawling
loudly. Then it saw me, stared at me for a second, gave a
great bawl and rushed down over the snowy slope. I got my
first bead on it while it was running up the opposite side;
at the crack of the rifle it fell and rolled down a hundred feet.
At the same moment the old bear suddenly tumbled over the

edge and slid down on the snow to near the bottom of the canyon, where she lay stretched on her back.

I photographed the bears as they lay, and then, as the twilight darkened, took off the skins and skulls and went back over the divide. The old bear was not large. Her stomach was full of roots of the pea vine and contained also a few mice. The cub was a male of the second year. His stomach was full of the same roots, but contained no mice. The pelage of both was long and full, in perfect condition, the color light buffy on the head and body, dark brown on the belly, legs, and tail.

The tramp down the mountain was made during the darkest hours, but it was only a deep dusk; the stars were faintly visible and the footing could be plainly seen. Many ptarmigan were disturbed and flew about me with noisy croaking; short-eared owls were hooting high in the heavens and many were flying close to the ground, hunting. Several times I rested, reclining on the soft skins to smoke my pipe, listen to the unseen owls, and enjoy the solitude. On reaching the creek however, much of the romance was destroyed. The snow had been rapidly melting all day, and the entire bottom was slush. There being no other course, I had to wade through it, always up to my hips, many times sinking to my chest. After two hours of severe work in forcing my way through for a quarter of a mile, I came to the bar, cold and exhausted. It was again dawn when the cabin was reached at 2.30 in the morning.

May 6–7. Considerable snow and hail fell on May 6 and 7. The 6th was occupied in preparing and salting the bear skins. On the 7th I tramped over the Polychrome Pass, climbed that end of Forks Mountain and watched for bears without success. Forty or fifty ewes were peacefully feeding all day on the mountain slopes, twelve rams were in sight farther east, and through the glasses many bands of ewes were visible on Polychrome Mountain. Again a light snow covered the slopes, but late in the afternoon much of it melted. Most of the sheep were then reclining either on the crest or on the saddles of the spurs, and several small bands were settled for the night. A common resting habit was to select crests

from which both sides below could be watched for approaching enemies—lynxes, wolverines, or more rarely wolves.

At dusk that evening, when I reached the timber, robins
were again singing from the spruce tops. I stopped to listen,
thinking how different the song seemed from that heard in
the south, and how appropriate it was to the wild environment. Tree sparrows and Gambel sparrows were singing more,
and ground squirrels were resuming their chatter when approached. Up to this time these squirrels had been much more
silent than during the summer and fall. No green vegetation
of any kind had yet been observed.

May 8. Great horned owls were now more frequently
heard hooting in these upper reaches of timber, probably attracted by the noisy ptarmigan and the abundant mice, although the latter had not been so evident since the melting
of the snow. For some time no rabbit tracks had been seen
anywhere in the upper country, but redpolls, absent lately,
had again appeared and continued to increase and remained
to breed.

May 8 was a fine clear day and I was out early, tramping
up the river. As I emerged from the Cabin Woods and looked
across to the higher slopes of Intermediate Mountain, my
glasses showed a bear's trail in the snow. Not being able to
see the animal, I kept on and soon saw tracks of a fairly large
bear on the glacier bar, evidently made early this morning.
When the bear came to the tracks made by me while going
up the river the day before, it followed them for a few feet
and then ran diagonally up toward the sloping banks bordering the bar. After running a hundred yards it reached my
return tracks and followed them on a walk for eight feet,
then turned and ran directly to the bank and across the rolling pastures in the direction of Bear Draw. Crossing these
pastures to the foot of Cabin Peak I again saw the tracks on
the snow leading to the creek bed, which was now wholly free
from snow. The bear, even after traveling half a mile or
more, was still running.

Following the creek to the divide behind Cabin Peak, where
the snow was still deep, and finding no tracks, I knew the

bear had continued up the Draw and felt quite confident that before the day passed it would be seen among the slopes surrounding the head. But not a track was seen anywhere as I climbed to the crests on the north side and continued to one of the higher peaks, where I sat down and for two hours kept a careful watch.

High among the peaks was a single ewe accompanied by her lamb of the preceding year. Other single ewes had been observed three or four times during the past few days and I thought it possible that they had begun to retire for the purpose of bringing forth their lambs. Rosy finches were abundant along the crest, many golden eagles were soaring above and below, and for the first time a marsh hawk was seen. I climbed over the peaks at the very head of the Draw and watched until late, but no sign of the bear appeared. The landscape was clear, Denali was immaculate, and the surrounding views were a compensation for the failure of the hunt.

While returning around the north crests I suddenly saw two large rams about two hundred yards below on the north slope. Dropping out of their sight I worked toward them until only a hundred yards away. Their horns were large and their winter coats had been shed except for small patches just above the tail and along the spine from the withers to a little way up the neck. Parts of the new coats were fairly clean, other parts very dirty. Their method of feeding, however, was the thing that most interested me. They kept searching along with their noses close to the ground and when they smelled the root of a particular plant, which had not then grown above the surface, they dug down for it with the forefeet, often digging with both feet at the same time. Then they would pull it out with their teeth and eat it. They continued feeding in this manner for half an hour—as long as I watched them. At last I had discovered what for some time had perplexed me: why all the sheep had been feeding so high in places where there was no vegetation. At this period apparently they feed almost exclusively on this root, which I could not identify.

Keeping out of sight of the rams so as not to disturb

them, I came into a breeze flowing from me directly toward them, and looking over the crest saw them running over a spur. They soon climbed an opposite spur, still running, and about three hundred yards from me. On reaching the top they began to feed, slowly working upward toward the main crest. I am sure they became frightened, but not badly frightened, by scenting me.

About ten that night we felt an earthquake tremor, light but unmistakable.

May 9. Early in the morning I collected one of the few yellow-rumped warblers in the woods near the cabin, and asked Karstens to go below with the shotgun to collect other birds. Then I took the up-river trail, and emerging from the woods, paused to look over the slopes of Intermediate Mountain across the bar. All along the east slopes the snow had melted in places, leaving bare areas, while between them, in the canyons and gullies, were deep snowbanks, giving the striated appearance already described.

I was high on one of these snowbanks where yesterday I had seen the big alternate footholes of the bear, when as I scanned the slope through the glasses, a bear suddenly came in the field, traveling north exactly in the old trail. Seating myself, I watched him. He walked along playfully, sometimes pausing to toss his nose backward and forward or from side to side to discover any possible taint in the air; sometimes loitering for no apparent reason; sometimes jumping about from mere excess of animal vigor; then again resuming his march and repeating his antics. Not once did he attempt to feed. In passing over the bare ground he blended with the surface and seemed to glide along, but against backgrounds of snow he stood out in bold relief. Whenever he reached the steep side of a canyon he would gallop down at speed, disappear, and quickly reappear, climbing rapidly on the opposite snowbank.

I had long dreaded a climb for bear on this mountain, because the timber extended up a mile from the river bluffs and in it the snow was soft and three feet deep—deeper in the drifts. Since there was no alternative, however, the situation was studied and a plan of possible stalk decided upon. It was necessary to reach as quickly as possible the north slope of the mountain rising from the canyon that separates it from Sheldon Mountain. By observing the snow there I would learn whether or not the bear had passed, and if not, the wind blowing north would be favorable for an approach. The bar, half a mile wide, was still covered with the great ice sheet through which the river, then at flood, had cut several channels, and was rushing with tremendous force, bearing huge cakes of ice, which, grinding against the icy sides, added rumbling and crashing sounds to the noise of the roaring currents. I was soon on the bar and crossed the several channels on ice bridges, still watching the bear. It finally went out of sight just before I reached the bluffs—but not before the spot where it disappeared had been carefully marked.

Quickly climbing the bluffs, I entered the woods and plunged into the snow to begin the severe struggle upward. Toiling on a few steps at a time, I finally reached the north end of the mountain, but no bear tracks were found. Then slowly zigzagging up to the crest, I looked over on the snow of the other side, but still no bear trail was visible. The bear, therefore, unless he had reversed his direction, which was not probable, must be somewhere between me and the point where he had last been seen. Recalling my failure to find a bear under somewhat similar conditions the preceding day, I determined to search with the utmost care every spot where he might be lying down. At first I could not resist loitering to watch a band of large rams opposite me on Sheldon Mountain, peacefully feeding in their accustomed place high on the slope, giving life and added wildness to these rugged mountains. Some were actively pawing away the snow and rocks to expose the roots, then full of juice, while others rested, looking over the landscape below. But before me was more serious work, for then followed one of the most fascinating bear hunts I have ever had. The slopes were broken and very steep and slippery. Only a very limited area below was visible at any one time. After going a short distance along the crest a slow descent was made to the edge of the woods and every spot carefully scanned as it came in view. Then, after a short advance, I climbed up again, circling when necessary to face the wind when passing places where the bear might be sleeping. Three times during as many hours, with equal care and caution, I climbed down from the crest to the foot of the slopes and up again without seeing anything of the bear.

When on the crest the third time, I rested, ate a piece of bread, and enjoyed the landscape. Flocks of beautiful little rosy finches, then migrating, kept flying about me; tree sparrows were singing sweetly below in the woods, and once a robin flew over so near me that it fluttered away with startled chirping. The ground squirrels, now in their rich spring coats, were again active, running about on the snow, sitting up, or as they dived into their holes, uttering their familiar chatter. Now and then the shrill prolonged whistle of a marmot sounded below, and twice a golden eagle soared along the crest very near.

The search was resumed in the same manner until, after descending and ascending three more times, I reached the crest at the head of the canyon, high above the point where the bear had last been seen. There were no tracks on the snow, either in the canyon or over the crest. Descending to a point where all parts of the slope between me and the woods were exposed to sight, I still found no signs. Feeling certain that the bear must be somewhere directly below, I began methodically to scruntinize every spot exposed to view in the woods.

Suddenly there came into the field of the glasses, a hundred and fifty yards below the edge of the timber, a large whitish object on a snowdrift among the spruces. It was the bear, sleeping. To have found him after such prolonged effort was an intense satisfaction. He was curled up with his head under his chest and looked like a huge white ball of shaggy fur. His hind quarters were toward me, his brown hind legs protruding slightly. The sight of a grizzly bear sleeping in the woods, high on a mountainside under the graceful spruces in the midst of such a stupendous landscape, was a wonderful picture of wilderness life.

Below the dark fringe of timber was the ice field, resounding with the roar and booming of the ice-laden river as the torrent rushed through the gorged channels. Directly opposite were the Cabin Woods, looking hospitable and gentle, isolated as they were in the seemingly desolate country. To the north, Sheldon Mountain presented a bold rugged crest against the darkening sky; while through the canyon of the Toklat below could be seen the timber of the outside country and the vast forested wilderness beyond. Across the canyon stood the Outside Range, beautiful now with its bare gray south slopes of limestone. Beyond the divides, on either side of Cabin Divide Mountain to the east, were the ragged peaks facing the East Fork and the Teklanika, and also the Bear Draw, that beautiful basin surrounded by imposing peaks. Old Camp Mountain fairly frowned above me, while the dark cloudy sky deepened the severity of the wild picture.

After studying the ground and selecting a course with a favorable wind, I began the descent, all the time in plain sight of, and closely watching, the huge animal on the snow. The bear proved a restless sleeper. Every few moments he would raise his head and prick up his ears, seeming to take only snatches of sleep between listenings. It was extremely interesting to work slowly downward step by step over steep and slippery ground, gradually getting nearer. I wanted to reach a point just above the edge of the woods, not far from which was a deep hollow filled with snow that had to be crossed. Finally, without having aroused his suspicion, I arrived at the hollow and waded into the snow, sinking to my hips at each step. After forcing my way through I walked upward and with intense anxiety looked. The bear was still sleeping in the same spot, without showing any symptoms of alarm. Fifty feet remained to be covered, although I was even then within shooting distance.

Cocking my rifle I moved slowly on. Suddenly, from the bar two miles below I heard, faintly but plainly, a shot from Karstens' shotgun. The bear heard it also, for his head was quickly elevated. I squatted motionless, and in a moment the head went down. I had advanced only a few steps when the report of the gun again sounded, and the bear again raised his head listening, but without taking alarm. I soon reached the selected point, a little more than a hundred and fifty yards from the bear, which was still curled up, apparently sleeping, with hind quarters and back toward me, entirely unsuspicious. Putting my elbows on my knees, I considered for a moment whether to whistle and start him up so that a vital shot might be obtained, or to fire at the centre of his back. Realizing however that if he were startled a single jump might take him out of sight in the willows, I aimed and fired. He gave a great leap upward, whirled, staggered panting, and stood facing me, his mouth open. As he turned, my rifle sight quickly covered his chest, and at the shot he bit his foreshoulder where the bullet entered, and dropped dead—without making a single movement. There he lay, a fine mature male grizzly in full and perfect pelage.

I rested awhile, smoked my pipe, and enjoyed the exultation of success. It was late, and after cutting away the willows, I took several photographs of the bear and carefully measured him. His length was 5 feet 7 inches, tail 4½ inches additional, hind foot 11 inches. His height could not be determined in the snow. I had never seen a bear with such long full pelage. The color of the upper parts was buffy white; of legs, belly, and tail, dark brown.

Then began the long and difficult task of taking off the skin in the deep snow. The sky was very dark, snow began to fall, and soon a heavy silent snowstorm descended over the woods. It was a strange, almost weird, task to skin that animal while great flakes of wet snow densely filled the air, wetting me thoroughly, and what was worse, soaking the bearskin and thus adding to the weight I was to carry. Clouds and mists shut off the view, so I could see but a short distance in the silent woods as I worked on in the increasing darkness. The sense of loneliness was broken by the twittering of flocks of snowflakes, and later by the songs of tree sparrows, sweet and cheerful, sounding in the trees; and just as darkness was about to fall, when the woods, filled with falling snow, were silent and mystic, a robin on a nearby treetop poured forth one full thrush-like song—a final lullaby ushering out the twilight. Then came darkness and silence, broken only by the distant rumbling of ice in the river.

Finally the skin was off, and such fat as could be found (very little) was cut from the carcass. Then, after trimming some flesh from the skull, I opened the stomach and found it empty and clean. The bear evidently had just left his winter den and had not begun to feed. The first bullet would have killed him, having entered the back, cut through the lungs, and remained under the skin at the side of a foreshoulder. The second shattered the heart, tore through the stomach and the flesh of the hind leg, broke the bone and lodged under the skin.

Arranging the heavy green skin in a pack, and taking the fat, skull, and rifle in my hands, I began the return struggle through the deep snow. A crust had formed, hard enough to support my foot until I put my weight on it before taking the next step; then it would break, plunging me to my hips in the deep snow. Thus I toiled through the woods and thick brush for more than two hours to make slightly more than a mile to the bar, which I reached thoroughly wet and exhausted. A short rest, then a walk over the hard ice, crossing ice bridges while the river dashed in a wild torrent below, and I reached the cabin at one in the morning to find Karstens soundly sleeping. Quickly making a fire and taking soup, bread, and tea, I smoked my pipe and made the day's record in my journal.

May 10–11. After preparing the bearskin, I walked through the woods and collected the first rusty blackbird I had seen. Two of the jays were still in the woods, but they no longer frequented the vicinity of the cabin. They were rather wild, yet now and then one would answer a call and alight on my hand. Robins were daily increasing in abundance, and the thin piping song of the juncos sounded everywhere among the trees.

On May 11 I followed up the river against a strong wind, observing many bands of sheep, and also the track of a wolverine. After reaching my old camp I turned and tramped to the west divide, where the snow was still so deep that no attempt was made to cross it. Several small bands of ewes were on the mountains along the creek, all feeding very high. From an elevation, the country was watched for a long time but neither a bear nor its tracks were seen.

An interesting sight, however, was a marsh hawk performing flight evolutions I had never witnessed before. It would soar upward in circles to a height of six or seven hundred feet, and then descend rapidly in continuous successions of loop-the-loop circles to within a hundred feet of the ground, when it would again soar and repeat its performance. During one descent I counted twelve circles, in another nine, and in still another eleven. While so doing its wings were kept spread, without a flap. The back dive carried it a long distance downward, when from the momentum gained, it would curve upward twenty or thirty feet, and dive backward again without a pause.

Later in the day Sam Means came along on snowshoes, telling me that his dogs were in a camp a mile behind and that he was hunting ptarmigan to provide food for them, adding that later in the afternoon he would come to my cabin. After a chat with him I returned to the Forks, climbed the point and watched for bears until dusk without result, and then started for the cabin.

Not far below the Forks is the entrance to a long deep canyon leading back to a narrow basin in the mountains, connecting Bear Draw with the Forks Range. A creek from this canyon flows through a narrow flat outside the timber to the bar. While approaching this flat I saw a very large bear digging roots. Quickly circling out on the bar so that the approach might be made in a cross wind, I carefully advanced to a point eighty-five paces away, and sat down with elbows on my knees ready for a shot. The bear never once looked up but continued busily digging roots. At first his hind quarters were toward me, so I waited for him to turn broadside. It was quite dark and his body, blending with the bare ground and willows, was somewhat indistinct, but after twice trying my rifle sight against him I found that there was still plenty of light for accurate aim. For five minutes at least I sat there ready to fire, confident that the bear was mine. I even planned to put the carcass on Sam Means' sled within half an hour, haul it to the cabin, and surprise Karstens.

But suddenly the bear threw up his head and swung around in an alert attitude. Knowing by the way he moved his head that he had winded me, I fired quickly, aiming behind his fore-shoulder. He whirled, grabbed his chest, and fell. I leisurely threw in another cartridge, expecting to witness his dying struggles. But he jumped up and with one spring was in the willows, and the next shot missed him. Partly hidden in the brush he continued to run, and had gone sixty or seventy feet before I could get a bead on him. Then I heard the bullet strike and he fell again, but quickly sprang up and ran into the woods. Hastening to a point where I could see the clear space above, I watched for awhile, but did not see him. Concluding that he was dying, I went forward to take his trail, but before reaching it discovered him climbing a snowbank far up the slope. His head was hanging down, his walk labored, yet he kept on to the edge of the canyon; then, after trying once or twice to run, walked upward a long distance and finally went down into the canyon. By the time I reached the place it was too dark to follow. The character of the blood on the snow showed that he had received a lung shot.

Returning to the cabin, I suffered the disappointment and disgust that usually follow bad work and over-confidence.

May 12. Sam Means arrived early in the morning, just before Karstens and I started with the dog *Silas* to find the bear. *Silas* was so attached to Karstens that, even after my kind treatment throughout the winter, he would not follow me when Karstens was there.

Since the wounded animal might have crossed the bare mountainsides, I thought the dog might help in following the trail. Entering the canyon we found the bottom filled with such soft snow that without snowshoes it was tiresome to tramp through it. Reaching the trail, we followed it up the canyon. At intervals the bear had stopped and lost much blood —in some stretches the whole trail was bloody. The dog took the lead, walking directly in the trail, which once led over a bare slope on a spur. In the snow the bear's feet at each step had sunk down eight or nine inches, yet except in this one place he had not chosen the hard bare ground where the walking was much easier.

This canyon is deep and imposing, the high slopes on either side rising abruptly, narrowing farther up, the summit capped with cliffs, crags, buttes, and turreted columns. As we proceeded the mountains seemed to enclose us, and the incline became so sharp that our progress was slow. After going a mile and a half we looked back through the deep channel between the rocky walls, obtaining splendid vistas of the country beyond.

Another half mile and we were in a narrow amphitheater so completely enclosed by rough sharp peaks that we seemed imprisoned in a deep mountain recess.

We had followed the bear's trail with eager anticipation, expecting at every turn that the wounded animal would come in sight. But when at the head of the canyon we saw the trail zigzagging up a very steep snowdrift, extending three hundred or more yards to the crest, it seemed incredible that any animal after losing so much blood could still have the vitality to make the ascent. As we toiled upward through the snow the surroundings were wild indeed, the rocks about us eroded in such complexity as to give an impression of confused grandeur. Reaching the crest at last we saw, not the expected bear, but his trail leading diagonally down over the snow and across two short rocky spurs, then zigzagging upward and again disappearing. It was discouraging to realize the possibility that the bear had crossed the summit to the bare slopes on the south side. As we started on the trail again, the slope was so steep that I was obliged to dig my cold hands into the snow to prevent pitching down.

Going by one spur, the next shut off the view of the open space above, to which the trail led. Karstens, closely following the dog, passed me and rounding the spur, exclaimed that the bear was ours—that he was so weak he could not walk. He was just below a heavy snowbank that overhung the crest. With his head close to the ground, he was still trying to climb.

Seeing the dog, the bear made a sudden rush of ten or fifteen feet toward him, bawling loudly three or four times and displaying decided rage. But seeing me—I believe for the first time—he stopped, looked at me a moment, turned, and tried again to climb the slope. With rifle across my arm I went fifty feet nearer and then, as he stood still for a moment, took a snapshot with the kodak, and had begun to approach still closer when he actually made another effort to climb. Thinking he would stop, I waited, but he kept on until so near the crest that I knew he would make it. The slope was so steep that I could not keep my balance and at the same time hold the rifle steady, yet at the shot the bear fell, grazed by the bullet (as I learned later), but immediately recovering began again to climb. Another bullet grazed him and he started quartering downward, soon going out of sight behind the jutting rocks.

His course was directly toward me, so, dropping to my knees, I held the rifle ready for a quick shot, for it seemed certain that he would come in sight only eight or ten feet above me. For several minutes he did not appear; then I saw him not a hundred feet away, and he moved another fifty feet to the edge of a rocky slope and stood while I took several photographs. While I was doing this he once or twice raised his head in a threatening manner.

Knowing he was so weak that he could not charge upward through the deep snow, I approached with rifle cocked and kodak ready. When I was about fifteen feet away, he suddenly began to rise, his ears laid flat, he eyes snapping viciously, his expression one of fierce rage. Karstens shouted: "Look out! Shoot!" I pressed the button, dropped the kodak and fired into his chest. He sank back in the snow, dead.

We made a level place and measured him with the utmost care. His length was 5 feet 9½ inches; tail, 5 inches; sole of hind foot with claws, 12 inches. His real length was probably several inches more but the body could not be properly straightened. He was the largest bear I had ever shot in the interior of Alaska. His color was like that of the last bear killed, and the pelage was perfect though not quite so long as that of the last. His claws were strikingly and uniformly white, and slightly translucent. Like the other bear, he had practically no fat. His stomach was full of the same kind of roots and contained also one ground squirrel but no mice.

My first bullet, fired the evening before, had gone low behind his foreshoulder and merely touched the point of one lung, making an inch cut at the lowest edge, and then had passed clear through the body and out through the skin. The bullet that hit him while he was running in the willows had passed through the flesh of one of the hind legs without touching the bone.

While we were taking off the skin, snow began to fall and we felt the cold, so we were glad to start back and warm up by the exertion of wading down through the snow.

Today the first pipits (titlarks) were seen, also a pair of Baird sandpipers and some Alaska longspurs; and in the evening an olive-backed thrush was heard singing in the woods. It was a happy evening we spent in the cabin.

May 13–14. Most of May 13 was occupied in preparing the bear's skin and some bird skins. Late in the afternoon I crossed the bar and watched the large band of rams that still occupied the same area as before high on Sheldon Mountain. May 14 was a lovely clear day with the wind blowing steadily from the south. I was off early to hunt up the river, and when rounding the point at the Forks was surprised to see a ewe and her two yearling lambs feeding a shot distance out on the bar near the farther end of the broken cliffs. In a short time both lambs lay down. Leaving my rifle, I worked forward among the rocks and took several photographs of them —not, however, until they had returned to the cliffs and had climbed upward a few feet. A little higher up I saw some ewes and photographed them also. Keeping concealed behind a rock I shouted several times, but although they looked alertly about, none were frightened enough to leave.

We had entirely consumed the meat of the last rams—those killed on March 11—so I took this opportunity to replenish the supply at a place convenient for getting the meat back to the cabin. Withdrawing under cover and taking my rifle, I again crept forward. A yearling ram fell at the shot and rolled dead to the bar. That was the last sheep I attempted to shoot in Alaska. All the others quickly walked upward and apparently feeling secure among such broken precipices, continued to feed without alarm. The wind was strong, whistling against the cliffs, and I was certain that neither my shouting nor the sound of the shot was clearly heard by them. The winter coat of this yearling lamb and that of many of the others had not yet been shed. The lamb had no fat and its stomach contained some green grass and other green plants and also a much larger quantity of the roots which lately the sheep had been eating almost exclusively. It was clear that although I could not find green vegetation anywhere, the sheep had discovered some.

Leaving the carcass behind some rocks, I crossed the river and went out on the bar. About twenty more sheep were in sight along the south face of Forks Mountain and, what was of extreme interest, eleven big rams were feeding on a low bluff above the mouth of the creek that flows from Polychrome Pass and is connected to the mountain slope by rolling pastures. Later, all lay down and rested for an hour or more. This was most significant, showing that at this time of year the sheep were searching for green vegetation and had to go to unusual spots to find it. Through generations of experience they doubtless knew all the areas where fresh green vegetation first appears in spring. From this time until early June numerous sheep frequented the south slopes of Forks Mountain. Often the rams wandered here from their summer feeding ground in the canyons to the east, though in summer sheep are seldom seen on that side of the mountain.

After crossing the bar and mounting the cut bank leading to the flats, I was gratified to see—what I was always eagerly looking for—the trail of a bear crossing the snowbanks. It was high on the north side of Divide Mountain. Climbing an isolated knoll fifteen or twenty feet high near the foot of the slopes, and searching through the field glasses, I failed to see the animal. The trail proved to be fresh and showed that the bear had come up on the east corner of the mountain and had gone around to the west. I knew that at that time of day it would be resting somewhere on the west face of the mountain and that later it would probably go down and feed on the long wide flats of the Upper West Branch. It would have been unwise for me to tramp up there at that hour, leaving a trail which, should the bear cross it, would frighten it into running a long distance.

Therefore, going back behind the knoll I made a small fire and lunched on tea and bread. A stiff warm wind blowing down the branch prevented the smoke and my scent from reaching the bear. While waiting until three in the afternoon I watched the sheep on Forks Mountain and frequently climbed the knoll to inspect such areas of the flats as were in view, and then started up the flats, keeping close to the foot of the west slope. The weather was clear and delightfully warm—in fact, after the exertion of wading through the snow banks, I perspired freely.

About two miles from the knoll, the bear had left a trail leading down to a thick clump of willows, about which it had tramped down the snow—so I knew it had been sleeping. I was elated that my experience with bears had prevented me in my eagerness from passing this point earlier in the day. The trail led from the willows diagonally to the flat, where fresh diggings proved that the animal was ahead and might be seen at any moment. After climbing some distance, I finally discovered it nearly two miles ahead, pottering about digging roots on the flat opposite Ram Canyon.

Descending to the flat, I went far out from the mountain so that the sun might be more directly behind me and make it more difficult for the bear to see me. Then began a most fascinating stalk over a wide flat, the bear continually in sight, the wind wholly favorable. The bear kept changing its position, walking short distances irregularly in different directions, stopping every few moments to dig and feed, and in this way advancing slowly up the flat. From a distance it looked very large, and at times, when the sun shone at certain angles on its buffy coat, it appeared almost pure white. When its head was turned away from me I moved forward, but stooped low when it was in a position to see me. Proceeding in this way I rapidly gained on it until within half a mile, when it turned at a right angle and without loitering walked toward the river half a mile distant.

It was headed slightly up the river, enabling me to follow in a parallel course. Yet the river was nearer to it than to me, and it waded through the slushy snow and crossed before I reached the bar. The old channels were full of soft snow, some of them deep, retarding my progress; and when I reached the passages of running water they were full of slush and I had difficulty in forcing my way through, often wading higher than my hips. By this time the bear had turned and was coming at a quick pace directly down the river. It would soon be opposite me and when a little farther would get my wind. It was only after a severe struggle that I finally crossed the last channel, thoroughly chilled, and hastened on. The bear was hidden by a ten-foot snowbank through which I sank to my chest and for five or six minutes could not extricate myself. When at last I did reach the top, the bear was three hundred and twenty-two paces ahead—as shown by measurement later—and had just turned to climb the mountain. It was in a position where it might get my scent at any instant.

Seating myself, I aimed directly at its hind quarters and heard the bullet strike. The bear whirled, fell, quickly recovered, ran down the eight-foot slope and out a few feet on the level, then turned up again. Once more I fired at its hind quarters. It struck the wound with one paw and stood a moment facing in my direction. I saw that a hind leg had been broken and knew that the bear could not escape. It floundered into deep snow and stopped, sinking to its belly. It was then broadside and at my shot sank motionless. At my approach it tried to rise but sank again. Going ten feet ahead I piled up a column of snow and placing my kodak on it, took six photographs.

While following that bear I did not once see it *look* for danger. It was killed at 6.15 in the evening, and after photographing it I promptly began to take off the skin. It was a female, not very large, and its color was the same as that of those previously shot. It had practically no fat; its stomach was full of roots of the pea vine and contained also two mice. It was clear that up to that time these roots were the main food of the bears—the mice and ground squirrels being captured incidentally. The teats were full of stale milk, but none of the fur about them showed that a cub had been sucking. Possibly she had had a cub in the winter, which for some reason had not survived.

On reaching the river, loaded with the skin and skull, I found that the water had dammed and that the whole snow field was slush. It was a long struggle, not without danger, but after an hour of severe labor I got through. Reaching the Forks, I added the sheep to the pack and staggered on toward the cabin. The moon was then full, the stars faintly visible. Reaching the cabin shortly after midnight I enjoyed a good supper, and while the awakening songs of robins sounded outside, wrote an account of the bear hunt in my journal.

Along the slope of Divide Mountain conies were more abundant than at any other place in the region tributary to the main Toklat River, and on this warm day they were continually bleating and dodging among the rocks on the slopes. All over the flat ground squirrels were numerous, and the tree sparrows and Gambel sparrows kept up a constant singing, while the robins flew about chirping, their cheery songs sounding everywhere among the willows on the mountain slopes. Today the first Wilson snipe was seen on the flats.

Signs of Spring.
Trip to Stony Creek.
Cock Ptarmigan Fights.
Eagles Attacking Lambs.
Birds Indicate Movements of Grizzly Bear.

May 15–16. Minimum temperatures, 25 degrees and 28 degrees above zero. On May 15 the first indications of green grass were seen, both in the woods and on the bars. May 16 I spent on the elevated slopes near the Forks, watching unsuccessfully for bears. Near there I first observed the arrival of a pair of short-billed gulls, which several times chased an eagle that was nesting there, darting at it whenever it flew near the bar. Once they chased it nearly to the mountain crest. The eagle when thus attacked paid little attention to them other than to dodge. Other spring arrivals first observed today were a pair of harlequin ducks in the swift water at the Forks, a pair of mallards flying over, and a flock of Hudsonian curlews on the bars. The ice had fallen in all the river channels, and the dryas on the flats was beginning to show green. The snow had departed from the cabin woods except in places on my snowshoe trail, where the narrow strip remaining was a reminder of my constant winter tramps over it when the snow was hard and covered all the brush. Then, during the cold months, I was in a state of exhilaration that always urged me to hasten along, eager to observe the sights beyond the woods, and when returning, to anticipate the cheerful welcome of the dogs. Now the last vestiges of the snowshoe trail caused keen regret, for the happy winter days were gone, never to return in this delightful region.

May 17. I went far down the river to the outside mountains but saw practically no bear signs. It was evident that the bears, on coming out from winter quarters, at once traveled up near the main ranges or climbed over them. The day

was hot and all the channels of the river were running at flood.
The current was cutting deep into the bars below the ice, and
soon the various branches would unite and the whole volume
of water would find a main channel through which it would
continue for another year.

In this lower country nearly all the lower slopes were now
bare and had a faded brown appearance quite tame in contrast with the snow-striped slope above. A few sheep were on
the outside mountain, but very few as compared with the
numbers farther up the river. The first pair of semipalmated
plovers was observed.

May 18. May 18 was a beautiful day, very warm, and
notable for the first appearance of spring flowers. The bright
hot days and long hours of sunlight were having a decided
effect on the vegetation, for daily the dryas became greener
and everywhere grass began to shoot up. Very large windflowers, both white and yellow, were in full bloom; also milk
vetch, purple saxifrage, and Alpine bearberry; and catkins
were now showing on the willows. I crossed Cabin Divide to
the mountains clustered at the southeast end between the Divide and Upper East Branch.

The first wandering tattlers were seen. Pipits (titlarks)
were abundant along the slopes of the mountains, and singing
robins, both high and low, were even more plentiful. Between the Divide and Upper East Branch there was still much
snow and great numbers of lemmings were running over it.
No signs of bears were seen, but many bands of ewes, comprising in all more than 250, were constantly in sight. Having observed the sheep in this region quite regularly since the
preceding July, I had learned to recognize many of the bands,
which, except at certain periods, had kept fairly intact. This
was possible because the bands contained individual sheep
with peculiar horns—broken or differing from the normal in
form; or because some of the ewes possessed habits that were
irregular—as for example, pairing out of season with small
rams. My numerous records of the daily operation of these
bands indicate that the regular range is very limited, covering only a few miles, and in many cases much less. When a

wolf visits the sheep country, all the sheep become terrified and run well back in the mountains, not resuming their normal ranging habits for several days.

For more than a week there had been no wind, and mosquitoes had been increasing in the higher country. Today they were about me in clouds and not being prepared for them I suffered accordingly. On the bars below, they had not yet become a nuisance.

Returning late through the pass leading to Bear Draw, I regretted that snowshoe days were gone, for I could no longer glide over a surface free from obstructions, since now the walking was impeded by 'nigger heads,' dwarf birches, and willows.

On Cabin Peak were ten sheep, nine feeding and one lying down on a large rock twenty feet above. Some observers would have called it a 'sentinel,' but when I got closer and looked at it through the field glasses, it was seen to be stretched out on its side, its head pointing upward, resting on one cheek, apparently sound asleep. I deliberately walked nearer, keeping in sight. All the sheep below saw me long before the 'sentinel' discovered me; but when it did see me it got up and proved to be a yearling lamb! It was dusk when I came down through the Draw. The tree sparrows were all hiding in the willows, sometimes ten or a dozen beneath a single bush. When disturbed all would rise, fly up into the willows and as was their delightful habit at that period, sing vigorously.

May 19. More of the flowers that began blooming yesterday were out, and the marsh grass along the bars was becoming green. The south wind was fairly stiff when I reached the Forks. Three or four sheep, discovered on the bluffs, were stalked with the kodak, but after two or three exposures they ran. Looking up I saw a fine ram quietly feeding on the slope near the edge of Wounded-Bear Canyon. Climbing, creeping, and crawling I finally came near enough to photograph him, though at some little distance, but he continued feeding, headed away from me. When I turned the roll for a fresh film he heard me, and quickly seeing me, bounded over into the canyon. It had taken half an hour to approach him and a strong wind was blowing directly from me toward him, yet not once did he show any evidence of scenting me. At this time, all about the mountains, it was common to see the shed hair of sheep. Often the wind would drive it fairly high through the air.

Later, after looking down on the two eggs in the eagle's nest, I remained for some time scanning the flats for the sight of a bear—but saw none. On the slopes above me four sheep were resting peacefully, and farther along still others were lying down.

A marsh hawk was sailing about the bars below, a short-eared owl was hooting high above, and a ptarmigan, appearing like a white reflection, was restlessly flying about the flats. The tree sparrows and robins, before going into the willows for the night, gave their evening songs.

May 20. The day was even warmer, large clusters of saxifrage were blossoming on the bars, and yellow and white windflowers were more abundant. The river was running at a great flood, bearing larger cakes of ice than at any previous time, and the bars, except where covered by the icecap, were bare. Here the ice had granulated to a depth of five or six inches and soon melted. The water quickly ran through numerous holes and cracks and the granulation began again.

Not wishing to alarm the bears by extending my trails through the country, and believing that the best opportunity to see them was on the flats, I spent another day watching from the same point on the bluffs above the Forks, but without result. This evening the skies were even more beautiful, the clouds becoming purple, while the mountain slopes below were deep carmine. These rich skies continued only a few days longer, giving place to the usual glow of summer sunsets.

Today I watched a ground squirrel gathering food. With its teeth it would pull a plant out of the ground, then, sitting squirrel-like on its haunches, would hold it in one paw and so maneuver it that the seeds were taken out and stored in its cheek pouches.

Now that parts of the bars were clear of ice, I noticed an occasional area among the willows where the meadow mice had been isolated in the ice field all winter. Here they had survived by eating willow bark—whole patches of willow had been thus denuded.

For several days I had noticed only single short-eared owls, indicating that the females were nesting. Also for the first time I saw—what soon became a common sight—a cock ptarmigan on the top of a spruce tree guarding its mate on her nest below. Near the Forks a pileolated warbler was seen.

Gambel sparrows were almost as common as tree sparrows. I had been deeply impressed by their song, which is constantly repeated and continued far into the evening hours. There are five notes, one or two of which are a little wheezy, in a descending minor key. Though deeply melancholy, they are sweet; though mournful and sad, they hint cheer. The theme is haunting, the strain repeating itself in the mind. The song was in complete harmony with my moods of these days, for I knew the time was soon approaching when I must leave. In the wild Canadian forests of the East the notes of the white-throated sparrows cause similar emotions.

Thrush songs in the wilderness break the mystic evening calm in tones that arouse deep emotions, attuned to the hour and environment in which they are heard. They are ethereal. No other music of the wilds can equal them, no other bird melody so affects the spirit with dreamy joy.

May 21. Preparations were made for a short trip to Stony Creek, and a tramp through the woods occupied the day. The first herring gull was seen on the bar. The number of redpolls passing over during the last few days clearly indicated a second migration, notwithstanding the fact that many remained to breed throughout this region, even as far down at the Tanana River.

I examined the recently deserted winter nest of the red squirrel near the cabin. It was about fifteen feet up in a small spruce and was composed of a bunch of leaves, twigs, and sphagnum moss a foot or more in diameter. A single small hole led into the centre, which was filled with the hair of sheep, evidently gathered about the cabin. It was well adapted to protect the squirrel from the Arctic winter temperatures.

May 22. Putting a pack on the horse *Toklat* we set out over the north Stony Divide. The frozen ground made the traveling good except for frequent snowdrifts, which were difficult for the horse. A number of ewes, all heavy with lambs, were feeding on Intermediate Mountain south of the divide. The rams on Sheldon Mountain were in their accustomed place; some had splendid horns. On the divide were fresh tracks of a caribou, the first seen this spring. By the shore of a little lake, nestled in the rolling hills of the divide, a pair of wandering tattlers were running about feeding; one, which proved to be a female, I collected.

On the other side the snow-filled ravines and furrows made the task of getting *Toklat* across very difficult. Often it was necessary to cut willows and pack them on the snow thickly enough to support his weight, and two hours were consumed in going down the last three hundred yards. Our shelter was built on level ground beneath the uppermost spruces on this fork. Robins, thrushes, and sparrows were singing, and a large flock of yellow-rumped warblers was flitting about the willows near camp.

May 23. Here very little green grass was available, and during the night *Toklat,* after unsuccessfully trying to satisfy his hunger, started back over the divide, where Karstens overtook him and brought him back. Meanwhile, I went up the river, which was clear and of small volume—it could be waded anywhere. The bars were free of ice and snow, and a large bear track led upstream.

Four short-billed gulls were flying about, but the most interesting birds were a pair of wandering tattlers playing on the bars. From this time on these birds, always in pairs, were abundant. They were most common on the creeks and lakes on the divides, yet it was not unusual to see them along streams high up in the canyons among craggy mountains. They were tame and allowed a close approach. Sometimes one would fly toward me with curiosity. As long as I remained there the birds of each pair kept constantly playing together, chasing, circling, and flying at each other. At times one would fly rapidly close to the ground, the other chasing it a hundred yards or more, then, alighting close to the creek, mutual activities would be resumed. They were constantly teetering their tails in the manner of the spotted sandpiper. There seemed something mysterious about these friendly birds, perhaps because of the remoteness of the areas they frequented. Undoubtedly the pairs bred in June near the places where I saw them.

A hundred feet above this bar was a well-defined bear trail—that had been traveled for many years. It passed through canyons and over rough rocks and broken surfaces. Similarly I had observed that other trails in this region were high and on rocky or rough ground, never along the flats or bars. Why bears should thus prefer high rough or rocky slopes instead of the smooth bars below is a mystery. Proceeding up the river to its forks—one branch heading east of Bog Hill, the other in the mountains at the head of Moose Creek—I climbed high and watched all day without seeing a bear.

On this day I again noticed the delicate white flower of the Alpine bearberry, which soon covered the mountain slopes.

This was the nesting season of the ptarmigan, when the peculiar activities of the cock were at their height. High on the mountains and even on the bars, cocks were stationed on the tops of spruce trees or on large hummocks or rocks, guarding their mates, which were near by on the nests. If a male were approached within a hundred yards, often at double that distance, he would utter a series of noisy croaks and move his head in agitation. Evidently this was a warning to the female to sneak off, for I found several nests with eggs (one to five each) within a hundred feet of the male on his lookout, but did not once detect the female. The nests were on knolls covered with willows or dwarf birches.

I could not resist certain reflections on these habits. When the female is laying and sitting she needs concealment more than at any other time. Why then should her mate advertise her near presence so continually? Why should he render himself so conspicuous in positions where, even from a long distance, he can be so easily observed? It might be concluded that this habit would result in attracting enemies, enabling them better to find the female or her eggs.* These habits may be the result of the accumulated experiences of countless generations, teaching that such activities better protect the female during the egg-laying period.

On all sides the cocks were fighting and chasing each other, often attacking in the air and continually uttering their croaks. Sometimes one would chase another across the valley—a distance of more than a mile and a half. Once two of them flew upward, circling and fighting all the way to the mountain crest, when one returned and resumed his perch. Often two would alight on the ground and fight a battle, continually pecking at each other until one was worsted and flew; then he was pursued by the other. In every direction, all through the day, the air was full of the noisy fighting ptarmigan. These activities continued for slightly more than a week, probably during the period of egg-laying, after which neither male nor female was conspicuous.

On reaching the tent I found that *Toklat* had again rebelled against being kept at a place where there was so little feed, and had once more departed. Knowing he had returned to the cabin, we did not follow him.

May 24. The voice of the varied thrush was now heard constantly in the evening and occasionally during the day among the more frequent songs of the olive-backed thrush. The day was spent on a tramp far down the river, climbing the mountains and watching for bears, but other than an old track on the bars no signs were seen.

The first foliage of any kind observed were leaves of the dwarf birch, first seen yesterday, and today beginning to

---

* Sheldon's explanation of the performance of the cock ptarmigan does not seem to fit the case. E. A. Preble, whose observations of these birds in the far north have been ample, tells me that while the conspicuous actions of the male willow ptarmigan might be presumed to attract enemies, it should be borne in mind that it is *the male, not* the female, that exposes itself, thus decoying the marauder away—or at least attracting his attention so he would be less likely to find her. In dozens of cases Preble has seen the males act as described while the female was leading away her young. We feel that the male instead of advertising her presence is attracting attention to himself, thus increasing her chances to escape observation.—C. H. M.

grow. When coming forth they are exquisite, well curled, and resemble rosebuds. They add green patches to the mountain slopes, varying the darker green of the lowly dryas. The following day willow leaves, and also those of stunted aspens, were just beginning to show. The long blue flower of *Synthyris* was first observed; also a yellow species of windflower, and small ferns were noticeable on the rocks.

During all the spring I made it a practice to measure carefully and repeatedly the tracks of bears, but only on hard surfaces where the impressions were clearly defined. Three of the largest measurements of the hind feet showed a length of ten inches from heel to the end of the toe, the claw punctures extending from an inch to an inch and a half farther. The hind foot of the largest measured ten-and-a-half inches, the claw punctures extending an inch beyond; the width of the paw, six inches.

Many root diggings of bears were found, showing that the young tender roots were carefully selected. These were delicious when eaten raw, tasting something like raw chestnuts; though when cooked, they tasted more like parsnips. The old roots, which the bears did not touch, were too coarse and tough to eat.

Returning over a bar late in the evening when the dusk was falling, the birds hushed, and the mountains beginning to look shadowy, my eye caught a moving object among the willows. Thinking it a bear, I seated myself with rifle ready, and in another moment saw a lynx silently stealing along. It entered a clear space over eighty yards away, then sat on its haunches and calmly looked about. It fell dead to my shot, and proved to be a very fat old female.* Putting it in my rucksack I returned to the cabin. It was shedding and full of fleas; its stomach was filled with mice and contained also one ground squirrel. Its length was 37 inches; tail, 4¾ inches; hind foot, 9¾ inches.

---

* This was the only fat lynx noted that year—the others being lean or half-starved. It was exceptional also in that its stomach was "filled with mice"—thus accounting for its condition. The others apparently were not eating mice. See also footnote, p. 329.

May 25. Going up the river I turned up a creek heading on Middle Stony Divide and flowing through a canyon with rough precipitous slopes on the north. Well up the canyon five sheep were seen high on the north slope, one an old ewe very much swollen, near by her two yearling lambs and two other yearlings, undoubtedly separated from their mother. One was stretched at full length, headed downward on the slope, with all four legs held out straight. Soon after on a rough craggy slope high above them I saw two ewes, each accompanied by a tiny newborn lamb. The lambs may have arrived a day or two before, and possibly others had been born a week or more earlier, yet these were the first I had seen; every day after that others were noticed. These ewes were feeding actively, and as they moved, the lambs followed, running with ease and agility. Both ewes, though in a spot so difficult of access, were very nervous and watchful. They saw me two thousand feet below and quickly ran over the crest.

Reaching the carcass of the bear killed on May 5 I climbed the spur and remained there watching until the sun was low. While sitting on this spur I was surprised to see a short-billed gull come flying up the canyon and after rising high above the divide, turn and fly back to the river bars.

Descending for some distance I saw the two ewes with their newly born lambs going down a deep boxed canyon not far below the crest. It was at least a couple of hundred feet deep and from a distance the walls seemed perpendicular. Not believing that such tiny newborn lambs could descend such precipitous slopes I thought they had merely gone down to some safe spot to rest. My surprise was complete when later the two ewes came climbing up the walls of the other side from the bottom of the canyon, the lambs following with ease, jumping and running up places so steep that, had I not witnessed the act, I should have thought it impossible. After they had gone over the upper edge of the canyon and walked upward the lambs began to suckle, each standing behind its mother.

While watching through my field glasses, a golden eagle suddenly came over the crest and with wings extended, made

a swoop at the ewes, coming within three feet of them. They
jerked up their heads, trying to strike the eagle with their
horns, and though unsuccessful they made it shoot upward
and fly back over the crest. This was the first time in all my
experience among the northern sheep that I had actually seen
an eagle attack or even seem to notice them; nor had I ever
seen a sheep notice an eagle, though many times I have seen
eagles and sheep very near to each other.

After this attack the ewes, keeping the lambs directly under
them, watched alertly for five minutes for the reappearance
of the eagle, and then nervously quartered toward the crest,
the lambs following close beside them. After another five
minutes the eagle came soaring from behind them. But they
quickly saw it and stood over their lambs. The heads of the
ewes were held stiffly up, tipped a little to one side, ready to
hook at the eagle should it come too close. As it passed fifteen feet above them it swooped somewhat indifferently and
quickly rose, both ewes at the same time shaking their heads
in a threatening manner. In a few moments the sheep walked
upward and passed over the crest.

Not having seen any signs of bears, I concluded to return
to the cabin the following day.

May 26. The dog *Silas* carried his pack (made like a small
canvas alforhas—a kind of saddlebag) lashed over his back;
in it were the cooking pots, a fry pan, plates, and other small
articles. We were just approaching the divide when he dashed
forward, and at the same time I saw three small caribou bulls
standing on the slope a hundred yards ahead, looking at us.
Their horns were small, their coats light and ragged, not then
being completely shed. They galloped away at full speed, rushing down a canyon leading to Stony Fork. *Silas* could not be
restrained and rushed after them, the dishes rattling. He was
rapidly distanced by the caribou but kept on and soon passed
out of sight.

When we arrived at the lake there were three wandering
tattlers on the shore, a pair on the south side and a single bird
squatted on the ground on the north shore. Thinking that the
single bird might be the mate of the one I had killed, I col-

lected it and found it was a male, undoubtedly the mate; it had remained there alone for four days. When we reached the centre of the divide *Silas* returned, having been away nearly two hours. His pack was intact, nothing had been lost from it.

At that moment, a short distance ahead, I saw a three-year-old ram crossing the divide toward Intermediate Mountain. Here was a rare opportunity to observe the actions of a sheep when chased by a wolf. Quickly taking the pack off *Silas*, I led him ahead to within a hundred yards of the ram, which had not yet seen us. *Silas* dashed at him full speed. The ram rushed toward the slope a hundred yards ahead. For a hundred feet the dog did not gain, but during the next hundred he gained at least twenty-five feet, and during the next hundred he was gaining rapidly. Although the dog was clearly the speedier of the two, I thought that the ram deliberately slackened his speed as he neared the slope, which was sharply inclined. The dog was not forty feet behind when the ram reached it. Up he went bounding for forty feet; then turned and coolly stood a moment to watch the dog, which was running up at almost equal speed. Then the ram turned and rather leisurely ran upward a hundred feet, gaining somewhat on the dog, who by that time was going much more slowly. This time the ram stood and watched until the dog was within twenty feet, then easily ran up another hundred feet and again stood and looked at the dog. *Silas*, however, was now only trotting and his panting showed that he could not run upward any more. Yet he followed the ram, which kept repeating the same tactics, never losing sight of the progress of the dog, until within a hundred feet of the crest, where a sharp projecting rock rose almost perpendicularly from the slope. The ram quickly climbed to the top and looked down at the dog, which now was only walking. Nor did he move when *Silas* reached a point fifty feet below him. Then the two stood looking at each other. Finally the dog turned and trotted back to us.

Not once, after the first burst of speed on the level, did the ram show any fright. When he knew he could reach the slope he was deliberate in every movement, and after reaching it he coolly played with the eager dog. After each advance, however, he was careful to turn and watch his pursuer. He seemed to know that the dog would soon give up the chase, yet I believe he did not credit *Silas* with the persistence he had displayed. The actions of the ram led me to suspect that a wolf would not have followed more than a few feet up such a slope, its experience, which *Silas* lacked, having taught it that a sheep could easily escape when once headed upward on a steep slope.

Rounding Intermediate Mountain I discovered, high among the crags, a mother ewe with a newborn lamb, her two yearling lambs following at a short distance. Twice when they came too close, she faced them in a threatening manner and stamped her feet as a warning.

As we approached the cabin, *Toklat* stepped out of the woods and watched us. Then following us home he soon pushed his head into the window, begging for a portion of the few oats that remained.

May 27. Karstens left very early, taking the horse to bring back the camp equipment, while I took the field glasses and went to the bar to look over the mountain slopes. Arriving at the corner of the woods I saw two caribou half a mile below on the bar, coming directly to the point where I was standing. The meat of the last ram killed, though of poor flavor, was being rapidly consumed, and we should soon need more. Here was an opportunity to shoot a caribou at the door of the cabin. Hastening back for my rifle, I returned, placed my kodak in position, and waited, well concealed at the edge of the woods, the wind favorable from the north, As the caribou came on, side by side, I was impressed by the ease with which they glided along, their loose-jointed gait deceiving one as to the rapidity of their walk, which was really very fast. They were small bulls, their horns only a few inches long and in the velvet.

When they approached Karstens' trail, about five hundred yards from me, I carefully observed their actions. On reaching it, both stopped, gave a spring backward, and stood a moment, apparently confused. Looking nervously about they advanced a few feet near the trail, then turned and walked toward Cabin Divide Creek, stopping every two or three steps to look back, continually smelling the ground; then moved in a wide circle and headed for the flat east of the woods. I hastened across the woods and watched them approach the flat where Karstens had walked earlier in the morning in going to catch the horse. When they again reached his tracks they immediately turned and trotted past the mouth of Cabin Creek, climbed the steep bluffs, and made off out of sight over the rolling hills.

The previous evening I had heard a dwarf hermit thrush singing in the woods and now collected one for a specimen; and while walking in the woods, heard the first pigeon hawk.

Recently the red-back mice and shrews had been very scarce and now most of the lemmings had left the woods—at least none were taken in the traps. Meadow mice however suddenly became very abundant and invaded my cabin in large numbers. They were evidently moving through the woods toward the bars to occupy their summer homes, from which the winter ice had driven them. The more I saw of the mice of this region the more convinced I became that large numbers of them move about from certain areas to others according to the season.

Going out on the bars to look at the rams on Sheldon Mountain, I found more than twenty in their usual place, quietly feeding high, near the spot where I had wounded the bear the preceding fall.

While I was watching them through the glasses, a bear came into the field feeding at this exact spot, not a hundred yards from, and in plain sight of, the rams; they paid no attention to it. In fact, the bear moved toward the rams without disturbing them in the least, and then began to work downward on the slope. Wading the river I hastened across the bar toward North Stony Divide. That day, practically from my cabin door I had seen caribou, sheep, and a grizzly bear!

The bear had been last seen descending into a canyon. Hurrying up through the woods to an opposite point I climbed high enough to look into the upper reaches of the canyon, but saw no animal; then continuing to the top of the high bluffs rising up to Intermediate Mountain I examined the opposite slopes of Sheldon Mountain, but no bear was visible anywhere.

Following the edge of the bluffs to a higher point not far from the divide itself, I had below me the whole belt of timber extending up the creek and around the slope of the mountain. Looking down among the scattered spruces I caught a glimpse of the bear. It seemed to glide through the scattered brush, then disappeared. Quickly going to a point opposite it, I watched. The spruces were so large and so far apart that it seemed possible to see even a squirrel among them. But I could not see the bear. Suddenly a tree sparrow piped its song, and a few feet farther on a bird flew up; then again I caught a glimpse of the bear, but it quickly passed out of sight. Twice more I saw it in a strip of willows, and again it disappeared. For ten minutes more I watched without seeing any other signs and concluded that the bear was lying down in the willows.

Then suddenly, three hundred yards from me, a robin flew up on a tree chirping, and a small dark object near the tree caught my eye. Turning the glasses on it I discovered the head of the bear protruding from the willows—its body not visible. It was motionless and seemed to be carefully watching something. How it had reached that spot without having been detected was a mystery I could not explain. For another two or three minutes it remained motionless, but I did not care to risk a shot and spoil the skull. Then the bear turned and went downward through the forest toward the bars. Only occasional glimpses of it could be had, and although it often stopped to look, with ears cocked up, there was never an opportunity to get my rifle sight on it long enough for a shot.

Its course could be followed only by noticing the startled birds that were alarmed as it passed near them. Robins flew up chirping, tree sparrows flew into the trees and began to sing, juncos and warblers flitted, and other birds made its presence known. The woods were so open and the brush so thin, it was difficult to realize that so large an animal could continue to move and still keep concealed. Its color blended with the background, it made no sound, but seemed to glide stealthily, making a conscious effort to render itself unseen. I had seen bears in the open, among rough mountains, crags, and canyons, and on the flats and bars; I had seen them running through the woods in alarm; I had even shot them in the forest; but never before had I observed a grizzly bear moving concealed for such a long time.

I hastened in the direction the bear had taken, while all the rams above were peacefully feeding in the exact spot on the slope where it had been. They were completely unconcerned by the scent of its recent tracks, which, as they fed with their noses to the ground, must have been very strong to their nostrils. For a long time I remained high on a bluff overlooking the bars and willow flats in the hope that the bear had gone there to feed; but it did not reappear. Then the fog poured up through the canyon of the main river and settled over the country and for some time everything was obscured.

It was late when I started up the river, and dark thin mists filled the valley until it resembled a vast calm lake between the mountain slopes. All the crests and peaks were brilliantly lighted by the sun. As I walked, this shining upper world seemed suspended, its outlines softened by the mist—a scene of indescribable beauty.

Before I slept, olive-backed, hermit, and varied thrushes were singing in the woods; later a wet snow fell, lasting all through the night.

More Grizzlies.
Last Days on the Toklat.

May 28. The mountains were white when I started up the river in the morning, and it was much colder, resembling a fall day. But later the sun was hot and by the time I had reached the bars the snow had melted and a stiff south wind was blowing. The bars were mostly clear, the ice cap only remaining where it had been very thick; they were now covered with windflowers, yellow and white, which softened the harshness of their usual appearance and warmed the landscape with color. The river had made new channels, quite different from those through which it had flowed the preceding summer and fall. The water was clear and so low that it could be easily waded at almost any point. Near the mouth of Bear Draw a bank swallow was seen and pigeon hawks were as abundant as they were last summer. The tracks of two caribou led up the bar.

I had just passed Wounded Bear Canyon when, far ahead on the flat near the northwest corner of Divide Mountain, my eye caught an object that could not deceive it—a bear. A look through the glasses gave the impression of a 'very large' bear, and a large cub was seen running about with her. The dense interfering light waves leaping and dancing along the bars no doubt magnified their size. The hour was shortly before one, the wind was right for the only possible stalk—an approach in plain sight.

When I reached the point of the mountain the bear was less than a mile ahead, exactly opposite my old camp, and feeding on the grassy flat of an ancient bar, elevated five or six feet above the bars of the river. She was about three hundred yards from the foot of the north slopes of Divide Mountain near the western end. There were no willows or shrubs of any kind between us. At first I went out on the bar at right angles in order to advance in a wind blowing from her to me. Taking advantage of her movements I crossed the river and went forward over the bar to the bank rising up to the flat. During this time my line of vision had not been high enough to see the cub, but after creeping up the bank, I was in full view of both animals. The old bear was actively digging roots, the cub running about in play.

I thought that in order to get near enough for a good shot it was necessary to advance about five hundred yards. The bear kept moving in all directions, stopping every few feet to dig and eat roots. This compelled me to follow parallel with her courses, so I should always be directly against the wind. After an advance of a hundred yards an unexpected difficulty presented itself, for the cub took a notion to race for a hundred yards in my direction and continued dashing about, so that my advances must be made only at times when neither animal would be likely to see me. The cub would run at speed for some distance, stop and dig a moment, and then race in another direction. Then it might run to its mother, then charge again in my direction, only to turn and speed off again. Stooping low or creeping forward I was a long time gaining ground toward the bear. Often it was necessary to lie flat for some time until the cub ran in a favorable direction. The old bear seldom looked up but the cub seemed always to be in the way of my advance. Yet it was a beautiful sight to see such a display of youthful animal vigor enlivening the flat around the grim looking mother.

Once the old bear caught a mouse. She made a wide sweep through the air with her big paw and seized the tiny thing as she half arose on her haunches. Such great motions for the purpose of capturing a mouse seemed grotesque and ludicrous. At length, in spite of the cub, I got nearer, and still nearer. Once the cub started straight toward me and kept coming. I thought surely it would see me although I was lying flat on the ground. It came to within a hundred and fifty feet, stood for a moment and looked about without suspecting me, then turned and raced back to its mother. Her back was then turned and I made a good gain. Under the bright sun she seemed much nearer than she was. She looked very large, perhaps because of the light waves and her long pelage.

When one gets close to a bear and realizes its activity and power, it is difficult to restrain the feeling of danger—partly, doubtless, because of impressions received in childhood. The long fur encircling the neck makes the bear's head look big and fierce, and the beast itself looks formidable. And when close, one feels that in case of a determined charge it might be impossible to stop it. However confident one may be, as I was during those moments, that the bear would try to escape, nevertheless one is keyed up to a high tension.

During this stalk the bear had been gradually nearing the mountain and finally started toward it, the cub close by. Fearing she might be going for a rest on the slopes, I waited until she turned broadside, and fired. She rose straight up on her hind legs, clapped her paw on her chest and turned completely around, all the time bending her head trying to look at the wound. The cub ran about her once or twice and stood looking at her. I thought she was beginning to totter, and waited; but she turned and dropped on her feet. As she started to walk, I fired again. She seized the same spot, rose on her hind legs a second time, but only for a moment before she dropped on all fours and sank down. The cub had gone a short distance to one side, but when its mother fell it ran a little way and then back to her, showing the first sign of alarm. It started back toward the mountain, and I was surprised to see the old bear attempt to follow. As she tried to rise I fired again and she dropped dead. Then the cub ran at full speed but did not go more than a hundred yards before it stopped, rose on its hind legs and looked back at its mother. It then ran in my direction, stopped again, rose on its hind legs, and stood for at least two minutes looking at the old bear. It was running at full speed not a hundred yards distant when I fired and killed it. Neither the old bear nor the cub seemed aware of my presence; both were completely bewildered as to what was happening.

I was surprised to count three hundred and nineteen paces before reaching the bear. She was old, and probably as large as females of this species grow. The hard level surface gave an unusual opportunity, and she was stretched on the ground and measured with great care, and then measured a second time. Her length was 5 feet 4 inches; tail, 5¼ inches additional; height 37 inches; hind foot with claws, 10¼ inches. Her color was pale, like that of the other bears; that of the cub, a male of the second year, was slightly darker. Her teats still contained small qantities of milk. Her stomach was full of roots of the pea vine and contained also one mouse. The stomach of the cub, in addition to roots, likewise included one mouse.

While I took off the skins after the wind had stopped, an upland plover, the first seen, walked by and others were calling on all sides. Small birds were constantly singing; eagles were screaming and flying around their nest; and several flocks of sheep were in sight as the sky took on its evening colors. On my return to the cabin, Karstens was already there, having brought back the camp material.

May 29. While preparing the skins of the bear and cub I was surprised to find them swarming with the largest species of flea I had ever seen. Many hundreds of them kept crawling out of the fur and it was several days before they left the skins. They immediately attacked me, biting severely as soon as they reached my skin. These bears were the only ones I have ever seen infested with fleas.

Today the first kingfisher was observed.

May 30. While passing Wounded Bear Canyon in the morning I saw the tracks of a fairly large bear coming down from the canyon onto the bar, and followed them to the point where they met my own, made the night before. Here had happened just what I expected: the bear, on reaching my tracks, had immediately started to run and had continued running to the mountain slope.

I climbed the bluffs above the forks and remained watching the flats. All the time I was up there the eagles kept flying about screaming. Evidently their eggs had hatched.

Many bands of ewes were in sight, most of them accompanied by their new lambs, yet many had not yet yeaned. Now a few of the sheep were coming down to the bars to eat a green herb which was sprouting there. A band of fourteen small rams was feeding on the bar near the east corner of Divide Mountain, and at one time all lay down and rested. In the middle of the day I descended into a hollow to make tea and eat a little bread.

After lunch, as I slowly turned the glasses over the flat—for the twentieth time—a bear came into the field, feeding opposite Ram Canyon, about three miles away. As I hastened on until near enough to be seen by it, great caution became necessary. The flat was alive with upland plovers, and it was a further reminder of summer to see for the first time three Arctic terns.

The wind was blowing strong directly from the west, a most unusual direction. It was necessary to cross the flat nearly to the river to gain a point from which the wind would be coming from the bear to me. The bear was only a mile ahead, but a long time was required to see it.

The first animals seen were four small rams, feeding a hundred yards out on the flat on or near the spot where I had last seen the bear. They were feeding in apparent unconcern, not keeping the nervous watch usual to sheep, especially when in a smooth country, unprotected by steep or rocky slopes. Finally, seeing the bear emerge from a small hollow not eighty yards from the rams, I watched them with intense interest. The bear kept moving about actively digging roots without once looking up, and the rams kept on feeding without paying any attention. When it moved a short distance toward them they were completely indifferent. They often threw up their heads to watch, but apparently did not even look at the bear.

The presence of the sheep made the stalk very much more difficult. The bear never once looked for danger, its whole attention being concentrated on smelling and digging the roots. But the rams looked about sufficiently to cause me to approach by stooping or creeping for at least an hour. At last the bear had gradually worked out toward the middle of the flat while the rams, still indifferent to its proximity, remained in the same place. It was necessary for me to move parallel to the course of the bear until finally the rams saw me and at once began to move toward the mountain. They reached it while I was lying flat, and walking rapidly up the slope paused every few moments to look at me.

The bear kept on digging without showing any sign of suspicion. At last I reached a cutbank five feet high, bordering a creek bed leading directly to it. By stooping a little I could advance rapidly, often raising my head to look. The approach seemed so safe and easy that I thought I might be able, before shooting, to photograph the bear. The wind was still strong, at right angles to my approach until I was about five hundred yards away, when suddenly I felt it on my back. Foreseeing the immediate result, I sprang up the bank for a long shot—but it was too late. The bear rose on his hind legs for a second, then dropped and ran at full speed toward the mountain south of Ram Canyon. Four shots in rapid succession missed; then I sat down and watched the flight. For a hundred yards the bear went in great leaps; then slowed to a run and kept on across the flat. It was a fairly large bear and although its lumbering gallop did not seem speedy, it covered the ground rapidly. At the foot of the mountain, instead of selecting an ascent up a smooth slope, it went directly up a rocky ravine, taking the roughest course I could see anywhere on that side of the mountain. It kept running until half way up, never turning aside for deep snowbanks, but wading through them. Then it began to walk, stopping frequently to look back down its trail, and finally went over the crest. Thus was lost the opportunity to kill the last bear I saw.

When climbing at a walk the bear looked like a huge spider, and at times even suggested a great crawling worm.

Going back to the flat to ascertain the cause of the sudden change of wind, I soon found it. The west wind in striking the face of Divide Mountain near the saddle leading to Upper East Branch, was whirled in a wide circle across the bar and deflected toward the south for half a mile. Into this area I had unwittingly passed.

This bear was of the same color as those already described. It seemed clear that while the bears vary much in color when they hibernate in the fall, they all emerge from the winter dens with coats of uniform color.

A study by Dr. C. Hart Merriam of the grizzly bears collected by me in this region resulted in the conclusion that they were a distinct species, which he named *Ursus toklat,* belonging to the *Alascensis Group*—a group extending westerly over the Nushagak and Kuskokwim hills to near the shores of Bering Sea. Yet grizzlies of the region to the eastward, belonging to the *Hylodromus Group,* occasionally stray into these mountains, for a female I killed on August 5, 1906, and the skull of an old male that I picked up on the Upper East Branch, were referred by Doctor Merriam to *Ursus kluane.**

May 31. I had planned to leave early in June, and to start Karstens for Glacier on June 1, with the horse and a pack-load of material. He would then return with two other horses (to be obtained at Glacier) with which to pack out the remainder of my material and equipment, to be taken by boat down the Bearpaw and Kantishna Rivers to the Tanana, from which point he could get a steamboat for his return to Fairbanks. I intended to take the horse *Toklat* and strike across country alone for Nenana on the Tanana River. Most of the day was given to packing the natural history specimens to be taken out, part of the afternoon to watching the sheep.

June 1. Karstens, as planned, left with the horse for Glacier early in the morning and I remained to enjoy the last few days in undisturbed possession of this, my wilderness. Summer had arrived. The month of May had departed—the month when the warm sun had destroyed the winter, practically completing the cycle of the year. May had brought out from winter sleep the marmots, ground squirrels, and bears; it had attracted the caribou and the sheep to their summer haunts; the ewes were yeaning. Love was finding expression in the music of the birds; vegetation was green; flowers were blooming. During May the weather had been glorious; the floods had given life to the landscape, the mountains in their contrasts were more beautiful than at any other period; the sunset skies

* *North American Fauna,* No. 41: 'A Review of the Grizzly and Big Brown Bears of North America,' by C. Hart Merriam, Washington, 1918.

were full of exquisite color, the twilights deep and mysterious until the sun had finally climbed high enough to conquer the darkness of night.

During the morning I chopped wood, and after lunch went up the river to again watch for bears. Bands of sheep were in their usual haunts. Before reaching Wounded Bear Canyon I saw an old ewe with two yearling lambs lying down on the bar. She was very thin and evidently had lost her spring lamb. Then, above some cliffs near the entrance to the canyon I saw three large rams. Two of them had large horns; those of the other were the grandest and most striking horns I had ever seen on the head of a live ram. They were of the closely coiled type, massive and heavy, wrinkled with age, and with tips sweeping outward from the high upward curl. Taking my kodak, after maneuvering a long time among willows on the opposite canyon walls, I succeeded in photographing the rams, but could not get near enough to have the horns show in the picture. The rams still had long hair on their necks, and in many instances the younger ewes and many of the yearlings has as yet scarcely shed at all. It is doubtful if all the sheep finish shedding before late in June.

More than two hundred sheep were constantly in sight. Every day recently I had noticed more ewes with new lambs. These lambs were very active and constantly skipped about in play, completely at home among the cliffs and crags and able to follow the ewes anywhere. In most cases, the ewes with new lambs were followed at a distance by their yearling lambs. Yet in some cases the yearlings had completely separated from the old ewes and were feeding independently. For some days after the birth of her lamb the ewe would remain high up in remote rough sections of the mountains.

The leaves of the willows were just becoming green and I noticed a ram or two browsing on them. Flowers of dryas, of a second species of milk vetch, and a yellow whitlow grass began to bloom.

June 2. The wind blew a gale from the south and I remained at the cabin arranging various things preparatory to leaving. Late in the afternoon I went back on the ridge, taking shelter from the wind behind some willows, and watched a few bands of sheep.

June 3 and 4. On the morning of June 3 a flock of black-poll warblers was feeding in the woods, and pileolated warblers were abundant, most of them doubtless remaining to breed. Their cheerful songs added to the variety of bird music now sounding everywhere. The ptarmigan were not now in evidence, though occasionally cocks were seen flying short distances close to the ground.

While tramping up the river many bands of sheep were visible, the ewes with newborn young having begun to assemble, some of their yearling lambs still following at a distance. The Upper West Branch began for the first time to run full of muddy water, evidence that the glacier at the head had begun to melt. The Upper East Branch was still clear. The willows were beginning to sprout, giving a shade of light green along the bars, where a species of astragalus (*Astragalus arcticus?*) first appeared.

June 4 was cooler, the sky heavily overcast, and a gloom hung over the landscape. The day was passed up the river observing the sheep. A wolverine track was seen on the bar. This animal must be associated with winter, when it is often seen and its tracks everywhere are a reminder of its constant presence.

June 5. June 5 reminded me of the climate in the coastal region of southeastern Alaska, for clouds swept the mountains, mist filled the valleys or draped the slopes, and showers fell at intervals all through the day. While going up the bar I saw a large bear's track approaching my tracks of the previous evening. When he had reached them, his tracks showed that he had run across the bar to the woods near Wounded Bear Canyon. Search for him in the mountains would be in vain, for as usual when a bear is frightened by the scent of a man's trail, he had doubtless gone a long distance.

Late in the afternoon I watched for bears from an elevated point above the Forks, but saw nothing except seven caribou bulls feeding on the bar near the West Branch. All had small antlers—apparently spreading spikes eight of ten inches in length.

For some days many bands of sheep had been feeding low on the slopes and my passing near had not frightened any except those with newborn lambs. They had become so accustomed to seeing me that they merely watched me alertly, continuing to feed after I had passed. But all through the year I had noticed that sheep were badly frightened whenever they saw me wearing my squirrel-skin parka, probably because of its resemblance to some enemy animal. Before starting back I put it on in order to make a final test of its effect. No fewer than six bands of sheep were feeding low. On seeing me all of these, and several others higher up, quickly ran upward to the crests or crags. There was no doubt whatever of its effect. The color of the parka resembled that of a wolf.

At this time the grass was growing rapidly, yet when I left, there was not enough above timber to support horses, at least not for more than half a day.

June 6 and 7. Since rain fell most of the day, June 6 was passed about the cabin, but on June 7 I went up the river. For some time golden eagles had been continually soaring, apparently watching for a good opportunity to capture the newborn lambs; but although I often saw them swooping at the lambs, no capture was observed. The ewes were very watchful and in each attack protected their lambs by standing over them and thrusting their horns upward at the swooping eagle. The lambs often remained in concealment while the ewes fed twenty-five yards or more away. Several times I saw a lamb following the ewe at a distance of fifteen or twenty yards. In each instance, on the appearance of an eagle, the ewe would rush toward the lamb to protect it.

Arriving at the Forks I saw an eagle dashing down at a lamb. But the ewe was on guard and after a couple of swoops the bird circled and flew back to her young. Climbing above the nest I looked down and saw the eagle sitting on it. On the rocks nearby were strips of skin and other remains of lambs, demonstrating that this eagle at least had been successful. Probably all the eagles of the region had done the same. I had already noticed an occasional ewe without a lamb, yet showing every evidence of having given birth to one. It is undoubtedly true that golden eagles take a heavy toll of the newly born lambs. After they are a month old they are seldom molested. In July both ewes and lambs seem completely indifferent to the eagles. I shot this one, the bullet at the same time killing two of the nestlings. Her stomach contained the remains of a ground squirrel.

June 8 and 9. June 8 and 9 were occupied in tramping the country tributary to the Forks watching sheep and caribou. Bears were now scattered, having resumed their summer habit of traveling actively about the mountains. None visited the region under my observation during the last few days of my stay. Except for some ice on the bar above the cabin and the lack of green, owing to the late growth of grass and willow leaves, the country had taken on the aspect of summer. The birds were constantly singing. Upland plovers were very numerous on the flats; wandering tattlers were on the bars; single short-eared owls were occasionally seen high in the air; varied thrushes were abundant in the woods, and restless redpolls still flew overhead.

On June 8 I first noticed the flowers of the rose bay or rhododendron and the stitchwort, and also those of the net-veined willow. No other flowers than those mentioned were seen before I left, though undoubtedly there may have been others that I did not discover.

Everywhere on the mountains the detached ewe bands were gathering and many were joined by the ewes with new lambs. These were the units that in July unite to form the large ewe bands—or rather, groups of bands. The ewes of the smaller independent bands hold together year after year, but the young rams, after reaching the age of three years, leave them. To understand the formation of the ewe bands, both large and small, one must see them in early June, when they form with the new lambs. Many of the ewes had not yet lambed. Most of them had only one lamb—only about one in fifteen having twins. All ewes with new lambs were extremely nervous and when they saw me, even if high and distant, at once retired. The tiny lambs were actively frolicking and playing with each other, chasing, clambering up rocks, trotting and running in sheer excess of animal spirits. The yearling lambs, which usually follow their mothers only ten days or two weeks after the new lambs are born, were now practically independent and were taking care of themselves. The original units of the bands, I believe, are families.

At this time the old hair along the back of the neck on many of the ewes was not shed, and many of the yearlings had not shed at all. The sheep would not all be completely free from their winter coats before the first of July. The new pelage on all the sheep, including the lambs, was now extremely dirty, much more so than at any other time of year. This is due to the muddy soil caused by melting snow and rain. The staining of the hollow hairs at this time is permanent, lasting throughout the year. In the fall, after the first snows and before the slopes become windswept and bare, the pelage is cleaner than at any other season.

Several bands of bull caribou were observed well up the bars and on the flats. No cows had yet come up into this region; all were below with their calves, outside of the ranges. Early in July the cows would return. Even when the antlers of the bulls were so light, I noticed that while lying down resting, their necks were usually extended on the ground.

On reaching the cabin late in the evening of June 9 I found Karstens and Merrifield there with two extra horses, anxious to hasten back with such material as was necessary to take out of the country. I had made my last tramp in this wilderness. That day Denali was clear and wonderful in its overpowering majesty.

June 10. After we had completed the packing, the day was given to caching the extra food and other things to be left well back in the woods, safe from any possible intruder, so that Karstens, should he return to the cabin, would find them unmolested.

Farewell to Denali.
Swimming the Nenana on Horseback.
Down the Tanana and Yukon to St. Michael.
Thence to Nome and Seattle.
Plea for the Name Denali.

June 11. Early in the morning I put the saddle on *Toklat,* together with a pack containing a little tea, sugar, rice, flour, an ax, and the .22 rifle. I did not take even my large rifle, kodak, field glasses, or other equipment. Karstens and Merrifield packed the other two horses to take to Glacier City, from which Karstens was to bring my material by canoe down the Bearpaw and Kantishna to the Tanana, thence returning to Fairbanks by the first steamer. I intended, alone, to lead *Toklat* across country to Nenana on the Tanana.

No words can describe my sorrow and regret as I led the horse out of the woods from the cabin to the bar and started down the river. I was leaving forever this region in which I had lived and hunted with a feeling of complete possession— leaving the joys I have tried to describe in this book.

It was a beautiful clear day. Sheep were in their usual haunts on Cabin Peak, others on the slopes of Bear Draw, and all the rams were feeding on Sheldon Mountain in the spot where I had watched them almost every day during the spring.

I walked rapidly down the bar and on reaching the canyon paused for a long last look, then turned my back and went through the canyon, where most of the higher region was lost to sight.

After passing outside of the mountains I found the summer more advanced. Mosquitoes, which had been sufficiently abundant above, were at their maximum below, beyond the ranges. Flowers were larger and much more numerous, the leaves of the willows and other shrubs were nearly full grown and the country presented the appearance of summer. Yet for two or three miles near the canyon at the Forks of the Toklat,

I led my horse over thick ice that covered the bars on both sides of the river.

Spotted sandpipers were now abundant; also herring gulls and a few short-billed gulls. All the familiar small birds were singing, and the nest of a Gambel sparrow with one fresh egg was found in a tuft of grass near the centre of the bar. A colony of cliff swallows had finished their nests on the cliffs at the Forks and were already laying eggs. Fresh tracks of caribou at the crossing places indicated that these animals were still traveling in the lower country.

At a trapper's cabin below the Forks I removed the pack from *Toklat,* put on his hobbles, and built a fire to cook some rice and bacon before sleeping. There was little grass, and the mosquitoes were so numerous that the horse would not leave the smoke. So I tied my sleeping-blanket around him, and thus protected he ranged short distances to feed. Putting more wood on the fire, I wrapped the saddle canvas around my face and head, and with my hands in my pockets slept at intervals through the night. For the three following nights I was obliged to get my rest in this way, the sleeping-blanket being required to protect the horse.

June 12. After tramping more than ten hours I reached the Cutoff in the evening. Clouds obscured the mountains up the river and several times during the day I was soaked by a succession of heavy thunder showers. Here on the bar I found another Gambel sparrow's nest with three young and one egg, indicating that here they had begun to breed a little earlier than twenty-five miles above. Neither ducks nor short-billed gulls were at the Cutoff, only herring gulls. The last song of the tree sparrow was heard yesterday, but Gambel sparrows were common all the way to Tanana River. Thrushes were more abundant in the woods here than in the mountains higher up, and kept singing all through the night.

June 13. Early in the morning I saw the last of the Toklat waters. The mountains were not visible, being hidden by the clouds. Traveling east through the woods, I frequently lost the indistinct old Indian trail, but by the aid of the compass managed each time to pick it up again. It led mostly through swamps and bogs and passed around several small lakes. Again there were heavy thunder-storms in the mountains to the south and rain poured down steadily all day. After tramping for five hours I reached the Teklanika River; it was running at high flood, but I finally found a place where the horse could ford it.

After leading *Toklat* around a fairly large lake and through dense brush in search of the trail, I saw a fine bull moose lying down not seventy-five feet away. His short branching antlers were in the velvet and he remained motionless, gazing at me while I turned *Toklat's* head away so he might not become frightened if the moose should jump up. Then for a few moments I watched the bull, surrounded by the deep forest. I believe he thought I might pass on without noticing him. But the horse evidently smelled him, for he became nervous and moved. This made the moose get up and trot off.

He was the last game animal seen by me in the interior of Alaska. After a tramp of eleven hours I reached the Nenana River, which was roaring by at such a high flood that it was doubtful if I could cross it. That evening I enjoyed eating a fine Alaska spruce grouse shot near the trail, and grass was so abundant that *Toklat* could satisfy his hunger without leaving the smudges built to protect him from the mosquitoes.

June 14. The day was beautiful and clear. Early in the morning the river was eighteen inches higher than the night before, so there was no possible chance of fording. After an hour it had fallen four inches, but then began to rise again rapidly. The current was rushing by, foaming and roaring and bearing along trees and driftwood. Some distance above was a long tangent where the current was smoother, the river about a hundred yards wide. Leading *Toklat* up this tangent for three hundred yards I determined to swim the river.

But first I placed enough provisions on the bank so that in case of accident—if I should be fortunate enough to get back to this side of the river—I would have food while returning to my cabin. Then, tightening the cinch and lashing the pack firmly behind the saddle, I mounted *Toklat* and forced him to plunge into the river, at the same time keeping him headed diagonally up the current. As I leaned forward, tightly grasping his mane, he struck out and was carried swiftly toward the other side. Although I was nearly swept off two or three times—particularly once when he almost rolled over—yet finally his feet struck the rocky bottom within a few feet of the opposite side, at least a hundred yards below the point from which we had started. He almost fell as he scrambled up under a high cut bank and I jumped off. My relief at escaping the danger of this crossing was profound. When I found a place to climb the bank, there was *Toklat* quietly feeding, apparently not in the least excited after his perilous swim. Those who love a good horse may imagine my feelings.

It was then after eleven in the morning and I led the horse along the east side of the river until nearly eleven that night, when we came to a stream where, after trying for a long time, no ford could be found. The Tanana River was not far ahead, but the day's work had been long so I decided to sleep on the bar and find a crossing in the morning.

June 15. Early in the morning I heard an approaching canoe and soon two prospectors rounded a curve, one paddling in the stern; the other picked up his rifle, mistaking the horse on the bar for a moose. He was surprised to hear my shout, and still more to learn that I had crossed the river with the horse the day before. The men soon found a hard bottom with their poles, and after fording, I reached Nenana in two hours.

At that time there were only the mission and a trading-store at Nenana, and the Nenana Indians were camped along the river. The mission was presided over by that refined, zealous, unselfish, and able woman, Miss Annie Cragg Farthing, who had spent the best years of her life helping Alaska Indians—first along the Yukon River and then for five years at this Mission, where she suddenly died in 1911, a martyr to the work she had ennobled by her devotion. Of all the missionary workers I had met in the North she was by far the most efficient and the most charming.

For three days I remained at Nenana, occupied in boxing my trophies and natural history specimens, visiting the Indians to obtain information from them about the wild ani-

mals, and enjoying the delightful companionship of Miss
Farthing. On June 19 I took *Toklat* aboard the small river
steamer *Tanana* and reached Fairbanks the next day. On
June 21 Karstens arrived, and three days later we parted, but
not without sincere regret at severing ties formed by long
companionship in the wilderness. Taking a steamer down the
river to Tanana, I caught the big packet *Sarah* bound for
St. Michaels, which we reached on July 1 after an enjoyable
trip down the broad Yukon. Three days later the *Corwin*
brought me to Nome, where I was obliged to remain until
July 18, the ice to the south having delayed the arrival of the
Seattle boats until the 17th. After a delightful voyage of eight
days over calm seas I arrived in Seattle, and on August 3
reached New York.

Recollections of my life in this vast interior wilderness
will ever remain fresh and vivid. But the impressions of the
inspiring majesty of Denali dominate every recurring thought
—"*Denali, The High One*"; "*Sultana, His Wife*"; the former more sublime perhaps than any other mountain in the
world. The Indians who have lived for countless generations
in the presence of these colossal mountains have given them
names that are both euphonious and appropriate. In a comparatively short time the Indians will become extinct. Can it
be denied that the names they gave to the most imposing features of their country should be preserved? Can it be too late
to make an exception to current geographic rules and restore
these beautiful names—names so expressive of the mountains
themselves, and so symbolic of the Indians who bestowed
them?

CHAPTER 34

Trees and Shrubs of the Toklat Region on the North Side of the Alaska Range.

The spruce, the aspen, the balsam poplar, the dwarf birch, and the willow are the trees and shrubs that fill the landscape of interior Alaska and Yukon Territory at timberline. Still higher are willows and a few other bushes.

The willows (*Salix*) cover broad areas along the bars, the borders of rivers, creeks and streams, and abound in the spruce or poplar woods, the canyons, the swamps and everywhere on boggy ground. They grow on all the mountain slopes —most abundantly on south exposures—and on soft boggy ground. At moderate elevations they often attain a height of fifteen feet, but at greater elevations are usually shrubby. Growing in dense patches, very stiff and unyielding, they offer stout resistence to the mountain climber who has to force his way through them.

When one attempts to stalk a moose above timberline one must count on having to contend with the willow. It may hide the game, and will surely obstruct his progress and cause noise as he pushes through it. When one is tired after a hard tramp and has to force his way through a willow patch, the unyielding growth tearing his clothes and making him stumble again and again, he heaps imprecations on it. When he can find no other wood to burn and has to endure its strong disagreeable smoke, he curses it. When taking horses across the rolling country the sight of a long line of willows ahead is most unwelcome, signifying a bog that may be crossed only after much difficulty and delay. It is in fact one of the most obnoxious obstacles to the passage of pack trains, not only tearing the packs and bogging the animals, but in many cases requiring the axe to chop out a trail. And when, as often happens, the willows are encountered after dark, the annoyance increases, particularly if one is obliged to force his way upward through them on the steep mountain slopes. But of all the evils inflicted by the willows the most exasperating perhaps is that imposed upon the man on snowshoes, for if the snow is not deep enough to completely bury the brush, the stiff bushes catch in his snowshoes, often tearing the webbing and tripping him so that he stumbles and falls—not once, but again and again—until he wishes he could destroy all the willows in the North.

But there is another side to the willows, as one learns by long experience and familiarity with them. When necessary to camp above timberline, either in winter or summer, one seeks the willows. They provide shelter from the wind, boughs for the bed, poles for the tent, and fuel for the fire. There is no other wood. They alone make traveling in such areas possible. The north side of the Alaska Range is largely timberless. At and above timberline one must depend on the willow for many uses. It comes handy for any purpose where tough fiber is necessary. Snowshoes may be repaired with it, and it may serve even for a temporary frame. Spruce, even when it can be obtained, is not a substitute, being too brittle. While willows often impede progress up a mountain slope, yet in places where the slopes are steep, they offer the only support— for one may hold on to them. There are many areas where, if bare of willows, one could not climb at all. While they often conceal the animals and render a stalk more difficult, they equally conceal the stalker. Often they alone make a successful stalk possible. So also, while their presence indicating a bog may be discouraging, they serve as a warning to avoid it; and they alone supply the material for corduroying the boggy places—thus making crossings possible.

During the greater part of the year willows form the sole food of the moose—without them this great game animal could not live in the region. The moose is abundant in proportion to the abundance of willows. In winter they support the ptarmigan, and their bark supplies food, often the only food, for the rabbits that are so necessary to the welfare of the natives. They also provide food for the mountain sheep and certain birds, and afford shelter to many birds, both from the elements and from their enemies.

Not only does one become dependent on the willows for many of his comforts in the North, but the soft light green of their foliage, dotting, streaking, and patching the valleys, river courses, and lower slopes, adds a pleasant element to the landscape; and in fall, when the leaves have turned bright yellow shading into golden, how beautiful they are in the bright sun! Later they don their rich brown coats, which in places continue into winter, softening the bleak inhospitable appearance of the mountain world, the last reminder of the brilliant autumn days. In October, when the thin mists of approaching winter drape the multiform branches of the willows in a delicate crystalline film of exquisite gauzes and laces, the landscape sparkles in the sunlight with a brilliant sheen of color—the most gorgeous sight in the northern wilderness.

Yes, I had learned to love the willow; it was continuously associated with all my experiences in the North.

Other friends are the cottonwood and aspen. In many places groves of the balsam poplar or black cottonwood (*Populus balsamifera*), tall, stately, and inviting, line the banks of the larger rivers. It is smaller on the bars, but ever welcome, affording delightful camping spots where the ground is clear and dry. Its wood when dry makes a splendid fire, although quickly consumed; the flame is hot and burns steadily, emitting little smoke. The fire is excellent for baking bread. The ash is so thick that if the fire is left too long without replenishing, it has a tendency to smother. Above timberline it is replaced by the aspen (*Populus tremuloides*), often the only wood besides the willow. In the mountains it does not grow so tall as it does lower down, and usually occurs along running water. Unlike the willow, it is not ever-present, yet it is common. Sometimes it forms thickets so dense as to annoy the hunter and interfere with the passage of horses.

The cottonwood and aspen cannot rank as useful woods except for fuel and tent poles. Nevertheless, they are easy to chop and the logs have several unimportant uses. Moreover, the bark provides the chief winter food of the beaver—a furbearer of great value to Alaska. Without it, beaver would be scarce. In winter, because so often exposed to wind, aspens seem bleak and cold, and seldom offer shelter; but in the summer their leaves give a shade of green different from that of the other trees, while in fall they are yellow and golden, adding variety to the colors of the landscape. Hence the aspen is ever welcome to the wanderer in the North.

The dwarf birch (*Betula nana?*) in many places is abundant at and above timberline, sometimes growing fairly high on the mountains, and densest on the south slopes. It is torture to push through it when climbing a slope, but when the way is very steep the hand welcomes it for support. Its thickets afford shelter from the wind, and owing to their flexibility may be traversed without noise—thus most welcome during a stalk. It furnishes abundant food for rabbits, provides shelter for birds, and at times its bark may yield food for moose as asserted by the Indians—though I could never find evidence of it. Its dry twigs provide kindling to start the fire, but their chief use is for sweeping the cabin floor. Cut in straight lengths and lashed together they make the only durable and satisfactory broom. Dwarf birch adds a darker shade of green to the landscape, while in the fall the deep red of its leaves contributes brilliant contrasts. This shrub is an ever-present associate of the high northern wilderness.

The white spruce (*Picea canadensis*) would require a whole chapter to do it justice. In the northern wilderness this tree is the emblem of hospitality. It provides a home for the wanderer. It gives him his shelter, his fuel, his bed, his cabin logs and tent poles, and lumber for numerous uses. In fact, the spruce is *home,* with all its connotations. How often during the winds, the rains, and the cold of winter have I felt the glow of warmth, the sense of shelter, and the congeniality of the spruces! They always invite. They add to the wilderness the mystery and strength of the vast forest. Their spired tops adorn the horizon with outlines of extraordinary beauty. Without them the land would be barren and inhospitable, albeit there might be, as in the Barren Grounds, a greater sense of freedom.

35 ❦ 1907-1908

Table of Minimum Temperatures at Base Cabin Three Miles below Upper Forks of Toklat.

TEMPERATURES RECORDED BY CHARLES SHELDON
BY SELF-REGISTERING THERMOMETER

DATE	MIN. TEMP.	DATE	MIN. TEMP.	DATE	MIN. TEMP.
1907		1907		1908	
Sept. 27	+ 40	Nov. 5	− 36	Jan. 22	− 25
Oct. 4	+ 20	6	− 32	23	− 12
5	+ 16	7	− 34	24	− 3
6	+ 13	8	− 5	25	− 1
7	− 1	9	− 5	26	+ 6
8	+ 1	10	+ 12	27–30	+ 4
9	+ 7	11	+ 5	31	+ 8
10	+ 13	12	− 1	Feb. 1	− 7
11	+ 9	13	+ 2	2	− 19
12	+ 4	14	+ 20	3	− 15
13	− 7	19	− 7	4	− 6
14	− 5	20	− 12	5	− 9
15	− 18	21	− 13	6	− 3
16	− 10	22	− 18	7	− 9
17	− 1	Nov. 23 ⎫		8	− 10
18	− 11	to ⎬ − 26		9	− 2
19	0	Dec. 3 ⎭		10	+ 1
20	+ 2	4	− 8	11	− 7
21	+ 26	5	− 12	12	− 2
22	+ 7	6	− 8	13	+ 18
23	+ 7	7	− 5	14	− 4
24	+ 11	8	− 1	15	+ 1
25	+ 12	9	− 1	16	+ 2
26	+ 27	10	+ 12	17	+ 20
27	+ 14	11	0	18	+ 8
28	+ 14	12	− 3	19	+ 6
29	+ 1	13	− 23	20	+ 24
30	− 17	Dec. 14 ⎫		21	+ 27
31	− 24	to ⎬ − 37		22	+ 22
Nov. 1	− 26	Jan. 19, ⎭		23	+ 15
2	− 26	1908		24	+ 5
3	− 30	20	− 35	25	− 9
4	− 29	21	− 34	26	+ 6

DATE	MIN. TEMP.	DATE	MIN. TEMP.	DATE	MIN. TEMP.
1908		1908		1908	
Feb. 27	+ 4	Apr. 10	+ 15	May 9	+ 23
28	+ 4	11	− 1	10	+ 25
29	− 4	12	− 2	11	+ 24
Mar. 1	− 3	13	+ 15	12	+ 20
2	+ 12	14	+ 6	13	+ 24
3	+ 9	15	+ 4	14	+ 24
4	+ 28	16	0	15	+ 25
5–19	− 41	17	0	16	+ 28
20	− 19	18	+ 2	17	+ 24
21	− 12	19	+ 7	18	+ 24
22	− 26	20	+ 20	19	+ 27
23	− 21	21	+ 8	20	+ 32
24	+ 12	22	+ 21	21	+ 34
25	+ 19	23	+ 5	22	+ 29
26	+ 13	24	+ 15	27	+ 30
27	+ 5	25	+ 17	28	+ 30
28	+ 14	26	+ 9	29	+ 28
29	+ 6	27	+ 10	30	+ 25
30	− 7	28	+ 32	31	+ 30
31	− 1	29	+ 26	June 1	+ 34
Apr. 1	+ 12	30	+ 32	2	+ 40
2	+ 6	May 1	+ 24	3	+ 42
3	− 2	2	+ 29	4	+ 35
4	− 12	3	+ 21	5	+ 34
5	− 16	4	+ 15	6	+ 30
6	− 5	5	+ 23	7	+ 35
7	+ 5	6	+ 22	8	+ 30
8	− 6	7	+ 20	9	+ 23
9	+ 8	8	+ 18	10	+ 33

Minimum Temperatures on Trips away from Cabin.

BY SELF-REGISTERING THERMOMETER

DATE	MIN. TEMP.	LOCALITY	DATE	MIN. TEMP.	LOCALITY
1907			1907		
Nov. 15	+ 6	Camp on Toklat River short distance below Forks.	Dec. 26	− 31	
16	− 2		27	− 32	
17	− 3		28	− 33	
18	− 3		29	− 38	
23	− 11	Camp near Caribou Camp and East Fork Toklat.	30	− 38	
24	− 15		31	− 35	
25	− 16		1908		
26	− 20		Jan. 1	− 37	Camp on moraine of Peters Glacier, Denali.
27	− 22		2	− 31	
28	− 12		3	− 23	
29	+ 12		4	− 20	
30	− 5		5	− 4	
Dec. 1	− 10		6	− 2	
2	− 5		7	− 8	
3	+ 8		8	− 16	
14	− 20	Camp short distance above Forks.	9	− 26	
			10	− 26	
			11	− 20	
15	+ 23	Camp near Bog Hill, south of McKinley Fork, apparently near end of Muldrow Glacier.	12	− 14	
			13	− 21	
			14	− 12	Eureka Mining Camp, Upper Moose Creek.
16	+ 3	Near McKinley Fork.	15	+ 12	Tom Lloyd's cabin, head of Glen Creek.
17	− 5	Camp on McKinley Fork.	16	+ 11	
18	+ 8		17	+ 6	
19	+ 15		18	+ 8	Clearwater Creek.
20	+ 13		19	− 12	Toklat River.
21	− 1	Camp on moraine of Peters Glacier, Denali.	27	+ 18	Near mouth Clearwater Creek.
22	− 4		28	− 1	Cutoff on Toklat River.
23	− 4		29	− 1	
24	− 18		30	+ 13	Mouth of Clearwater Creek.
25	− 29				

DATE	MIN. TEMP.	LOCALITY	DATE	MIN. TEMP.	LOCALITY
1908			1908		
Mar. 5	+ 24		Mar. 15	− 19	
6	+ 13		16	− 23	
7	+ 14		17	− 23	Forks of Toklat.
8	+ 3		18	− 24	
9	− 18	Forks of Toklat.	19	− 19	
10	− 20		May 23	+ 28	
11	− 19		24	+ 33	Camp on North
12	− 22		25	+ 31	Stony Divide.
13	− 33		26	+ 34	
14	− 25				

APPENDICES

BY CHARLES SHELDON

List of Birds Observed on the Upper Toklat River near Mt. McKinley, Alaska, 1907-1908.

REPRINTED VERBATIM FROM *The Auk*, VOL. XXVI, NO. 1, JANUARY, 1909.

The birds noted in this list were observed incidentally while hunting and studying the habits of some of the larger animals at the head of the Middle Fork of Toklat River, Alaska, practically at the north base of Mount McKinley in the main Alaskan range, latitude about 63° 30'. The river has its sources in the glaciers of the main range and flows through four high ranges before it emerges outside, where the main body of the timber ends. From its entrance into the outside range, however, there is a fringe of spruces on both sides from two to three hundred yards wide extending up the mountain slopes and thus continuing to within a few miles of the source. I built my cabin in the extreme upper end of this tongue of timber, 10 miles above the point where the river emerges from the outside range. The birds mentioned in this list were observed at and above that point, mostly above all timber. The variety of bird life in the region is not great. I arrived about the 1st of August, 1907, and left June 11, 1908. Careful attention was given to recording the spring arrivals, but the fall departures, in most cases, were not observed. By the latter part of September, 1907, all birds but the residents had gone, except in the few cases mentioned. The dates given show when the bird was first seen in the spring of 1908 or last seen in the fall of 1907. Thirty miles below, in the vast timbered area, bird life may be more varied and abundant.

The river is a silt-laden stream, dashing swiftly and often in several channels through a broad glacial valley with wide bars extending from a quarter to a half mile on each side. In some places willows grow abundantly; in others there is grass, but most of the country is bare. The mountains are high and rugged, with much snow on the north slopes the year round; they are usually bordered by narrow rolling hills, all above timber, and contain numerous small lakes of a few acres only. The trees are spruces and willows; willows often extend well up on the slopes and up the creeks. The poplar is practically absent. Dwarf birch grows abundantly in places.

The specimens of birds collected were presented to the U. S. Biological Survey.

BIRDS OF TOKLAT RIVER REGION

Larus argentatus. HERRING GULL. Commonly breeding June 12, forty miles below my cabin.

Larus brachyrhynchus. SHORT-BILLED GULL. Seen commonly in pairs along the bars in spring. Probably breeds. First seen May 16.

Sterna paradisæa. ARCTIC TERN. Common summer resident about the small lakes in the rolling country above timberline. Breeds. First seen May 30. Mature young observed August 2.

Anas platyrhynchus. MALLARD. Summer resident below the mountain ranges. One migrating pair observed May 16. About 40 miles above the mouth of the river there is a stretch of 3 miles where the water does not freeze but remains open all winter. This is the end of the salmon run. About 300 mallards were there all winter. They fed on dead salmon and salmon eggs in the pools. White men have observed these ducks wintering there for seven years. Indians tell me they have always wintered there. I visited the spot on January 3 [-28], 1908, and secured two males and a female.

Sixteen mallards wintered on Moose Creek in the open water about 100 miles southwest of those in the Toklat. These also were in open water at the head of the salmon run.

Mallards winter also just below Gulkana Lake in the outlet which flows into Copper River, and a few have been observed wintering in a small tributary of the Tanana River just below the Delta River. Undoubtedly there are many other places in the interior of Alaska where Mallards winter.

Nettion carolinense. GREEN-WINGED TEAL. Commonly seen with young in the small lakes in the rolling country above timber. So observed in July and August.

Histrionicus histrionicus. HARLEQUIN DUCK. One pair seen May 16.

Chen hyperborea. LESSER SNOW GOOSE. Flock of three seen migrating October 10.

Grus canadensis. LITTLE BROWN CRANE. Seen only in fall migration, from Sept. 10 to early October. All flocks followed the same course.

Gallinago delicata. WILSON SNIPE. Common summer resident. Arrived May 14.

Pisobia bairdi. BAIRD SANDPIPER. One migrating pair seen May 12.

Heteractitis incana. WANDERING TATTLER. Very abundant in spring. Arrived May 18. A female was secured May 22. They appeared mated in pairs and their actions showed they were preparing to breed. They were still about in abundance when I left, June 11, but probably had not begun to breed. They occurred along the river bars and at the lakes and even on the small creeks high on the mountains. Not observed in the lower country.

Bartramia longicauda. UPLAND PLOVER. Common summer resident; breeds. Arrived May 28.

Actitis macularia. SPOTTED SANDPIPER. Common summer resident. First observed a few miles below my cabin June 11, but undoubtedly arrived earlier. Breeds.

Numenius hudsonicus. HUDSONIAN CURLEW. Summer resident in rolling country above timber. Arrived May 16.

Squatarola squatarola. BLACK-BELLIED PLOVER. Observed occasionally late in July about the lakes.

Ægialitis semapalmata. SEMIPALMATED PLOVER. Common on bars in spring migration. Arrived May 17 and still about June 11.

Canachites canadensis osgoodi. ALASKA SPRUCE GROUSE. Resident. From time to time through the winter one would appear in the woods near my cabin. Two fine males were secured in October, 1907. Abundant below, in the timbered region.

Lagopus lagopus. WILLOW PTARMIGAN. Very abundant resident. Began to pair for breeding April 20.

Lagopus rupestris. ROCK PTARMIGAN. A male was killed March 5 in the rolling country above timber.

Lagopus leucurus peninsularis. ALASKA WHITE-TAILED PTARMIGAN Not uncommon high on some of the mountains.

Circus hudsonius. MARSH HAWK. Common summer resident. Arrived May 12. Breeds.

Aquila chrysaetos. GOLDEN EAGLE. Common summer resident. Breeds, nesting in cliffs. Arrived April 8. Last observed September 21. Arrived paired and went directly to old nest and remained about it. One nest contained two eggs when I examined it April 29. When next I examined it, June 7, it contained two fledglings.

Gyrfalcon. A large grayish hawk was observed at times through the winter, always on and about the creeks of the mountains.

Falco columbarius. PIGEON HAWK. Common summer resident. Breeds. Arrived May 27. Large hawks were occasionally seen in summer, but the species were not recognized.

Asio flammeus. SHORT-EARED OWL. Exceedingly abundant everywhere above timber in spring. Arrived April 30 in pairs. Breeds.

Glaux funerea richardsoni. RICHARDSON OWL. A male killed May 4, 1908.

Bubo virginianus subsp.? HORNED OWL. Common resident in the woods.

Nyctea nyctea. SNOWY OWL. Very common above timber from November to early May.

Surnia ulula caparoch. AMERICAN HAWK OWL. Common summer resident. Arrived April 10.

Ceryl alcyon. BELTED KINGFISHER. Summer resident. Breeds. Arrived May 29.

Dryobates pubescens nelsoni. ALASKA DOWNY WOODPECKER. Resident. Not uncommon; always seen feeding in willows and sometimes as high as willows grow in the mountains. A male secured in December, 1907.

Picoides americanus fasciatus. ALASKA THREE-TOED WOODPECKER. Resident in spruce woods. Common. A male secured October, 1907.

Sayornis saya. SAY PHOEBE. Common. Arrived June 5.

Pica pica hudsonia. BLACK-BILLED MAGPIE. One seen Sept. 22 in some high cliffs.

Perisoreus canadensis fumifrons. ALASKA JAY. Resident. Very abundant.

Corvus corax principalis. NORTHERN RAVEN. Resident. Abundant.

Euphagus carolinus. RUSTY GRACKLE. Summer resident. Common. Arrived May 10, when a male was secured.

Pinicola enucleator alescensis. ALASKA PINE GROSBEAK. Common in migrations but not observed at timberline between migrations. Few seen in spring, abundant in fall. First bird to arrive in spring; paired by March 12; migrated in flocks through October; last seen November 7. A male and a female were preserved in October, 1907, and a male March 11, 1908.

Leucosticte sp.? Common in spring migration. Arrived May 3. Seen usually high above timberline in pairs.

Acanthis linalia. REDPOLL. Resident. All through October numerous flocks appeared at timberline, but very few remained at timberline in winter. Common below the mountain ranges in winter. Again at timberline numerous flocks appeared in spring, beginning about April 15, and continued through May. Many remained near timberline to breed. In winter it feeds exclusively among willows. Males were secured in November, 1907, and May 24, 1908.

Plectrophenax nivalis. SNOWFLAKE. Common spring migrant. Arrived April 8, when a specimen was secured.

Calcarius lapponicus alescensis. ALASKA LONGSPUR. Abundant in spring migration. Arrived May 12, when a male was secured.

Zonotrichia leucophrys gambeli. INTERMEDIATE SPARROW. Abundant summer resident. Arrived May 3, when a male was secured. Nest with one egg observed on a bar, in a small grass tuft. Next day, outside the ranges, 30 miles below, I found another nest on the bar with 3 young ones and one egg.

Zonotrichia coronata. GOLDEN-CROWNED SPARROW. Commonly seen in spring. Arrived May 26.

Spizella monticola ochracea. WESTERN TREE SPARROW. Summer resident. Breeds. Commonest of sparrows at timberline. Arrived April 26. Last sparrow to leave in fall, late in September.

Junco hyemalis. SLATE-COLORED JUNCO. Common summer resident. Breeds. A male was secured April 30, 1908.

Passerella iliaca. FOX SPARROW. Common summer resident. Arrived May 4.

Petrochelidon lunifrons. CLIFF SWALLOW. Seen breeding in cliffs 25 miles below my cabin on June 11.

Riparia riparia. BANK SWALLOW. Abundant summer resident. Breeds. Arrived May 18.

Lanius borealis. NORTHERN SHRIKE. Common summer resident. Breeds. Arrived April 26.

Dendroica coronata. YELLOW-RUMPED WARBLER. Common summer resident. Most abundant of warblers. Arrived May 9.

Dendroica striata. BLACK-POLL WARBLER. Flock observed migrating, June 3.

Wilsonia pusilla pileolata. PILEOLATED WARBLER. Common summer resident. Arrived May 20.

Anthus rubescens. Pipit; Titlark. Very common summer resident. Breeds. Keeps mostly above timberline. A male secured May 12, 1908.

Cinclus mexicanus unicolor. Water Ouzel. Common resident. Abundant in winter on the open water where Mallards winter on the Toklat, mostly below the mountain ranges, and keeps constantly singing for two hours after dawn. Specimen secured.

Certhia familiaris montana. Rocky Mountain Creeper. Male killed near cabin in woods October 21.

Penthestes hudsonicus. Hudsonian Chickadee. Common resident.

Regulus calendula. Ruby-crowned Kinglet. Common summer resident. Arrived April 29.

Hylocichla ustulata swainsoni. Olive-backed Thrush. Common summer resident. Arrived May 12. Keeps singing all night when breeding. A male secured May 27, 1908.

Hylocichla guttata. Dwarf Hermit Thrush. Summer resident; fairly common. Breeds. Arrived May 26, when a female was secured.

Planesticus migratorius. Robin. Very abundant summer resident. Almost as common high in the mountains, at upper limit of willows, as it is below. Breeds usually in small spruces, occasionally in willows and on the ground. Arrived May 3. Last seen October 4.

Ixoreus nævius meruloides. Pale Varied Thrush. Common summer resident. Breeds. Arrived May 15. Last seen October 7.

BY THE EDITORS

Mammals of North Side Alaska Range, Toklat Region.

Mammals collected by Charles Sheldon on Upper Toklat River and along base of Alaska Range in 1906–1908, and presented to the Biological Survey Collection of the U. S. National Museum.

Caribou, *Rangifer arcticus stonei* J. A. Allen.
Alaska Moose, *Alce americanus gigas* Miller.
White Sheep, *Ovis dalli* Nelson.
Red Squirrel, *Sciurus hudsonicus* Erxleben.
Yukon Ground Squirrel, *Citellus plesius ablusus* Osgood.
Hoary Marmot, *Marmota caligata* Eschscholtz.
Beaver, *Castor canadensis* Kuhl.
Red-backed Mouse, *Evotomys dawsoni* Merriam.
Meadow Mouse, *Microtus drummondi* (Audubon and Bachman).
    "   " *Microtus operarius endœcus* Osgood.
    "   " *Microtus xanthognathus* (Leach).
    "   " *Microtus miurus oreas* Osgood.
Muskrat, *Fiber spatulatus* Osgood. [No specimen.]
Lemming, *Lemmus yukonensis* Merriam.
Rock Cony, *Ochotona collaris* Nelson.
White Rabbit, *Lepus americanus macfarlani* Merriam.
Canada Lynx, *Lynx canadensis* Kerr.
Red Fox (including Black and Cross Foxes), *Vulpes kenaiensis* Merriam.

Toklat Grizzly, *Ursus toklat* Merriam.
Kluane Grizzly, *Ursus kluane* Merriam.
Black Bear, *Ursus americanus* Pallas. Seen on Kantishna River and
    common in timbered region.
Weasel, *Mustela arctica* (Merriam).
Mink, *Lutreola vison ingens* Osgood. [No specimen.]
Marten, *Martes americana actuosa* Osgood.
Wolverine, *Gulo luscus hylæus* Elliot.
Wolf, *Canis tundrarum* Miller [No specimen.]
Shrew, *Sorex personatus* Geof. St. Hilaire.
    "   *Sorex obscurus* Merriam.
    "   *Sorex tundrensis* Merriam.
    "   *Microsorex hoyi eximius* Osgood.

New Species of Mammals (previously unknown) Discovered and Collected by Charles Sheldon in Alaska and Elsewhere

AND PRESENTED TO THE BIOLOGICAL SURVEY COLLECTION, U. S. NATIONAL MUSEUM

Five species named in his honor by naturalists:

Ursus sheldoni Merriam, Montague Island, Alaska.
Ovis sheldoni Merriam, El Rosario Peak, Sonora, Mexico.
Marmota caligata sheldoni Howell, Montague Island, Alaska.
Neotoma sheldoni Goldman, Pinacate Mts., Sonora, Mexico.
Thomomys sheldoni Bailey, Santa Teresa, Nayarit, Mexico.

Five additional new species, the type specimens of which were collected by Sheldon:

Ursus toklat Merriam, Head of Toklat River, Alaska.
Microtus elymocetes Osgood, Montague Island, Alaska.
Microtus miurus oreas Osgood, Head of Toklat River, Alaska.
Peromyscus eremicus papagensis Goldman, Pinacate Mts., Sonora, Mexico.
Dipodomys deserti sonoriensis Goldman, La Libertad Ranch, Sonora,
    Mexico.

Five hundred and fifty-four specimens of mammals collected by Charles Sheldon and presented to the Biological Survey Collection, U. S. National Museum:

Big Game Animals
35 skins with skulls.
85 additional skulls.
———
120

Small Mammals
373 skins with skulls.
61 additional skulls.
———
434

Localities in Which Sheldon Hunted.

In Alaska:

Alaska Range, Mt. McKinley National Park.
Admiralty Island.
Katzehin River, tributary to Lynn Canal.
Montague Island, Prince William Sound.
Head of Toklat, Alaska Range and base of Denali.

In British Columbia (Canada):

Queen Charlotte Islands.
Vancouver Island.

In Province of Quebec (Canada):

Magdalen Islands.

In Yukon Territory (Canada):

Forks of MacMillan River.
Glenlyon Mountains.
Mount Sheldon.
Ogilvie Rockies.
Pelly Mountains.
Pelly River.
Plateau Mountain.
Rose Mountains.
Ross River.
Selwin Rockies.

In Arizona:

Gila Range.
Grand and Havasu Canyons.
Tule Range.

In Mexico:

Cocopa Mountains, Lower California.
Santa Maria Mountains, Chihuahua.
Seriland and deserts of western Sonora.
Viejo and Pinacate Ranges, northwestern Sonora.
Sierra del Rosario, northwestern Sonora.
Tiburon Island, Gulf of California.

List of Tribes and Bands Mentioned in the Journals.

(SEVERAL UNDER GEOGRAPHIC NAME ONLY)

In Alaska:

Chilkat, southeastern Alaska.
Innuit [Eskimo], Prince William Sound.
Minchumina, about lake of same name.
Nenana.
Tanana [Tenankuchin].

In Yukon Territory:
Nahane, Nahanni House region.
Pelly [Espatotina], Pelly River.
Selkirk.

In British Columbia:
Haida, Queen Charlotte Islands.
Koskimo Kwakiutl, Vancouver Island.

In Arizona:
Havasupai, Havasu or Cataract Canyon.
Yuma.

In Mexico:
Cocopa [Kokopah], northern Lower California.
Sére, Tiburon Island and adjacent part of Sonora.
Tarahumara, Chihuahua.